Indexed in

<u>EGLI 1996</u>

Joyce in the
Hibernian
Metropolis

Joyce in the
Hibernian
Metropolis

Essays

Edited by Morris Beja and David Norris

Ohio State University Press
Columbus

A different version of Mark Osteen's chapter originally appeared in his *The Economy of "Ulysses": Making Both Ends Meet* (Syracuse University Press, 1995)

The excerpts from Friedrich von Flotow's opera *Martha, or The Fair at Richmond* in Sebastian Knowles's chapter is reprinted by permission of G. Schirmer, Inc. International copyright secured. All rights reserved.

Library of Congress Cataloging-in-Publication Data

Joyce in the Hibernian Metropolis : essays / edited by Morris Beja and David Norris.
    p. cm.
    Collection of essays from the 13th International James Joyce Symposium, held in Dublin, June 1992.
    Includes bibliographical references and index.
    ISBN 0-8142-0685-9 (cloth).
    1. Joyce, James, 1882–1941—Criticism and interpretation—Congresses.   I. Beja, Morris. II. Norris, David, 1944–   .   III. International James Joyce Symposium (13th : 1992 : Dublin, Ireland)
PR6019.09Z6343   1996
823'.912—dc20
                                                                                                95-50446
                                                                                                  CIP

Text and jacket design by Hunter Design Associates.
Type set in Goudy Oldstyle by Connell-Zeko Type and Graphics, Kansas City, Missouri.
Printed by Thomson-Shore, Inc., Dexter, Michigan.

The paper in this publication meets the minimum requirements of American National Standard for Information Sciences—Permanence of Paper for Printed Library Materials. ANSI 239.48-1992.

9 8 7 6 5 4 3 2 1

For
Ellen Carol Jones
and
Ken Monaghan
and, in memoriam,
Augustine Martin

Contents

Contents

Contents

The Novels

Preface: A View from Dublin

The overall title of the Thirteenth International James Joyce Symposium, held in Dublin in June 1992, was "In the Heart of the Hibernian Metropolis," and Joyce's native city certainly took to its heart once more the 600-odd [*sic*] symposiasts who participated.

Dublin, of course, has a special attraction for Joyceans as both the source and subject matter of Joyce's genius. Some have feelings about the city as ambiguous as those that characterize Joyce's own love/hate relationship. As a Dubliner, a Joycean, and one who has attended almost all the International Symposia since their inception, I can understand the complex interaction between Joyce's readers and his native city.

The first two Symposia were held in Dublin in the late 1960s. They were comparatively small but lively affairs, full of good humor, extravagant wit, and—as will never again be possible—graced by the presence of people who had known Joyce intimately at school, at university, and from his Trieste and Paris days. There were also the freshness and sparkle of literary and topographical discovery in the air. Much of the motivating energy and many of the participants came from the United States, and the natives tended, when mocking what they regarded as the frequent excesses of Joycean scholarship, to adopt an American accent in the retelling of countless barroom stories about the academic obsession with the trivia of Dublin's street life. The initial puzzlement and amusement at the appetite for minutiae occasionally led to a bantering and dismissive approach that extended to the whole of American scholarship. This reaction was not only naturally resented but was also obviously a mistake.

The scholarly interest in Joyce in the United States is so enormous and covers such a wide range of approaches, subject matter, and talent that it inevitably includes both the best and the worst, the brilliant and the dull, the stimulating as well as the soporific. Many Dubliners and non-Dublin Joyceans in those days regarded each other with amused skepticism, and some even engaged in barbed incivilities. There was also a small minority who happened to be both Dubliners and Joyceans and consequently received the barbs of both sides, but I am glad to say that these were confined to flesh wounds.

Almost thirty years on, the atmosphere tends more toward sweetness and light than to shite and onions. Directing the festivities in Ireland for the Symposium were Sean J. White, the late Augustine Martin, and myself; and in the United States the academic program was directed by Morris Beja. The emergence of a new intellectually progressive Ireland was signalled with the election of Mary Robinson as President of Ireland; she very graciously consented to perform the opening ceremony of the Thirteenth Symposium in the National Concert Hall in Dublin. Although unwell with gastric flu, the President left her bed against doctors' orders and delivered the opening address with such panache that few in the audience realized she was ill. Her genuine interest, which had already been shown when she quoted Joyce at her inauguration in Dublin Castle, and the warmth of her words of welcome, completely won over her listeners and got the Symposium off to a fine start.

Nearly 120 different sessions, ranging from major addresses to panel discussions, covered topics as diverse as parlor games and Joyce, the Joyce papers of the National Library, living book reviews, sessions on Joyce and cinema, Joyce and fashion, Joyce and commodity culture, *Finnegans Wake* and sexuality, and Joyce and homosexuality. These various activities generated over a hundred submissions for inclusion in the present volume.

Confronted by this rich harvest, Morris Beja and I sat down on opposite sides of the Atlantic to produce a book that would reflect something, at least, of the flavor and intellectual range not only of our Dublin discussions but also, and more significantly, the world of Joyce studies as we head toward the end of the century—Joyce's century. We were reassured to find when we exchanged views that there was, despite our frequently very different perspectives on Joyce and Joyce scholarship and criticism, a remarkable degree of coincidence in our judgement of specific submissions. Above all, we tried to select essays by which we felt enlightened. Not every valuable discussion, of course, translates well from the auditorium to the printed page, and that fact and the inevitable considerations of space have led us—at times with some frustration in regard to exclusions—to a collection of about thirty contributions. We have divided the volume into a section of general essays, several groupings deriving from specific panel sessions ("Hostile Responses to Joyce," "Male Feminisms," and "'Aeolus' without Wind"), and sections dealing with the shorter works and the novels. I feel it would be both invidious and impertinent to comment here upon the merits of individual pieces. Suffice it to say that both Morris Beja and I admire all the essays, however much our personal taste did, on occasion, indicate a slightly different order of priority.

One element that it is impossible to reflect adequately in this volume is what I might call the fringe. These fringe events provided the opportunity for visitors to acquaint themselves with Joycean locations such as Clongowes Wood College in Sallins, County Kildare, where we were graciously received by Father Rowland Burke Savage. There were also memorable evening events, such as the songfest orchestrated by Zack Bowen in the Aula Maxima, for which there was standing room only, and the poetry reading in the Physics Theatre in Earlsford Terrace by Seamus Heaney and Mark Strand. This was followed by a reception hosted by Baileys Irish Cream, who sponsored the entire Symposium. As chair of the organizing committee, I can say that Baileys proved themselves to be generous, effective, and tactful, and I was amused by occasional outbreaks of fastidiousness, usually from participants whose cultural backgrounds tended to endorse rather than disdain corporate sponsorship and commodity culture. But goodwill ruled the day, and some of those who came to scoff stayed to ask for the address of the sponsors!

This was the third International James Joyce Symposium in which I played a role in the management; I chaired the host committee in 1977, 1982, and 1992. It was also the last time I shall fulfill such a role, as I intend from now on to enjoy myself on the back benches. I may therefore, I hope, be permitted a few valedictory remarks.

Joyceanity has now achieved the status of a kind of secular religion, with its martyred god-king, holy books, high priests, heretics, fanatics, free thinkers, witch hunts, schisms—and weirdos. This development coincides with a time when not only the heart of the Hibernian metropolis but the heart of much of the intellectual world—and certainly that of academe—is in turmoil. Most of the ancient European seats of learning—including my own university, Trinity College, founded by Queen Elizabeth in a vain attempt to civilize the Irish by turning them Protestant—were created by an impulse that was in part religious as well as intellectual, thereby reflecting a coherent view of the universe and its function. In the late twentieth century we live in a very much more complex world, in which there is no such certainty, and the boundaries of reality are fluid and shifting; and while the academic form remains, there is no longer any consensus about a governing set of ideas. Rationality, along with God herself, is dead, the universe is absurd, communication is impossible, and the right hemisphere of the brain is at war with the left. Yet faced with the collapse of meaning, we still insist on awarding precise grades to treatises on intellectual angst in Beckett and we calmly dock marks from students for the late presentation of essays on *Finnegans Wake*. Personally I am quite comfortable with incoherence, but I like it to remain at least consistently incoherent.

For me (much more, I should say, than for my coeditor) the cross-fertilization of continental psychoanalysis and literary theory has produced some bizarre results. Meaning in a work of art, we are sometimes told, is unstable and something over which the artist cannot be assumed to be in control. No such restrictions, however, are placed on the critic, who may happily continue to pontificate on the absence of meaning and the paucity of language as a means of communication. We may have outgrown Wilde, but we have obviously not outgrown the paradoxical. None of this would matter very much were it not for the absence of joy, celebration, and humanity from much of the academic diet. Moreover, it is strange that a number of those who are disposed to be precious about the inadequacies of language should so frequently retreat into dull jargon as if to prove their point. It is an unpleasant reality not confined to Joyce studies that one may be compelled to wade through pages of turgid prose resembling a railway timetable with a gloss by Gertrude Stein only to discover after a lengthy process of decoding that the insights artfully concealed therein may be banal in the extreme. Those who scorn the confines of stylistic simplicity often do so for good if varied motives. Nevertheless, there are times indeed when I give a heartfelt echo to Molly Bloom's "O, rocks . . . Tell us in plain words."

Some years ago, having given an introductory lecture on Joyce, I was approached by a young man who told me that my lecture had been brilliant and illuminating. I primped at first at what I took to be praise, anticipating basking further in the balm of his adulation, but this was far from the case. He went on to denounce me in quite strident terms, telling me that the experience had been one of intellectual imperialism and that what I had been doing was colonizing the imagination of my audience. The duty of the critic, he sternly rebuked me, was not to clarify or illuminate but to obfuscate and mystify. My antennae tell me that this young person was probably a good deal more in tune with the intellectual zeitgeist than I am. Yet Joyceanity is a broad and inclusive church, and I very much hope that there will always be room for those like myself who do not disdain Joyce the man or the writer with all his faults, and who grant to him, as an artist, at least as much "intentionality" as they cede to his text.

DAVID NORRIS

Acknowledgments

The editors are grateful to the contributors, of course. They would also like to express their special gratitude to all those who made the Symposium itself so special; we could not name them all, but we must mention a few people: Sean J. White, Ken Monaghan, and the late Augustine Martin. The original plan was that there would be three editors of this volume, ourselves and Gus Martin, but the pressure of other commitments led Gus to feel compelled to withdraw from the project, with his blessings on it. As the book goes to press, we have just heard of his untimely death. He shall be greatly missed.

Welcome Address
by the President of Ireland, Mary Robinson, on the Occasion of the Opening of the Thirteenth International James Joyce Symposium, 15 June 1992

Ladies and Gentlemen,

It gives me great pleasure to be with you today to officially open this Thirteenth International James Joyce Symposium.

It's particularly moving for me to be here today because I feel a special connection to this occasion. When I was inaugurated as President I spoke of the fifth province: a place without visible boundaries or actual geography, but that territory within the mind and the spirit that gives us access to the other four historic provinces of Ireland. That makes us conscious that a nation is a place of the mind and spirit as well as a place of event and actual day-to-day history.

Well, there are many treasures in that fifth province. And I feel Joyce's Ireland is definitely one of them. Again, it's not a place of territories or boundaries. For all his wonderfully accurate local detail, it's not a place of regional interest. It's that fierce territory where nothing is taken for granted, where love is frequently expressed as anger and enquiry. It's those great gifts he left us of rebellion and uncompromising self-inquiry that prevent us ever being complacent about being Irish. In any national experience there are many smaller ones. Joyce's Ireland may not be the most visible Ireland to me, but it is certainly one of the most precious.

This is the sixth occasion on which Dublin has played host to this distinguished group. It is fitting that you return to the city that is not only Joyce's birthplace but the wellspring of so much of his inspiration. Joyce saw his departure from Dublin in terms of "exile," but such was his lifelong obsession with the city that he later came to say he had never really left it. He carried Dublin in his imagination, and he never missed an opportunity to quiz visitors from Dublin on the latest news. Desmond Harmsworth recalls that Joyce tried to extract from him an admission of a feeling of affinity with Dublin. Harmsworth had demurred, pointing out that as a Londoner and a Cockney he was not bound to feel for any place but his own. This, however, did not satisfy Joyce: "Do you not feel that Dublin is your town," he insisted, "your, shall I say, spiritual home?" I know that because of Joyce and his works, Dublin occupies a unique place in your imagination and affections and in those of Joyceans throughout the world. Your gathering today is testament to the universal appeal and fascination that Joyce's works hold, and in welcoming your Symposium to Dublin I am delighted that I also welcome each one of you "home."

For Joyceans, this is a particularly exciting time to be in Dublin. The recent unveiling by the National Library of the James Joyce/Paul Léon papers has shed further light on Joyce's life and work in Paris. Few who were present at the official opening will forget how movingly Paul Léon's son, Alexis, spoke of his father's work and friendship with Joyce. The collection that is now open to the public in the National Library was the final act in many years of devoted service to Joyce. Joyce's own tribute to Paul Léon is worth recalling: "For the last dozen years in sickness or health, night and day, he has been an absolutely disinterested and devoted friend and I could never have done what I did without him."

Poised on the eve of another Bloomsday, it is, perhaps, appropriate to consider the debt that society owes to artists such as James Joyce. When Joyce and Nora eloped in 1904 they could have had little notion of the difficulties they were to face over the coming years. In a remarkable love story, they were to remain devoted to each other through family tragedies and professional controversy. Joyce's work outraged conventional wisdom of his time and was widely banned. Here in Ireland Joyce fared no better, and we were, perhaps, more suspicious of his motives than most. To have moved from that position to the situation today, where Bloomsday is fast becoming our second great national day, is a testament not only to Joyce's genius and artistic integrity but also to our growing maturity and confidence as a nation. We are no longer afraid to see ourselves in the mirror that the artist holds up to us and now appreciate artists like Joyce who were prepared to challenge the orthodox and to shatter complacency.

The debt we owe to the artist is that he impels us to address moral issues honestly while offering imaginative insights into the human condition. It is hard to imagine what progress would be possible without the efforts of the artist who liberates us from cant and paralysis. Ireland today is an outward looking country that is proud of its role as an equal partner in the new Europe. Without the efforts of Joyce, who was himself the quintessential European, it might have taken considerably longer for Ireland as a nation to come of age.

I have studied your program of events, and it certainly is a demanding and exciting schedule. However, Joyce, who was something of a Greek scholar, would not have been slow to point out that *symposium* is made up of the Greek words *syn*, "together," and *posis*, "drinking." If, therefore, you fail to solve Bloom's puzzle while crossing the city and find yourself in convivial company, I am sure your memories of this Symposium and of Dublin will be all the richer.

I wish you every success in both the serious work you do and in the enjoyment of your time in our capital city.

Abbreviations

The following abbreviations are standard for references to Joyce's works and important secondary texts. Where contributors have used alternative editions, the edition used will be noted in the Works Cited.

CP	Joyce, James. *Collected Poems*. New York: Viking Press, 1957.
CW	Joyce, James. *The Critical Writings of James Joyce*. Ed. Ellsworth Mason and Richard Ellmann. New York: Viking Press, 1959.
D67	Joyce, James. *Dubliners*. Ed. Robert Scholes in consultation with Richard Ellmann. New York: Viking Press, 1967.
D69	Joyce, James. *"Dubliners": Text, Criticism, and Notes*. Ed. Robert Scholes and A. Walton Litz. New York: Viking Press, 1969.
E	Joyce, James. *Exiles*. New York: Viking Press, 1951.
FW	Joyce, James. *Finnegans Wake*. New York: Viking Press, 1939; London: Faber & Faber, 1939.
GJ	Joyce, James. *Giacomo Joyce*. Ed. Richard Ellmann. New York: Viking Press, 1968.
JJI	Ellmann, Richard. *James Joyce*. New York: Oxford University Press, 1959.
JJII	Ellmann, Richard. *James Joyce*. New York: Oxford University Press, 1982.
JJA	*The James Joyce Archive*. Ed. Michael Groden, et al. New York: Garland Publishing, 1978–79.
Letters I, II, III	Joyce, James. *Letters of James Joyce*. Vol. 1, ed. Stuart Gilbert. New York: Viking Press, 1957; reissued with corrections 1966. Vols. 2 and 3, ed. Richard Ellmann. New York: Viking Press, 1966.
P64	Joyce, James. *A Portrait of the Artist as a Young Man*. The definitive text corrected from Dublin Holograph by Chester G. Anderson and edited by Richard Ellmann. New York: Viking Press, 1964.
P68	Joyce, James. *A Portrait of the Artist as a Young Man: Text, Criticism, and Notes*. Ed. Chester G. Anderson. New York: Viking Press, 1968.

SH   Joyce, James. *Stephen Hero.* Ed. John J. Slocum and Herbert Cahoon. New York: New Directions, 1944, 1963.

SL   Joyce, James. *Selected Letters of James Joyce.* Ed. Richard Ellmann. New York: Viking Press, 1975.

U   Joyce, James. *Ulysses.* New York: Random House, Vintage Books, 1934; edited, reset, and corrected 1961.

U-G   Joyce, James. *Ulysses: A Critical and Synoptic Edition.* Ed. Hans Walter Gabler, et al. New York and London: Garland Publishing, 1984.

U-GP   Joyce, James. *Ulysses: The Corrected Text.* Ed. Hans Walter Gabler, et al. New York: Random House, Vintage Books, 1986; London: Bodley Head, 1986; and Harmondsworth: Penguin, 1986. (These editions have identical pagination.)

General Essays

Joyce's AquaCities

Robert Adams Day

If you were to ask me how the second word of my title should be pronounced—Aqua Cities? A *quay* cities? Aquassities?—I should have to reply either that I don't know, or any one you like, or all three. But that should not trouble aficionados of *Finnegans Wake*, who know that words polysemous to the eye are often not so to the ear. And it is no good asking me why I didn't take the trouble to consult the dictionary, because I did, and discovered, to my mild astonishment (which no doubt you will share) that the word is not to be found—not in any of the various standard unabridged English dictionaries, not even in the latest edition, with supplements, of the great *Oxford English Dictionary*, whose harmless drudges pride themselves on picking up unconsidered trifles, nor yet in the standard French dictionaries of Robert and Harrap, nor the latest multivolume Italian *Vocabolario*. The word appears to be a coinage of the master, and therefore all the more appropriate to what I am going to talk about. But it evidently means waterinesses, so there we are. But stay! What are waterinesses? Transparencies, clarities, pellucidities, as in the mineral waters to which all card-carrying intellectuals are now addicted? Or are they more-diluted-than-they-should-bes, as in the third cup of watery tea that Stephen, in *Portrait*, drains to the dregs before attacking his fried bread (*P64* 174)? Or are they sogginesses, as in the prose of postmodernists and the linens of damp places like Dublin? And why do I say that Joyce must

---

Since the following discourse was intended to be delivered before a large audience, "on a semifestive occasion," and was designed almost as much to amuse as to instruct, it seemed to me that little would be gained and a good deal lost if the facetious tone were removed by eliminating the asides to the audience. I therefore decided that it would be best to present my readers with what the audience heard and to rely on their indulgence. The talk was dedicated, when given, to the memory of Maria Jolas.

have invented the word? Where is it found? It's used in *Ulysses,* and if you don't know where, I'll tell you—but not yet. A discourse of some length aimed at a large audience on a semifestive occasion ought not to be very technical; and since we are gathered here to celebrate Joyce and Dublin or Joyce *in* Dublin—moreover, since I am one of the few present over the age of thirty who has not written a doctor's thesis on Joyce—it behooves this Joycean autodidact to say something simple. So I am going to undertake a meditation on Joyce and water and cities, among them Dublin, concerning which I am also no expert. Modernist authors are apt to be rather watery—think of Eliot, think of Pound and Hart Crane—and water is indeed very simple—H_2O— but if we consider water in Joyce, its existence, its qualities and attributes, its power as presence and metaphor, we may be able to make out that Joyce outdoes them all in his imbricated relations with the element.

John Keats, we remember, wanted his epitaph to read, "Here lies one whose name was writ in water," alluding not only to his fear that he would cease to be but that he would soon be forgotten. Joyce left no instructions about his epitaph, and if he had, he might well have said that *his* name had been written in Fendant de Sion, the white Swiss wine that he called the urine of an archduchess (Budgen 168) and that so nobly stimulated both his Muse and the stomach ulcer that finished him off. But, be that as it may, once when he was asked if he had any plans for further writing, now that *Finnegans Wake* was finally achieved, he replied that he wanted to write a short book about the sea (Potts 202). And we remember that, whatever the *Wake's* circularity (if we should wish, after 628 pages, to go back to the "riverrun" at the beginning) the book ends with Anna Liffey losing her individuality as her waters and her words are diffused into the sea.

Speaking in praise of water, to be sure, is not a very original or uncommon thing to do. The very first line of Pindar's first Olympian ode reads, "Best of all things is water," and the pre-Socratic philosopher Thales maintained that all things were but water in different forms. Even those of us who have never struggled through Xenophon's *Anabasis* will have heard of the weary, parched soldiers' glad shout, *"Thalassa! Thalassa!"* (The sea! The sea!) as they came in sight of water. Buck Mulligan certainly remembers it, for the benefit (or a mild put-down) of Greekless Stephen (*U-GP* 1:80). Anyone who has been to Greece, especially during the hotter months, will understand why the Greeks set such store by water; but Dubliners, habituated to fog, mist, rain, mizzle, lakes, rivers, pools, and bogs, and seldom visited by the sun, might be inclined to take water for granted and place a higher value on what they used to call the craythur, as dispensed by the brothers Guinness and by John Jameson. But even *uisge beatha* means "water of life," Dublin means "black pool," *Baile atha Cliath* means "ford of the hurdles," and Eire would not be the Emerald Isle if it did not have lots of water as well as lots of chlorophyll. Water, if not the best of things, is, next to air, the most necessary to personkind.

4

But not necessarily necessary to literature. How much water do you find in Flaubert or Balzac or Thackeray or Dreiser? Joyce, though, spent a lifetime close to water, and most of it in cities bisected by rivers: Dublin, by the Liffey; Rome, by the Tiber; Paris, by the Seine; Zurich, by the Limmat; and Trieste, washed by the Adriatic, whose "dark streets down by the river" he evoked in *Giacomo Joyce* (3). He might well have echoed the medieval monk (well thought of, if not authentic) who observed how benevolently thoughtful it was of God to have made rivers run by cities. Joyce's infancy was passed in Bray, with its "cold seawall"; his adolescence and young manhood were spent not far from the Grand Canal, the Royal Canal, the Poddle, with its "tongue of liquid sewage" (*U-GP* 10:1197), the Dodder, the trees along whose banks were more sinned against than sinning (by Joyce and Nora, among others [Delaney 157]), the quays along the Liffey, Dalkey, the Bull, the North Wall, Sandymount Strand—a decidedly aqueous existence. And even when he turned to the haunts of men, Mooney's *en ville* was balanced by Mooney's *sur mer*—one frequently had to step to the rear of the premises to pump ship—and in between pubs there were the greenhouses, over one of which Tom Moore's roguishly pointing finger indicated the meeting of the waters (*U-GP* 8:414).

There is yet further testimony to the aqueous influences on Joyce's youth. The Liffey flows near Clongowes, and among the Joyce memorabilia is a little volume bound in blue paper, which Joyce almost certainly was obliged to read there, containing a tribute to that stream. It is T. J. Lyster's anthology, *Poems for the Young Student,* and it contains "Mesgedra," a poem about Ireland's heroic past, by Sir Samuel Ferguson. Ferguson was partial to the Liffey; he observed,

> Not all inglorious in thy elder day
> Art thou, Moy-Liffey. . . .

He wanted

> To fling my votive garland on thy wave. . . .

He rhapsodized,

> Delicious Liffey! From thy bosoming hills
> What man who sees thee issuing strong and pure,
> But with some wistful, fresh, emotion fills,
> Akin to Nature's own clear temperature?

But at the beginning of the poem Ferguson pulled out all the stops:

> When glades were green where Dublin stands today
> And limpid Liffey, fresh from wood and wold,
> Bridgeless and fordless, in the lonely Bay
> Sunk to her rest on sands of stainless gold. . . .
> (*Poems* 42, 40, 33)

Bloom remembers this "schoolpoem" in the Burton restaurant (*U-GP* 8:664), and Peter Costello, in a recently published biographical work, is quite sure that reminiscences of "Mesgedra" must have influenced the closing paragraphs of *Finnegans Wake* (83–84). If he is correct, that is proof positive that sometimes, at least, you can make a silk purse out of a sow's ear.

And when it came time for the exile to sing, it is no wonder that *super flumina Babylonis* seemed to be his motto, from his first anthologized poem, which is about the waves like an army advancing on the shore, to the stitching of eight hundred or more river names into "Anna Livia Plurabelle." Joyce never got very far from the waters of Babble-on; and though it may be pure coincidence, it does not surprise me at all that Thomas Wolfe, a mountain boy who was infatuated with Joyce, chose to call his immense autobiographical *omnium gatherum*, which largely takes place on dry land, *Of Time and the River*. "A wind is rising, and the rivers flow," said he, as though they hadn't been doing it before.

William York Tindall, dead some years now (and I fear little regarded in these days of grand theory except by the oldest of Joyceans) was, along with Edmund Wilson and Harry Levin, a founder of such Joycean scholarship as was not initiated by the master himself among his Paris circle. And I think it was Tindall who first drew our attention to the importance of water and water imagery in Joyce. Indeed, he went so far as to call it Joyce's principal symbol. In his *Reader's Guide*, the fruit of many years of seminars explicating Joyce, Tindall speaks of baby Stephen wetting the bed on the first page of *Portrait*, and says, among other things, "From this infantile beginning the great image proceeds, becoming the sea at last and Anna Livia Plurabelle, the 'riverrun' of life and time in *Finnegans Wake*. . . . by itself water carries the meanings of life and death, for it is our origin and our goal. . . . In the first half of *A Portrait* water is commonly disagreeable, agreeable in the second. . . . the image of water changes and expands" (88–89). And in his edition of *Chamber Music*, Tindall wrote at great length, though dispersedly, of the waters in those lyrics, ranging from the sea and its advancing waves to the waters deposited in chamberpots by gentle ladies.

Some later students of Joyce have waxed indignant about Tindall's preoccupation with tinkling ladies and with urine as a mode of water in Joyce's thought. But even if we argue that the "shell of night" in *Chamber Music* 26 is a seashell rather than a *vase de nuit*, such shells do bring to our ears the roar of waters, as they do to the barmaids in "Sirens"; and only yesterday, so to speak, John Bishop contended, in *Joyce's Book of the Dark*, that *Finnegans Wake*, a book of sleep, arises in many ways, literal and figurative, from the rush of waters that the sleeping ear hears in the tides of its own blood (336–46), or, as Joyce put it: "Tides, myriadislanded, within her, blood not mine, *oinopa ponton*, a wine-dark sea. . . . In sleep the wet sign calls her hour, bids her rise" (*U-GP* 3:394–97), neatly equating the Virgin Mary, Stephen Dedalus's mother, Molly

Bloom, and perhaps even the leaning lady of *Chamber Music*. Tindall may have been slightly cranky in pursuing images, but he was dead right regarding the importance of water in Joyce's life and thought (which are, after all, inseparable). Yeats too, after reading *Chamber Music*, wondered, borrowing the terms of his wonderment from Blake, whether Joyce was a fountain or a cistern (quoted in CM 78), and more recently Dennis Brown, characterizing the "men of 1914," chose to compare Eliot to fire, Joyce to water (Trotter 11). The idea of water, being an infinity of things, doing an infinity of things, dominated Joyce's creation; and the idea of a "great image" beginning in tentative dribbles and expanding to infinity throughout the chronological sequence of Joyce's work, is the theme I have chosen.

But how to deal with this tasteless, soundless, odorless, solid, liquid, or gaseous element? Water takes on color, odor, sound, and tactile presence from its circumstances, as we see when contemplating an ice cube or the ocean; and Joyce's narrative utterance is the water that sustains and interpenetrates his creation. If you are writing a realistic story set in Dublin, you are bound to come to water, and had better not make too much of it. (I remember being tartly cautioned, as a symbol-hunting graduate student, by a professor who reminded us that a mutton chop in Trollope is probably *not* intended to evoke the Lamb of God.) But when Joyce says in his notes to *Exiles* (not written for publication) that the dead lover's symbols "are music and the sea" (118), we are bound to sit up and take notice.

The mature Joyce had a unique and unrivaled creation machine in his head; he did not, like Little Chandler, consider anxiously that he must put in allusions (*D69* 74); they arose as needed when preconsciously summoned and flowed out of his pen. But clearly he saw the advantage of starting from somewhere important, and his notebooks are guideposts or collections of gnomons, or perhaps beacons amid the sea of images and stories. However, until we get to *Finnegans Wake*, concerning which none of the conventional tools of fictional criticism work very well, we can proceed on the assumption that protean water, or water as multivalent image, takes on its colors and shapes from being perceived through the sensibilities of relatively conventional characters. Joycean characters characterize water as they think about it, and it tests and judges them through their reactions to it. Perhaps the most general and traditional meanings of water by itself are life and death, and I think that we may trace a consistent pattern through Joyce's aquacities and his aqua cities as his characters interact with them. Some choose life, some elect death by water; *Finnegans Wake* embraces and dissolves both, holding them in solution. But, as everything in Joyce can seemingly be taken in two ways, I think that here we shall discover a paradox. Those who fear water fear death by drowning or, if the water is figurative, fear the abandonment of their integrity and shape for fluidity and mutation. But by remaining timidly landlocked they enter a living death. Eliot's mummified Prufrock is not the only character in a modernist fiction who walks fruitlessly (or peachlessly?) on the beach dreaming vaguely of being a lobster, or alternatively of being entertained by sea girls. Joycean characters who are hydrophile, on the other hand, risk losing life; but the saying "he that loseth his life shall find it" was not deprived of its validity by the death of Jesus.

Joyceans are all too prone to fancy that the mind of Joyce was like the mind of God, existing in an eternal present and containing all that is and may be. We must be careful and remember that the hand that wrote *Ulysses* did a lot of other things, too (Ellmann 190). But it is tantalizing to reflect that, like *Finnegans Wake*, *Chamber Music* begins with a river and ends with the sea. Water figures in only seven of its thirty-odd lyrics, but unless we choose to claim that its connotations in these are pure happenstance, we have to conclude that the youthful lutanist already knew what he meant to do with water and waters. In the first poem Love wanders aimlessly by the river, pallidly Pre-Raphaelite in costume, with his fingers straying upon an instrument (which phrase only the perverse could see, surely, as alluding to onanism?). In poem 9 the May breezes play merrily with the seafoam, but love is unhappy when love is away. The timorous lady in 26, unwilling to abandon herself to the lover, is filled with fear at what she hears as she leans to the shell of night: rushing rivers scare her. Rain in 32 has fallen all the day, and separation is foretold. And in the last two poems many waters flow to and fro, making moan as cold winds accompany lonely exile, or resembling a cruel invading army as the abandoned lover wails in despair. Clearly, for the youthful lyricist, when he sings of undirected, absent, frustrated, desiring, unfulfilled, or in short, pre-Nora love, rain and rivers and seas are bad medicine. The poems of happy union, physical or not, take place in unwetted woodlands and vales. May we speculate that *Chamber Music*, exquisite though it is, is about a fictive lover who never wet the tea?

As good modernists we have been taught by *The Waste Land*, if we hadn't thought of it before, to see water and dryness as life and suspended animation or living death, respectively, and so we will not be surprised to find *Dubliners* a pretty arid collection of scenes; but water figures significantly in at least four of the fifteen tales. We are not likely to forget the image of the "dark mutinous Shannon waves" (D69 223) into which the snowflakes disappear, an image of the metamorphosis of water in the magniloquent last paragraph of "The Dead," but the yacht on which Jimmy Doyle loses his shirt in "After the Race" might just as well be a landlocked hotel room. Much more significant are the quayside scenes in "An Encounter" and "Eveline"; and here we might again, if inclined to speculate, continue to see the outlines of an emerging pattern. Water can bring life to deadness and dryness; it can be a road to adventure and freedom; but it can kill by drowning. The boy in "An Encounter" crosses the Liffey, looks at sailors, and thinks vaguely of escape and textbook geography made real; but it is Mahony, whom he had "always despised . . . a little," who

8

proposes that "it would be right skit to run away to sea on one of those ships" (*D69* 28, 23). Do we have an anticipation here of Stephen versus Mulligan, W. B. Murphy, and Bloom? Eveline desires and fears a sailor; she lives amid dust and dusty cretonne, but she has been shown fear in a handful of dust— "she wondered where on earth all the dust came from" (*D69* 37); like Stephen she might say, "Dead breaths I living breathe, tread dead dust" (*U-GP* 3:479). Alas, at the final moment, at the dock, "All the seas of the world tumbled about her heart. He was drawing her into them; he would drown her" (*D69* 41). In *Dubliners*, the promise of life and freedom is just that: a promise. The boy's romantic longings are stifled and end, as the old man's mind "circled slowly round and round" (*D69* 26), in disgust at sordid old age and at onanism; Eveline, paralyzed by timidity, retreats forever to her dusty cretonne and alcoholic father. And even if she *had* eloped with Frank, she might have ended her days in Liverpool, seduced and abandoned, as Hugh Kenner thinks (quoted in Feshbach 223), or as I think, amid the dusty cretonne of a Buenos Aires brothel, as a commodity in the then flourishing transatlantic white slave trade. The water of *Dubliners* cannot redeem the city; it is only a deceptive mirage.

But just before writing the first *Dubliners* stories Joyce's talent had taken a new and promising, though temporarily abortive, direction. In January 1904 he dashed off the sketch "A Portrait of the Artist," which was rejected by *Dana* as being incomprehensible; but a month later, on his Dedalian twenty-second birthday, he decided that it would be the germ of *Stephen Hero*, on which he immediately set to work. "Germ" is an appropriate word to use, for not only is the sketch packed with images that recur transformed in the later work, but it marks the birth of Stephen Fitzjames, or rather of the Joycean persona that generations of critics have endlessly dissected, trying to find out which trait is autobiographical, which is not, and why. It also marks, far more than the relatively objective *Dubliners* stories, Joyce's fateful decision to use what I like to call his "personal myth" as a matrix for his work—the disguised saga of James Joyce as Everyman, to say nothing of God the Father, William Blake, and the quintessence of Ireland.

I have said nothing so far about the real James Joyce—rather than his narrative voice—in his fictions, nor yet about Joyce *in* water rather than merely living near it; but at this point those of us who have not recently read *My Brother's Keeper* with attention may be in for a surprise. Whatever his thoughts about thunder and dogs, Joyce did not fear water. The half-blind, sedentary Joyce of the *Finnegans Wake* years was far in the future; young Jim not only won track trophies at Clongowes, but, Stanislaus tells us, he was "very fond of swimming, too. He was a splashy swimmer, but fast. Over a short distance he could beat his burly friend Gogarty, who was, of course, a far stronger swimmer" (42). A water baby, in short; and so it is no surprise to find that the artist-figure in his first avatar is hydrophile. "An impulse led him forth . . . where the mists hung streamerwise . . . amid the fragrant rain. . . . In summer it had led him seaward. . . . as evening deepened the grey glow above the sea, he had gone out, out among the shallow waters . . . singing passionately to the tide" (Scholes and Kain 64–65). Nor is it surprising that this passage also contains material that would become the celebrated "wading girl" episode. Stephen as persona would seem to be firmly set as a lover of water and the sea.

But another surprise awaits us. It is always unwise to extrapolate the Joycean artist from *Stephen Hero,* because it represents only a fragment of the whole that eventually was epiphanized into *Portrait;* but for what it is worth we can say that that work is almost wholly free from water. Almost, that is: for a few pages from the end of that fragment we hear that "Stephen spent the great part of the summer on the rocks of the North Bull." On the rocks, we note, while his brother Maurice "stretched idly on the rocks or plunged into the water" (230). Stephen remains high and dry, and while on the next page he responds affirmatively to his father's question, "Had a dip?" he is perhaps merely being soothingly mendacious, for drunken Mr. Dedalus says, "Well, there is some sense in that. I like to see that" (231). And at the very end of the fragment we have, Stephen is seen staring in fascinated revulsion at the body of a woman, escaped from the asylum, who had drowned in the canal. Insignificant, perhaps; but maybe a pattern is beginning to take shape.

When the great metamorphosis takes place in Joyce's mind, and he passes from scrupulous meanness to gorgeous polyphony, or, in C. S. Lewis' phrase, from the drab to the golden style, the fictions become, as we are all aware, decidedly more aqueous. Everyone knows about the significant use of water and watery images in *Portrait*—I count at least twenty-one appearances, large and small, literal and metaphoric—and most Joyceans if you asked them would doubtless concur with the received doctrine that water has negative connotations in the first half of *Portrait,* positive in the second. They think of Stephen's abhorrence, several times repeated, of the cold slimy water in the square ditch at Clongowes, and, in Tindall's phrase, of "wading with the wading girl that brings renewal" (89). But if one examines all the watery images in *Portrait,* it becomes clear that Stephen's affirmative contacts with the element are oddly tentative. When he is not flinching with revulsion from real or figurative water, he is merely getting his feet wet.

Stephen is not seen bathing at Clongowes, he only remembers "with a vague fear the warm turfcolored bogwater" (P64 22), and when he does wade, it is not in the sea but in "a long rivulet in the strand" full of seaweed (P64 170). The wading girl's thighs, which he sees from a considerable distance, are bare almost to the hips, but Stephen, like Prufrock, does not even roll up his trousers; and he soon begins striding over the strand and then turns landward. Most Joyceans are apt to transfer their admiration of Joyce to his persona, and to hope that Stephen will shortly write *Ulysses;* and so they tend to forget that nearly everything in Joyce can be taken in two ways. Stephen may be a genius, but he is also an insufferable prig; and moreover, unlike his fastidious creator, he is dirty. "—Well, it's a poor case," says Mrs. Dedalus,

> when a university student is so dirty that his mother has to wash him.
> —But it gives you pleasure, said Stephen calmly. (*P64* 175)

We might sympathize with Stephen as he turns away from the porcine Christian brothers, come from bathing at the Bull, or when his flesh "dreaded the cold infrahuman odour of the sea" (*P64* 167), or when the "corpsewhite" "medley of wet nakedness" of his fellow students "chilled him to the bone" (*P64* 168), but the possibility of joining them in the purifying water for a splash and a shout does not enter his thoughts; no, "he, apart from them and in silence, remembered in what dread he stood of the mystery of his own body" (*P64* 168). Stephen is high and dry, and remains so.

It is true that chapters 2 and 3 of *Portrait* are entirely dry, and that Stephen's vision of Hell is of a field of dry weeds, but when he thinks of water in a favorable way, as with his concluding visions of the sea, he is never *in* it, but *on* or *over* it. Icarus, as he well knows, died by drowning. Much more often Stephen uses imagery of the sea as an insidious but all-powerful threat. "He had tried to build a breakwater of order and elegance against the sordid tide of life without him and to dam up . . . the powerful recurrence of the tides within him. . . . The water had flowed over his barriers: their tides began once more to jostle fiercely above the crumbled mole" (*P64* 98). For Stephen the waters, if you are not well inland or able to fly or sail over them, mean destruction. During one of his spasms of piety, "He seemed to feel a flood slowly advancing towards his naked feet and to be waiting for the first faint timid noiseless wavelet to touch his fevered skin. Then . . . he found himself standing far away from the flood upon a dry shore, saved by a sudden act of the will or a sudden ejaculation: . . . seeing the silver line of the flood far away and beginning again its slow advance towards his feet" (*P64* 152). The waves that talk among themselves in young Stephen's dreamy imagination, as he snoozes in the Clongowes infirmary, might seem to speak of hope, but they herald the death of Parnell (*P64* 26–27). In short, if water fascinates Stephen it is with the terror of its depths, and if some might argue that the scene of composing the villanelle is pretty watery, it is Stephen's soul that is "dewy wet," and it is bathed in waves of light (*P64* 217). He may scorn the dean of studies; but as regards the use of sea images, they are as one. The dean says of Stephen's tentatives at an esthetic theory: "—These questions are very profound, Mr. Dedalus. It is like looking down from the cliffs of Moher into the depths. Many go down into the depths and never come up. Only the trained diver can go down into those depths and explore them and come to the surface again" (*P64* 187). Stephen, at the end of *Portrait*, is no trained diver.

Nor is he as *Ulysses* opens. The central action of Joyce's model, the *Odyssey*, you may remember, begins with wily Odysseus at sea, not on or over it, but in

11

it. The man of many shifts, however, will not drown; he is afloat on a wimple, donated by a goddess known as fair-ankled Ino in the words of the Victorian abridgment that I, and perhaps Joyce, read in school. Daughter of Cadmus, she was driven mad by Hera for having nursed Dionysus; she leaped into the sea and became alternatively a seagull or the goddess Leucothea, whichever you like. The sea has no terrors for Odysseus and his ilk, even if Poseidon is irritated with him on account of Polyphemus: the aquatic goddess has an eye for an all-round gentleman. Telemachus, like Stephen, is of course a landlubber; and I do not think it is accidental that the first personage we see in *Ulysses* is Buck Mulligan, who right after breakfast plunges boldly into the sea: "You saved men from drowning. I'm not a hero, however," says Stephen (*U-GP* 1:62).

Joyce disliked Gogarty, and Stephen disloves Mulligan; but we are not compelled to agree with them. Stephen, as I observed before, is a gloomy, insufferable prig, and dirty to boot; Mulligan, and a fortiori Bloom, are physically if not mentally clean, they like people, and they have an earthy sense of humor, very much like the artist who created them.

The sea embraces the text of *Ulysses*. Almost at the very beginning Mulligan parodies Homer and quotes Xenophon: "The snotgreen sea. The scrotumtightening sea. *Epi oinopa ponton*. Ah, Dedalus, the Greeks! I must teach you. *Thalatta! Thalatta!*" (*U-GP* 1:79–80). And almost at the very end, Greekless Molly, who doesn't comprehend "met him pike hoses," echoes Buck and Xenophon and proleptically echoes Anna Liffey at the end of *Finnegans Wake*: "O that awful deepdown torrent O and the sea the sea" (*U-GP* 18:1597–98).

As regards water, *Ulysses* is in a state of saturation. Water figures in every episode, and if I were to discuss all of its manifestations in the significant detail they deserve we should be here until tomorrow—or rather *I* should, bombinating in a void. As I said before, a realistic fiction about Dublin is bound to have rivers and canals in it; and so I prefer to consider what characters think about water, in water, or near water as an index of their ultimate Joycean merit. And first, for Stephen.

The sea, which Mulligan bids him behold, is "a dull green mass of liquid" (*U-GP* 1:108). Haines, not Stephen, is the "seas' ruler" (*U-GP* 1:574). The "unclean bard makes a point of washing once a month" (*U-GP* 1:475). Although "Lycidas . . . is not dead, / sunk though he be beneath the watery floor, / . . . Through the dear might of him that walked the waves," the point is lost on Stephen, who says in the schoolroom, "I don't see anything" (*U-GP* 2:80). The bay is "empty." Stephen in "Proteus," walking on the "unwholesome sandflats" (*U-GP* 3:150), fears falling over a cliff that "beetles o'er his base into the sea," into "Elsinore's *tempting* flood," a suggestion of suicide (*U-GP* 3:281; italics mine). "The flood is following me," he thinks in a terror-stricken moment reminiscent of *Portrait*, and decides to go inland, where "I can watch it flow past from here" (*U-GP* 3:282). Watching it flow is supremely tempting; flowing with it is abhorrent.

Would you do what he [Mulligan] did? A boat would be near . . . I would want to. I would try. I am not a strong swimmer. Water cold soft [like Eileen's hands in *Portrait?*] . . . Do you see the tide flowing quickly in? . . . If I had land under my feet. I want his life still to be his, mine to be mine. A drowning man. His human eyes scream to me . . . I . . . with him together down . . . I could not save her. Waters: bitter death: lost. (*U-GP* 3:320–30)

And Stephen's vampire poem, as I once pointed out, is partly inspired by a picture in a book of woodcuts he had bought, introduced by Yeats, showing an agonized bat-winged figure, like drowned Icarus, about to disappear beneath huge threatening waves (Day, "How Stephen Wrote").

But, as we have begun to see, if Stephen fears annihilation by drowning whenever he thinks of the depths or the encroaching tide, he has another fear, equally strong but more obscurely voiced. He fears flow, change, dissolution, metamorphosis. "I want his life still to be his, mine to be mine" (*U-GP* 3:327–28). He fears that his ashplant—solid prop, phallic symbol if you will, or magic wand—"will float away" (*U-GP* 3:454). Images of flux swirl through his head as he contemplates the sluggish tide: "It flows purling, widely flowing, floating foampool, flower unfurling. . . . To no end gathered; vainly then released, forthflowing, wending back. . . . Full fathom five thy father lies. . . . Sunk though he be beneath the watery floor. . . . God becomes man becomes fish becomes barnacle goose becomes featherbed mountain. . . . A seachange this" (*U-GP* 3:459–482).[1] But Stephen does not take the hints that his store of images extends to him. The drowned man does not change into something rich and strange; he remains a "bag of corpsegas, sopping in foul brine" (*U-GP* 3:476). High and dry again, Stephen breathes dead breaths, treads dead dust (*U-GP* 3:479), even though the great sweet mother of "Telemachus" has become "Old Father Ocean" (*U-GP* 3:483). *This* old father, old artificer, will not stand forgetful Stephen in good stead. He relies rather on his "salteaten stick"; all that dust has had its natural effect, and amid all that water Stephen becomes a parched, weeping Jesus on the cross: "I thirst" (*U-GP* 3:485). A pilgrim with Hamlet hat and staff and Mulligan's sandal shoon, he turns resolutely away from the temptations of dissolving water to seek solace in another kind of foam, at "The Ship. Half twelve" (*U-GP* 1:733), though he does not manage to get there after all.

No one is going to pin down "Proteus" and his images to the satisfaction of all; but it is clear enough that Stephen's meditations are sterile, self-regarding, limited to the perceptions and to the past, present, and future of toothless Kinch, the superman. He wants to gain love ("Touch, touch me"; *U-GP* 3:486), not offer it; he will not leave his self-enclosed identity or enter the lives of others for more than a moment. He is of the company of Joycean figures who hover at the verge of the water, safely dry, but who will not float, perhaps drown, in any case be changed. The case is similar in the metaphorical seas of "Scylla and Charybdis," the cave-bound monster and the whirlpool: *Stephanos contra mundum.* He fools the company of wits to the top of their bent but remains fixed, parrying every thrust, as they swirl around him. True, he reflects on "the sea's voice, a voice heard only in the heart of him who is the substance of his shadow, the son consubstantial with the father" (*U-GP* 9:479–81), but, as a recent critic has noted, "he misses his own cue" (Cope 237), and, when he fades temporarily out of sight in "Wandering Rocks" with his sister Dilly, he is still singing the old song: "She is drowning. . . . She will drown me with her, eyes and hair. Lank coils of seaweed around me, my heart, my soul. Salt green death" (*U-GP* 10:875–77), although he has his wages in his pocket and Dilly could use a few shillings. Stephen is entirely preoccupied with the future of toothless Kinch—to be "seabedabbled, fallen, weltering" (*U-GP* 9:954).

Curiously, though, Stephen drunk may be wiser than Stephen sober. When he comes onstage in "Circe" he is chanting: "Vidi aquam egredientem de templo a latere dextro. Alleluia. Et omnes ad quos pervenit aqua ista / Salvi facti sunt" (*U-GP* 15:77–98). "And I saw the waters coming forth from the right side of the temple. And all to whom those waters come / shall be saved." Stephen knows, or should know, that these waters come from Ezekiel's prophecies, that they become "waters to *swim* in," that when they come to the sea they "shall be healed," and that "every thing shall live whither the river cometh" (Ezekiel 47:1–9). But although Joyce makes Stephen utter the last words "Triumphaliter" (*U-GP* 15:98), he also disjoints the quotation into three parts, suggesting distraction; and Stephen's thoughts immediately veer toward Georgina Johnson, "the goddess who rejoices my youth" (*U-GP* 15:122–23), as he disappears from view, in search of her. Stephen will need a good deal of psychotherapy, or hydrotherapy, before he can come to terms with water and understand how much he needs it.

If Buck Mulligan, at home both in water and in Dublin society, *bon viveur* and obscene jester, will not fill the bill as a plausible antithesis to Stephen, Leopold Bloom, of whom we see a great deal more in *Ulysses*, will do very well. *His* head has no objection to simply swirling when he thinks of seaside girls; but unlike them (if we remember all the lyrics of the song), his daughter Milly did not suffer from *mal de mer* when he took her around the Kish in *Erin's King*. "Not a bit funky," he remembers with pleasure, in his second evocation of water in "Calypso." The lively waters that "made the damned old tub pitch about" produced no fear (*U-GP* 4:434–35). It is true that Bloom's *first* watery thoughts, of the Dead Sea, sear his flesh with "grey horror," but those waters are stagnant: "no fish, weedless . . . no wind would lift those waves" (*U-GP* 4:230, 220). The Dead Sea does not flow.

As we all know, Mr. Bloom, who has no bathroom, nevertheless does not use the washstand like Molly but makes a visit to the public baths one of the first tasks of his day; no unwashed bard he. And as if to point up the parallel, Joyce as "the arranger" allows Bloom a soupçon of Stephen's "Proteus" imagery: "a huge dull flood leaked out, flowing together, winding through mudflats all over the level land, a lazy pooling swirl of liquor bearing along wideleaved flowers of its froth" (*U-GP* 5:315–17). Both men reflect on drowning; but for Stephen it is the "*mildest*" death (*U-GP* 3:482–83); "Drowning they say is the *pleasantest*," ruminates Bloom in "Hades" (*U-GP* 6:988). Although he is by no means ready to die ("They are not going to get me this innings" [*U-GP* 6:1004]), the idea of dissolution does not appall him. "How can you own water really? It's always flowing in a stream, never the same, which in the stream of life we trace. Because life is a stream" (*U-GP* 8:93–95).

Accordingly, we ought not be surprised to find that in "Circe," where battered and bruised Stephen stubbornly clings to his identity, Bloom turns into so many things (including a woman) that I am not going to list them, because my space is limited. Bloom is a cultured allround man, the new womanly man; and I think that when Joyce told Frank Budgen that he was tired of Stephen because he had a shape that couldn't be changed (Budgen 105) he was making a much less petulant and a much profounder statement about Stephen, and himself as artist and thinker about life, than we have been giving him credit for. In any case, he next went on to *Finnegans Wake*, where the characters have no recognizable shape at all—drowned, dissolved, and metamorphosed in a rich linguistic Irish stew.

It may be, though, if you believe, as I do, that symbolic or fantastic events in *Ulysses* are just as "real" as making cocoa or restoring Parnell's hat, that it is Bloom after all who saves Stephen from drowning. For at the end of "Circe," after Stephen has murmured "white breast . . . dim sea," and curled up in a fetal position, Bloom, holding hat and ashplant, stands guard over the prostrate bard "in the attitude of secret master," and curiously enough, murmurs "in the rough sands of the sea . . . a cabletow's length from the shore . . . where the tide ebbs . . . and flows" (*U-GP* 15:4942–54). Whereupon the vision of Rudy appears. One can drown just as well in the stream of life as in the sea, after all, unless a helping hand is ready.

But it is time to return to aquacities (which you may have wondered if I was going to mention again). As I noted before, Joyce seems to have invented the word; and if you look at the Gabler edition (*U-GP* 1472) and the British Museum notes (Herring 445), you find that at first he wasn't sure how to spell it, making two tries. It occurs, for the first and only time, in "Ithaca." And it also occurs, significantly or not, just after one of those curious "ruptures" in the text of which the deconstructionists are so enamored. To illustrate: On entering the basement kitchen, Bloom draws water, which gets by far the longest description, apart from the inventories, in the entire chapter. He then, having put the filled saucepan on the hob, washes his hands, in fresh, cold, neverchanging, everchanging water, appropriately for a Joycean priest who is about to celebrate a parody communion with the creature cocoa. The very next line reads: "What reason did Stephen give for declining Bloom's offer?" (*U-GP* 17:263). But oddly, in this fanatically detailed chapter, no offer or declination has been made. Was Joyce so intoxicated with the implications of his imagery that he left out a needful link? Being no deconstructionist, and disliking *aporia*, I shall simply say flatly that we shall never know and get on with it. Nevertheless, this enchanting rupture is surrounded by fascinating matter, which I do want to explore.

The silent oration of Bloom, water lover, drawer of water, water carrier, in admiration of that element, is too long to quote (it was expanded from the first manuscript to the final version by a factor of five), but I want to cite a few significant phrases: universality, unplumbed profundity, hydrostatic quiescence, hydrokinetic turgidity, preponderance of three to one over the dry land, indisputable hegemony, capacity to dissolve and hold in solution all soluble substances including millions of tons of the most precious metals, seaquakes, waterspouts (and sixteen other violent manifestations), persevering penetrativeness, properties for cleansing, quenching thirst and fire, nourishing vegetation, infallibility as paradigm and paragon, metamorphoses, variety of forms, ubiquity as constituting ninety percent of the human body (*U-GP* 17:185–227). Now the language of this aria is not Bloom's; it is, of course, that of the arranger, as usual in "Ithaca," and the notes are full of hydrostatistics, about eighty of them (Herring 417–93). But however we may feel about it, clearly Joyce wants us to feel the impact of this torrent of watery qualities and to apprehend what water can do, through Bloom.

Stephen, on the other hand, is curtly handled: "he was hydrophobe [is it going too far to think of hydrophobia?], hating partial contact by immersion or total by submersion in cold water, (his last bath having taken place [ugh!] in the month of October of the preceding year [is the interval of eight months intended to be significant?], disliking the aqueous substances of glass and crystal [no wonder he broke his spectacles!], distrusting aquacities of thought and language" (*U-GP* 17:237–40). Bloom then keeps quiet, stifling his good intentions by thinking of "the incompatibility of aquacity with the erratic originality of genius" (*U-GP* 17:147) and struck by Stephen's *seemingly* "predominant qualities": "Confidence in himself, an equal and opposite power of abandonment and recuperation" (*U-GP* 17:253–54). But is aquacity incompatible with genius? Perhaps, if it merely means see-throughability; but certainly, in view of the Rabelaisian hodgepodge of watery qualities and powers with which we have just been deluged, it is not incompatible with the genius of such as James Joyce. Stephen, like unwary Oedipus, or like Hamlet before he learns to relax and trust in God,[2] is leaning on a weak reed (or ashplant) if he is only confident in himself. He needs to find a father, or Old Father Ocean, or perhaps a Molly or Nora, if his genius is to be sustained and fertilized. When he exits he is still very much of the company of those who shun water only to find a living death.

Molly, of course, as we immediately see, is full of liquid and of life. She urinates and menstruates; more, her discourse, with no beginning and no end, is

16

verbal water, in which shapeless thoughts flow, eddy, and are transformed. Her symbols, like those of the dead lover in the notes to *Exiles*, might very well be music and the sea. As with Anna Livia, in her thoughts the "awful deep-down torrent" (*U-GP* 18:1598) has the penultimate word.

Neither space nor my knowledge in progress allows me to make more than a few random observations about *Finnegans Wake* with respect to water, cities, and aquacities. Transparency it certainly has not got; and anyone can see that half or more of the words in it are dissolved, like the digested peas that at one point turn into eaps (*FW* 456.22); or else they are solvents like the word "peatrick" (*FW* 1.10), which simultaneously holds Saint Peter, Irish Patrick, the Irish peat rick, and the quasi-Irish shell game or pea trick, in its tiny but capacious depths. Words in *Finnegans Wake* can do everything that Andrew Marvell's marvelous drop of dew can do, only better. It is a sea of stories in which people and things, like the city of Dublin, are often submerged but always glimmer through the depths or bob up like corks in the Liffey, or like throwaways. We all know that Joyce brocaded about eight hundred river names into "Anna Livia Plurabelle," and that the river, like the mountain, is never far away; but consider also that of the 124 songs from Moore's *Irish Melodies*, all woven into the *Wake*, no less than 40 contain water in one way or another, from the title or first line, like "Silent, O Moyle," or "As a Beam o'er the Face of the Waters may Glow," "The Meeting of the Waters," "By that Lake Whose Gloomy Shore," "Come o'er the Sea," "I Saw from the Beach," "As Slow Our Ship," "Sail On, Sail On," "The Boyne's Ill-fated River," "I Wish I was by that Dim Lake," to the waters of Babylon evoked in "The Parallel," to the seas, rivers, dews, mists, and rain that share Moore's imagery with tears and "balmy drops" of wine. Even to enumerate the ways in which water and bodies of water penetrate the *Wake* would take a very long time. But I cannot forget what Brendan O'Hehir tells us about the word "Liffey": it has several possible etymologies, but, he says, we should always expect to find a play on "leaf" and, most significantly, "life" (392). Bloom was not alone in remembering that life is a stream. Nor can I forget what we are also told about the completion of the *Wake*. "Joyce finally, with agonizing effort, brought himself to terminate his task by composing 'Soft morning city.' We may say that he had hung up his harp. And thereupon he went down to the river and wept. By the waters of" (Rose 964). I have quoted a secondary source, and one may be skeptical about its reliability; but we have confirmation of the state of Joyce's emotions and thoughts as he brought his task to an end in his own words. Joyce, you remember, had ceased to correspond with his benefactress Harriet Weaver, and was using Paul Léon as an epistolary go-between. Some time in December 1938 he wrote a memorandum for Léon (Fahy 31); Léon was to say that Nora had told him that Joyce was in a state of exhaustion over the final pages of the *Wake*, written in the most extreme emotional tension. "It deals with the merging of the fresh waters of the Liffey and the salt waters o the Irish Sea at the

Dublin Estuary!!! Ha! Ha! Ha!" What we are to make of the ha-has (sarcasm, hysteria, triumph) I cannot tell; but exhaustion, tension, closure, and the meeting of the waters are there, and they are vouched for by unimpeachable authority.[3]

All this may sound somewhat airy and theoretical to those who, like older Joyceans, have not learned to reject the idea of authorial intention. All this water could be just adventitious; but we have testimonies from life about Joyce's views concerning water and watery cities. Paul Léon tells us that "Joyce's feeling for all bodies of water amounted almost to nostalgia, and he was drawn to the seashore by an irresistible attraction. Wherever he went on holiday, he immediately looked for a river, a stream, or even a brook, and his first walks led him along its banks. How many hours we passed together, watching the calm flow of the Seine" (Potts 289–90). And he extravagantly admired Pare Lorentz's *The River*, calling its script "the most beautiful I have heard in ten years" (Obituary). Carola Giedion-Welcker is even more explicit: "'What a city!' he would exclaim [of Zurich]. 'A lake, a mountain, and two rivers are its treasures. . . . [Ireland]' he said, 'has two voices, one comes from the mountains and the other from the sea'" (Potts 261). And again, "He observed the life of waters, the ocean and above all the rivers, as he observed the life of people. River-nature, river-myth merged with that 'river-civilization' which to him seemed fundamental. Repeatedly he sought out regions with rivers" (Potts 265). Joyce begged the Giedions never to give up their house in Zurich, because it had a little creek rushing past the garden (Potts 265). "To him the confluence of the Limmat and Sihl was an elemental and dramatic meeting, and when I once wanted to take a picture of him in Zurich, it had to be at exactly this spot and with this river background" (Potts 265). Joyce, in Zurich, it seems, "took frequent boat trips on the lake . . . to serve his art. . . . From the water, the fish smell, the blue-green color, the misty haze . . . he hoped one word would be born" (Potts 265), but he refused to say whether he had found this quarry, which surely would have had to be a thunderword to include all that.

But the last and most poignant of these testimonies comes again from Paul Léon. *Finnegans Wake* had appeared, but such acclaim as it had received had been drowned out by the outbreak of war. The exhausted Joyce had moved to La Baule to be near Lucia in her nursing home, but he could visit her only a few minutes a day. Léon remembered:

> The rest of the day wore away in walks on the beach. They reminded him of the time when on the seashore of Ireland he had spoken about matters of heaven and earth . . . and where the waves had brought him the smile of Nausicaa. He remembered also the quays of Trieste and the sails on Ulysses' sea. Now his work was done. . . . But the waves roared as ever . . . the Ocean continued beating the shore and chafing on its edges. And in his mind was rising the idea of a new poem whose fundamental theme would be the murmur of the sea. (Potts 203)

Clearly, as had not been the case with callow Stephen Dedalus, only half of Joyce at best, "the seas' voice" persisted in being still heard "in the heart of him who is the substance of his shadow, the son consubstantial with the father," and still wanted to be given expression in a new way, in spite of all that had been accomplished in the exhaustive and exhausting *Finnegans Wake*. And if the artist could have lived, yet another book about the sea would have been created. How could this be? Such an effort might seem impossible, but Joyce's mind, even if wretched and fatigued, remained limitless, and, to finish my meditation on aquacity and answer that last question, I can find no better phrase than the beautiful dying fall that Eleanor Clark uses to end her essay on Hadrian's Villa: "After all, all that water had to come from somewhere" (194).

NOTES

1. I discuss the implications of this mysterious sentence at length in my "Joyce, Stoom, King Mark."
2. This view of Hamlet's character is forcefully argued in Johnson's "The Regeneration of Hamlet."
3. Léon wrote the letter to Weaver; it is dated 16 December 1938, and it contains the words precisely as quoted above, but omitting the exclamation points and the ha-has. We are told that Harriet Weaver was much moved by its contents (Lidderdale and Nicholson 373).

WORKS CITED

Bishop, John. *Joyce's Book of the Dark: "Finnegans Wake."* Madison: University of Wisconsin Press, 1986.

Budgen, Frank. *James Joyce and the Making of "Ulysses."* Bloomington: Indiana University Press, 1960.

Clark, Eleanor. *Rome and a Villa.* Garden City, N.Y.: Doubleday, 1952.

Cope, Jackson I. "Sirens." In *James Joyce's "Ulysses": Critical Essays*, ed. Clive Hart and David Hayman. Berkeley and Los Angeles: University of California Press, 1974.

Costello, Peter. *James Joyce: The Years of Growth, 1882–1915.* Dublin: Roberts Rinehart, 1992.

Day, Robert Adams. "How Stephen Wrote His Vampire Poem." *James Joyce Quarterly* 17 (1980): 183–97.

———. "Joyce, Stoom, King Mark: 'Glorious Name of Irish Goose.'" *James Joyce Quarterly* 12 (1975): 211–50.

Delaney, Frank. *James Joyce's Odyssey: A Guide to the Dublin of "Ulysses."* New York: Holt, Rinehart & Winston, 1981.

Ellmann, Maud. "Disremembering Dedalus: A *Portrait of the Artist As a Young Man*." In *Untying the Text*, ed. Robert Young. Boston: Routledge & Kegan Paul, 1981.

Fahy, Catherine, comp. *The James Joyce–Paul Léon Papers in the National Library of Ireland*. Dublin: National Library of Ireland, 1992.

Ferguson, Sir Samuel. *Poems*. Dublin, 1880.

Feshbach, Sidney. "'Fallen on His Feet in Buenos Ayres': Frank in 'Eveline.'" *James Joyce Quarterly* 20 (1983): 223–27.

Herring, Phillip F., ed. *Joyce's "Ulysses" Notesheets in the British Museum*. Charlottesville: University Press of Virginia, 1972.

Johnson, Samuel Frederick. "The Regeneration of Hamlet." *Shakespeare Quarterly* 3 (1952): 187–207.

Joyce, James. *Chamber Music*. Ed. William York Tindall. New York: Octagon Books, 1982.

Joyce, Stanislaus. *My Brother's Keeper: James Joyce's Early Years*. Ed. Richard Ellmann. New York: Viking Press, 1958.

Lidderdale, Jane, and Mary Nicholson. *Dear Miss Weaver: Harriet Shaw Weaver, 1876–1961*. New York: Viking, 1970.

Moore, Thomas. *The Poetical Works*. London: Oxford University Press, 1910.

Obituary of Pare Lorentz. *New York Times*, 4 March 1992, sec. B, p. 15.

O'Hehir, Brendan. *A Gaelic Lexicon for "Finnegans Wake."* Berkeley and Los Angeles: University of California Press, 1967.

Potts, Willard, ed. *Portraits of the Artist in Exile: Recollections of James Joyce by Europeans*. Seattle and London: University of Washington Press, 1979.

Rose, Danis. "The Beginning of All Thisorder of 'Work in Progress.'" *James Joyce Quarterly* 28 (1991): 957–65.

Scholes, Robert, and Richard M. Kain. *The Workshop of Daedalus*. Evanston, Ill.: Northwestern University Press, 1965.

Tindall, William York. *A Reader's Guide to James Joyce*. New York: Noonday Press, 1959.

Trotter, David. "Six Hands at an Open Door." *London Review of Books* 13 (21 March 1991): 11–12.

Catching the Conscience of a Race: Joyce and Celticism

Vincent J. Cheng

James Joyce opens his essay "Ireland, Island of Saints and Sages" thus: "Nations have their ego, just like individuals. The case of a people who like to attribute to themselves qualities and glories foreign to other people has not been entirely unknown in history, from the time of our ancestors, who called themselves Aryans and nobles, or that of the Greeks, who called all those who lived outside the sacrosanct land of Hellas barbarians" (CW 154). Even as early as 1907, when this essay was written, Joyce was aware that nations participate in the activities of the ego/self, and in the consequent dynamics of self and other in which the self attributes to itself qualities "foreign to other people," who are thus labeled "barbarians." At the national and ethnic levels, these are discursive processes that participate in the dynamics of "othering" that create and consolidate an imagined national "character," a sovereign Self—most usually by defining "others" in terms of clearly defined essences and comfortable, essentialized stereotypes (of "barbarians"). For example, in 1836 Benjamin Disraeli railed about the Irish, who, he claimed, "hate our free and fertile isle. They hate our order, our civilization, our enterprising industry, our sustained courage, our decorous liberty, our pure religion. This wild, reckless, indolent, uncertain, and superstitious race have no sympathy with the English character" (Curtis, *Anglo-Saxons* 51). Disraeli's description is classic in what it reveals, which is that "they" are everything that "we" are not (or at least prefer to think that we are not): subservient, disorderly, uncivilized, unenterprising, cowardly,

---

This essay is abstracted from several sections of a long chapter (chap. 2) from my recently completed study *Joyce, Race, and Empire* (Cambridge: Cambridge University Press, 1995).

21

indecorous, and so on. In fact, then, as Joyce's comments on the national "ego" also suggest, the nature of what one formulates as "other" and "barbarian" tells us much more about the self than about the other.

In particular the "Irishman"—an expression that Conor Cruise O'Brien has referred to as the "pejorative singular"—was endowed by Anglo-Saxonists with those traits most feared or despised in respectable English society.[1] This process, of course, was basically similar to the way the English formed their images of Africans and Orientals, too, based on their particular needs at the time, in a universalized essentialism of the other as primitive, barbaric, and uncivilized/uncivilizable. During the nineteenth century the Irish were repeatedly (including through scientific arguments) "racialized" by the English as "White Negroes" or savage Orientals, and functioned as belonging to a primitive race much more closely related to African Hottentots and Bushmen, or to native Maoris or savage Chinese. Eventually, in the latter half of the century, the Irish were relegated to a subhuman status, to anthropoid apes.[2]

In "Ireland, Island of Saints and Sages" Joyce expresses his awareness of such stereotyping mechanisms, in which "the English now disparage the Irish because they are Catholic, poor, and ignorant," whereas in fact "Ireland is poor because English laws ruined the country's industries"; and in which Ireland has been made into "the everlasting caricature of the serious world" (CW 167, 168). But, as Joyce goes on to point out about such English stereotypes, "That the Irish are really the unbalanced, helpless idiots about whom we read in the lead articles of the *Standard* and the *Morning Post* is denied by the names of the three greatest translators in English literature—FitzGerald, translator of the *Rubaiyat* of the Persian poet Omar Khayyam, Burton, translator of the Arabian masterpieces, and Cary, the classic translator of the *Divine Comedy*" (CW 171; significantly, Joyce's examples were able to prove themselves by going *outside* the English/Irish cultural borders into broader, international cultural perspectives, through acts of cultural "translation").

Such derogatory images of "other" cultures conjoin in what Edward Said calls an "essentialist universalism" in which the Other is constructed to seem unchanging, unalterable, and universal along essentialized stereotypes, which serve to consolidate a comfortable us/them binarity and distinction that operates along lines similar to Freud's concept of projection—a projection that, as Curtis notes, is a "refracted image" that "worked to enhance the self-esteem of the beholder at the expense of those being stereotyped" (*Apes* 14), much like Virginia Woolf's depiction in *A Room of One's Own* of the female as a mirror that allows the male to see himself as twice his actual size.

In such essentializing of a universal primitivism, these racial stereotypes create comfortably, securely, clearly defined boundaries between the self and the other, within the dynamics of what Derrida has taught us to recognize as Western logocentrism—a clearly demarcated us/them binarity and difference that functions to reify the dominant Western culture's sense of itself as civilized and rational by contrast while repressing or occluding the knowledge that the qualities of primitive otherness are already contained (but repressed) within the self. In this way, Anglo-Saxonists could proclaim, as did Joseph Chamberlain in 1895, in all good conscience (or at least in all good "conscious"), that "the British race is the greatest governing race the world has ever seen" (Banton 76).

During the nineteenth century the popular English conception of the Irish as a backward, primitive, "native" Celtic race attained the broad cultural force behind it consistent with the Gramscian notion of "hegemony" or the Foucauldian notion of "discourse" and discursive formations, along the lines of Said's concept of Orientalism, in which "such [Orientalist] texts can *create* not only knowledge but also the very reality they appear to describe" (Said 94). Consequently, by the 1860s the popular image of the Irishman in both popular cartoons and in written discourse was an anthropoid ape. L. P. Curtis's *Apes and Angels: The Irishman in Victorian Caricature* convincingly documents how Victorian cartoons and illustrations transformed "peasant Paddy into an ape-man or simianized Caliban . . . by the 1860s and 1870s, when for various reasons it became necessary for a number of Victorians to assign Irishmen to a place closer to the apes than the angels" (2). The English, of course, reserved the designation of angels for themselves, frequently punning on angels, Angles, and Anglo-Saxons. The timing of this culturally created image (of Irish apes) was not accidental, for it was when the Irish turned to political activism and agitation in their demands for Home Rule that *Punch* and other English periodicals began to "picture the Irish political outrage-mongering peasant as a cross between a garrotter and a gorilla" (Curtis, *Apes* 31). Bolstered by such scientific, anthropological reasoning as Robert Knox's pseudoscientific Celtophobic racism, John Beddoe's "index of nigrescence," which purported to show that Celts were Africanoid in physical characteristics, and Daniel Mackintosh's data claiming that the heads of Irish people were characterized by absent chins, receding foreheads, large mouths, thick lips, melanous and prognathous features, and so on,[3] it was perhaps inevitable that Anglo-Saxonist racism would turn the "white Negro" into a simian Celt.

While there were many equations made between the Irish and apes in both literature and nonfictive writing, the most prevalent manifestations of the equation of the Irish Celt with an ape appeared in the popular cartoons of the day, in English periodicals such as *Punch* and *Judy*, in which any character with a prognathous jaw and simian features was readily recognized as representing an Irishman, without any need for further identification. Joyce reveals his pained awareness of such derogatory stereotyping in *Stephen Hero*, when Madden (Davin in *Portrait*) speaks of those "old stale libels—the drunken Irishman, the baboon-faced Irishman that we see in *Punch*" (*SH* 64). To illustrate Madden's point, I have included a small but striking selection of such cartoons here (selected from Curtis's *Apes and Angels* pp. 41, 42, 43, 59, 60, 66, and 63, respectively). They depict Anarchy as an Irish agitator with repellent features

PUNCH, OR THE LONDON CHARIVARI.—October 29, 1881.

TWO FORCES.

Figure 1. *"Two Forces"*: *Britannia vs. Anarchy.* John Tenniel's illustration in *Punch* underscored the Manichean, colonialist images of Good and Evil: a frightened, vulnerable, and feminized Hibernia has to be protected from the savage, stone-wielding Irish male, representing Anarchy; her protector is none other than a majestic Britannia, wielding the sword of the Law and standing upon the lawless banner of the Irish Land League. (*Punch*, 29 October 1881.)

evoking simianness (figs. 1 and 2); an "Irish Frankenstein" described by *Punch* as a bestial *"Caliban* in revolt" (fig. 3); St. Patrick's Day as a stereotyped "shindy" or "donnybrook" involving Irish-Americans in the form of gorillas bashing each others' heads (fig. 4); a cartoon in *Harper's Weekly* balancing (as equal in weight) black slaves in the South with simian Irish-Americans (fig. 5); a degenerate "Simian Irish Celt" doing a jig while John Bull and Uncle Sam look on disapprovingly (fig. 6). The last example (fig. 7) is perhaps the most strik-

Figure 2. *Anarchy: detail from "Two Forces."* The close-up underscores how Paddy, as the stereotyped Irishman, has been fully simianized as a repellent Irish agitator with apelike nose, lips, jaws, and teeth. (*Punch,* 29 October 1881.)

ing: Paddy and Bridget, as the essentialized Irish pair, are portrayed as living in their native habitat, a shanty; the rather Wakean title of "The King of A-Shantee" connects the Irish Celt with the African Ashanti, and Paddy's clearly apelike features imply that he may be the "missing link" in the evolution between the lower species of apes and Africans.

This, then, was part of the context and discourse of race at the end of the nineteenth century: a discourse racialized along a binary axis that posited the English "race" as one pole (the positive) and the Irish as the other (the negative),

PUNCH, OR THE LONDON CHARIVARI.—May 20, 1882.

THE IRISH FRANKENSTEIN.

"The baneful and blood-stained Monster * * * yet was it not my Master to the very extent that it was my Creature? * * * Had I not breathed into it my own spirit?" * * * (*Extract from the Works of* C. S. P-RN-LL, M.P.)

Figure 3. "*The Irish Frankenstein.*" Tenniel's stereotype of the Irish assassin appeared in *Punch* just two weeks after the Phoenix Park murders, in which two English emissaries were assassinated in Phoenix Park. The prognathous jaw and simian nose of this monster/assassin—shown carrying pistol and a bloodied dagger, standing over its maker, a respectable and law-abiding English gentleman—were features that the English considered distinctly Irish. *Punch* described this Frankenstein as a Celtic Caliban: "Hideous, blood-stained, bestial, ruthless in its rage, implacable in its revengefulness, cynical in its contemptuous challenge of my authority, it seemed another and a fouler *Caliban* in revolt, and successful revolt, against the framer and fosterer of its maleficent existence." (*Punch*, 20 May 1882, pp. 234–35.)

26

Figure 4. *"The Day We Celebrate: St. Patrick's Day, 1867."* St. Patrick's Day is depicted by Thomas Nast in *Harper's Weekly* as a stereotyped "shindy" or "donnybrook" involving Irish-Americans in the form of gorillas beating up policemen and law-abiding citizens. (*Harper's Weekly*, 6 April 1867.)

in which "Irish" was defined as everything not desirably "English." Thus, the conception of an essentialized and racialized Irishness depended, for its very definition and formulation, on the English ideal of Englishness, a national ego-ideal (assuming that "Nations have their ego, just like individuals").

Joyce was certainly very aware of and very sensitive to such stereotyping and essentializing. Having denied (in his 1907 essay) "that the Irish are really the unbalanced, helpless idiots about whom we read in the lead articles of the *Standard* and the *Morning Post*," Joyce goes on to argue that these stereotypes have their origin in the oppressive conditions of an Irish environment long suffering under the cruel Penal Laws (which forbade Irish Catholics to vote, become government employees, practice a trade or profession, sit in parliament, own land, keep a horse, and so on) imposed until recently by England (see *CW* 168–71); but, as he further comments about the constructed stereotypes, "this pejorative conception of Ireland is given the lie by the fact that when the Irishman is found outside of Ireland in another environment, he very often becomes a respected man. The economic and intellectual conditions that prevail in his own country do not permit the development of individuality" (*CW* 171).

That same year (1907) Joyce wrote an essay for *Il Piccolo della Sera* in Trieste titled "Ireland at the Bar," in which he narrated a very suggestive story (which I quote at length):

Figure 5. *"The Ignorant Vote: Honors are Easy"* (black slaves and white apes). Nast's cartoon in *Harper's Weekly* suggests that emancipated Southern slaves were equivalent in weight to the brutish Irish-American voters in the North. The Northern voter is characterized by simian features and the identifying clay pipe and hat of the stereotypical Irishman. (*Harper's Weekly*, 9 December 1876.)

Several years ago a sensational trial was held in Ireland. In a lonely place in a western province, called Maamtrasna, a murder was committed. Four or five townsmen, all belonging to the ancient tribe of the Joyces, were arrested. The oldest of them, the seventy year old Myles Joyce, was the prime suspect. Public opinion at the time thought him innocent and today considers him a martyr. Neither the old man nor the others accused knew English. The court had to resort to the services of an interpreter. The questioning, conducted through the interpreter, was at times comic and at times tragic. On one side was the excessively ceremonious interpreter, on the other the patriarch of a miserable

Figure 6. *"An Irish Jig."* James A. Wales's cartoon in *Puck* of "An Irish Jig" shows both John Bull and Uncle Sam unable to tame the wildness of the Irish ape, fattened on English and American food supplies (and also on "drugs") and sporting distinctly apelike features (as well as the sterotypic Celtic clay pipe and hat). (*Puck*, 3 November 1880, p. 150.)

Figure 7. *"The King of A-Shantee."* In Frederick B. Opper's cartoon for *Puck* titled "The King of A-Shantee," "Paddy" and "Bridget" are portrayed as the stereotypical Irish peasant couple living in their lowly shanty; the Irishman is connected through the pun of "A-Shantee" with the African Ashanti, just as his prognathous, simian features suggest that he may be the theorized "missing link" in the evolution between apes and black Africans. (*Puck*, 15 February 1882, p. 378.)

tribe unused to civilized customs, who seemed stupefied by all the judicial ceremony. The magistrate said:

"Ask the accused if he saw the lady that night." The question was referred to him in Irish, and the old man broke out into an involved explanation, gesticulating, appealing to the others accused and to heaven. Then he quieted down, worn out by his effort, and the interpreter turned to the magistrate and said:

"He says no, 'your worship.'"

"Ask him if he was in that neighbourhood at that hour." The old man again began to talk, to protest, to shout, almost beside himself with the anguish of being unable to understand or to make himself understood, weeping in anger and terror. And the interpreter, again, dryly:

"He says no, 'your worship.'"

When the questioning was over, the guilt of the poor old man was declared proved, and he was remanded to a superior court which condemned him to the noose. On the day the sentence was executed, the square in front of the prison was jammed full of kneeling people shouting prayers in Irish for the repose of Myles Joyce's soul. The story was told that the executioner, unable to make the victim understand him, kicked at the miserable man's head in anger to shove it into the noose. (CW 197–98)

In December of 1882 an old man named Myles Joyce had indeed been hanged, along with two other men, in County Galway for murder; he "was generally considered to be an innocent victim of public indignation" (Mason and Ellmann in CW 197). Joyce's narrative emphasizes the fact that, as a Gaelic-speaking Irish Celt, Myles Joyce was allowed no voice of his own in an English-speaking forum. The story serves as an allegory of the Irish "race" under English domination. As Gayatri Spivak has asked, can the subaltern speak? Or must we conclude, along with Karl Marx, that "they cannot represent themselves; they must be represented"? If so, that representation is often, as in this story, distorted and peremptory, resulting in public execution or personal immolation. As Spivak has argued about the subaltern woman under imperialism, she is allowed no subject position from which to speak: "There is no space from where the subaltern (sexed) subject can speak" (Young 163); thus everyone else speaks for her but herself. And if the racialized and colonized Irish subalterns "must be represented," how can they be represented? How can a young Joyce represent them, and thus create/represent the uncreated/unrepresented conscience of his race? Should he speak as an Irishman, or must he use the language and cultural systems of the oppressors? (As Stephen Dedalus thinks about the English dean of studies in Portrait: "How different are the words home, Christ, ale, master, on his lips and on mine! . . . His language, so familiar and so foreign, will always be for me an acquired speech" [P68 189].) To speak as an "Irishman" means that, like Myles Joyce, one will not be heard: surely it did not escape Joyce's linguistic sensitivity that the de-speeched subaltern here has the same name as himself and is of "the ancient tribe of the Joyces."

Joyce's own comment after telling this story is revealing precisely along these lines:

The figure of this dumbfounded old man, a remnant of a civilization not ours, deaf and dumb before his judge, is a symbol of the Irish nation at the bar of public opinion. Like him, she is unable to appeal to the modern conscience

of England and other countries. The English journalists act as interpreters between Ireland and the English electorate. . . . Skimming over the dispatches
from London (which . . . have something of the laconic quality of the interpreter mentioned above), the public conceives of the Irish as highwaymen
with distorted faces, roaming the night with the object of taking the hide of
every Unionist. (CW 198)

Joyce is aware that being-spoken-for ("interpreted" and represented) results in
the essentialized negative stereotypes of the race ("the Irish as highwaymen
with distorted faces, roaming the night"). Unable to speak, Ireland is "unable
to appeal to the modern conscience of England and other countries." Along
with Joyce, Ireland herself was acutely aware of the trap involved in this pattern of being "represented" and essentialized, as illustrated in a telling Irish
political cartoon ("Pat" in fig. 8), in which an English journalist sent to Ireland to "furnish truthful sketches of Irish character" encounters a handsome
and respectable looking Irish gentleman and draws/represents him instead as
a frighteningly bestial and vampiric gorilla (Curtis, Apes 71). As Joyce has
Madden point out in Stephen Hero, the Irish Celt is labeled/libeled as "the baboon-faced Irishman that we see in Punch" (SH 64). How can one break this
pattern and represent oneself and one's own "race" and conscience?

For this binary pattern is a trap that essentializes and limits representation
to precisely its own terms, terms one must play by if one accepts the binary oppositions. In other words, if you try to prove that you aren't what "they" say
you are, you are judging/arguing by the same rules/categories "they" are, and so
you end up reifying/maintaining those categories in place as functional realities. For example, if you try to prove that you are more angel than ape, that
you aren't a Hottentot or Maori, then you are only reinforcing and reinscrib-
ing the terms of a hierarchy that places angels (and Anglos) at the top and
"Negroes" and Orientals near the bottom. A textbook example of the dangers
of such totalizing binaries is the case of Benjamin Disraeli, who, as an English
Jew trying to exculpate Jews from English and European anti-Semitism, proved
more English than the English and more racist than the Anglo-Saxonist.
John Tenniel's cartoon (fig. 9) in Punch of Disraeli masquerading as an angel
brilliantly underscores the racial supremacist's motivating fear and anxiety of
being seen or represented as an ape instead (Curtis, Apes 106). Consequently,
Disraeli's attitudes toward "other" races were, in spite of his own marginal-
ized/othered status, essentialist and prejudicial, resulting in his opinion that
the Irish are a "wild, reckless, indolent, uncertain, and superstitious race" who
"hate our order, our civilization, our enterprising industry, our sustained courage, our decorous liberty, our pure religion" (Curtis, Anglo-Saxons 51; one wonders which "pure religion" Disraeli meant).

Is it possible to break this pattern, to step outside its functions? Joyce, as
his essays exemplify, "tells his compatriots that they must cease to be provin-

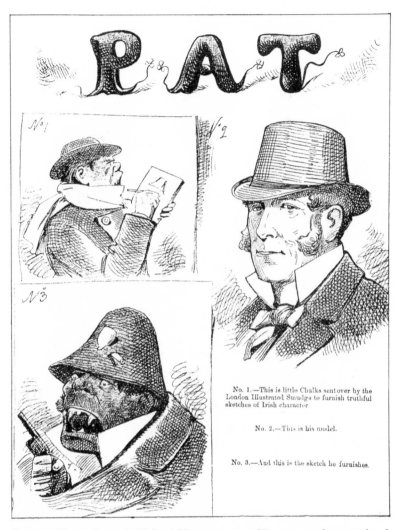

Figure 8. "*Setting Down in Malice.*" The cartoonist of *Pat* suggests the typical and distorted representation of Irish features and character by the English press. In his representation an English reporter, "Chalks" (no. 1), portrays a handsome and respectable Irishman (no. 2) as a bestial and vampiric gorilla instead (no. 3). (*Pat*, n.s. 1, no. 2, 22 January 1881.)

Figure 9. *"Dressing for an Oxford Bal Masqué."* In Tenniel's cartoon Disraeli's masquerade as an Oxonian angel underscores the central fear by racial supremacists of being thought of as apes rather than angels. (*Punch*, 10 December 1864.)

cial and folklorist and mere Irish" (Mason and Ellmann in CW 8); he rejected the limitations of a narrow and provincial nationalism in order to speak to a wider, international (and not purely "English") forum, advocating internationalism over provincialism, advising the Irish to look toward Europe and the international community as its "bar of public opinion," rather than trying to define itself within English constructions of empire, race, and nationhood.[4]

Joyce's logic might be seen as a choice not to play by the same terms as the binary system that would function him as a primitive and racialized Celtic other, but to "play along" with such terms and racial comparisons—by refunctioning them and activating them in an enabling (rather than disabling) fashion. As Michael Banton has noted about attitudes toward racial difference and sameness, "Ideas about race have mostly been used to exclude people from privilege while ideas about shared ethnicity have been used to create bonds of belonging together" (126). In *Ulysses* and *Finnegans Wake,* Joyce repeatedly rejects and reverses all these racialized, derogatory analogies (of the Irish as racial others) by using them in a positive, vital, and enabling manner, by turning them into bonds of shared ethnicity, analogizing and equating the Irish with other races and colonized peoples by suggesting a solidarity of the marginalized and othered.[5]

If the Irish were depicted as other races, Joyce shows that being like (or just being) other races is a positive thing. As early as 1907 he was arguing that the Celtic race in Ireland has Oriental roots: "This language [Gaelic] is oriental in origin, and has been identified by many philologists with the ancient language of the Phoenicians," a racialized analogy clearly meant to be positive rather than pejorative, since the Phoenicians were (he tells us) "an adventurous people, who had a monopoly of the sea" and were "the originators of trade and navigation, according to historians"; Joyce goes on to argue that this ancient people's Druidic religion and civilization were also transplanted to Ireland (*CW* 156). Later Joyce points out that Irish civilization is "almost as old as the Chinese," dating back "to a time when England was an uncivilized country" (173).

The Orientalist comparison had already provided the Irish with the enabling analogy of themselves as Israelites (led by Parnell as another Moses) searching for freedom from a tyrannical Egyptian empire, an analogy Joyce would play with in the "Aeolus" episode of *Ulysses* and which he first evoked in his 1912 essay "The Shade of Parnell," who "like another Moses, led a turbulent and unstable people from the house of shame to the verge of the Promised Land" (*CW* 225). None of these equations/analogies between the Irish and other "races" has derogatory implications for the peoples being compared; rather, they argue that the Irish share in and participate in the strengths and glories of these other civilizations. Joyce is able to employ the racialized analogies positively, even if only by suggesting a solidarity of the marginalized, as when he warns that the English, "if they are wise . . . will hesitate to alienate the sympathy of the Irish for constitutional agitation; especially now that India and Egypt are in an uproar and the overseas colonies are asking for an imperial federation" (*CW* 194).

By the time Joyce came to write *Ulysses* he would equate the Irish with the Greeks as well as with the Phoenicians and the Jews, citing Victor Bérard's arguments about Homer in *Les Phéniciens et l'Odyssée*; as Richard Ellmann has pointed out, "Joyce could [thus] claim Bérard's authority for that climactic encounter in *Ulysses* when 'jewgreek meets greekjew.' . . . In other words, the whole Middle East played its part" (27). Which is to say that the very conception of *Ulysses* is based on an implied equation of Otherness with the Self, of Oriental/Jew with West/Greek, denying the comfort and clarity of binary distinctions based on an essentialized (and fetishized) notion of inherent difference.

Conversely, to base a nationalist response upon the terms of these essentializing binary distinctions is to play by the same rules of that binarity and thus to take on the same hierarchical assumptions. Thus, as Luke Gibbons argues, "many of the conceptions requisitioned by nationalist propagandists in defence of Irish culture are, in fact, an extension of colonialism, rather than a repudiation of it. The racial concept of an Irish national character is a case in point" (104). By positing a countering notion of Irish racial/national character to combat the English stereotype, Irish nationalists were themselves performing an act of static stereotyping; "the 'Celt,' and by implication the Celtic revival, owed as much to the benevolent colonialism of Matthew Arnold as it did to the inner recesses of hidden Ireland" (Gibbons 104).[6]

Such binary logic is predicated on an Us/Them distinction that argues for racial purity and superiority, Us always being valued above Them. Buying into those terms means simply reversing the terms, and claiming that "no, it's *we* who are better than *you*" in an act of reverse racism. Irish Nationalism and the Celtic Revival, or Celticism, were in large measure just this sort of response; thus, for example, Arthur Griffith could (much like Disraeli), while arguing for Irish autonomy and freedom, be so otherwise bigoted as to approve of black slavery (see Gibbons 104).

Celticism or Irish Nationalism tried to do for the "Irish race" what Anglo-Saxonist racism had done for the "English race," by exalting the Self's own proclaimed racial and cultural superiority in comparison to all other races/cultures. Thus, Irish scholars involved in the Celtic Revival during the latter decades of the nineteenth century argued that they were "the direct descendants of a pure and holy race, composed of Firbolgs, Tuatha de Dananns, and Milesians, whose ancient institutions, veneration for learning, and religious zeal made Saxon culture . . . look nothing less than Barbarian"; as Curtis concludes, "ethnocentric Irish men and women sought to combat heavy doses of Anglo-Saxonist venom with a Celticist serum of their own making" (*Anglo-Saxons* 15), seeking to provoke patriotic fervor by being "racy of the soil." Ernest Renan's (whom Stephen cites three times in *Stephen Hero*) lyrical and ecstatic views of the Celtic race in his *La poésie des Races Celtiques*, which argued that the Celts were unmatched in the world in both their purity of blood and their strength of character, were sounded by the Gaelic League and the Irish Literary Revival; similarly Irish apologists like Charles Gavan Duffy had already proclaimed that "the history of Ireland abounded in noble lessons, and had the unity and purpose of an epic poem" (see Lloyd 68). The collusion and mirrored quality of such ethnocentrisms is suggested by the fact that the same logic and the same stereotypes were invoked by both sides: Matthew Arnold's analyses of the distinctive character of the Irish genius (such as that "he is truly sentimental") were in fact largely derived from Renan, which also explains why the Arnoldian image should have so appealed to the Irish Literary Revival. The ease with which Irish apologists could accept "the Arnoldian stereotype as benign—in fact, as not a stereotype at all—explains how it could be taken to heart by Irish revivalists," as Gibbons suggests (104).

In fact, the very notion that there was still a pure and distinct Celtic race living in Ireland was an essentialist construction that, ironically enough, was equally acceptable (in fact essential) to *both* the Irish Nationalist and to the Anglo-Saxon imperialist, for both depended (emotionally and psychologically) on the notion of themselves as a race pure and distinct from others. Thus, the Celticist response was a mirror image of Anglo-Saxonist racism, resulting in the ancestor worship and racial mythology espoused by the Gaelic League, the Gaelic Athletic Association, the Ancient Order of Hibernians, and so on.

In 1892 Douglas Hyde delivered in Dublin his powerful and influential lecture "The Necessity for De-Anglicising Ireland," which advocated that the noble Celtic race should divest itself of the despicable culture of the "bloody brutal Sassenachs" and return to Irish cultural purity by studying Gaelic, "our once great national tongue" (Hyde 160). This nationalist nostalgia for origins argues for the same kind of cultural purity and superiority that the Anglo-Saxonist supremacists had long advocated for the English "race." In spite of all the bloody invasions, settlements, and migrations in Irish history—Celts, Romans, Danes, Normans, Saxons, and so on—the Irish were somehow still held up as being pure of blood. Arguments were even made by Celticist enthusiasts that America had been discovered in A.D. 545 by Saint Brendan, or that Shakespeare had been a Celt (suggestions Joyce roundly mocks and parodies in the "Cyclops" episode of *Ulysses*).

Such Celtic ethnocentrism was most fervently espoused by the Fenians (whose very name reflects a commitment to Celtic mythology and militarism), espousing an ancient mythology that seemed to justify war, bloodshed, and heroic death, adding the likes of Shane O'Neill, Wolfe Tone, and Robert Emmet to the mythological pantheon of Cuchulain and Finn MacCool.[7] Joyce, who found Emmet's uprising and the Young Ireland movement to risk foolish and pointless spilling of blood (CW 189), would have none of this Celtic ethnocentrism, blood cult, and originary nostalgia, and refused to be involved in the Revival and in the public activities of Irish Nationalism. His parody of Fenian Celticism in the "Cyclops" chapter of *Ulysses* skewers such blindly racist logic as that espoused by the "Citizen," in real life Michael Cusack, treasurer of the Gaelic Union (see Fig. 10). For the pacifist, exiled, and multilingual Joyce, the "spiritual liberation" of Ireland and the creation of the "conscience of my race" involved getting out of the binary structure and into an internationalist, multilingual, and multiculturalist perspective.

What Joyce grew increasingly to understand is that, whereas racism and ethnocentrism depend on static essences and absolute difference, peoples and

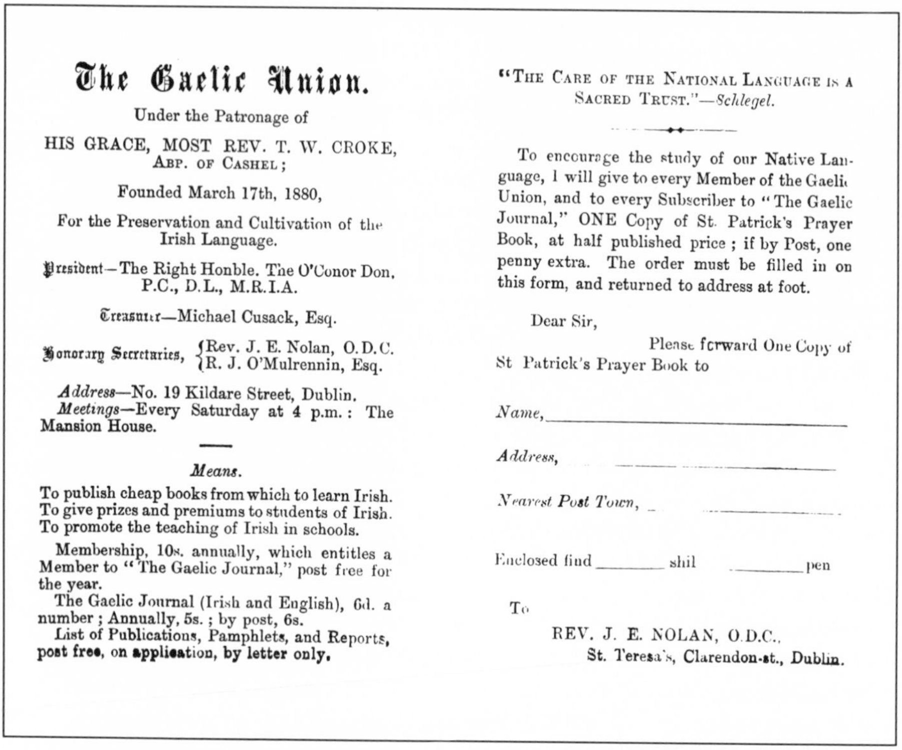

The Gaelic Union.

Under the Patronage of

HIS GRACE, MOST REV. T. W. CROKE,
ABP. OF CASHEL;

Founded March 17th, 1880,

For the Preservation and Cultivation of the Irish Language.

President—The Right Honble. The O'Conor Don, P.C., D.L., M.R.I.A.

Treasurer—Michael Cusack, Esq.

Honorary Secretaries, {Rev. J. E. Nolan, O.D.C. / R. J. O'Mulrennin, Esq.

Address—No. 19 Kildare Street, Dublin.
Meetings—Every Saturday at 4 p.m.: The Mansion House.

Means.

To publish cheap books from which to learn Irish.
To give prizes and premiums to students of Irish.
To promote the teaching of Irish in schools.

Membership, 10s. annually, which entitles a Member to "The Gaelic Journal," post free for the year.

The Gaelic Journal (Irish and English), 6d. a number; Annually, 5s.; by post, 6s.

List of Publications, Pamphlets, and Reports, post free, on application, by letter only.

"THE CARE OF THE NATIONAL LANGUAGE IS A SACRED TRUST."—*Schlegel.*

To encourage the study of our Native Language, I will give to every Member of the Gaelic Union, and to every Subscriber to "The Gaelic Journal," ONE Copy of St. Patrick's Prayer Book, at half published price; if by Post, one penny extra. The order must be filled in on this form, and returned to address at foot.

Dear Sir,

Please forward One Copy of St Patrick's Prayer Book to

Name, ______

Address, ______

Nearest Post Town, ______

Enclosed find ______ shil ______ pen

To

REV. J. E. NOLAN, O.D.C.,
St. Teresa's, Clarendon-st., Dublin.

Figure 10. "*The Gaelic Union.*" Pamphlet put out by the Gaelic Union "to encourage the study of our Native Language," an activity it refers to (citing Schlegel) as "a sacred trust." Michael Cusack is listed as Treasurer. (My thanks to Theresa O'Connor for providing a copy of this pamphlet.)

populations contain multiplicitous and heterogeneous characteristics of both individual and cultural difference that cannot be so conveniently (and logocentrically) named and essentialized. In such binary operations both self and other get conveniently and comfortably demarcated (and *bordered* by an essentialist Pale), and the consequent totalizing (and Manichean) mechanics of absolute differences "left no loophole for the Irish to share much in common with their English rulers" (Curtis, *Anglo-Saxons* 53), allowing neither for shared traits nor for heterogeneity within each individual group characterized.

The result is a form of reverse ethnocentrism in which the racialized and colonized subaltern group (Ireland) searches for its own native origins and cultural superiority in order to proclaim a racial purity with which to match and mirror the claims of its imperial oppressor. In *White Mythologies: Writing History and the West,* Robert Young points out that "those who evoke the 'nativist' position through a nostalgia for a lost or repressed culture idealize the possibility of that lost origin being recoverable in all its former plenitude without allowing for the fact that the figure of the lost origin, the 'other' that the colonizer has repressed, has itself been constructed in terms of the colonizer's own self-image" (168). As Spivak and Homi Bhabha have argued, and as the Celticist case illustrates, such a "nativist" position merely mirrors the hierarchical fantasies of the colonizer's culture, now projected onto the fantasized originary culture of the other, and that all such arguments, from either side, employ the terms and logic constructed by the dominant, colonizing culture. Or, as Frantz Fanon writes: "Western bourgeois racial . . . ideology . . . manages to appear logical in its own eyes by inviting the sub-men to become human, and to take as their prototype Western humanity as incarnated in the Western bourgeoisie" (163).

One of the colonizer's rules/terms by which both sides of such a binary dialectic play is a "purer than thou" racial claim, arguing the purity and essence of one's own racial group. But arguments for either an Anglo-Saxon or a Celtic racial essence/purity are but wishful thinking, since they suppress the specific heterogeneities, differences, and slippages within each individual notion. As early as 1895 William D. Babington and George Sigerson had both tried to refute the notion that either the English or the Irish were separate races, noting that the concept of "the English race" itself willfully ignored the fluid mixture of races in Britain over many centuries, that "the Irish race" was the composite result of waves of invasions and strife over many centuries, that there were thus no such things as inherently Celtic (or English) virtues or vices, and that the specific differences between cultures resulted from social and environmental influences (see Curtis, *Anglo-Saxons* 104 and Gibbons 105).

Instead of a pure lineage of cultural inheritance, composite cultures might more fruitfully be theorized not on a notion of difference based on rigid binarisms but on a heterogeneity resulting from porous borders and live spheres of influence and interaction. After all, the very activities and characteristics that the self would expel and represent as primitive and other in fact shape the self's own culture and constitution. What gets occluded is not only the actual heterogeneous specificities of different cultures but also the presence of the other within the self, the willingness to acknowledge that not only does the other-within shape the self, but that in very real ways it *is* the self. What is denied is an awareness of the fluid and reciprocal nature of influence and cultural formation, in which the self both acts and is acted on. As James Clifford puts it in his essay "Traveling Cultures," "what's elided is the wider global world of intercultural import-export in which" the encounter with the other "is always already enmeshed" (100). The physical as well as figural topos of a conquered culture (as also of the conqueror's culture) is already what Mary Pratt calls a "contact zone," composed of porous or fluid "borders" that blur and deny any clear markers of absolute difference (in this sense, Gloria Anzaldua's figuration of "borderlands" functions similarly).[8]

Finally, this was a reality Joyce was well aware of in his choice to reject the Celticism of Irish Nationalism, founded as it was on this binary trap. His argument that the Irish should look beyond their narrow provincialism and their affairs with England and develop a more international consciousness was an attempt to break out of such constricting dynamics and terms, in which an Irish essence could be defined only on the conqueror's terms (such as those posited by Arnold) and in reaction/response to English claims. For Joyce rejected wholesale the Celticist argument for racial purity and national characteristics, which he found to be as specious as the English stereotyping of the Irish character as the "baboon-faced figures" (SH 64) and "the unbalanced helpless idiots we read about" (CW 171) in the English papers and magazines. Like Babington and Sigerson, we find him (in "Ireland, Island of Saints and Sages") reminding us that "the Celtic race" was "compounded of the old Celtic stock and the Scandinavian, Anglo-Saxon and Norman races . . . with the various elements mingling and renewing the ancient body." The Irish, Joyce argues, are in fact a very mixed race—"Do we not see that in Ireland the Danes, the Firbolgs, the Milesians from Spain, the Norman invaders, and the Anglo-Saxon settlers have united to form a new entity?" (CW 166)—including many Irish patriots such as Parnell "in whose veins there was not even a drop of Celtic blood" (CW 161–62; the then mayor of Dublin, Mr. Nannetti, he informed his Triestine audience, was Italian). Joyce's representation of the Irish "race," cogently articulated in a significant passage, is very much a vision of a complex mix of racial and cultural strains operating within a fluid "contact zone":

> Our civilization is a vast fabric, in which the most diverse elements are mingled, in which nordic aggressiveness and Roman law, the new bourgeois conventions and the remnant of a Syriac religion [Christianity] are reconciled. In such a fabric, it is useless to look for a thread that may have remained pure and virgin without having undergone the influence of a neighbouring thread. What race, or what language . . . can boast of being pure today? And no race has less right to utter such a boast than the race now living in Ireland. (CW 165–66)

In rejecting the argument that the "race now living in Ireland" has somehow remained "pure and virgin," Joyce is rejecting the ideological foundation behind the Citizen's, the Gaelic League's, and the Literary Revival's motivations. In arguing that in Irish civilization "the most diverse elements are mingled," Joyce is acknowledging the hybridity and collaboration of discursive influences and cultural formations. His subsequent fictional works become increasingly informed by his sensitivity toward the nature of the hybridity, ambivalences, and interpenetrations involved in hegemonic and discursive formations. This was, of course, the understanding of discourses that Foucault advanced in The Order of Things when he suggested that the histories of the same (self) and the other were inextricably implicated and interpenetrated: "the history of the order imposed on things would be the history of the Same—of that which, for a given culture, is both dispersed and related" (xxiv); as Shem/Mercius would say to Shaun/Justius in *Finnegans Wake*, "the days of youyouth are evermixed mimine" (*FW* 194.4). Joyce would go on, especially in *Ulysses* and *Finnegans Wake*, increasingly self-consciously to blur the racialized demarcations of difference between a dark other and an imperial self. For Joyce was consciously rejecting the rigid simplicity of the mirrored racial arguments and characters posited by both Anglo-Saxonism and Celticism, as he attempted more fruitfully to engage in the "spiritual liberation of my country" and to "create the uncreated conscience of my race" by representing Ireland in "my nicely polished looking-glass" instead, a representation not mirrored in the haze of a Celtic twilight but, in Seamus Deane's phrase, as a "mirror held up to Culture" (41).

NOTES

1. Cited in Curtis, *Anglo-Saxons and Celts*, p. 22. Curtis adds: "So persistent has been this theme of English cultural and racial superiority over the Irish that one begins to suspect the existence among those who tried to subdue and rule the Irish of a deep-seated need to justify their confiscatory and homicidal habits in that country" (18).

2. Joyce himself has been, in our own century, a recipient/victim of this racialized discourse of Irishness, for—as Gibbons points out—it was the Unionist provost of Trinity College, J. P. Mahaffy, who asserted that "James Joyce is a living argument in favour of my contention that it was a mistake to establish a separate university for the aborigines of this island—for the corner boys who spit in the Liffey" (113).

3. "The stereotype of the primitive, melancholic, and prognathous Irish Celt was documented by anthropologists and ethnologists who constructed impressive typologies of the physiognomies of the British and Irish peoples" (Curtis, *Apes* 94).

4. Joyce's portrayal of Davin, Stephen's young Nationalist friend in *Portrait*, whom Stephen mocks as a "rude Firbolg Mind" with a "delight in rude bodily skill—for Davin had sat at the feet of Michael Cusack, the Gael" (*P68* 180), is of a character trapped precisely inside the binary logic and limits of Celticism. Stephen describes Davin as "the young peasant worshipp[ing] the sorrowful legend of Ireland. . . . His nurse had taught him Irish and shaped his rude imagination by the broken lights of Irish myth . . . [with] the attitude of a dullwitted loyal serf"; as a result, "whatsoever of thought or of feeling came to him from England or by way of English culture his mind stood armed against in obedience to a password: and of the world that lay beyond England he knew only the foreign legion of France in which he spoke of serving" (*P68* 181). In effect, such a closed system is trapped within the oscillation of an English/Irish dialectic, in which everything is still finally defined around Englishness.

5. This was also the basic logic and strategy behind a recent popular film, *The Commitments*. In this engaging Alan Parker movie, a young man named Jimmy Rabbitte organizes a rock-and-roll band in Dublin that he trains to perform black "soul music." When one of the skeptical band members asks, "D'ya think maybe we're a little white for that kind of thing?" Jimmy points out, "You don't get it, lads. The Irish are the

blacks of Europe. And Dubliners are the blacks of Ireland." The poor Dublin young-
sters in the band then take on as their motto "I'm black and I'm proud." At another
point, standing in a welfare queue and finding another band member also on the dole,
Jimmy notes, "We're a Third World country, what can you do?" Finally, in a resonant
comment that speaks to the racialized discourse of the Irish as apes, Jimmy describes
his band thus: "We're the guerillas of soul. That's guerilla with a 'u', not an 'o'".

6. Gibbons goes on to suggest that "the racial mode is, moreover, the version of
Irish nationalism which has passed into general academic circulation in recent years
through the 'revisionist' writings of Conor Cruise O'Brien and F. S. L. Lyons (among
others)—largely, one suspects, because it redefines even resistance within the colonial
frame and thus neutralizes the very idea of anti-colonial discourse" (104).

7. Theresa O'Connor's essay "Demythologizing Nationalism: Joyce's Dialogized
Grail Myth" (in Cheng and Martin, 100-21) demonstrates how Joyce subverts such a
Celtic mythological discourse of war and blood by replacing it with a mythos of life,
birth, and renewal.

8. Pratt defines "contact zone" in this way: "I use this term to refer to the social
spaces where cultures meet, clash, and grapple with each other, often in contexts of
highly asymmetrical relations of power, such as colonialism, slavery, or their aftermaths
as they are lived out in many parts of the world today" (34).

WORKS CITED

Anzaldua, Gloria. *Borderlands/La Frontera: The New Mestiza*. San Francisco: Spin-
sters/Aunt Lute, 1987.

Banton, Michael. *Racial Theories*. Cambridge: Cambridge University Press, 1987.

Cheng, Vincent J., and Timothy Martin, eds. *Joyce in Context*. Cambridge: Cambridge
University Press, 1992.

Clifford, James. "Traveling Cultures." In *Cultural Studies*, ed. Lawrence Grossberg, Cary
Nelson, and Paul Treichler. London: Routledge, 1991.

Curtis, L. P., Jr. *Anglo-Saxons and Celts: A Study of Anti-Irish Prejudice in Victorian England*. Bridgeport, Conn.: University of Bridgeport, 1968.

———. *Apes and Angels: The Irishman in Victorian Caricature*. Washington, D.C.:
Smithsonian Institution Press, 1971.

Deane, Seamus. "Joyce the Irishman." In *The Cambridge Companion to James Joyce*, ed.
Derek Attridge. Cambridge and New York: Cambridge University Press, 1990.

Ellmann, Richard. *The Consciousness of Joyce*. New York: Oxford University Press, 1977.

Fanon, Frantz. *The Wretched of the Earth*. Trans. Constance Farrington. New York:
Grove Press, 1965.

Foucault, Michel. *The Order of Things: An Archaeology of the Human Sciences*. London: Tavistock Publications, 1970.

Gibbons, Luke. "Race against Time: Racial Discourse and Irish History." *Oxford Literary Review* 13, nos. 1–2, *Neocolonialism* (1991): 95–117.

Hyde, Douglas. "The Necessity for De-Anglicising Ireland." In *Language, Lore and Lyrics,* ed. Breandan O Conaire. Dublin: Irish Academic Press, 1986.

Joyce, James. *The Critical Writings of James Joyce.* Ed. Ellsworth Mason and Richard Ellmann. New York: Viking Press, 1959; reprint, 1964.

Lloyd, David. *Nationalism and Minor Literature: James Clarence Mangan and the Emergence of Irish Cultural Nationalism.* Berkeley: University of California Press, 1987.

O'Brien, Maire, and Conor Cruise O'Brien. *A Concise History of Ireland.* 3rd ed. New York: Thames & Hudson, 1985.

O'Connor, Theresa. "Demythologizing Nationalism: Joyce's Dialogized Grail Myth." In *Joyce in Context,* ed. Cheng and Martin.

Pratt, Mary Louise. "Arts of the Contact Zone." In *Profession 91,* ed. Phyllis Franklin. New York: Modern Language Association, 1991.

Said, Edward W. *Orientalism.* New York: Vintage Books, 1979.

Spivak, Gayatri Chakravorty. "Can the Subaltern Speak?" In *Marxism and the Interpretation of Culture,* ed. Cary Nelson and Lawrence Grossberg. Champaign: University of Illinois Press, 1988.

———. "The Rani of Sirmur." In *Europe and Its Others,* vol. I, ed. Francis Barker, et al. Colchester: University of Essex, 1985.

Woolf, Virginia. *A Room of One's Own.* New York: Harcourt, Brace, Jovanovich, 1929.

Young, Robert. *White Mythologies: Writing History and the West.* London: Routledge, 1990.

43

OndtHarriet, PoldyLeon and Shem the Conman

David Norris

The deposit of the Léon/Joyce correspondence with the National Library of Ireland bears eloquent and moving testament to the friendship of two remarkable men and to the qualities of integrity and dedication that each of them possessed in different ways. The basic elements of this story have been known for some time, and it is not for me, today, to rehearse these details. I would like, however, to take this opportunity once more to reiterate my profound respect for both the principal protagonists in this affair. Neither do I seek to use this occasion to ventilate in any extended way my own personal position in the controversy that regrettably surrounded the ceremony revealing this important cache of material to the public, which took place at the beginning of April this year.

However it is not, I think, entirely inappropriate for me to summarize the grounds of my reservation as a preamble to what I have to say about the contents of the correspondence itself. At the opening it was revealed that a certain number of papers of what were described as a purely personal family nature had been released to Stephen James Joyce, grandson of James Joyce, and also that another section of the correspondence was placed under a further embargo until 31 December 2050. This announcement shocked me, and I was further disturbed by the tone of the contribution made by Mr. Stephen Joyce and consequently left the library. I felt it to be ironic that this announcement should be made in the very place where, in the "Scylla and Charybdis" section of *Ulysses*, James Joyce—in the person of his alter ego, Stephen Dedalus—made what amounts to a strong plea for full access to the most private and intimate details of an artist's life in order to understand the nature of human genius and its impact upon literary creation. Moreover, the material involved was the property of the Léon family and not the Joyce family. Indeed, a reading of the accompa-

44

nying notes from Paul Léon and Constantine Curran, which I have before me, does not seem to me to require the action that was taken by the Library and that, indeed, established a very dangerous precedent in dealing with such items.

On the other hand, I would like to pay tribute to the very careful, painstaking and scholarly work undertaken on behalf of the Library by its staff and, in particular, by Catherine Fahy. The collection itself is divided into sixteen sections ranging from a detailed correspondence between James Joyce and Paul Léon and Léon acting on behalf of Joyce and Harriet Weaver, Joyce's benefactor, down to bundles of gas bills, sheafs of bank accounts, documents relating to home insurance, Joyce's many moves, the decoration of his flats, and his daughter Lucia's medical bills and receipts. The principal sections are

1. Direct correspondence between Joyce and Léon
2. Correspondence between Joyce, Léon and Harriet Weaver
3. General correspondence
4. Business correspondence with
    a. agents and solicitors,
    b. publishers, broadcasting corporations, etc., and
    c. film proposals, translation rights, etc., and
5. Manuscript and typescript drafts of poems and pages from "Work in Progress."

I propose to deal almost entirely with the first two sections, which, from a biographical point of view, considerably amplify our understanding of Joyce's personality.

The correspondence with Léon opens and closes with Léon employed on errands regarding the money, clothing, health, and publishing problems that beset Joyce and his family. The correspondence with Weaver follows a parallel pattern. I have to say at the outset that I retain with some modification my profound respect for Joyce and his single-minded devotion to his artistic mission. I have also, however, to state that the picture of Joyce presented by the late Richard Ellmann—of Joyce's qualities, of James Joyce as a man—seem now to me more representative of that gentle and humane scholar himself than of James Joyce, and that we may, perhaps reluctantly, have to modify our view of Joyce somewhat in the direction of the long-held popular image of Joyce as manipulative, arrogant, and, in times of crisis, frequently indifferent to the feelings of those who became his helpers.

Each of the three letters referred to in detail on page 1 of the Library's catalogue starts with a peremptory order to Léon to make telephone calls on Joyce's account. This is strikingly reminiscent of the opening scene of *Ulysses*, in which Buck Mulligan conducts his relationship with Stephen Dedalus by barking out a series of commands. "Come up, Kinch! Come up, you fearful jesuit!" "lend us a loan of your noserag," and finally, "give us that key," a scene that probably echoes real life and Joyce's resentment at what he felt was his cavalier treatment by Oliver St. John Gogarty. Throughout this correspondence there are ironic distorted echoes in Joyce's own personality of traits that in literature he held up to disdainful examination.

On the other hand, endlessly patient and good humoured, Paul Léon emerges from the correspondence as an incarnation of some aspects of the spirit of Leopold Bloom. It is clear throughout that Léon had a genuine affection for Joyce the man, and in an early letter of 14 July 1932, Léon engagingly acknowledges, like Yeats and Mrs. Joyce before him, that he has not yet read *Ulysses* but he does promise to try. What Joyce made of this admission was not recorded in the correspondence, but in an obvious assertion of power, Joyce seeks from the beginning to control the tone, form, and content of the correspondence: 20 July 1932, Léon should type his letters to Joyce; 31 July 1932, Léon should not write funny messages; 8 September 1932, Léon should not employ "such phrases." The balance of power is very clearly indicated by the fact that the blizzard of commands for Léon to make telephone calls is curiously counterpointed by Joyce's instruction of 20 September 1932 that Léon should not telephone Joyce unless the matter is of exceptional importance because the phones of the Hotel Metropole were located on the ground floor. The master, it seems, was not to be inconvenienced in the carrying out of Léon's largely self-imposed duties. However on 16 February 1933 Joyce did, at least—acting, perhaps, as the new womanly man—send Léon a valentine!

Léon was a man of profound common sense who frequently gave Joyce good advice with regard to legal matters concerning agents and publishers. For example on 4 May 1937 he writes to Joyce, who wanted to dismiss J. Ralph Pinker as his agent, and demonstrates that severing the connection with Pinker's firm would result neither in any saving nor in any simplification of procedures for collection of royalties. Pinker's had been Joyce's agents for twenty-one years, and now, as Léon points out, their files were useful and Pinker was not in a position to damage Joyce's interests, as he was not involved in any negotiations with publishers. Moreover, as Pinker would continue to draw commission in any case, there was little practical value to be obtained by firing him.

When, as frequently happened, Joyce became coy about direct contact with his patroness, Miss Harriet Weaver, Léon was used by both as an intermediary. This appears from time to time to have irritated Nora Joyce, who may, indeed, have been slightly jealous of the fact that another woman was secretly in communication with her husband through a third party. A letter of Joyce dated 6 October 1939 thanks Léon for a letter and an enclosure that he has not seen, since Nora tore up the enclosure, which was a letter from Harriet Weaver. Joyce also relays to Léon a message from his wife indicating that it was her intention to tear up any other letters that Weaver enclosed in future correspondence.

Both the Joyces, in fact, appear frequently to have placed an interdict on correspondence between their friends and relatives. In 1935 Joyce made substantial use of his sister Eileen Schaurek in dealing with his daughter, Lucia. Mrs. Schaurek generously, if a little foolishly, took Lucia into her home at Bray, where for a time Lucia seemed to settle down in the company of her cousins Nora and Boezema. She ran away on several occasions and she appears to have made at least one attempt to burn the bungalow down. Joyce seems to have felt that his sister did not sacrifice herself sufficiently in looking after his daughter and was angry with Miss Weaver for presuming to have suggested any resemblance between Lucia and her aunt. On 15 April 1935 we find Harriet Weaver grovelling to Joyce with an apology for having failed with Lucia and for appearing to compare Lucia with Eileen. A few months later, on 17 August 1935, she writes to Léon, confirming that a final set of instructions had been relayed to Eileen and that, presumably on Joyce's direct instructions, she has agreed to a complete termination of correspondence with Mrs. Schaurek.

Toward the end of the direct Joyce/Léon correspondence comes one of the saddest items, recounting an incident already known through Ellmann's biography, when, after a disagreement occasioned by Léon's refusal to be partisan in the divorce between Giorgio and Helen, Joyce demanded the return of all his business papers and contracts. A letter of 19 November 1939 in response to this request from Joyce encloses the dossier on Lucia, an envelope containing cuttings about *Finnegans Wake* and all the contracts that were then in his possession. However, characteristically, the last dated letter from Léon to Joyce, of 5 February 1940, shows the good and faithful friend in his familiar posture of service. It ends by stating that he "will be glad to do anything urgent that Mr. Joyce wants."

The three-cornered correspondence of Joyce, Léon, and Weaver, which forms the second main division, consists of 213 letters exchanged between 1930 and 1939. It thus covers the period of composition and revision of much of *Finnegans Wake*. Comparatively early in the correspondence, by 1 March 1932, it is clear from remarks contained in a letter of that date from Weaver to Léon that he has been imposed as an intermediary: she writes to thank Léon for having sent her so many letters on Joyce's behalf. This hint was presumably taken on board by Joyce, as a reply is forthcoming by return from Léon in which he indicates that Joyce is overwhelmed by dealing with simultaneous offers of publication for *Ulysses* by four separate American publishers and that he asks Léon to apologise for him for not having written personally.

Inevitably, we come early to the basis for the financial situation between Weaver and Joyce. In a letter dated merely as 1933, Miss Weaver writes that she has instructed Joyce's solicitors to sell £100 of stock. This is a recurrent theme of the correspondence, the sums becoming rapidly larger and the demands more frequent. It is clear that Joyce was determined to live on the capital that Miss Weaver had transferred to him rather than attempting to live within the income provided by interest and dividends, an extremely foolish strategy for someone in his position and one that Miss Weaver was later to blame herself for permitting. The tone of Miss Weaver's letters is sometimes like that of a hybrid of sympathetic nanny and professional victim. She was clearly looking for a cause, a need that Joyce was quite capable of adequately satisfying. She seems indeed, in these letters, to live vicariously through the exciting vicissitudes of the Joyce family and their doings. She did not always do so, however, without the occasional mild Quakerish protest, asking on 4 March 1933 could the Joyces not manage to stay in Zurich longer than seven days for 4,000 francs, which she points out was more than double for each of them what she had paid herself for her stay in Paris.

Relentlessly, however, the selling went on. On 30 March 1933 Léon writes to Weaver to announce the departure of the Joyces for Zurich and to request the sale of another £200 worth of stock. This is followed immediately by a letter of 31 March, in which Léon gives details of the proposed expenses necessitating the sale, suggesting that Miss Weaver's Quaker instincts had once more asserted themselves and she was requiring justification—a justification that appears to have been satisfied, since the same day, 31 March 1933, she writes to Léon indicating compliance with the request. However, on 2 April 1933 Léon is bewailing to Miss Weaver the inevitable consequence in terms of a reduction of Joyce's income. Just under a month later she is agreeing to sell another £100 of stock, the last in this portfolio, and offers to pay £100 herself for the Joyces' trip to Zurich, although she remarks ominously that her own finances are not good. On 13 May 1933, apparently to demonstrate the strength of her friendship for Joyce in the teeth of his accusation that he was being treated like a schoolboy, she increases the Johannesburg stock that she made over to him to £500. Joyce, meanwhile, celebrated the Bloomsday of 1933 by selling yet another £100 of stock. August of that year finds the public trustee expressing concern at the constant realization of capital and the beginning of a long and unsuccessful campaign by Weaver to get Joyce to sign the official application for funds together with details of Lucia's expenses.

On 26 September 1933 Harriet Weaver wrote to Léon a letter whose import was principally addressed to Joyce and that is poignantly reminiscent of a letter addressed to the young Joyce in the same city some thirty years previously by his mother. In this letter Mrs. Joyce wrote to her son, "My Dear Jim, If you are disappointed in my letter and if, as usual, I fail to understand what you wish to explain, believe me it is not from any want of a longing desire to do so and speak the words you want. As you so often said, I am stupid and cannot grasp the great thoughts which are yours much as I desire to do so." In her letter Miss Weaver pathetically asks Léon, if he ever finds Joyce in a mood to listen to a message from her, to tell him that she is "trying very hard to understand and appreciate Work in Progress despite [her] slow, dull and unimaginative mind." Miss Weaver, in fact, was part of a scene in which Joyce continually reconstructed the psychological elements of his childhood and youth in Dublin, reconstituting her as archetypal mother, his own favourite role being that of wayward son.

There is little doubt that Joyce enjoyed manipulating his circle, and the tripartite correspondence between Léon, Joyce, and Weaver indicates Joyce's considerable skill as a ventriloquist. While alternately sympathising, empathising, scolding, and, like many victims, ultimately being induced to blame herself, Miss Weaver provided the perfect audience for his talents. As Christmas approached, Léon himself appears to have been in trouble with Joyce, apologising to Miss Weaver for not being able to keep her au courant with the doings of the Joyce household and explaining that he has seen Joyce only rarely and that his visits have often been short and curt. When the spring of 1934 "sprang" the "gracehoper" was troubled in mind rather than "hoppy" on "akant" of his "Joyicity," and was actually writing lines of dialogue for Miss Weaver at a second remove. On 11 March Léon writes that Joyce is adamant in his refusal to sign the letter for the public trustee and indicates that instead Miss Weaver should write directly to Mr. Joyce saying that she has not forgotten him and that she will always assist him. She should also send over Joyce's books, which were in storage in London. On 17 March 1934 she acknowledges to Léon that she has performed the required contortions. Miss Weaver's unselfishness conveniently knew no bounds.

By autumn (5 October 1934) she is resigned to Joyce's obduracy in refusing to write to the public trustee and offers instead to exchange some of her own stock for the Canadian and Pacific stock. She points, however, to the fact that this will lead to a reduction in her own income and render her less able to help in the future. Her thought, as usual, is ever for Joyce rather than herself. Matters continue to deteriorate until 29 January 1936, on which date a worried Weaver writes to Léon about the financial situation. She fears that if she has to subsidize Joyce from her own resources these will be exhausted in less than ten years. In the light of the prevailing circumstances, it was perhaps optimistic of her to think that even her considerable means, which she placed virtually entirely at Joyce's disposal, would have lasted another decade. She also indicates that she has been secretly providing money for Joyce to make up for the fact that some Canadian and Pacific stock has not been paying dividends for three years. By 7 February, shortly after Joyce's birthday, she is offering to sell more of her own stock, although she insists that Joyce must economize, stating quite flatly that she herself cannot economise any further unless she parts with her flat, an astonishing suggestion. Characteristically, she takes the blame on herself and castigates herself for not having made the capital more inaccessible to Joyce, saying very sensibly that it should have been available only for needs and not for luxuries. She further reproves herself for not having protected Joyce from himself. On 18 February 1936 Joyce in a rather grand gesture declines to accept the transfer of stock, which he had not realized "meant any sacrifice on Miss Weaver's part." This does not, however, prevent him "directing" Léon to write to Munro Saw for £200 to be realized out of her benefaction instead. This has curious and ironic echoes of Joyce's early short story "Eveline," in which the young woman of that title surrenders her wages to her dissipated father, who then responds to her request for housekeeping money by retorting that he does not intend to give her any of his hard earned money to throw about the streets.

Once more Miss Weaver masochistically obliges by abasing herself, writing on 19 February 1936 to Léon requesting him to ask Mr. Joyce to allow her to visit him in Paris. She apparently hoped to be allowed as a supplicant into the presence in order to "clear up misunderstandings." Things did not improve immediately, for on 22 March 1936 we have a letter in which she inquires plaintively whether Mr. Joyce is still too antagonistic toward her to send a message. A letter of 18 September discloses that, unknown to Joyce, she has made good her suggestion of 7 February and acquired Joyce's Canadian and Pacific stock, which has fallen in value and which she would hold to in the hopes of its rising again, at which point she would sell out and make good the difference to Joyce.

Léon, at least, appreciated the nature and extent of Weaver's patronage and vicariously expressed gratitude on behalf of Joyce, a gratitude that she deprecates in a letter of 21 December 1938 while heaping praise on Léon for his assistance to the writer. Joyce apparently did not, however, at this time attempt to offend her by his gratitude, for on 30 December 1938 she tells Léon that she has received a series of registered envelopes but is afraid that she has upset Joyce in some way, as for the first time in twenty-three years he has not sent her Christmas greetings nor did he inscribe the copy of the U.S.A. Matisse edition of *Ulysses* that he had sent to her. The last letter in the collection carries no date but imposes an artistically satisfying symmetry—Paul Léon to Harriet Weaver, money to be sent from Munro Saw.

As the four volumes of Joyce's correspondence amply illustrate, Joyce could be a witty, charming, and engaging correspondent. He was also very human, in addition to being an artist of heroic determination. The letters in the Léon Collection at the National Library of Ireland amplify our knowledge of Joyce, although they do not place him in a flattering light. The baldness of the summaries given in the catalogue minimizes the charm of expression as it exposes the degree of exploitation involved in many of the transactions recorded. Joyce himself might have been surprised at this interpretation. When Beckett, stung by Joyce's rebuff of a growing intimacy between them, stated gloomily that Joyce had no human feeling, Joyce replied, "no feelings, I, My God," indicating that such an attitude showed an incomprehensible misunderstanding of his life and works. The Joyce-Léon-Weaver correspondence gives us an additional context within which to place some of the letters already known to scholars. Nevertheless, despite some negative impact of that context, nothing could diminish the humanity and profound feeling of Joyce's letter to Harriet Weaver in which he defends the expense of his desperate attempts to save his daughter's sanity:

> I believe I can cover most of the expenses of publication of my daughter's alphabet. My idea is not to persuade her that she is a Cézanne but that on her 29th birthday . . . she may see something to persuade her that her whole past has not been a failure. The reason I keep on trying by every means to find a solution for her case (which may come at any time as it did with my eyes) is that she may not think that she is left with a blank future as well. I am aware that I am blamed by everybody for sacrificing that precious metal money to such an extent for such a purpose when it would be done so cheaply and quietly by locking her up in an economical mental prison for the rest of her life.
>
> I will not do so as long as I see a single chance of hope for her recovery, nor blame her or punish her for the great crime she has committed in being a victim to one of the most elusive diseases known to men and unknown to medicine. And I imagine that if you were where she is and felt as she must you would perhaps feel some hope if you felt that you were neither abandoned nor forgotten.

Whatever reservations one may have about Joyce, either as a writer or a man, one is inevitably reminded of the old proverb "show me your friends and I'll show you your worth." There must have been some very remarkable quality in the living reality of James Joyce that drew devoted friendship from people such as Paul Léon and Harriet Weaver. Of Joyce it can be said with truth that part, at least, of his glory was that he had such friends.

Czech *Ulysses:*
Joyce and Political Correctness, East and West

Jeffrey Segall

Although to many Joyce readers the juxtaposition of "Joyce" and "politics" still has a jarring, oxymoronic ring, more and more Joyce scholars in recent years have turned their attention to exploring the relationship between politics and the production and reception of Joyce's work. Interest in the politics of and around Joyce's work originates in two current and often complementary dispositions of Joyce criticism, the one toward a greater historical contextualization of Joyce studies, the other toward a desire to "locate" Joyce's politics in some broad or specific ideological landscape that liberalizes or radicalizes Joyce, especially in contrast to his Modernist contemporaries.

Several essays and books in recent years have followed in the wake of Richard Ellmann's and Dominic Manganiello's pioneering research in the general area of Joyce's political beliefs, including Robert Scholes's "Joyce and Modernist Ideology," G. J. Watson's "The Politics of *Ulysses,*" Richard Brown's *James Joyce and Sexuality,* and Franco Moretti's *Signs Taken for Wonders.* In the effort to better situate Joyce's work ideologically, most of these critics restore controversial aspects of *Ulysses* in particular that have been diminished in the process of canonization. The challenge to the critic-cum-cultural-archaeologist is to sift with fine tools for what constitutes satisfactory evidence in the portrait of our artist as a political man. The polemicists from the twenties and thirties who swung their cudgels over the text of *Ulysses* remind us today that the ideological decoding of a literary text is risky business. Particularly in the case of Joyce, "ideology" is not translatable into doctrine but is more a direction of mind and sensibility—nuanced, ambivalent, even self-contradictory. It is not decipherable by explicit ideas but by a panoply of aesthetic choices.

This, in a typically Joycean circumlocuitous manner, moves me to my broad subject, "Joyce and Political Correctness." My title refracts in several tantalizing directions, only one or two of which I'll be able to explore in this essay. My concern has been chiefly with the impact of politics on Joyce criticism, primarily American Joyce criticism, beginning with the cultural warfare among Stalinists, Trotskyists, and New Humanists in the twenties and thirties and continuing with the war hysteria of the early forties and the post-war ascension of the New Critics. The "political correctness" controversy began in earnest in the twenties and thirties, when the political consequences of cultural activity were debated more vigorously than ever before in our history. If we adopt Denis Donoghue's useful paradigm of cultural history, we may read the publication of Ulysses as a "cultural event" of major significance around which the "lore" of varied and contestatory critical responses followed. If I may paraphrase A. Walton Litz, the seventy year history of Ulysses criticism affords us the chance not to reach a "magisterial synthesis" of the novel but to understand what the book has meant in history.

Political controversies over Ulysses have crossed more borders than Joyce did, and my experience teaching as a Fulbright Lecturer at Charles University in Prague during 1991 and 1992 gave me a glimpse of what the novel endured behind what we used to call the Iron Curtain. I was able to trace a part of the novel's publication odyssey in pre-Velvet Revolution Czechoslovakia, from translator to publishing house to government bureaucracy to academic mediator. The struggle to publish a new translation of Ulysses in Czech in 1976 and 1977 is a fascinating story, one that lends a different perspective to the "political correctness" controversy that currently so absorbs us in America.

The authoritative Czech translation of Ulysses was completed in 1976 and published by Odeon publishers of Prague in 1977. (The first Czech translation of Ulysses—preceded only, remarkably enough, by the French and German translations—was a group effort and appeared in 1930.) At the time the Czech translation was completed (by Prelozil Aloys Skoumal), the authorities at the Czech Ministry of Culture would not allow it to be published, citing the usual Marxist objections to Joyce's work: it was formalist rubbish, overly subjective, unconcerned with social problems; it was, in sum, the fruit of decadent bourgeois culture. Mirek Jindra, one of my colleagues on the Philosophical faculty at Charles University, was well aware of the objections of the authorities. When he was asked by Odeon to write an introduction that might placate the powers that be, he incorporated—with a degree of cunning Joyce himself would have admired—many of their objections into his argument for the novel's publication. His goal, as he recently explained to me, was simply to get this fine new translation of the novel into print. His method, he admitted, was to distract and mislead, while upholding the prejudices of the

53

authorities. He had to continually massage the egos of the petty bureaucrats who, with a simple phone call or stroke of the pen, could block the publication of a work that was ten years in the making. (Such intervention was usually accomplished with a phone call, Mirek told me. One never knew when the next purge—or, as it turned out, the unthought-of revolution—might occur, and it was always better not to leave fingerprints.) But before discussing Mirek's method in detail, consider for a moment these excerpts from his introduction, which he kindly translated for me in Prague.

Jindra begins by quoting F. X. Salda, an eminent Czech writer and critic (not a Marxist) between the wars who previewed the first Czech translation of *Ulysses,* published in 1930, in his *Salda's Diary* in 1929. He writes,

> [*Ulysses* is a great] Leviathan, a giant whale which has torn the nets of so many literary critics, the delusory monster which has attacked many other countries, and is now prepared to attack us aggressively next year.

Jindra goes on with his own commentary:

> *Ulysses* appears to be a literary boulder crushing, destructive, yet at the same time, devilishly tempting: a hardly digestable conundrum for a normal, average reader, and a disquieting problem for all those deeply involved in literary studies.
>
> To read *Ulysses,* that is to get into the book and understand it, is a task for long years, and nearly impossible. You may be reading a passage for the 5th or maybe the 20th time, and all of a sudden, you begin to feel you are penetrating Joyce's microcosm. But on the next page, the author prepares a trap and kicks you out of his space into which, it seems, nobody is invited, and in which he doesn't permit anybody to stand for very long. This universal subjectivism of the author may be the key sign of *Ulysses.* Joyce seems to forget that that which he lets out of his inner world in tremendous solipsistic associations will be read by somebody else.
>
> [The] 1st World War catastrophe, which reflected the inner contradictions of disintegrating capitalist society, added to [Joyce's] perception of man as a creature forced into a sort of blind alley. He didn't succeed in condensing out of the chaotic nebulae of the world of his time a new star which could help man see the further azimuth of his road. But he did succeed in shouting his deafening "Ecce Homo" from the moment of history to which he belonged.
>
> *Ulysses* is something which cannot be evaded; it must be respected. But we cannot accept the "ideology" of this book; this is not the ultimate way to write books. Even if there may be many reservations, even objections to *Ulysses,* we must take it as one of the milestones in the cultural history of mankind—even if we would try hard to get around it on our roads through the world of literature.

The syntax and reasoning of this last paragraph are tortured, full of reversals and qualifiers that loop back upon the assertions so tentatively offered earlier. Jindra's praise of the novel is tepid, offered grudgingly, and, in the third sentence, deflated by its very generality (a "milestone in the cultural history of mankind"), then rescinded following the dash ("we would try hard to get around it"). Jindra's prose is continually looking over its shoulder; his juggling or balancing act is difficult to maintain here.

Mirek's strategy, evidently, was to express many reservations about *Ulysses*; to doff his cap in the direction of the standard Marxist objections to *Ulysses*, complaining of its subjectivism and of Joyce's inattentiveness to the reader (both of which complaints, by the way, were made by Edmund Wilson, and by others less sympathetic to the novel); to suggest that the novel was an aberration and a product of the late crisis of capitalism; to adopt a tone neither of sanction nor of dismissal, but of grudging tolerance; and to employ a kind of literary Doublespeak by making ambiguous statements that could be read two ways—or perhaps one way by simple-minded bureaucrats eager to seize upon the images offered specifically for their consumption. Thus, in the first quote, Jindra cites F. X. Salda in his 1929 reference to *Ulysses* as a "Leviathan," a "delusory monster . . . prepared to attack us aggressively." Salda's reference is ironic, of course: he suggests the monster of *Ulysses* is a delusion. But either the authorities didn't catch this, or, as Jindra suggested to me, they were so convinced of their own strength, and perhaps their own enlightened status as Czech Marxists nearly fifty years after the crude Stalinism of Salda's period, that they allowed the book to be published.

Planting an array of images and associations, Jindra works as artfully as Roger Ailes in discrediting his subject. *Ulysses* is conjured up as destructive, evil, elitist; it is more noise than sense, reflecting chaos, affirming nothing. In his masterstroke, Jindra deftly adds quotation marks around "ideology" in his final dismissal of *Ulysses*. The quotes flag the word "ideology" for the inattentive bureaucrat who will ultimately decide on the fate of the novel, and Jindra's conclusion ("we cannot accept the 'ideology' of this book") was no doubt pleasing. But the quotation marks have the additional effect of blunting the very attack Jindra appears to be making, by ironically suggesting that "ideology" is a construct rather than a natural or integral part of the text.

Although Jindra's presentation of the novel was, he can now admit, farcical and disingenuous, his intervention did, in fact, make it possible for *Ulysses* to be published in Prague. Jindra made a cameo appearance as *Ulysses*' sly Czech fairy godmother, providing the gown the novel would need to dance in at the prince's ball. His efforts on behalf of the novel seem to me to be an almost parodic reenactment of other attacks on the novel before other audiences in other times and places. Like others before him, Jindra wrestled the leviathan of *Ulysses* into some satisfactory shape, bending to ideological pressures that have shaped so much twentieth-century cultural debate in the West as well as the East. The aura, if not always the text, of *Ulysses* has served historically as a site of political contestation. The objective of a good deal of *Ulysses* criticism, early and late, has been to legitimize Joyce, to give him the stamp of political correctness, as that term has been variously defined by time and place and political circumstance.

It is one of the fascinating ironies in the critical history of *Ulysses* to discover that what often appears to be a hostile response to the novel may in fact be a defense of it (Jindra's introduction), or at times may reflect a greater apprehension of what the text is about; and what appears to be praise for the novel may conceal appropriative or manipulative moves that do the text greater injustice. Viewed with some historical detachment, Jindra's efforts on behalf of *Ulysses* were not in principle so different—nor any less cagey—than Morris Ernst's legal defense of the novel before Judge John M. Woolsey in U.S. District Court in 1933. However, the effect of efforts to at least legitimize or, in the work of later critics, to canonize *Ulysses* is that edges are sometimes smoothed, gaps and deletions occur. The "politically correct" Joyce, no matter what version that is or who sits in the court of judgment, leaves us always with an edited manuscript, and as readers and critics we are obliged to confess our sins of omission.

The term "political correctness" has been much bandied about lately, and we would do well to remember that the phrase is not a new one but originated in the twenties and thirties with the ascendancy of Stalinism and its encroachment internationally into many spheres of social and cultural life. Philip Rahv, for example, uses the term "correct politics" in his 1939 essay "Proletarian Literature: A Political Autopsy" to describe the American Communist Party's efforts to produce an American proletarian literature, one in which, as Rahv explained, "a novel or a play was certified 'revolutionary' only when its political ideas—existing or latent—corresponded to those of the Party" (296). Of course, political litmus tests—then and now—were as likely to be administered to literature from the Right as from the Left, and Joyce's work, along with that of other Modernists, suffered under the scrutiny of ideologues from both sides.

Perhaps in the spirit of Joycean perversity, what I would like to offer here is a celebration of the politically incorrect, at least insofar as that term was—and continues to be—loosely applied to Joyce's work. In part, the inspiration for this essay was the comment of one of my colleagues at the University of California who, during a conversation about American stand-up comedians, sagely, surreptitiously, but allowing no opportunity for argument, confided that David Letterman was "not PC." I was so startled by his comment that I could hardly form a reply. Later, I couldn't help but think of Joyce and wondered how he—fresh, raw, absent his place in the canon—would have fared under the scrutiny of my colleague. Joyce and other Modernists had been savagely ridiculed and caricatured by Soviet and American ideologues on the Left during the twenties and thirties. Was I naive to assume that Stalinist cultural injunctions had passed with the thirties, or at least with Brezhnev?

Joyce himself has outlasted, if not transcended, simple-minded efforts to categorize his work ideologically. On the larger canvas of twentieth-century culture, Joyce's oeuvre may be viewed in three dimensions: as a cultural commodity, as a cultural problem, and most provocatively, as a cultural catalyst. Joyce's work exists simultaneously in these three dimensions. What sustains it, I believe, is its intractability and the implicit demands it makes upon the readers and the cultures that receive it. Because of its breadth and complexity, *Ulysses* resists pressures of cultural appropriation and critical exegesis. It exerts a counterpressure of its own, creating us as we create it, reading us as we read it. It makes us aware of our own limits and shortcomings as readers, our cultural predispositions and our political predilections. If we are persistent, energetic, and intellectually supple enough to negotiate our way to Ithaca and embrace Penelope, we find ourselves ineffably altered, awed, imaginatively exhausted and exhilarated. It is in the difficulties of *Ulysses*—in its equivocations, its tensions, its modulations, and its ambiguities—that we find the pulse of the book. These warn us quietly, if persistently, of the dangers of coding and simplifying. "He had a mind so fine no idea could penetrate it," said T. S. Eliot of Henry James. I wish he had said it of Joyce.

At a time in our intellectual history when revolutionary and reactionary currents ran strong and polemics dominated literary discourse, Joyce moved against the illiberal spirit of his time. Joyce ushered in a post-ideological age, and his ideal reader was not one with an ideal insomnia so much as one who was not married to an idea. This is not to say his work lacks a value center or a moral dimension, but that the affirmations his work contains are always nuanced, circumscribed by comic irony, ambivalence, and evasion. Edmund Wilson heralded Joyce as "the great poet of a new phase of the human consciousness," a phase for which, we might add, applications are still being accepted.

Some might accuse me of having taken on the protective coloration of my temporary Eastern European home as I imply my own skepticism about the tendentiousness of some current criticism. My Czech colleagues and students are much warier than I about the deployment of generalizing theory in all spheres. After forty years of Doublespeak, Czechs are stubbornly empirical, relentlessly ironic, and reflexively mistrustful of "those big words that cause us so much pain." Recent polls assessing national moods, which included former Eastern Bloc countries in their surveys for the first time, concluded that the Czechs are the most pessimistic people in the world. Yet, out of that unlikely soil rises a reed of hope and faith, chastened by difficulty, and perhaps most eloquently expressed by that most self-effacing of politicians (so self-effacing that he recently resigned), Vaclav Havel. These lines are taken from a recent speech titled "The Post-Modern World Is Sick of Systems," which Havel delivered at the World Economic Forum in Davos, Switzerland:

> We are looking for new scientific recipes, new ideologies, new control systems, new institutions, new instruments to eliminate the dreadful consequences of previous recipes, ideologies, control systems, institutions and instruments.

Everything would seem to suggest that this is not the way to go. Man's attitude to the world must be radically changed. We have to abandon the arrogant belief that the world is merely a puzzle to be solved, a machine with instructions for use waiting to be discovered, a body of information to be fed into a computer.

It is my profound conviction that we have to release from the sphere of private whim such forces as a natural, unique and unrepeatable experience of the world, an elementary sense of justice, the ability to see things as others do, a sense of transcendental responsibility, archetypal wisdom, good taste, courage, compassion and faith in the importance of particular measures that do not aspire to be a universal key to salvation. Such forces must be rehabilitated.

Is it not both fitting and ironic that here, in this modest expression of faith born of and bounded by skepticism; in this extolling of civic virtue over messianic ambition; in this paradoxical grasp of the limits and powers of the human soul, we find something of the spirit of Joyce evoked?

APPENDIX

What follows is a fuller, though still excerpted version of the preface to the Czech translation of *Ulysses*, translated by the author of the preface, Mirek Jindra. "Joyce's *Ulysses* Today," by Mirek Jindra; preface to Czech translation of *Ulysses*. Translated by P. A. Skoumal. Odeon Publishers: Prague, 1977.

In December 1929, F. X. Salda's *Notebook*, a rather prestigious literary journal of the inter-war period, brought out several pages where the author writes about the "Leviathan," that "giant whale which has torn the nets of so many literary critics, the delusory monster which has attacked many other countries, and is now prepared to attack us aggressively next year."

With admirable foresight, F. X. Salda has prepared his readers for the first Czech translation of *Ulysses*. It was prepared by Ladislav Vimietol and Jarmel Fastroeva and was published by the publishing house Petra in 1930, as the 3rd translation of *Ulysses* (German in 1922, French in 1929). Several decades have elapsed since, but even now, *Ulysses* appears to be a literary boulder crushing, destructive, yet at the same time, devilishly tempting: a hardly digestable conundrum for a normal, average reader, and a disquieting problem for all those deeply involved in literary studies. More than a half century after the work was written, it still irritates and provokes and becomes a starting point of new breakthroughs; it is still the object of devoted adoration and passionate condemnation. To read *Ulysses*, that is to get into the book and understand it, is a task for long years, and nearly impossible. You may be reading a passage for the 5th or maybe the 20th time, and all of a sudden, you begin to feel you are penetrating Joyce's microcosm. But on the next page, the author prepares a trap and kicks you out of his space into which, it seems, nobody is invited, and in which he doesn't permit anybody to stand for very long. This universal subjectivism of the author may be the key sign of *Ulysses*. Joyce seems to forget that that which he lets out of his inner world in tremendous solipsistic associations will be read by somebody else.

Maybe this is just the first impression because the other side of this ego-centric, precious coin of Joyce's is represented by a cold-blooded, calculated basic intention to masterfully manipulate literary techniques and construction procedures to prepare the response which the work should provoke. Joyce wants to stand before the eyes of the enchanted audience an integrated model of the modern man with all the attributes in an apocalyptic dimension, the model of a modern man with his complicated inner life, consciously and unconsciously influenced by the disintegration of moral values and social values which have so far governed his fate.

We should not forget that *Ulysses* was written in the years of the 1st World War catastrophe, which reflected the inner contradictions of disintegrating capitalist society. Although Joyce seemingly ignored the war, we can't believe that it wouldn't be a shock to the soul of a man as sensitive as Joyce. Most probably, it added to his perception of man as a creature forced into a sort of blind alley. And so the evidence he has given about what the situation is may be historically limited. He didn't succeed in condensing out of the chaotic nebulae the world of his time a new star which could help man to show the further azimuth of his road. But he did succeed in shouting his deafening "Ecce Homo" from the moment of history to which he belonged.

Marxist literary history describes Joyce as the unique delineator of the disintegration of the values of bourgeois values at the beginning of the 20th century—an author who saw the antagonisms of capitalistic society surrounding him but didn't understand its course and rejected the new optimistic moments which were born in the beginning of the century. (Again, the formulation of Dmitri Ztomsky, the Soviet literary critic.)

. . . Each chapter of *Ulysses* corresponds to the main episodes of the Odyssey. The parodic sequences in *Ulysses* give some sort of irrational mysticism of the myth. A special dialectic of Joyce's figure is developed in this way, since Joyce's man is at the same time a beast and a victim of the beast, master and at the same time, slave.

Language is maybe the main character of *Ulysses*. Language seems to have an independent quality, reflecting a very free creativity which doesn't put any limits on the geyser of language fantasy, which doesn't put any taboos on the sexual sphere, or anywhere else, which doesn't respect normal syntax.

. . . This manipulation of language is going further and further, especially in *FW*.

The Czech translation is the fruition of deep study. . . . it is one of the best translations of *Ulysses* in world literature.

E. M. Foerster said of *Ulysses*: "*Ulysses* is a simplification in the interests of Hell." Compared with Picasso's model in the fine arts.

Ulysses is something which cannot be evaded; it must be respected. It provides material used by new generations of writers from around the world—France, USA, Russia, Japan. Even if there may be many reservations, even objections to *Ulysses*, we must take it as one of the milestones in the cultural history of mankind—even if we would try hard to get around it on our roads through the world of literature.

WORKS CITED

Brown, Richard. *James Joyce and Sexuality.* Cambridge and New York: Cambridge University Press, 1985.

Ellmann, Richard. *The Consciousness of Joyce.* New York: Oxford University Press, 1977.

Havel, Vaclav. "The Post-Modern World Is Sick of Systems." Speech delivered at the World Economic Forum, Davos, Switzerland; published as "The End of the Modern Era," *New York Times,* 1 March 1992, sec. 4, p. 15.

Jindra, Mirek. "Joyce's *Ulysses* Today." Trans. Mirek Jindra. Preface to *Ulysses,* translated into Czech by P. A. Skoumal. Prague: Odeon Publishers, 1977.

Litz, A. Walton. "*Ulysses* and Its Audience." In *James Joyce: The Centennial Symposium,* ed. Morris Beja, et al. Urbana: University of Illinois Press, 1986.

Manganiello, Dominic. *Joyce's Politics.* London: Routledge & Kegan Paul, 1980.

Moretti, Franco. *Signs Taken for Wonders: Essays in the Sociology of Literary Forms.* London: NLB, 1983.

Rahv, Philip. *Essays on Literature and Politics, 1932–1972.* Ed. Arabel J. Porter and Andrew J. Dvosin. Boston: Houghton Mifflin, 1978.

Scholes, Robert. "Joyce and Modernist Ideology." In *Coping with Joyce: Essays from the Copenhagen Symposium,* ed. Morris Beja and Shari Benstock. Columbus: Ohio State University Press, 1989.

Watson, G. J. "The Politics of Ulysses." In *Joyce's "Ulysses": The Larger Perspective,* ed. Fritz Senn. Newark: University of Delaware Press, 1987.

Wilson, Edmund. *Axel's Castle.* New York: Scribner's, 1931.

I Don't Understand. I Fail To Say. I Dearsee You Too

Louis Lentin

Before the nightmare "creaseword" puzzle of *Finnegans Wake* can dissolve, "and the nightmail afarfrom morning nears" (*FW* 565.32), "while the dapplegray dawn drags nearing nigh for to wake all droners that drowse in Dublin" (585.20–21), the corpse of Finnegan suddenly sits erect in his coffin, stares about him and cries out, as well he might, "Where are we at all? and whenabouts in the name of space?" To which reasonable demand he himself replies with the semi-mortal words, "I don't understand. I fail to say. I dearsee you too" (558.33–34).

That, at least, was part of the scenario in *The Voice of Shem*, Mary Manning's fine stage adaptation of extracts from the *Wake* that I directed for the stage many years ago. At that point in the "continuarration," "dadad's lottiest duaghterpearl" (561.15), having just been married to the strains of "Hymnumber twentynine" (234.34) in a setting by Father Blesius Mindelsinn, now dies, with the immortal cry of *Mild und Leise*. The audience was by now understandably just as confused and flabbergasted as poor old Bygmester Finnegan himself, who was, of course, about to begin again. So the line that I have appropriated as the title for this homily—"I don't understand. I fail to say. I dearsee you too"—coming from Earwicker/Finnegan, by now well and truly waked in his coffin, usually brought down the house.

However, I don't wish to loft the smog from Finnegan, but rather—as we are now rather fittingly gathered in this "waalworth of a skyerscape" (4.35–36), one of the old hearts of Dublin's Jewish community—to conduct a Jewish wake, sit shivah, for Leopold Bloom, *meshumed* extraordinaire. So "siddle down and lissle all" (432.21–22), and join me on my personal and hopefully not

---

The following was a talk delivered at the Irish Jewish Museum, Dublin.

too incommodious vicus into the heart of this Hibernian metropolis, while I attempt to interweave three strands.

First is the fact that Leopold Bloom, although constantly referred to throughout *Ulysses* and since as a Jew, is in strict Jewish religious terms a fake, not a Jew at all.

Second, although Joyce has set his masterpiece, for very specific reasons, on June 16, 1904, apart from one small and perhaps questionable reference the book completely ignores the largest anti-Semitic outbreak in Ireland up to that time and indeed since. I refer to the 1904 pogrom in Limerick, when the small Jewish community of that time was subjected to vilification and indeed physical attack, which led within a year to its decimation. Those events were fully reported in both the Irish and London press of the time, and there is little doubt but that Joyce must have been aware of them.

The third strand is made of some personal experiences, provoked perhaps by my own position as an Irish Jew in Catholic Ireland. The anti-Semitism is in no way unfamiliar to me but rather is part of the growing pains and indeed the pains of many grown Irish Jews. There can be few among us, or indeed few Jews in any country in the Diaspora, who have gone through life without some anti-Semitic experience, no matter how mild. I recall as a very young boy not being invited to the annual school Christmas party—not because I was the only Jewish boy in the school (in Limerick, as it happens) but because, as it was pointedly put to my father, it was a party only for "children of the parish." One went through unimportant experiences of that nature, but suddenly one day my position as an outsider was indelibly imprinted on me by a remark from an elderly English colleague. We were at the time discussing a television play I was to direct that revolved around events during the Irish Civil War, and in particular the dramatist's rather watery theme of understanding or indeed misunderstanding between Free Staters and Republicans, when suddenly my colleague said—and I will never forget the moment—"How could you understand, you're not Irish, you're Jewish." The remark was not meant to hurt but simply to state that, in the context of matters specifically Irish, there were things I could not be expected to comprehend.

Of course, "who has ever heard of an Irish Jew?" It does sound a bit of a joke. Bloom may be a bit of a cod, but I assure you that Gerald Goldberg—the Dick Whittington of Cork—is very much an Irish Jew. It is the only possible label I can give myself as well. And the author of the collection of short stories published under the title, *Who Has Ever Heard of an Irish Jew?*—David Marcus— is also very much a member of the clan, as indeed are many others.

Irish Jewry may on occasion prefer to bury its collective head in the sand, but many of us stand up for the pot shots. Nevertheless, the title *Who Has Ever Heard of an Irish Jew?* has a faint aura of truth about it, although not perhaps as strong as the tang of urine in Poldy's pork kidney. But despite Jewish Lord Mayors of Irish Catholic cities, judges, members of Dail Eireann (three, I believe, at the present count), writers, performers, musicians, and even film and television directors for God's sake, and apart from the odd eminent doctor, dentist, lawyer, and accountant, the aptness of Mr. Deasy's anti-Semitic remark in the "Nestor" episode of *Ulysses* still holds somewhat. Ireland, he says, "had the honor of being the only country which never persecuted the jews. . . . And do you know why? . . . Because she never let them in" (*U-GP* 2:439, 442).

The vitally important word being *in*—fully in—not half in, or with a foot in the door. My English dictionary defines the word *in* as, among other things, belonging to, being a member of, having a share or part in. So maybe Mr. Deasy is right after all.

The supposed split allegiance of many Jewish communities is often thrown up as if to say, how can there be such a thing as an Irish or a French or a Swiss Jew, for that matter? Of course there can. I suggest that the question arises only in the minds of those citizens who have some difficulty letting Jews in—in the complete sense. So perhaps Irish Jews should fully support the Maastricht treaty, if for no other reason than that a full European Community would hopefully allow us once again to be considered Europeans.

Leopold Bloom, when questioned "What is your nation if I may ask?" can only reply, as we all would, "Ireland . . . I was born here" (*U-GP* 12:1430–31). But the very asking of it begs the question, and though many Irish Jews may be all-arounders like Bloom, until relatively recently, when we wanted to play ball it could only be done in Jewish alleys.

John Wyse Nolan may come to the rescue and ask, "why can't a jew love his country like the next fellow?" but someone like J. J. O'Molloy is bound to respond, "Why not? . . . when he's quite sure which country it is" (*U-GP* 12:1628–30).

I am not being anti-Irish; what I say now is not intended in any way as an attack on a society that has an extremely low level of anti-Semitism. My very personal experiences are not unique to this country. No doubt others will have had their own anonymous mail, such as two letters I received while head of television drama at RTE: one threatening me with the "Irish army" if I as a Jew continued to decide which plays Irish viewers could see; and the other denouncing me for attempting to produce a play that had as its central character a fanatical Roman Catholic, unacceptable in his fanaticism even to his own community, but that in reality dealt with other outsiders, this time Irish/Italian owners of a fish-and-chip shop in a small country town.

So I feel that it is worth asking if there really is any difference between the attitudes and opinions Joyce provides for his acutely observed cast of Dubliners in 1904 and those expressed to me both openly and anonymously more than sixty years later. Do we Jews of the Diaspora, like Leopold Bloom, still exist only in a limbo of alienation? Have we still only cherished expectations? *Plus ça change, plus c'est la même chose.*

However, let me continue on my vicus and wander with Leopold Bloom on

16 June 1904: Bloom the Yiddishe Goy. Or, if I may present you with a riddle (three *aliyahs* for the first correct answer): When is a Jew not a Jew? Answer: when he is in bloom.

It's an oft quoted couplet: "How odd of God to choose the Jews. . . ." Maybe so, but how very odd of Shem to pen a Jew who is not a Jew and as a jest, or indeed maybe out of ignorance, ironically to give him as wife a Maid Marion who, although brought up a Catholic, is in fact the daughter of a Jewess from Gibraltar. I can find no reference to either mother or daughter having ever converted, so strictly speaking Molly Bloom is a more fully paid-up member of the tribe than her husband.

Joyce, of course, liked to have his little joke, but his knowledge of Judaism was garnered from many sources, some perhaps—as far as the required Hallachic law was concerned—not quite the full shekel.

Bloom as a total Jew, not an ersatz one! Why did Joyce carefully set out his genealogy, which states without question that his peripatetic hero was anything but kosher, yet have him regarded without question by all and sundry then and since as a Jew? What would the book have lost or gained had Joyce gone the whole hog? This is not something that, as a casual paddler in the Joycean stream, I am going to dip my tumpty-tum toes into, but rather leave it to the deep-sea anglers. But may I remind you that if your mother is Jewish, then so are you. In this sense your father's religion is totally unimportant.

Let's take a brief look at the Bloom family tree. Rudolph Virag—Leopold Bloom's father, a Hungarian Jew—decides in 1850 or so to emigrate, first to London, then finally to Dublin, where he is no doubt welcomed by his bearded coreligionists. In 1865, after a visit to the society for promoting Christianity among Jews, he becomes a "souper" and is converted to Protestantism. In that year—and the events may not be unconnected—he marries Ellen Higgins, and although there has been a Dublin Jewish family of that name, Ellen Higgins is a Protestant.

Virag now changes his name to Bloom; *virag* is Hungarian for flower, so that *bloom*, while having a decided Jewish ring to it, has the added attraction of not being too far removed from the original. Then in 1866 our very own Leopold Bloom is born and promptly baptized a Protestant. To be sure, old man Rudolph passes on to the boy a certain amount of *yiddiskeit*, the *aleph bet*, parts of the Haggadah, the Shema, but Joyce—as if to make assurance triply sure—has Poldy dipped not once but thrice at baptism, again by doubting Irish boys under the parish pump in "Swords," and finally, irony of ironies, in order to enable him to marry his Maid Marion, makes him as Irish as could possibly be and has him finally doused in oil, this time as a Roman Catholic.

You might say that Joyce has done his best for old Bloom: Jewish father, Protestant at birth, Roman Catholic by choice, but still regarded for all time as a Jew. How far do you have to go to be let in?

Both Bloom's children, Rudy and Milly—assuming neither Molly nor her mother ever converted to Catholicism—are, paradoxically, also Jewish. Joyce deprived Poldy of his only son, Rudy, but Milly, if she hangs in there, will produce Jewish offspring. So in 1904 we have the all-round Bloom, a *meshugenner meshumed* if ever there was one, no less adrift in his own personal odyssey than Homer's Semitic hero.

What a glorious hoax! The most dissected Jewish literary creation of the twentieth century, perhaps of all time—if we fight shy of Shylock—regarded by all and sundry as a Jew, but in fact in strict religious terms not a Jew at all. That, if you don't mind me saying so, is more than a bit of a cod! But is it really of any importance, and if so, why? Why has Joyce chosen to place at the heart of *Ulysses*—and Bloom surely is its very heart—a wandering hapless citizen, to label him on all sides a Jew, to grant him humanitarian characteristics, thoughts and attitudes that place him apart from his fellow citizens, and yet to deny him the finest cut of all? Is Bloom, like Moses, only to be granted a Pisgah view of his promised land?

Bloom is certainly fully conscious of his Jewish heritage. He carries it with him, not only physically; he knows, remembers, retains, hangs on to threads of Jewish knowledge given him as a boy by his Jewish apostate father. He has as much Hebrew as many Jews wandering around Dublin today. He may start the day with a pork kidney, but he worries about the contents of Plumtree's Potted Meat.

In many ways he takes a Jewish stance, carries a candle, a light to enlighten the gentiles. Joyce grants him his culture—Mozart and Meyerbeer figure among his favorite composers—but I personally find his cultural judgments unreliable and only half assimilated. In this, as in so many other ways, Joyce never permits him to be a whole man; rather he has created a man adrift, Irish only by birth, Jewish only by inclination. Yet Bloom belongs only in Dublin, and it is fitting that he is the chief literary citizen of that city of paralysis. He is a member of the dominant Church, a Jew, yet not a Jew; a Christian, of course not. Mulligan calls him the wandering Jew: a neat label, but in many respects Bloom is more wandering than Jew.

Above all else this wandering Jew desires identity. Bloom's journey through Dublin on 16 June 1904, a journey he will repeat every day of his life, is a search for an identity that will always be denied him. Let me in, he cries; certainly Molly will not. He is even forced to climb over his own railings. No man needed a key more.

Of course all this suits Joyce's purpose admirably. Bloom corresponds to Ulysses, the wandering Greek. Joyce's masterpiece reeks with Homeric allusions; the structure is not only based on but stylistically reflects the Greek hero's adventures. Ulysses is of course a hero on the grand scale; Bloom is anything but. Or could it be part of Joyce's scheme of things that it takes certain heroic qualities to exist in an alien society?

Bloom is pathetically eager to claim himself as one hundred percent Irish.

He is careful not to go about proclaiming his Jewishness. Like Homer's hero, also a man of many devices, he knows that his modus operandi is to be circumspect; he can but wander and endure, without complaining too much about what the gods may send.

No doubt the incongruity of creating his central Dubliner as a Jew, yet not fully a Jew—moreover a Jew who has sampled three religions without accepting them—attracted Joyce with its satirical possibilities. And, of course, the theme parallels Joyce's own rejection of Catholicism. Bloom adrift in Catholic Ireland also mirrors Joyce's own increasing feeling of alienation in Europe, his place there being as ambiguous as that of the Jews in Ireland. Joyce, like Bloom, is not a citizen of no place but no accepted citizen of any place.

Despite his many efforts to be accepted, and except, it would seem, from buying his round, Bloom never fully gets a look in. You get the picture in Barney Kiernan's pub:

> So in comes Martin asking where was Bloom.
> —Where is he? says Lenehan. Defrauding widows and orphans.
> —Isn't that a fact, says John Wyse, what I was telling the citizen about Bloom and the Sinn Fein?
> —That's so, says Martin. Or so they allege.
> —Who made those allegations? says Alf.
> —I, says Joe. I'm the alligator.
> —And after all, says John Wyse, why can't a jew love his country like the next fellow?
> —Why not? says J. J., when he's quite sure which country it is.
> —Is he a jew or a gentile or a holy Roman or a swaddler or what the hell is he? says Ned. Or who is he? No offence, Crofton.
> —Who is Junius? says J. J.
> —We don't want him, says Crofter the Orangeman or presbyterian.
> —He's a perverted jew, says Martin, from a place in Hungary and it was he drew up all the plans according to the Hungarian system. We know that in the castle.
> —Isn't he a cousin of Bloom the dentist? says Jack Power.
> —Not at all, says Martin. Only namesakes. His name was Virag, the father's name that poisoned himself. He changed it by deedpoll, the father did.
> —That's the new Messiah for Ireland! says the citizen. Island of saints and sages! . . .
> —Charity to the neighbour, says Martin. But where is he? We can't wait.
> —A wolf in sheep's clothing, says the citizen. That's what he is. Virag from Hungary! Ahasuerus I call him. Cursed by God. . . .
> —Saint Patrick would want to land again at Ballykinlar and convert us, says the citizen, after allowing things like that to contaminate our shores.
> (U-GP 12:1621–73)

But now let me move on to my third strand: from the world of fiction to the harsh reality of life in Limerick for the Jewish community in 1904. You will recall that the Dreyfus affair, which continued until 1906, reached its crisis in 1902, just before Joyce's arrival in Paris.

In 1903 Joyce returned to Ireland just in time for the Limerick pogrom, a virulent and violent outburst of anti-Semitism that decimated that small community. While it was not a pogrom in the Russian sense, Jews were attacked and hurt, and a ruinous financial boycott was imposed on the community. Sides were taken by leading Irish figures, and the sorry event became in its own way a cause célèbre, of which, when he came to write *Ulysses*, Joyce must have been fully aware. He hunted up so much detail for the book that his seemingly deliberate choice not to touch on this event, which impinged on every Irish Jew, bears some consideration.

In June 1904 the Limerick pogrom was in full spate—I could say bloom—and one might have expected some reference to it in *Ulysses*, so specifically set in that same year. However, apart from one possible moment, again in Barney Kiernan's pub, and some oblique references by Molly in her final soliloquy, to which I have referred but which in my opinion fail to connect, it would appear to be absolutely ignored. Certainly, despite some scholarly claims, it never provides the book with any tension whatsoever. The moment in the pub:

> —And I belong to a race too, says Bloom, that is hated and persecuted. Also now. This very moment. This very instant.
> Gob, he near burnt his fingers with the butt of his old cigar.
> —Robbed, says he. Plundered. Insulted. Persecuted. Taking what belongs to us by right. At this very moment, says he, putting up his fist, sold by auction in Morocco like slaves or cattle.
> —Are you talking about the new Jerusalem? says the citizen.
> —I'm talking about injustice, says Bloom. (*U-GP* 12:1467–74)

If you examine this passage, what you perceive is a very persistent use of the present tense by Bloom. He speaks of persecution and insults "Also now. This very moment. This very instant." Then we hear, "sold by auction in Morocco." Why Morocco? Why not Egypt? If you substitute the old French name for Morocco, Le Maroc, the line read quickly now reads "sold by auction off in Le Maroc" and acquires much more significance, signaling perhaps that Joyce knew he had to make some reference, no matter how oblique, to parallel events in Limerick. But it does appear to be the only reference in the entire book, if indeed that is what it is. (This fascinating interpretation is not mine, but Dorith Ofri's.) Two words in *Finnegans Wake* may allude to the Limerick events: "limenick's disgrace" (434.21); but in the context of lace, for which Limerick was famous, and knickers, these words may of course be interpreted differently.

I can understand Bloom desperately seeking acceptance among his Gentile buddies, conscious both of his heritage and his present Roman Catholic status, being careful not to bring this contentious subject into the open, but there can be little doubt that Joyce deliberately goes out of his way to avoid it.

To have created Bloom as an all-round Jew would not have suited Joyce's purpose and would certainly not have allowed him to construct *Ulysses* as he did. Bloom as a Jew in the fullest sense must surely necessitate protagonists from the Jewish community, which in turn would have made it almost impossible for Joyce to avoid placing the Limerick events in a prominent position. It's a story worth writing, but not the book Joyce wished to write. Therefore I suggest that Leopold Bloom could be a Jew in every sense but the fully religious one. Otherwise the book could not have reflected, as it so wonderfully does, the triangular relationship and parallels among Ulysses the Greek; Leopold Bloom the non-Jew non-Christian just as much at sea in the streets of Dublin, unaccepted by both Jew and Christian alike; and Joyce, who, renouncing his own Catholic upbringing, committed himself to exile.

Some years ago, while working on another television production, I sat for a whole wonderful afternoon with an eminent American Jewish expert on another great Irish writer: there we were, one a Polack and the other a Litvak, both of us examining the *pilpulim* of Sean O'Casey's Protestant background. I suggest that if you ask the average Dubliner in the street what O'Casey's religion was, he will swear he was of course a Catholic. And as for our very own Bloom? You are more than likely to be told "sure that fellow was a Jewman." How wrong can you get.

Poor old Ben Bloom Elijah, doomed to be perpetually hounded by that mongrel Garryowen, and despite—or maybe, indeed, because—of his and our own cries of "Abba Adonai," forever, like the rest of us, to remain suspended "at an angle of fortyfive degrees over Donohoe's in Little Green street."

Hostile Responses to Joyce

Approaching Joyce with an Attitude

Morris Beja

The essays in this section came out of a session on "hostile responses to Joyce." It may seem odd to have arranged such a session during an International James Joyce Symposium, but in my role as coordinator of the program I came fairly soon to feel that it would be salutary to counter the danger of hagiography that such a conference might otherwise generate. In the context of a week during which his city and his nation, to say nothing of numerous people from many other cities and many other nations, came together at least in large part out of a fascination—even obsession—with his work, it seemed useful to recall how controversial James Joyce has been and can remain, to realize how negative reactions to his work can be (and not merely among readers who have difficulty getting through the longer entries in the weekly TV listings).

As Hans Robert Jauss has put it, in *Toward an Aesthetic of Reception*, "the way in which a literary work, at the historical moment of its appearance, satisfies, surpasses, disappoints, or refutes the expectations of its first audience obviously provides a criterion for the determination of its aesthetic value" (25). Often when we think of Joyce's early readers we tend to recall those to whom in the twenties and thirties he was a major hero: we retain images of William Faulkner and Thomas Wolfe as young writers visiting France and lurking in the background as they observe the Great Man, too diffident even to approach him; or of F. Scott Fitzgerald offering to jump out of a window to prove his devotion and admiration.

But an essential element of Joyce's heroism to such younger contemporaries was the way in which he triumphed over his rejection by the philistines. It is sobering to recognize that frequently the most vehement of the philistines were members of the literati—like the one who wrote in the review of *A*

71

Portrait of the Artist as a Young Man in the *Irish Book Lover* that "no clean-minded person could possibly allow it to remain within reach of his wife, his sons or daughters," and who ended that review with the question, "Above all, is it Art?"—and replied, "We doubt it."

The philistines are easily dismissed, while it is much more interesting to consider the genuine and thoughtful but quite negative reactions to Joyce in sensitive, often brilliant readers and writers who could not finally or truly admire his work—or worse, could not stomach it. In varying degrees we see such reactions in some of the major literary figures of his day, like Virginia Woolf, or Wyndham Lewis, or the writers discussed in the following two essays, D. H. Lawrence and Rebecca West. None of those four examples are after all lightweights in twentieth-century literary history.

Even when important literary figures were receptive, they frequently had major reservations, as in H. G. Wells's famous comment about Joyce's "cloacal obsession." Other figures who have honorable roles in literary history because of their ability to recognize and champion the value of the new in other writers often could not go so far as to accept the worth of Joyce's art: readers, for example, like Edward Garnett, who rejected the *Portrait* for the firm of Duckworth yet wrote enthusiastic reports on *Sons and Lovers* and *The Voyage Out*.

In some ways it is especially fascinating to examine the negative attitudes toward Joyce in the realms and cultures to which he—especially the artist as a young man—was and felt closest, however hostile and ambivalent his relationship might have been in countless ways: Ireland and England.

The fierce early Irish reaction to Joyce clearly came out of special needs—political, nationalistic, aesthetic, cultural, religious, even psychological—that made it difficult for his work to be widely admired in his homeland for many years. At his death the magazines of both his former schools—the *Clongownian* and the *Belvederian*—completely ignored the event (although fascinatingly the *Belvederian* did carry a notice of the death around the same time of Joyce's younger brother Charles). The later Irish author Benedict Kiely has reported the way in which the youth of Ireland reacted when a Dublin newspaper did them a favor "by failing to carry even a news report of the death of Joyce, and thus helping to identify and delineate the enemy."

Meanwhile, the England of Bloomsbury was notorious in its antipathy to what Joyce was doing—to what seemed to E. M. Forster a "dogged attempt to cover the universe with mud." Other elements of the British literary establishment of the time were even more vociferous in opposition to "Modernism"—although in fact nowadays most critics and scholars tend toward definitions of Modernism that embrace the work of a number of writers who would probably have resented being classified that way or being put together in a category with James Joyce.

Unfortunately, an unpleasant degree of classism was occasionally involved in the irritation with Joyce, as in Virginia Woolf's infamous comment about

Joyce's achievement as "underbred," that of a self-taught working man, while to Rebecca West he seemed "a great man who is entirely without taste." Ethnocentrism also figured in West's uneasiness, as suggested by her description of Joyce's mind as "furnished like a room in a Westland Row tenement": there is no Westland Row in London, although there is one in Dublin.

The British critical establishment was even less friendly, as personified in the enormously influential work of F. R. Leavis, who began a book on D. H. Lawrence with the claim that Joyce and Lawrence seem to be "the crucial authors" in determining one's attitudes toward modern literature, asserting that if you regard Joyce as a major writer, then you can have "no use for Lawrence," while if you regard Lawrence as a great novelist, "then you could hardly take a sustained interest in Joyce." I would maintain that the healthiest reaction to such a statement—or, in any case, to its apparent assumptions about the departmentalization of literary taste—is denial. Yet for decades there was and perhaps still is a tendency in some critical corners to feel that such a "choice" is inevitable.

Moreover, insofar as such a comparison has been made, it has been assumed in many quarters that it would be Lawrence who would emerge victorious. Joyce was granted certain advantages, such as technical mastery and a willingness to experiment, but aside from such matters it would have seemed to many readers during the decades from the twenties through the fifties and even into the sixties that posterity would belong to Lawrence. He was the prophet, the person to whom more and more people would turn for inspiration and wisdom, while Joyce represented a dead end, or worse. In Henry Miller's notebooks on Joyce and Lawrence, written during the thirties (but not published until the *Joyce Studies Annual* 1992), Miller contrasted Joyce "the doubter" with Lawrence "the apostle of a new order"; Joyce provided only a "cul-de-sac."

Among literary critics, one encountered that attitude not only in books by people like Leavis—that is, in Lawrentians writing books about Lawrence—but also in Joyceans writing books about Joyce: books like S. L. Goldberg's *The Classical Temper*, which in the early sixties claimed that, compared to Lawrence, Joyce's grasp of the nightmare of history "is not particularly impressive." A similar dichotomy appeared in Darcy O'Brien's *The Conscience of James Joyce*.

If Lawrence was seen as prophetic, Joyce was often regarded as a reactionary figure, an elitist whom it was best to ignore. The attacks on him on the Continent were frequently, in fact, political. For a long period a great many of the most virulent responses came from hard-line Marxists, as in the attack by the Russian critic R. Miller-Bunitskaya, for whom "Joyceism" was "a most reactionary philosophy of social pessimism, misanthropy, barrenness and doom, a hopeless negation of all creative, fruitful forces." Within the last couple of decades, however, scholarship and criticism have made myopic assertions about Joyce's reactionary politics, or about his political irrelevance, increasingly difficult to take seriously.

On the Continent the Joyce who aroused such negative responses could also be wildly and widely lionized—sometimes by the same people after what in some cases turned out to be little less than conversion experiences, as in the case of Louis Gillet, who went from writing an attack on Joyce in the *Revue des deux mondes* in 1925 to becoming a major champion of Joyce's work and a close friend.

In the United States, too, many of the attacks were basically political. The early acceptance of Joyce in the States by relatively large numbers of writers, critics, and academics was so notable that we tend to forget or be ignorant of the fierce rejection of his work by some extremely influential critics—like Paul Elmer More, who abhorred "the moral slough of *Ulysses*" and wrote (in an essay on Joyce) that he "should hate to believe that three thousand years have brought to mankind only weariness and ugliness from which no escape is possible save in a weary and ugly art" (70, 78): the art, that is, that he saw in *Ulysses*.

Later American critics have been more sophisticated in their critiques, but the attacks have not stopped, despite or perhaps because of the fact that Joyce has become the single most clearly canonical figure in twentieth-century literature and far and away the one about whom the most is written each year. Those on any side of the currently intense "canon wars" can hardly look to a more dramatic revolution in status than that achieved by the Joyce who was once banned or dismissed or both. In particular, the role of the academic world in changing general views toward his work can hardly be exaggerated. Even before his work became legal in the United States, for example, it was at times assigned in university courses or would in any case be available in university libraries. For admirers of Joyce's art, such a reversal has not been without its price, as we see new readers come to his work lacking a full realization of how subversive it can be. On the other hand, Joyce's standing has forced critics who rebel against his status to explore or explain their reactions in more sophisticated terms than were once deemed necessary.

But while more subtle, the negative responses have frequently retained a moral dimension, as in Wayne Booth's discomfort in *The Rhetoric of Fiction* over the ways in which "Joyce was always a bit uncertain about his attitude toward Stephen" (330). (Since Deconstruction and the vogue of indeterminacy, such an objection may seem a virtue, but it would also have seemed no problem to the New Critics, who would have recognized the profound possibilities for powerful literary effects within ambiguity—or irony, for that matter.)

In *No Man's Land*, Sandra Gilbert and Susan Gubar attack Joyce through his portrayal of women and the "parrot-like blankness with which Joyce's women respond to abstract concepts" (232). They argue for example that in the "Nausicaa" chapter of *Ulysses* "the commercial crap" of Gerty MacDowell's "genteel Victorian diction is at least in part associated with the reaction-formation of intensified misogyny with which male writers greeted the entrance of women into the literary marketplace" (233). (It should be mentioned that anyone familiar with the feminist criticism of Joyce during the last decade or so—arguably the single most powerful realm of Joyce studies during that time and ours—will realize that most feminist critics would go beyond that interpretation of Joyce's achievement. For many readers, including many feminist ones, Joyce has come to seem a liberating force: not a liberated man, necessarily—or at all—but a liberating force, the author that is of liberating work.)

A different moral urge seems to underlie Leo Bersani's 1990 essay "Against *Ulysses*" in his *The Culture of Redemption*. For him, *Ulysses* is "a model of interpretive nihilism," a "text to be deciphered but not read." There is an element of Leavisite high seriousness in Bersani's approach, so it is not surprising that once again Joyce is contrasted unfavorably with Lawrence, with Bersani asserting that "the experimentalism of *Ulysses* is far from the genuine avant-gardism of *Women in Love*" (174–75). But Bersani's attack is more informed and complex, and less dogmatic, than Leavis's, and his reaction is expressed with a tinge of regret, as when he says in his final sentence that "even in writing 'against *Ulysses*,' we can only feel a great sadness in leaving it—to stop working on *Ulysses* is like a fall from grace" (178).

I have not attempted in this short account to counter the attacks I have reported, except occasionally in brief comments I could not resist. Rather I have wanted to remind us of the sobering reality of the deep doubts many readers have had about the achievement of James Joyce. Such doubts will remind us that it is conceivable that the same writer who went from unpublishability to vilification to canonization within less than half a century could quite possibly be *de*-canonized in even less time.

Even those of us who regard that prospect as unlikely can learn by confronting and examining the hostility or relative hostility toward Joyce's work by people who are not easily dismissible. Above all, I would argue, we can attain a renewed and intensified awareness of Joyce as *other*: as disturbing, perplexing, dangerous and threatening: a writer—and a force—to conjure with.

WORKS CITED

Bersani, Leo. *The Culture of Redemption*. Cambridge, Mass.: Harvard University Press, 1990.

Booth, Wayne. *The Rhetoric of Fiction*. Chicago: University of Chicago Press, 1961.

Gilbert, Sandra M., and Susan Gubar. *No Man's Land: The Place of the Woman Writer in the Twentieth Century*. Vol. 1: *The War of the Words*. New Haven: Yale University Press, 1988.

Jauss, Hans Robert. *Toward an Aesthetics of Reception*. Trans. Timothy Bahti. Minneapolis: University of Minnesota Press, 1982.

More, Paul Elmer. *On Being Human*. Princeton: Princeton University Press, 1936.

"A Would-Be-Dirty Mind": D. H. Lawrence as an Enemy of Joyce

Paul Delany

You know that I need to go away, away, away: yes, yes, I can't go on here any-more. You know there are always the angels and the archangels, thrones, pow-ers, cherubims, seraphims—the whole choir there. But here these baptised beasts always make themselves heard, these and nothing else. I'm going away from here. Walking one arrives: if not to the grave, at least a little bit outside this human, too human world. (Lawrence, *Letters IV* 185)

D. H. Lawrence wrote these words on 2 February 1922, when he was prepar-ing to pack up his home in Sicily, turn his back on Europe, and sail around the world. I think they are a good entry into the question of why Lawrence and Joyce must be counted among the great pairs of literary enemies; for what di-vides them, finally, is their differing attitudes to "this human, too human world" below, and to "the angels and the archangels" above.

A few notes, first, on how much these adversaries knew about each other's work. Joyce was certainly prejudiced against Lawrence, both as a writer and as an Englishman, but probably knew more of him by hearsay than by close reading. In June 1918 he asked his agent, J. B. Pinker, to get him a copy of the American edition of *The Rainbow* (*Letters I* 115). The publisher, Huebsch, was being very careful about distributing copies, and Joyce may never have re-ceived the copy he ordered (Delany 166–167). The only other Lawrence book we know Joyce looked at was *Lady Chatterley's Lover,* and he probably did not look at it for very long (*SL* 359). Lawrence does not seem to have taken any interest in Joyce before 1922, and there is no sign that he ever read *Dubliners* or *Portrait.* Then the publicity surrounding the publication of *Ulysses* caught his attention and in July 1922, while living in Australia, he wrote to S. S. Koteliansky that "I shall be able to read this famous *Ulysses* when I get to America. I doubt (i.e. I suspect) he's a trickster." Lawrence was writing *Kangaroo* at the time, and said of it, "but such a novel! Even the Ulysseans will spit at it" (*Letters IV*, 275). He finally got hold of a borrowed copy of *Ulysses* in New Mexico in November 1922, and sent it back eight days later with the comment: "I am sorry, but I am one of the people who can't read *Ulysses*. Only bits. But I am glad I have seen the book, since in Europe they usually mention us together—James Joyce and D. H. Lawrence—and I feel I ought to know in what company I creep to immortality. I guess Joyce would look as much askance on me as I on him. We make a choice of Paola and Francesca floating down the winds of hell."[1] The needle of personal rivalry is already evident, reflecting Lawrence's uneasiness that he and Joyce had become strange bedfellows as the two most notorious banned authors in English.[2] Lawrence's literary judgement of the novel was guarded: "*Ulysses* wearied me: so like a schoolmaster with dirt and stuff in his head: sometimes good, though: but too mental" (*Letters IV*, 345). Lawrence would return regularly to this criticism of Joyce as someone who achieved his effects in too conscious a way. Two months after reading *Ulysses* he wrote "Surgery for the Novel—or a Bomb," and spoke of the "death-rattle" of the "serious" novel:

> "Did I feel a twinge in my little toe, or didn't I?" asks every character of Mr. Joyce or of Miss Richardson or M. Proust. . . . Through thousands and thousands of pages Mr. Joyce and Miss Richardson tear themselves to pieces, strip their smallest emotions to the finest threads, till you feel you are sewed inside a wool mattress that is being slowly shaken up, and you are turning to wool along with the rest of the woolliness.
>
> It's awful. And it's childish. It really is childish, after a certain age, to be absorbedly self-conscious. (*Selected Literary Criticism* 114–15)

When Lawrence came to read part of "Work in Progress" in the summer of 1928, he felt that Joyce was going much further down the wrong path: "Somebody sent me *Transition*—American number—that Paris modernissimo periodical, James Joyce and Gertrude Stein, etc. What a stupid *olla podrida* of the Bible and so forth James Joyce is: just stewed-up fragments of quotation in the sauce of a would-be-dirty mind."[3] Early in 1929 Harry Crosby tried to arrange a meeting between the two men, but Joyce refused. In whatever circle they inhabit on the opposite shore, presumably they are still passing each other without the tribute of recognition.

It would need a book to do justice to the rivalry between these two near-contemporaries whose literary careers and personal histories have so much in common, yet who remain so deeply opposed. In this brief essay I attempt only to identify two major points of contention: realism as a method and sexuality as a subject.

Much in Lawrence's judgment of Joyce derives from the assumption that Joyce was the inheritor of nineteenth-century realism. Lawrence's most eloquent statement on this tradition comes in his discussion of Flaubert:

> Realism is just one of the arbitrary views man takes of man. It sees us all as little ant-like creatures toiling against the odds of circumstance. . . . I think the inherent flaw in *Madame Bovary* is that individuals like Emma and Charles Bovary are too insignificant to carry the full weight of Gustave Flaubert's profound sense of tragedy. . . . Emma and Charles Bovary are two ordinary persons, chosen because they *are* ordinary. But Flaubert is by no means an ordinary person. Yet he insists on pouring his own deep and bitter tragic consciousness into the little skins of the country doctor and his dissatisfied wife. . . .
> . . . the human soul has supreme joy in true, vivid consciousness. And Flaubert's soul has this joy. But Emma Bovary's soul does not, poor thing, because she was deliberately chosen because her soul was ordinary. . . .
> [Yet] Even Emma Bovary has a certain extraordinary female energy of restlessness and unsatisfied desire. So that both Flaubert and Verga allow their heroes something of the hero, after all. The one thing they deny them is the consciousness of heroic effort. (*Phoenix II* 281–282)

Now if you substitute Molly and Leopold for Emma and Charles I think you have essentially the same point, though Lawrence would not be so generous to Joyce as to Flaubert. And how might one respond in Joyce's defense? First, that Joyce's "profound sense" is comic rather than tragic, and that *Ulysses* is not a nihilistic work, as *Madame Bovary* perhaps is. Second, that ordinary life *is* quite heroic enough for Joyce, provided one pays sufficiently close and respectful attention to it. Bloom may not be much bigger intrinsically than Charles Bovary, or Bouvard and Pécuchet, but he is imagined with affection rather than scorn, and that makes all the difference. Third, that the special effect of *Ulysses* depends on Molly and Bloom having "something of the hero" *without* being conscious of it, as Lawrence would want. Their greatness lies in, in other words, precisely in their lack of consciousness—*we* see the classical parallel, but they mustn't.

When we turn to the sexual opposition between Joyce and Lawrence, we need to fill in the background of the former's sly deflations and the latter's dismissive outbursts. Lawrence was two years dead when Joyce called the ending of *Lady Chatterley's Lover* "propaganda in favour of something which, outside of D.H.L.'s country at any rate, makes all the propaganda for itself" (*SL* 359). What Joyce did not know was that Connie Chatterley seems to have been conceived deliberately as the antidote to Molly Bloom! "The last part of [*Ulysses*]," Lawrence burst out, "is the dirtiest, most indecent, obscene thing ever written. Yes it is, Frieda. It is filthy. . . . This *Ulysses* muck is more disgusting than Casanova. I *must* show that it can be done without muck" (Mackenzie 167). One can make a joke of this, saying that Lawrence liked the idea of *Ulysses*—

"lusty woman has impotent husband, takes lover"—but not the way it was written up. But there is a serious point at issue, concerning the treatment of sexuality in nineteenth-century realism. Lawrence found that treatment a deliberate narrowing of human potential; whereas Joyce accepts realism's fundamental project of documenting, without moral preconceptions, people's everyday behavior.

Joyce regards with equanimity every possible sexual act that is freely chosen; but he does not stop there. His interest in the body is also a moral stance, taken up against the orthodox Christian hostility to "mere" flesh. More heretic than scientist, Joyce becomes a Manichean in reverse, preferring the flesh that affirms to the spirit that denies. Courting Marthe Fleischmann, he reminds her that "Jésus Christ a pris son corps humain: dans le ventre d'une femme juive" (SL 233). It is by woman's flesh, and especially her secret inner parts, that a world fallen into negation can be redeemed. At the same time, Joyce is fascinated by woman's double nature, combining the carnal with the transcendent. His sexual epiphanies are moments when the woman displays both qualities intensely and simultaneously. The whore in Portrait, for example, is a priestess of the body. A real priest would raise the host up to heaven then bring it down into the mouth of the communicant, who kneels below him. But the whore puts something even more potent into Stephen's mouth: her own tongue, in a direct communion of flesh with flesh.

In the vision of the bird-girl, and in the erotic letters to Nora, Joyce excites himself with a sacred love-object who displays for him her profane functions of excretion; the most intense sexual experience is one that mingles, sacrilegiously, the most exalted with the most vulgar.[4] Yet Joyce's sexuality remains catholic, in the sense of universal: it includes every possible means of communion between men and women, whether high or low. His letter to Nora of 2 December 1909 is a classic expression of his need to reconcile sacred and profane love: "side by side and inside this spiritual love I have for you there is also a wild beast-like craving for every inch of your body, for every secret and shameful part of it, for every odour and act of it."[5]

For Joyce, then, the spiritual idea adds spice to the raw hungers of sensuality; and this is precisely what offends the Lawrentian sexual ethic. The episodes I have discussed would be for Lawrence prime examples of "sex in the head," the subordination of the physical act to a sophisticated consciousness of it. In Women in Love, Birkin tells Hermione: "You don't want to be an animal, you want to observe your own animal functions, to get a mental thrill out of them" (41). The Lawrentian ideal of immediacy is the opposite of Joyce's "working up" of sexuality within a cultural and religious symbolic system. Hence Lawrence's complaint that Ulysses was "too mental." In Finnegans Wake he found a progression of the disease "too terribly would-be and done-on-purpose, utterly without spontaneity or real life" (Letters VI 548).

"Real life," for Lawrence, means striking through the mask of culture to get as close as possible to "the thing itself." Joyce, on the other hand, accepts that reality is inescapably textual. Stephen's maxim that absence is the highest form of presence argues that representations are more potent than whatever they are taken to represent. In sexual relations, Joyce dwells obsessively on in-direct or incomplete modes of consummation; he is fascinated by everything that may intervene between desire and performance. A partial list of these in-termediate conditions would include idealization (of the woman), fantasies of the inaccessible other, voyeurism, fetishism (of garments, symbols, the writ-ten word), fear of exposure, surrogate or vicarious satisfaction, complaisance, jealousy, the incest taboo, impotence. Most of these conditions can be found also in Joyce's personal sexual history.

Lawrence did not read Joyce closely enough to appreciate the full extent of his rejection of sexual immediacy. But he read enough to support a psychic in-dictment: that in Joyce the worm of consciousness preys on the living flesh of desire. To this Lawrence adds a moral judgement, directed against the demotic quality of sex in *Ulysses* and *Finnegans Wake*. When Lawrence was twenty-two, he told a congregational minister that he had "believed for many years that the Holy Ghost descended and took conscious possession of the 'elect'—the con-verted one" (*Letters I* 39). Lawrence ceased being a chapel-going orthodox Christian in his late teens; but there persisted in his emotional makeup much of the Calvinist division of mankind into the elect and the preterite (those who are without grace and rejected by God). Not unlike Joyce, Lawrence dares to be a heretic by making sexual union the center of his heterodox religion. But Joyce makes *all* sex sacramental in some degree—even, and especially, such stigmatized practices as prostitution or masturbation; Lawrence makes distinctions and excludes. In Lawrence's neo-Calvinist morality, sex becomes the predominant means and sign of grace; but, by the same token, the wrong kind of sex is the mark of preterition. From this comes Lawrence's preoccu-pation with the *signs* of sexual grace, such as the proper correspondence be-tween the man's and the woman's desire.[6] And just as in the orthodox Calvin-ist tradition, determining the exact degree of grace in the soul becomes an esoteric art. There is also a Calvinist anxiety about salvation, though now as-sociated with sexual instead of explicitly religious consciousness.

My general point here is that sexuality in both authors demonstrates the subtle complicity between Modernism and religion; Modernism might even be considered a religious revival, challenging the Victorian idea that religion would wither away and be replaced by science. Yet Joyce and Lawrence are firmly heterodox; it almost seems that they preserve religion because it *enables* heresy, perversion, and sacrilege. Within Catholicism, the use of ritual for profane purposes goes back to medieval love poetry and reaches its formal limit in the Marquis de Sade; Joyce's erotic letters to Nora continue and extend this tradition. For Joyce, before there can be sweets there must be sin. Calvinism has a different interplay between rule and transgression. There, Lawrence is best understood as an antinomian: one who believes that the elect are incapable of sin, following Titus 1:15: "Unto the pure all things are pure." In the antinomian system, the same act may be sinful or blameless; it all depends on whether the person acting is in a state of grace. Lawrence applies a similar rule to sexual acts. His antinomianism is most evident in his treatment of extreme or "unnatural" practices, such as anal intercourse. This can be sign of preterition, for acquaintances like J. M. Keynes (*Letters II* 320-21) or for the decadent Loerke in *Women in Love*. But for Will and Anna in *The Rainbow*, or for Mellors and Connie in *Lady Chatterley's Lover*, it is the most forbidden acts that confirm their love and raise them above the common run of humanity (*Rainbow* 218-20; *Lady Chatterley* 258-59).

When Lawrence says, "I hate sex, it is such a limitation," I think he is concerned with the unequal distribution of grace: sex is the most promising way of escaping this "human, all too human world," yet it too often fails to provide enough lift. Hence Lawrence's obsession with distinguishing between good sex and bad sex—that is, between the sacred and the profane. Joyce, on the other hand, wants the sacred and profane to merge, in bed, chamber pot, or individual pair of trousers. By Lawrence's standards, all of Bloom's sex is spectacularly bad—and Molly's, too, if for different reasons. But Joyce, like Father Conmee (*U-GP* 10:184-205), blesses on regardless; and this Lawrence cannot forgive.

NOTES

1. *Letters IV,* 340. The reference to Dante's Paolo and Francesca (*Inferno* V) is unclear. They are still united in death; Lawrence must have been thinking either of Francesca's hatred for the husband who murdered them, Giovanni da Malatesta (who was still alive when Dante composed the episode), or of some other pair who keep up their rivalry beyond the grave, such as Ulysses and Ajax (*Odyssey*, book II).

2. *The Rainbow* was banned in 1915; in 1921 it was reissued in the United States by subscription. *Women in Love* was privately published in the United States in 1920; an expurgated English edition appeared in the following year. In July 1922 copies of *Women in Love* were seized from the New York office of Lawrence's publisher, Thomas Seltzer, though in September the book was cleared for sale.

3. *Letters VI,* 507. Olla podrida: a spicy stew of meat and vegetables. The issue was presumably *Transition* 13 (Summer 1928), containing "Continuation of a Work in Progress," revised as *Finnegans Wake* III.ii.

4. I am assuming here that the bird-girl encourages Stephen to watch her urinate. See Joyce's confession to Gertrude Kaempffer that his first sexual experience was similarly provoked; also H.C.E.'s "sin in the park" (Ellmann 418–19).

5. *SL* 180–81. For Lawrence, Joyce's scatological interests prove his disgust with the body: "And now, man has begun to be overwhelmingly conscious of the repulsiveness of his neighbour, particularly of the physical repulsiveness. There it is, in James Joyce,

in Aldous Huxley, in André Gide, in modern Italian novels like *Parigi*—in all the very modern novels, the dominant note is the repulsiveness, intimate physical repulsiveness of human flesh" (*Criticism* 410–11). But I think Lawrence fails to see that the repulsion he feels in reading Joyce is his own, rather than the author's. Seated "above his own rising smell," Bloom remains "calm" (*Ulysses* 56). Joyce, too, relishes the body as it is—whereas Lawrence, much of the time, wrinkles his nose.

6. See, e.g., Compton Mackenzie's testimony: "What worried him particularly was his inability to attain consummation simultaneously with his wife, which according to him must mean that their marriage was still imperfect in spite of all they had both gone through" (167–68). Mellors makes a similar complaint about his first marriage.

WORKS CITED

Delany, Paul. *D. H. Lawrence's Nightmare: The Writer and His Circle in the Years of the Great War.* New York: Basic Books, 1978.

Ellmann, Richard. *James Joyce.* New and revised ed. Oxford: Oxford University Press, 1983.

Lawrence, D. H. *Lady Chatterley's Lover.* Harmondsworth: Penguin, 1961.

———. *The Letters of D. H. Lawrence.* 6 vols. Cambridge: Cambridge University Press, 1979–91. Vol. 1, ed. James T. Boulton, 1979; vol. 2, ed. George J. Zytaruk and James T. Boulton, 1981; vol. 4, ed. Warren Roberts, James T. Boulton, and Elizabeth Mansfield, 1987; vol. 6, ed. James T. Boulton and Margaret H. Boulton, with Gerald M. Lacy, 1991.

———. *Phoenix II.* Ed. Warren Roberts and Harry T. Moore. Harmondsworth: Penguin, 1978.

———. *The Rainbow.* Ed. Mark Kinkead-Weekes. Cambridge: Cambridge University Press, 1989.

———. *Selected Literary Criticism.* Ed. Anthony Beal. New York: Viking Press, 1956.

———. *Women in Love.* Ed. David Farmer, Lindeth Vasey, and John Worthen. Cambridge: Cambridge University Press, 1987.

Mackenzie, Compton. *My Life and Times: Octave V 1915-1923.* London: Chatto & Windus, 1966.

Rebecca West vs. James Joyce, Samuel Beckett, and William Carlos Williams

Austin Briggs

Reading Rebecca West, one understands why Max Beerbohm once sketched a caricature of her as "the Femme Shaw," and why Shaw himself wrote that West could "handle a pen as brilliantly as I ever could, and much more savagely" (Glendinning 4).[1] Like Shaw, one cannot but admire the flash and thrust of West's attack, whether she is describing Michael Arlen—"every other inch a gentleman"—or the Jamesian sentence—"a delicate creature swathed in relative clauses as an invalid in shawls" (Glendinning 111, 61).

West boldly defined her role as critic in the premiere issue of the *New Republic*, in an article that is what its title—"The Duty of Harsh Criticism"—suggests. Writing in 1914 (she was all of twenty-one at the time), West argued that living under the stress of war, "if we want to save our souls, the mind must lead a more athletic life than it has ever done before, and must more passionately than ever practise and rejoice in art" (18). The paragraphs that follow make clear that the athletic life of the mind is to be aerobic and high impact. Prescribing a "new and abusive school of criticism," West warmed up by flattening a pair of lightweights, A. C. Benson and Mrs. Humphrey Ward, before announcing the main event thus: "But there is a more serious duty than these before us, the duty of listening to our geniuses in a disrespectful manner." West then proceeded to point out deficiencies in George Bernard Shaw and H. G. Wells, "two great writers of to-day who greatly need correction" (19). In time, Rebecca West came to correct another genius, James Joyce, and—not surprisingly—she did so disrespectfully.

Most Joyceans probably know West's criticism of Joyce from selections in

Robert Deming's volumes on Joyce in the Critical Heritage series and from the contributions by Samuel Beckett and William Carlos Williams to *Our Exagmination Round His Factification for Incamination of Work in Progress*.[2] Beckett's "Dante . . . Bruno. Vico. ." is less than admirable when it pauses to snipe at West along the way. In "The Strange Necessity," West had tried to relate aesthetic response and the conditioned responses of Pavlov's experiments; taking the cheap shot, Beckett accuses her of a "continuous process of copious intellectual salivation." Irked by West's account of shopping for a dress and hats in Paris while reflecting on Joyce's work, Beckett goes on to say, "When Miss Rebecca West clears her decks for a sorrowful deprecation of the Narcisstic element in Mr. Joyce by the purchase of 3 hats, one feels that she might very well wear her bib at all her intellectual banquets, or alternatively, assert a more noteworthy control over her salivary glands than is possible for Monsieur Pavlo's [sic] unfortunate dogs" (13).

One senses here the animus that Susan Brienza describes in "Clods, Whores, and Bitches," and given Beckett's clear distress at West's daring to mention the purchase of millinery and the reading of Joyce's works in virtually the same breath, one suspects that animus again when, only four sentences further on, Beckett turns to a passage from "Work in Progress" that begins, "Who in his heart doubts either that the facts of feminine clothiering are there all the time or that the feminine fiction, stranger than the facts, is there also at the same time, only a little to the rere?" (13–14; the full passage Beckett quotes appears in a slightly different form as *FW* 109.30–33).

Unlike Beckett's essay, which devotes only a half page to her, William Carlos Williams's contribution to *Our Exagmination* is focused throughout on West. As Paul Mariani explains in his biography of the poet, when Williams read West's "The Strange Case of James Joyce" in the September 1928 New York *Bookman*, he found it "so condescending and reactionary . . . that he wrote at once to the editors demanding an opportunity to answer her 'High Church' attack, as he called it in a letter to Marianne Moore" (285). Though the *Bookman* refused, Williams was still working on his defense of Joyce when a letter arrived fortuitously from Sylvia Beach requesting an essay for *Our Exagmination*. (In 1927, reacting to a letter from Pound telling him to ignore "Work in Progress" as mere "backwash," Williams had published a defense, "A Note on the Recent Work of James Joyce," in *transition* [McMillan 185].) Williams accepted with alacrity, explaining that he had already drafted twenty-eight typewritten pages of a reply to West's article. In his letter to Beach, dated 4 November, Williams says, "Rebecca West praises Joyce in such a way that I felt ill over it. I had to answer her but found it extremely difficult so cleverly has she involved her hidden thesis in fine words. I can't tell you how it infuriated me." Williams begs Beach to wait for his essay; her project will "spur" him to complete what he terms "important work for me."[3]

Williams's contribution to *Our Exagmination*, "A Point for American Criticism," is a full-scale assault on West, mostly on the dubious grounds expressed in the letter to Marianne Moore, that West is "High Church"—English and insular. "This is the opportunity of America!" Williams yawps, "to see large, larger than England can" (180). Sounding a bit like George Bush, he continues, "This American thing it is that would better fit the Irish of Joyce" (181). "To me," Williams says, "Rebecca West's view seems incompatible with American appreciation, and though her observations appear mainly true, they seem narrow, inadequate, even provincial, certainly scared, protestant female—unsatisfactory" (184).

In a letter to Valery Larbaud, Joyce admits that he stood behind the "twelve Marshals" who contributed to *Our Exagmination*, "more or less directing them what lines of research to follow" (quoted in *JJII* 613). The letter leads one to ask to what degree the attacks on West by Beckett and Williams reflect Joyce's own reactions. As we have seen, Williams was already at work on a furious reply to West before Sylvia Beach invited him to contribute to *Our Exagmination*, but as Suzette Henke speculates, his "indictment of West as a 'scared protestant female,' probably pleased Joyce, despite (or even because of) its misogynist rhetorical ring" (77). And like Beckett, Joyce, too, was distressed by West's hats, so much so that they became, so to speak, bees in his bonnet. Padraic Colum explains an appearance of "forty bonnets" in the *Wake* (552.29–30) as expressive of Joyce's disdain for West and "the frivolousness of women who go off to buy bonnets after making snap judgments on books of manifold significance" (126).[4] "It is the masculine values that prevail," Virginia Woolf was to lament in *A Room of One's Own*; "the worship of fashion, the buying of clothes [are] 'trivial' " (77).

Just what did the DWPF (dead white provincial female) say that excited such reactions and that has led more recent readers to term her criticism of Joyce "malicious" (Reynolds 201) and "vicious" (Cumpiano 54)? Some years before, it was West who had suggested to H. G. Wells that he review *A Portrait of the Artist*, as he did in an appreciative and widely circulated notice that significantly promoted Joyce's reputation (Ellmann 414),[5] but presumably neither Joyce nor his defenders knew of her good service here; nor, presumably, did they know that West had given a lecture on *Exiles*, which she had liked "tremendously" (Scott 118); and, surely, they cannot have known, as we will never know, what remarks on "the defects of James Joyce's aesthetic theory" West cut from her lecture "The Spirit and Tendency of the Modern Novel" when she discovered that the Woman's Athletic Club of Chicago, an audience she had imagined a "collection of husky young women in sweaters" was composed instead of wealthy and overweight dowagers (letter, 25 Nov. 1923, quoted in Ray 153–54). We do know, however, that the criticism of Joyce's writing that West published in 1928 produced what Joyce himself would characterize two years later as a "great storm" (Hoffmeister 132).

Williams's hostility to West in *Our Exagmination* can be explained as being motivated by more than his habitual pugnacity toward writing in English not in the American vein (somehow the Irish were honorary Americans). The West whom Williams attacks in "A Point for American Criticism" is a critic he charges with putting both Joyce and the United States "in a bad light" through an unnamed article that had appeared in an *American* publication (173). As we have seen, the article in question—"The Strange Case of James Joyce"—appeared in the New York *Bookman* for September 1928. The *Bookman* did not identify it as such, but the article is a reprint of the first thirty-eight pages (13–50) of the title essay of *The Strange Necessity,* which had been published by Jonathan Cape in late July (the American edition would appear in early November [Hutchinson 3–4]). In other words, when Williams wrote his essay he had read only approximately the first fifth of "The Strange Necessity."

Although the references to Pavlov in "Dante . . . Bruno. Vico. ." make it clear that Beckett knew more of West's criticism of Joyce than merely the extract published in the *Bookman,* Joyce as well as Williams may not have known the complete text of "The Strange Necessity." In a letter dictated on 20 September 1928, during a bout of eye trouble, Joyce wrote to Harriet Weaver of having "about fifty pages" of West's book read aloud to him. "I cannot judge until I hear the whole essay," Joyce said. "I think that P.P. [*Pomes Penyeach*] had in her case the intended effect of blowing up some bogey bogus personality and that she is quite delighted with the explosion" (Ellmann 605; brackets his).

For at least a time, then, Joyce knew about as much of the full essay as Williams did, for "about fifty pages" would have run more or less through part 1 of "The Strange Necessity," pages 13–58 in the London edition, which must have been the one read to Joyce, given the date of his letter to Weaver. Whether he ever heard or read the entire 186 pages of the essay, however, Joyce did know something more of it than Williams; the first mention in "The Strange Necessity" of purchasing hats (51) appears immediately after the paragraph that concludes the excerpt published in the *Bookman.*

Joyce's initially positive reaction to West's essay is curious.[6] Why, in his letter to Weaver, does Joyce say of *Pomes Penyeach,* "It is a pity that W.L. [Wyndham Lewis] did not wait for its publication too as it would probably have mollified his attack" (Ellmann 605; brackets his)? One would expect, moreover, that a reader knowing only the opening fifty pages or so of "The Strange Necessity" would believe West's criticism to be much more negative than it actually is. (Robert Deming's *Critical Heritage* anthology offers passages from "The Strange Case" but nothing from the rest of "The Strange Necessity.")

The opening section of "The Strange Necessity" gives a misleading impression of the whole, because an unwary reader (circa 1920s at least)—even so wary an "unwary" reader as Joyce—might mistake the tone and miss a strategy that the Wife of Bath (circa 1380s) would have understood. West's associative flights often seem, well, flighty; she dismisses with equal peremptoriness such disparate matters as the game of boules and *Pomes Penyeach*; she shamelessly exposes a frivolous nature ("I had bought a black lace dress" [50]; "I had lunched in a divine house" [51]); and she betrays crassness in confessing that she spent part of her day in Paris with a lawyer discussing an investment.

The lengthy essay that makes up more than half *The Strange Necessity* and gives the volume its name opens with West's recollection of browsing through the copy of *Pomes Penyeach* that had just been sold to her at Shakespeare and Company "as they sell pious whatnots in a cathedral porch." Strolling along the boulevards of "the best of all cities," happily tracing the course of a dove overhead in the "clean French light" (13), West finds added pleasure in the discovery that the poem she has just read—"Alone"—closes with "words as blank as the back of a spoon": "And all my soul is a delight, / A swoon of shame" (14). Barely three pages into her essay, West tartly concludes that Mr. Joyce is "entirely without taste" (15).

West's adverse judgments on *Ulysses* are several. Joyce's most serious weakness is the "sentimentality" revealed in "Alone," a term West defines by free associating her way to Provence and the detested boules. The sentimental artist is a boule player, "moving certain objects according to certain rules in front of spectators" in order to produce shock after shock as object strikes object (17). In short, Joyce is a writer who sometimes plays to his audience shamelessly, like Dickens. (Had Dickens realized that "the logic of the book's being suddenly demanded an eleventh-hour recovery," West writes of Little Nell, "he would have hit the child on the head without the slightest compunction" [19].) Thus, West says, Joyce sets up the "Nausicaa" episode so that he can score with the surprise of Gerty MacDowell's lameness. The obvious obscenity of the novel is also objectionable as a sentimental effort to produce shock. Moreover, *Ulysses* is marred because Stephen is so transparently a hero: "his creator has given him eyelashes an inch long" (20). In West's reading, Stephen is a narcissistic self-portrait who "enjoys the unnatural immunity from interruption that one might encounter not in life but in a typical Freudian wish-fulfillment dream" (22).

West finds "two colossal finger-prints left by literary incompetence on *Ulysses*." First, the Homeric parallels that Joyce's apostles point to with ecstasy are a blunder because Greek unity is incompatible with what she takes to be the Manichaean duality of *Ulysses*. Second, Joyce misuses literary tradition, especially in the parodies of "Oxen of the Sun" that are so prized by Joyce's devotees as evidence of profound learning; supposing the parodies to originate in the mind of Stephen Dedalus, "translated . . . into terms of the literature in which he had been saturating himself," West finds them "noticeably bad" (28–29). Finally (in a passage that seems on the way to anticipating Chomsky's *Syntactic Structures* by almost thirty years), West argues that Joyce's "strings of words" do not accurately represent the stream of consciousness:

There is nothing more certain than that sentences were used by man before words and still come with the readiness of instinct to his lips. They, and not words, are the foundations of all language. . . . Your baby has no words, but it will use sentences for hours together, sentences sometimes pausing for thought and adding a pungent dependent clause, till it builds up a kind of argument-like mass. (32–33)

Given such an indictment and such a list of particulars, one understands why Patrick Parrinder borrowed West's "The Strange Necessity" for the title of the essay he subtitled "James Joyce's Rejection in England (1914–30)."[7] But the issue is not so simple. Bonnets aside, why did Joyce, if Ellmann is correct, line up the apostles of *Our Exagmination* to refute Rebecca West (along with Sean O'Faolain and Wyndham Lewis) as one of the three "chief critics" of "Work in Progress" at the time (613)? Astonishingly, given the counterattack in *Our Exagmination*, West's attention to "Work in Progress" in "The Strange Necessity" is limited exclusively to ninety-nine words at the close of a longish paragraph on stream of consciousness in *Ulysses*, and of those, sixty-one make up a quotation from Joyce. True, West does give summary judgment on the passage she quotes—"it is not true" (36)—but this can hardly be termed a broadside fired at the *Wake*.

In fact, for all its reservations, "The Strange Necessity" is unequivocal on the question of Joyce's genius and importance. West places "A Painful Case" (which she misnames "A Sad Case" but recalls in accurate detail) and "The Dead" among the "most beautiful short stories that have been written in our time" (24); "these two stories by themselves should explain why we rank James Joyce as a major writer" (28). West may object to what she takes to be lapses of taste in *Ulysses*, but she praises the beauty of the writing in the beach scene in "Telemachus" and in the "exquisitely pathetic picture of the visions of a sweet and ordered life" that come to Bloom in "Ithaca" (22–23).

Doubtless we judge West wrong (but by no means alone in this at the time) in failing to appreciate the distance that Joyce establishes between himself and Stephen. On the other hand, we may think that she was right to believe that interior monologue is not the objective recording many readers once took it to be, and right as well to think that contemporary enthusiasts made too much of the ingenuity of the Homeric parallels. Right or wrong, however, and whatever the criticism of *Pomes Penyeach* and—briefly— "Work in Progress," when taken in its entirety, "The Strange Necessity" simply cannot be read as an attack on Joyce. Discussing what she most admires in *Ulysses*, West is effusive. Molly's soliloquy lies "outside the sphere and beyond the power of any other writer alive or dead" (24); it offers "one of the most tremendous summations of life that have ever been caught in the net of art" (47). West's reading of Bloom as earth-bound jester is not persuasive, but the praise she gives to him is, if anything, more open-handed than that bestowed on Molly: "I do most solemnly maintain that Leopold Bloom is one of the greatest creations of all time: that in him something true is said about man" (43).

In a letter of 7 November 1958, West wrote to Richard Ellmann that in "The Strange Necessity" she was following a form of discursive personal criticism used by Rémy de Gourmont and other French writers; she might also have mentioned Virginia Woolf, for as Samuel Hynes observes, "The Strange Necessity" opens like an essay by Woolf, "mixing an account of a stroll in a city with thoughts about literature, making it all seem informal and easy, and consciously charming, and very womanly." But, even overlooking the implication that Woolf fell short in never conquering her "womanly" qualities, one must conclude that Hynes misses the point when he speaks of West "acting out her liberation from the stereotypes of her sex" (xii). The accounts of the "womanly" activities of buying hats and a black lace dress do not function to set up the reader of "The Strange Necessity" for West's escape to "serious" ("manly"?) matters like Joyce and Pavlov. Rather, West is arguing that Joyce is important because he can compete even with such matters of vital human importance as haute couture, three-star luncheons, and investments prudently laid by for a comfortable old age.

Also linking West and Woolf, but with far greater sensitivity than Hynes, Bonnie Kime Scott says that "The Strange Necessity" "might be described as a less disciplined version of Virginia Woolf's effort to understand human contexts in A Room of One's Own" (119). The fine insight is worth expanding on, especially because West seems to have associated attacks on her writing about Joyce with the attacks she anticipated falling on Woolf's essay. In her Letter from Abroad in the New York Bookman for January 1930, West follows an affectionate sketch of Woolf glimpsed on the street with glowing praise for Woolf's oeuvre as a whole and for the just-published A Room of One's Own, which she calls an "uncompromising piece of feminist propaganda . . . the ablest yet written" (553). West emphasizes that Woolf's new book is "all the more brave and defiant because antifeminism is so strikingly the correct fashion of the day among the intellectuals." As an example of the fashion, West notes that recently a male writer referred to "intellectualized women" with a "foul epithet" originally applied by Baudelaire to George Sand (554).[8] As we shall see, in her Bookman Letter the following month, West would cite Baudelaire again, this time quoting him directly to protest the misogyny that she feels has been directed at her for being a woman who dares find fault with James Joyce.

Woolf's essay cannot have influenced "The Strange Necessity," for the lectures upon which A Room of One's Own are based were delivered in October 1928, three months after West's essay appeared. Still, the resemblances between the two works are marked. Woolf creates a novelistic personal fiction of her stroll through the "courts and quadrangles of Oxbridge on a fine October morning" (6), and West takes her stroll along the boulevards and streets of Paris, musing on *Pomes Penyeach* and James Joyce on a "sun-gilded autumn day" (184). In a passage that West praised in the *Bookman*, Woolf digresses from the "serious" matters at hand to devote a page to a mouth-watering description (female salivation again!) of the sole à la crème and roast partridges, the sauces and salads and wines, served to men at an Oxbridge high table, and West strays from meditations on literature and painting to recall her pleasure in the notorious bonnets or in the delectable taste of preserved *fraise*. Woolf briefly relates the nourishment given women artists to experiments measuring the effect of Grade A and ordinary milk on the bodies of rats, and West trespasses at length into presumably masculine (and Wellsian) territory in order to relate artistic response to Pavlovian experiments with dogs.[9]

Woolf's brilliant essay suggests how much art and method lie in West's. More interesting than correspondences in detail is what Scott rightly calls the "lyrical" quality that the two essays share (119), and one notes as well a wicked wit in both that by turns charmingly disarms and uncompromisingly annihilates opposition. Thus West turns on its head the solemn assumption that in contrast to art, female pleasures are trivial and practical matters are low. What might have once seemed to some to be "womanly" digressions into the superficial are in fact intrinsic to West's argument for the "fundamental unity of all art and all experience" (189). Unapologetically embracing the pleasure principle, she discovers to her surprise that art is "not a luxury, but a necessity" (178); her emotions, "supporting and supported by the intellect," have urgently warned her that she "must read every word of *Ulysses*" (179).

"The Strange Necessity" is not an essay on Joyce or on modern letters (though it has a good deal to say about Yeats, Lawrence, George Moore, and Proust); it is, rather, a lengthy meditation on life and art, remarkably broad and eclectic in the range of its references. Anthony West writes that "The Strange Necessity" is "one of those mid-life wagers that the nonacademic literary figure must make in order to achieve recognition as a serious critic. It was intended to convince those who knew her only as a literary journalist and a writer of *Saturday Evening Post* short stories." Though characteristically unfair to his mother here, Anthony West at least recognizes that central to the essay are "laudatory considerations of the innovative fictions of Joyce and Proust" (368–69).

H. G. Wells, who offended Rebecca West by telling her that her essay "ought to have music by Stravinski" (Ray 176), gives a clue to what may be either a strength or a weakness of "The Strange Necessity," depending on the reader. Recalling his constant advice on her writing during the period of their intimacy ("Construct, construct"), Wells says that West "writes like a loom producing her broad rich fabric with hardly a thought of how it will make up a shape, while I write to cover a frame of ideas. . . . She splashed her colours about; she exalted James Joyce and D. H. Lawrence as if in defiance of me— and in despite of Jane [Mrs. Wells] and everything trim, cool, deliberate in the

world" (102). If a frame is the model, "The Strange Necessity" does lack structure. Along its nonlinear and far from cool personal course, West leaves Joyce
for long stretches to discuss not only many other authors, past and present, but
painting, music, Pavlovian psychology, and a host of other matters.

Had Williams read the whole of "The Strange Necessity," he would have
found Joyce almost disappearing from the essay after the introductory section
until the conclusion; after section 1, Joyce is mentioned only three times in the
next 117 pages of the London edition, once in a long paragraph (68–70), once
in a brief sentence (88), and once in a four-word parenthesis (114). In the summary final eighth of the essay (sections 6 and 7), however, West returns to
Joyce and modifies the negative commentary of the first section in significant
ways. If earlier she objected to the obscenity of Joyce, for example, now she
makes it clear that Joyce should under no circumstances be banned. ("The
Strange Case of James Joyce" was one of the documents filed in support of
Ulysses in the Woolsey case [Moscato 199]; in 1960, by then a Dame Com-
mander, Order of the British Empire, West would testify on behalf of publication in the *Lady Chatterley* case [Weldon 12–13].)

More important, as noted above, the summation clarifies the purpose behind what could be taken in the opening pages to be flighty digressions on the
pleasures of strolling and shopping and dining in Paris; in her closing pages,
West returns to her day in Paris to explain, "There was nothing here that did
not delight me, yet all the time I was plucked away by an urgent necessity to
think of James Joyce and the tedious schoolboy Stephen Dedalus and the
Dublin Jew Leopold Bloom and his trollop. . . . When I looked back on the
day, nothing seemed so real as this persistent, nagging preoccupation with
Ulysses" (185). Anticipating the kind of attacks women critics were all too
likely to receive, especially if they gave themselves away by admitting to delight in the fripperies of fashion houses, West concludes that there was "nothing illogical" in her preoccupation with *Ulysses* or in the pleasure she took in
discovering that Joyce had produced a bad poem, "nothing . . . inconsistent
with my great reverence for him" (191).

In short, "The Strange Necessity" of West's title refers to the human imperative that we experience life through art, and the form of the essay—associative, digressive, astonishingly allusive (Al Capone makes a brief appearance)—pays warm and knowing tribute to the authority that *Ulysses* has
exercised over her imagination. West may mock the "pilgrims" who come to
Shakespeare and Company as if for holy relics, but she unblushingly professes
her "great reverence" for Joyce; that reverence, however, does not still her critical faculties or smother her questions.

In 1930, one year after the appearance of *Our Exagmination* and two after
"The Strange Necessity," West published an essay on "Work in Progress"
titled "James Joyce and His Followers." After first brushing aside as foolishness the charge that Joyce's *"patés de langue gras"*—his "paste of words"—is

incomprehensible, she poses three main questions (6). Thus far she has found the entertainment derived from "Work in Progress" worth the effort expended in reading it, but if Joyce ends up devoting twenty to thirty years to the packing of portmanteau words with allusions, can readers be expected to devote half again as many years of their lives to the unpacking?

The remaining two questions undoubtedly reflect the Freudian analysis West began in 1927 (Glendinning 118). If the function of Joyce's new language is to carry us back into the experience of the race, why must we pass through obsolete words to reach a collective unconscious that Freud and Jung show is already accessible through the images that spring spontaneously from the unconscious? West's final question assumes that Joyce's concept of "word paste" derives from Freudian and Jungian analysis of the puns in dreams: "Why is there no sense of clarity, of the gratification that comes from comprehension, such as pervades an analysis that is successful in coping with its subject matter in the same way, and any work of art . . . that has resolved the matter in the terms of its age?" ("Joyce and His Followers" 6). Will a new kind of clarity emerge, West wonders, when "Work in Progress" is complete?

In her closing paragraph, West unequivocally defines the context in which her questions must be read: "I would not myself stake a penny on any of my objections. I state them only because it seems to me of interest to consider what points James Joyce will have to make if he is to quell all resistance in the minds of his age who are looking for the inheritor of art and would like to find it in him. . . . Can one," West asks, "think of any other writer concerning whose work such interesting considerations arise?" The followers of James Joyce are justified in their faith in him, she approvingly concludes, and "theirs, almost alone today, is a religious attitude to art" (6).

The language of "Joyce and His Followers" is notably respectful and the criticism strongly positive, and perhaps it is worth noting that the article appeared not in an avant-garde publication but in the Books section of the *New York Herald Tribune* at a time when the *New York Times* was editorializing that "Work in Progress" was "sleazy, broken, interrupted by surrenders to unintelligibility" (23 August 1929, quoted in Deming 503). West's article did not satisfy at least one follower, however. Two years after the appearance of "James Joyce and His Followers," in the Readers and Writers department of the *New English Weekly* for 21 July 1932, William Carlos Williams responded to a request from Gorham Munson, the American correspondent of the periodical, for an assessment of the current state of English letters. Williams has some good words for Maugham's *Cakes and Ale* and expresses appreciation of the crisp prose in English journalism and medical literature (a monograph "on, let us say, measles"); as for current writing in England otherwise, however, he professes indifference and ignorance in equal measure. In a style he must somehow have thought witty, Williams dismisses those few writers whose names he can recall, the likes of Eliot (whose "blindingly" stupid "religistic attitudes" are undoubtedly the result of residence in England) or Shaw ("Well, well, well, well") or "Wolf" ("who, good Lord, seems to me more like some creature from Hans Christian Andersen's fairy tales than a human being").

The full text of Williams's remarks on West, who receives more attention than anyone else in the brief letter, is as follows: "And Rebecca West, I never should forget her. Once she wrote a simple criticism of Joyce's beginning Anna Livia Pluribella [sic]. I answered her as best I could. When lo and behold a month later she recanted everything she had said in the first article and praised Joyce as the genius he is—using every point I had made against her in my defence of him. That wasn't nice" (331).[10]

The inevitable riposte from West appeared in the Letters columns of the *New English Weekly* five weeks later. Dismissing "A Point for American Criticism" out of hand, she terms Williams's defense of Wakean language "schoolboy cheers" and condemns his account of her criticism as "sheer moonshine . . . anti-English delirium . . . an orgy of obtuseness . . . crassly fatuous . . . [an] amalgam of hysterics and stupidity . . . irresponsible impudence." The only effect that Williams's attack on "The Strange Necessity" had on her, she says, was that insofar as possible, she wrote "James Joyce and His Followers" in words of one syllable to avoid any further "gross misapprehension."

More substantively, West insists on what we have seen, that "The Strange Necessity" is focused on *Ulysses*, not "Work in Progress." Yes, she concedes, she had criticized "sentimentality and lack of critical taste," but her overall estimate had been that Joyce was "a great genius." She had expressed doubts that posterity would adopt Joyce's innovations, West accurately recalls, but she had also expressed in equal measure her confidence that posterity would remember him as "a great creative artist." "James Joyce and His Followers," West insists, was not the recantation of her earlier estimation of Joyce that Williams described in the *New English Weekly*; it was an expression of a "much greater interest and hope regarding the experiments with a new language" based on a subsequent reading of all the installments of "Work in Progress" (458).

In the 1958 letter to Richard Ellmann cited earlier, West goes beyond his questions to volunteer an account of her exchange with Williams in the *New English Weekly*. A friend who taught at Columbia, she explains, had sent her a letter from a student raising several questions concerning "The Strange Necessity," which she tried to answer in "James Joyce and His Followers."[11] "Unfortunately," however, "these points were all taken from an article by Carlos Williams published in a volume of "Transition" devoted to Joyce which I had not then seen. . . . Williams was very angry indeed because I had not mentioned him. In the early thirties he wrote about this very bitterly, and I answered him, explaining the situation, in Orage's New Age." Why West recalls the *New English Weekly* as the *New Age* is easily explained, for A. R. Orage's *New English Weekly*, by then under another editor, became the *New English Weekly and The New Age* in 1939. More difficult to account for is West's confession to Ellmann that she agrees with Williams's charge that she had borrowed too freely from "A Point for American Criticism" (which ran in *Transition* before *Our Exagmination*, as did Beckett's "Dante . . . Bruno. Vico. ."): resemblances between the essays by West and Williams are incidental at most.

One needs a stronger word than "ingenuous" to cover West's plea to Ellmann that she is "completely innocent" and never "meant to be offensive" in the "most unfortunate incident" with Williams. To the contrary, West's letter in the *New English Weekly* is designed to give great offense; far from trying to explain matters, as she claims to Ellmann, West is out for blood. (In another time or place, Jane Marcus admiringly remarks, "West would have been required to register her pen as a deadly weapon" ["A Speaking Sphinx" 153]). "The Strange Necessity" supports West's claims in the *New English Weekly* in one crucial respect, however; she had presented Joyce from the start as a "great genius whose extraordinary powers must be recognized" (458).

Patricia Hutchins writes in *James Joyce's World* of the way comments like West's in "The Strange Necessity" apparently got "under Joyce's skin and worked their way through him like a needle" (182), and she repeats what West told her about Joyce's reaction to "The Strange Necessity": "[West] said that it must be taken into account that her essay, though it expressed deep admiration for the genius of Joyce, began with an unfavorable opinion on one of his poems, and that writers are often most sensitive about their lesser works; and that the essay, because of its particular form, perhaps seemed to Joyce too familiar in tone for a writer . . . of his stature."[12] But there was something more, West added, something inexplicable, "something mythic about the resentment" (247).

Still later in her 1958 letter to Ellmann West attempted to explain once more. Writing "in a personal and almost fictional framework" in "The Strange Necessity," she had tried "to show the power of James Joyce breaking into a mind unprepared for it." But her effort was taken literally and brought down many attacks on her, and "Joyce's resentment of the essay was extreme." West told Ellmann,

> when I heard that Joyce was offended by my essay, I did not dare to do anything that would have made him understand what I felt about him. This was certainly reverence (so far as his prose works were concerned) although I neither think that *Ulysses* is the only book in the world or believe that the hope for literature lies in the adoption of its form. (He is perhaps the one genius who invented a form and exhausted its possibilities at the same time.) It is simply a work of genius, and that surely is enough.

As we have seen, the essay supports West's view of her intentions; no wonder that she recalled even later, near the end of her life, in a 1981 interview with Bonnie Kime Scott, that she was bewildered by the "insane hostility" toward her that she found in the *Wake* and in Joyce's conversation as reported to her (121).[13]

West's lasting sense of persecution because of her criticism of Joyce may seem to lack proportion. Anthony West speaks harshly of a streak of "wild paranoia" in his mother (58), and Victoria Glendinning, though far more sympathetic, offers six entries in the index to her *Life* under the heading "character and personality of RW: paranoia and blaming others" (291). (The *Wake*, of course, is an ideal gift for a paranoiac.) When she discusses West's belief that the *Wake* is full of "spiteful references to her," Glendinning notes that West was constantly finding herself in other people's novels and offers an astonishing list of examples ranging from Wyndham Lewis's *The Roaring Queen* to Muriel Spark's *Memento Mori* and Iris Murdoch's *Sacred and Profane Love Machine* (124). West may have been defensive even to the point of paranoia, or—putting it more mildly—the references in the *Wake* may, as Scott suggests, be less consistently spiteful than West believed (119). Nevertheless, West's sense that they and the two essays in *Our Exagmination* and the subsequent writings by Williams were hostile must not be written off simply as a symptom of what Senators Specter and Hatch might term the delusional.

Joyce's unhappiness with West can be explained in a number of ways. We can decide, as Hutchins does, that Joyce was simply thin-skinned, and we can speculate with Scott that West's criticism was a "little more individually situated than Joyce would have wished" and that it also "may not have singled *Ulysses* out sufficiently from other stimuli" (121). We can wonder, furthermore, whether West's handsome tributes to other writers in "The Strange Necessity"—notably Lawrence, George Moore, and Proust—may not have aroused a twinge of jealousy, or whether, as James Atherton suggests, the efforts by West to locate the influence of Freud and Jung, which William Carlos Williams mocks in *Our Exagmination*, may have aroused Joyce's hostility to her (38). And we may ask whether possibly it was galling for Joyce—to whom *nomen* was *omen*—to be found wanting by a critic with a *nom de plume* out of his beloved Ibsen.

Any or all of these explanations seem plausible, and one more, equally plausible, remains. Suzette Henke and Bonnie Kime Scott are justified in suspecting that West's gender may also have been at issue (Henke 77; Scott 120–21).[14] As we have seen, West does hit hard (Scott calls much of "Necessity" "critical, even insulting" [119]), and readers were not always ready to accept a woman who was "unwomanly" enough to confront a man as an equal. In a generally admiring appraisal of West that appeared in 1929, Patrick Braybrooke cautions, "Lately she has written many superficial articles, in which she attacks men, in an extremely cheap kind of way" (141), and Fay Weldon quotes a colleague who protested West's reviews: "I do not think any female genius has eviscerated the unspeakable male so mercilessly" (33).

West may have been bewildered by the reaction to "Strange Necessity," but she also believed that her gender contributed to the hostility that set her up as a target in *Our Exagmination* and sent her bonnets floating into the vast recirculation of the *Wake*. Her suspicions in this regard are clear in the angry rejoinder to Williams's *Exagmination* essay that she published in her Letter from Abroad in the New York *Bookman* for February 1930, one month after the sweetly reasonable "James Joyce and His Followers" and, as we have seen, one month after she had written of Baudelaire's "foul epithet" in connection with the sexist reaction she believed *A Room of One's Own* was certain to elicit. Her profound offense against *Ulysses* in "The Strange Necessity," West protests in her Letter from Abroad, is that she "*read* the book, instead of taking it as an occasion for dandyism, a way of eclecticism, a fraternity pin." By doing so, she demonstrated to Joyce's champions the truth of Baudelaire's characterization of woman as a "brute—she has no dandyism—she eats when she is hungry and drinks when she is thirsty!" (664).

One must go to West's life to appreciate the full force of her reply to Williams. As Victoria Glendinning reports, West was "startlingly dark-skinned when young" and knew of a family legend of an African ancestor on her mother's side (28–29). Spurred by a recent viewing of the film *Carmen Jones* at which she and her companions were amused by the resemblance they perceived between her and Pearl Bailey, West wrote of the legend in a 1955 letter to Evelyn and Margaret Hutchinson. "I have, as I may have told you," she writes, "a remote strain of Berber blood." It seems that one of her eighteenth-century Highland ancestors "went soldiering in North Africa and brought back an African bride . . . —alas, my nearer ancestors were ashamed of this and destroyed all traces."[15]

To be sure, the passage in the letter is in the spirit of fun, and West obviously enjoys the romance of it all (sometimes, she says, she allows herself to believe that by way of her African ancestor she is related to Saint Augustine). Her feelings about the Berber bride were apparently complex, however, or so one may infer from a striking passage of self-revelation in "James Joyce and His Followers." Explaining the Wakean pun in terms of Freudian free association, West offers the example of a hypothetical analysand, a woman who dreams of someone remarking that her hair, which has grown very long, is dressed in the "criminolation" style. From "criminolation" through Latin *crinis* for "hair" and "crinkly," to an "ancient rumor of black blood in the family" and thence to the crinoline invented by the Empress Eugenie to conceal her pregnancy, the patient works back to her guilt feelings about sex and the resulting sense that "motherhood seems as 'incriminating' as black blood" (6). As noted earlier, West began psychoanalysis in 1927; given West's child out of wedlock by H. G. Wells and the rumor of the African bride, we may assume that it is West herself who is the hypothetical patient here. (It is entertaining but fruitless to speculate that "crimealine" [*FW* 8.30] might have somehow lodged in West's subconscious.)

With this background in mind, we feel an added weight of personal offense in West's reply to Williams in the *Bookman*, a bitter and fantastic expression of feeling utterly marginalized that marvelously links sexism, racism, and colonialism. West imagines the "Joyceite dandies" crowding round her jungle hut to gaze at the female brute, "watching me in horror while I squat in my lava-lava on the mud floor, flashing my beetle-stained teeth and waggling my nose-ring at them in barbaric good-fellowship that unspeakably revolts their lilyhood, eating my yam, raising to my lips the shell of palm-wine . . . reading a book . . . the book . . . Ulysses" (ellipses in original).

If female brute she is, says West, so be it: "The author, wearing a nose-ring, drops to her knees before the Ulysses of James Joyce." She demands equality, however, even as she submits: "But James Joyce, so different from his followers, in writing a book so eminently to be read, must wear a nose-ring too. His giving of reality to a world that needed reality shows that he too believes that one should eat when hungry and drink when thirsty. I continue to waggle my nose-ring" (664).

Having begun with West as Femme Shaw, I might note that one of Shaw's many services to letters was his rejection of bardolatry. So, too, West's criticism of James Joyce: she reminds us that one may revere an artistic achievement without setting it up as an idol for uncritical worship. Her judgments of Joyce's work are uneven—flawed, even foolish and rude at times—but they are often perceptive and, taken in their totality, they express enthusiastic admiration far more than reservation or detraction. Furthermore, West's writing on Joyce reminds us of what it must have been like to encounter Ulysses and Finnegans Wake for the first time, without an elaborate critical framework to guide and support.

The paradox of West's criticism of Joyce (and of others she greatly admired, such as Lawrence) is that she can be reverent yet never abandon the disrespectful "duty of harsh criticism" to which she dedicated herself at age twenty-one. A clue to the conundrum of her "disrespectful reverence" and to the gleeful pleasure she takes in discovering Joyce's sentimental weakness through Pomes Penyeach may lie in a book review that she published in the New Freewoman when she was nineteen. In "Spinsters and Art," West discusses the advantages that "non-celibate" writers have over "spinster" writers. Though a follow-up letter to the editor of the Freewoman makes it clear that men (e.g., Walter Pater and A. C. Benson) may be spinsters and that unmarried women (e.g., May Sinclair) may not be, the review treats spinsters as exclusively female. "It is not until one meets a man on the grounds of not duty, but attraction," West writes, "that his faults strike one with surprise" (47).

The discussion of noncelibate writers links up curiously with a question that West poses in the final paragraph of "The Strange Necessity": "Is it possible that the intense exaltation which comes to our knowledge of the greatest works of art and the milder pleasure that comes of our more everyday dealings with art, are phases of the same emotion, as passion and gentle affection are phases of love between a man and a woman? Is this exaltation the orgasm, as it were, of the artistic instinct, stimulated to its height by a work of art?" (196). A few pages earlier West also implies, though less explicitly, that she has experienced and enjoyed *Ulysses* not as an adoring spinster but as a critical (and "knowing") noncelibate, and she pays to *Ulysses* as charming a compliment as any book ever received. Reading *Ulysses*, West says, "was like standing up to dance the tango after one has not danced it for a very long time, with one who dances it very well" (203).

Given Joyce's lifelong interest in moo-cows, I might close on a bovine note. When West decided against publishing a letter responding to a man who had objected to the acerbity of her theater criticism in the *New Freewoman*, she did so, she explained, on the grounds that she was "old-fashioned enough to think that a superior cow ought to refrain from attacking an inferior bull" (Glendinning 50). Clearly, Rebecca West believed that in James Joyce she had encountered a blue-ribbon Irish bull.

NOTES

1. The caricature, drawn from imagination, is reproduced in Jane Marcus, *The Young Rebecca*, pl. 9, following 148.

2. In welcome contrast to the general run of commentary on West's criticism of Joyce are Bonnie Kime Scott's *Joyce and Feminism* (118–21 et passim) and "The Strange Necessity of Rebecca West." Rather than cite Scott at length, I would like to recommend her work as a complement to my essay. The best case for West as critic is made by Harold Orel in *The Literary Achievement of Rebecca West* (31–69).

3. Williams' unpublished letter is quoted with permission of the Manuscripts Division, Department of Rare Books and Special Collections, Princeton University Libraries. Arguing that Williams did not really understand *FW*, Marion Cumpiano quotes an interview in which he admitted years after his *transition* essays that he was still not sure what it was about (55).

4. Padraic Colum analyzes at length the reference to West and her bonnets in *FW* 552.23–30 (124–26), as does Nathan Halper, who concludes from the passage that Joyce regarded West, like her namesake in *Rosmersholm*, to be a "petty bourgeois" who "got away with murder" (763). "She sass her nach" (*FW* 552.29) suggests, as does Williams in *Our Exagmination*, that part of West's problem is that she is an Englishwoman (no Sassenach, West was Scots-Irish). Scott sees the references in *FW* as more than simply mocking (118–19). For more on West in *FW*, see Tindall 80 and the long note in Benstock 229. If Adaline Glasheen is correct in asserting that "almost any Wells" in *FW* can refer to H. G. Wells (303), what of all the "wests," beginning with "well to the west" on the very first page (*FW* 3.21)?

5. Ellmann says that, when asked to review *Portrait*, Wells protested he was too busy but, "spurred by Rebecca West, he thought better of his decision" (414). This exaggerates West's role. On 3 November 1958, Ellmann wrote to West requesting information about the review and other matters relating to Joyce. West's reply of 7 November acknowledged that, yes, she had recommended *Portrait* to Wells; "someone

else had sent it to him . . . but he had not read it till I drew his attention to it. But . . . he probably would have read it anyway." Ellmann's letter and West's copy of her reply, both unpublished, are in the Rebecca West Collection at Yale; I am grateful for permission from the Beinecke Library to quote from West's letter here and elsewhere in this essay.

6. Citing what Nathan Halper reported of a conversation with Padraic Colum, Bonnie Kime Scott concludes that Joyce reacted positively to the first fifty pages of West's essay but "after reading further, he was [in Halper's words] 'irritated profoundly'" (118); Scott's inference is certainly plausible, but Halper's article does not support it.

7. Parrinder is persuasive in his overall assessment of the rejection of Joyce in England but he is mistaken about West; for reasons that my essay makes clear, I cannot agree with his contention that Bloomsbury values lead her to conclude in "Strange Necessity" that Joyce "does not need to be taken seriously" (163).

8. In A Room of One's Own, Woolf analyzes the "protest against some infringement of his power to believe in himself" of one Z, "the most humane, most modest of men, [who] taking up some book by Rebecca West . . . exclaimed, 'The arrant feminist! She says that men are snobs!'" (35).

9. When on 28 November 1928 H. G. Wells wrote to turn down Joyce's request for support in pushing "Work in Progress" with the public, he explained that for all its faults, "Anrep's dreadful translation of Pavlov's badly written work on Conditioned Reflexes" was "new and illuminating" as Joyce's work was not. Ellmann, who quotes Wells's letter, says that Joyce was "not at all offended" by it (608), but I wonder whether West's discussion of Pavlov may not have unpleasantly recalled Wells's refusal to Joyce.

10. In the New English Weekly for 10 November 1932, Williams defended himself from criticism leveled at him there five weeks earlier by Austin Warren in "Some Periodicals of the American Intelligentsia." Still smarting from her counterattack of the preceding August, Williams cannot resist dragging West into his letter; he asks why she and Warren have been "so violent against me" (91) and after apologizing for going on so long about Warren, tacks on a final paragraph rehashing his earlier complaints in the Weekly about West's criticism of Joyce. This time he is milder, however, closing, "I did not mean, particularly, to offend [her], perhaps it was a fault of the language" (92). More to the point than this apology (if apology it be; the "particularly" falls oddly) is Williams' admission that he still has not read "The Strange Necessity" beyond the extract in the Bookman.

11. The friend at Columbia might have been Carl Van Doren (or his brother Mark), who was married to Irita Van Doren, to whom the American edition of Strange Necessity is dedicated; she was West's friend and editor at the New York Herald Tribune.

12. Hutchins's text reads, "not of his stature," but the not defies the sense of her sentence. Repeating what she earlier told Hutchins (247), West wrote in her letter to Ellmann of 7 November 1958 that matters with Joyce were exacerbated because of Joyce's impression that she and her American publisher, George Doran, had called on him in Paris and behaved rudely, but West insisted to both Hutchins and Ellmann that she was never in Paris with Doran and that she never met Joyce; whether Joyce was under any such misapprehension cannot be determined.

13. In The Court and The Castle, West's brief discussion of Joyce and Lawrence

(221–23), praises Joyce's "titanic genius" unstintingly (221). Nearing the end of her life, West may have still been trying to mend fences with the Joyceans. In his Publisher's Note to *Rebecca West: A Celebration* (1977), Marshall Best says that West herself edited the selections that were not complete works or independent portions from works (xix); the extracts mentioning Joyce from "Strange Necessity" (373–77) barely hint at the reservations in the full essay.

14. In support of the view we share that male chauvinism probably contributed to Joyce's reaction to West's criticism, Scott quotes a remark that he once directed at Mary Colum, "I hate women who know anything," which appears in Ellmann (without a citation) as "I hate intellectual women" (529); Karen Lawrence quotes it, correctly, in the opening sentence of her essay "Joyce and Feminism" in *The Cambridge Companion to James Joyce* (237), and I heard it quoted in Ellmann's incorrect version twice at the 1992 Dublin Symposium. Lest this remark become a locus classicus in Joyce studies, it may be useful to point out that in context this "apparently unequivocal attack," as Richard Brown terms it (91), is far from unequivocal. When Mary Colum protested his exaggerated expressions of indebtedness to Dujardin and his refusal to acknowledge any debt to Freud and Jung, she recalled, Joyce angrily interrupted. " 'I hate women who know anything,' he said. 'No, Joyce, you don't,' I said. 'You like them.' After a few seconds of silent annoyance, a whimsical smile came over his face, and the rest of the afternoon was pleasant . . ." (Colum 132–33).

15. West's unpublished letter to the Hutchinsons [Feb. 1955] is quoted by permission of the Beinecke Library, Yale University. Is there a connection between the legendary African ancestor and "Panther," Wells's pet name for West during their affair? (Wells, who was "Jaguar," implies that both nicknames were her inventions [111].) One of West's earliest memories, she recalls in *Family Memories*, was of Indian soldiers from a nearby billet who would admire her on the street with curious intensity. "It is just possible," she muses, "that it was because in my childhood I was very dark—but surely no darker than other children, and not so dark as them [the soldiers]" (200).

WORKS CITED

Atherton, James S. *The Books at the Wake*. Expanded and corrected ed. Mamaroneck, N.Y.: Paul P. Appel, 1974.

Beckett, Samuel. "Dante . . . Bruno. Vico. ." In *Our Exagmination round His Factification for Incamination of "Work in Progress,"* by Samuel Beckett, et al. 1929. Reprint, New York: New Directions, 1962.

Benstock, Bernard. *Joyce-again's Wake*. Seattle: University of Washington Press, 1965.

Best, Marshall A. Publisher's Note to *Rebecca West: A Celebration*, by Rebecca West. New York: Viking Press, 1977.

Braybrooke, Patrick. *Novelists: We Are Seven*. 1929. Reprint, Freeport, New York: Books for Libraries, 1966.

Brienza, Susan. "Clods, Whores, and Bitches: Misogyny in Beckett's Early Fiction." In *Women in Beckett*, ed. Linda Ben-Zvi. Urbana: University of Illinois Press, 1990.

Brown, Richard. *James Joyce and Sexuality.* Cambridge and New York: Cambridge University Press, 1985.

Colum, Mary, and Padraic Colum. *Our Friend James Joyce.* Garden City, N.Y.: Doubleday, 1958.

Cumpiano, Marion W. "The Impact of James Joyce on William Carlos Williams." *William Carlos Williams Review* 15 (Spring 1989): 48–58.

Deming, Robert H. *James Joyce: The Critical Heritage.* Vol. 2. New York: Barnes and Noble, 1970.

Glasheen, Adaline. *A Third Census of "Finnegans Wake."* Berkeley: University of California Press, 1977.

Glendinning, Victoria. *Rebecca West: A Life.* New York: Knopf, 1987.

Halper, Nathan. "James Joyce and Rebecca West." *Partisan Review* 16 (July 1949): 761–63.

Henke, Suzette A. "Exagmining Beckett and Company." In *Re-Viewing Classics of Joyce Criticism,* ed. Janet Egleson Dunleavy. Urbana: University of Illinois Press, 1991.

Hoffmeister, Adolf. "Portrait of Joyce." In *Portraits of the Artist in Exile,* ed. Willard Potts. Seattle: University of Washington Press, 1979.

Hutchins, Patricia. *James Joyce's World.* London: Methuen, 1957.

Hutchinson, G. Evelyn. *A Preliminary List of the Writings of Rebecca West, 1912–1951.* New Haven: Yale University Press, 1957.

Hynes, Samuel. "In Communion with Reality." Introduction to *Rebecca West: A Celebration,* by Rebecca West. New York: Viking Press, 1977.

Lawrence, Karen. "Joyce and Feminism." In *The Cambridge Companion to James Joyce,* ed. Derek Attridge. Cambridge and New York: Cambridge University Press, 1990.

Marcus, Jane, ed. "A Speaking Sphinx." *Tulsa Studies in Women's Literature* 2, no. 2 (1983): 151–54.

———, ed. *The Young Rebecca: Writings of Rebecca West, 1911–17.* New York: Viking Press, 1982.

Mariani, Paul. *William Carlos Williams: A New World Naked.* New York: McGraw-Hill, 1981.

McMillan, Dougald. *"transition": The History of a Literary Era, 1927-1938.* London: Calder & Boyars, 1975.

Moscato, Michael, and Leslie Le Blanc. *The United States of America vs. One Book Entitled "Ulysses."* Frederick, Md.: University Publications of America, 1984.

Orel, Harold. *The Literary Achievement of Rebecca West.* New York: St. Martin's Press, 1986.

Parrinder, Patrick. "The Strange Necessity: James Joyce's Rejection in England (1914–30)." In *James Joyce: New Perspectives,* ed. Colin MacCabe. Bloomington: Indiana University Press, 1982.

Ray, Gordon N. *H. G. Wells and Rebecca West.* New Haven: Yale University Press, 1974.

Reynolds, Mary T. *Joyce and Dante: The Shaping Imagination*. Princeton: Princeton University Press, 1981.

Scott, Bonnie Kime. *Joyce and Feminism*. Bloomington: Indiana University Press, 1984.

———. "The Strange Necessity of Rebecca West." In *Women Reading Women's Writing*, ed. Sue Roe. New York: St. Martin's, 1987.

Tindall, William York. *A Reader's Guide to "Finnegans Wake."* New York: Farrar, Straus & Giroux, 1969.

Weldon, Fay. *Rebecca West*. New York: Viking Press, 1985.

Wells, H. G. *H. G. Wells in Love*. Boston: Little, Brown, 1984.

West, Anthony. *H. G. Wells: Aspects of a Life*. New York: Random House, 1984.

West, Rebecca. *The Court and The Castle*. New Haven: Yale University Press, 1957.

———. "The Duty of Harsh Criticism." *New Republic*, 7 November 1914, 18–20.

———. *Family Memories*. New York: Penguin, 1988.

———. "James Joyce and His Followers." *New York Herald Tribune*, 12 January 1930, sec. 12 (Books), 1, 6.

———. A Letter from Abroad. *Bookman* (New York) 70 (January 1930): 551–57.

———. A Letter from Abroad. *Bookman* (New York) 70 (February 1930): 664–68.

———. Letter to G. Evelyn and Margaret Hutchinson, February 1955. Rebecca West Collection. Beinecke Library, Yale University.

———. Letter to Richard Ellmann, 7 November 1958. Rebecca West Collection. Beineke Library, Yale University.

———. Letter to the Editor. *Freewoman*, 1 August 1912. In *The Young Rebecca*, ed. Jane Marcus.

———. Letter to the Editor. *New English Weekly*, 25 August 1932, 458.

———. "Spinsters and Art." *Freewoman*, 11 July 1912. In *The Young Rebecca*, ed. Jane Marcus.

———. "The Strange Case of James Joyce." *Bookman* (New York) 68 (September 1928): 9–23.

———. "The Strange Necessity." In *The Strange Necessity*. London: Jonathan Cape, [1928].

Williams, William Carlos. Letters in Readers and Writers. *New English Weekly*, 21 July 1932, 331; 10 November 1932, 91–92.

———. Letter to Sylvia Beach, 4 November 1928. Box 235, folder 10, the Sylvia Beach Collection (Collection no. C0108). Princeton University Libraries.

———. "A Point for American Criticism." In *Our Exagmination round His Factification for Incamination of "Work in Progress,"* by Samuel Beckett, et al. 1929. Reprint, New York: New Directions, 1962.

Woolf, Virginia. *A Room of One's Own*. 1929. New York, Harcourt, Brace, Jovanovich, Harvest edition, n.d.

Male Feminisms:
Approaching "Nausicaa"

Introduction

Richard Pearce

Over the past ten years some of the most powerful and interesting work on Joyce has been done by feminists, some of whom have been men. The goal of this group of essays is twofold. The first is to focus some of the issues of male feminisms—and I am using the plural to emphasize the range of possible positions that male feminists can take, only a very few of which are represented in our essays. The second, and more important, is to bring a new, self-consciously gendered perspective to bear on "Nausicaa," which is the only episode in *Ulysses* with an equally male and female focus. Though most of the critical attention has centered on Gerty MacDowell, Philip Weinstein and I will begin by focusing on Gerty's relation to Bloom and problematizing Bloom, a feminized male, usually celebrated for the way he exposes and transvalues traditional male values. Patrick McGee will situate gender domination within the framework of imperialism. And Jennifer Levine will illuminate the opening frame of "Nausicaa," where Gerty, Cissy, and Edy are not only tending but educating three little boys.

"Nausicaa": Monologue as Monologic

Richard Pearce

As I approach the "Nausicaa" episode as a male feminist, I realize that I may not get much further than Leopold Bloom does as he bumbles along the strand trying to assess his encounter with Gerty MacDowell. For—despite his marginalization, feminization, and victimization, and despite the way he deconstructs traditional male power—he is both passively implicated and actively complicit in shaping the social discourses as well as the narrative frame in which the women in *Ulysses*, especially Gerty, must negotiate. My goal, therefore, is twofold: to develop a viable male feminist strategy, and to illuminate the complex narrative power relations in "Nausicaa." I will attempt to do this by foregrounding my problematic position, especially as I draw the threads of my argument together, and then by placing it within the theoretical context of positionality.

I want to start with the issue of "male feminisms," not just because this is the topic of this section but because of my self-consciousness as one of three males assuming and potentially appropriating the position of feminists, and, moreover, who are addressing readers—who may be, for the most part, women—about the episode that, as Marilyn French points out, takes us from "a world entirely male in its occupants and concerns" into "one exclusively female" (156). Although I believe that both men and women can bring our different, even gendered, resources to bear on understanding the forms and effects of patriarchy and changing social structures, I know that men speak from the historically constructed position that subordinates or appropriates women's voices and subjectivities. I also know that the term *male feminist* may be a contradiction, or as a colleague of mine says, an oxymoron. Indeed, men's relation to feminism may, as Stephen Heath says, be impossible.

My problem is partly personal, for until Wheaton went coed in 1988 I had been teaching for twenty-four years in one of the oldest women's colleges, and, during the last ten of those years, most of the faculty had been successfully engaged in integrating scholarship on women into the curriculum. Moreover, I'm the father of two daughters who grew up, attended Wheaton, and who, along with my wife, contributed to my education during the years when the college was most heavily involved in interdisciplinary feminist workshops and in learning feminist pedagogy. When Wheaton went coed I was anxious to teach what I had learned to young men, but I soon came to a new and troubling self-consciousness. I became aware that, while I had been learning for so long together with predominantly female colleagues, I had been identifying with them and taking their position, as much as a male could. Not that this was bad; there was plenty of work to be done, and a male perspective could certainly add a dimension. But I had been taking this perspective without being sufficiently self-conscious. Indeed, as I began to address men as well as women, I gained a new awareness of myself as a *male* feminist, or one of a variety of male feminists who, besides having different perspectives and resources to offer, are situated in different positions from those of women but who have built into our positions—as well as our voices, bodies, postures, and movements—a history of domination.

The inescapability of my position was driven home to me at the 1990 MLA convention as I took part in a dialogue with Pamela Caughie on questions of authority and gender in teaching Virginia Woolf. We had developed our dialogue in an exchange of letters over the previous year but had overlooked what became obvious as we read our paper. Caughie had just distinguished her problems in the classroom as different from mine because of our genders. I began to respond with, "Your view of yourself as a female feminist teacher is even more complicated than you describe." Oh, oh. I realized at this point in our presentation, as did everyone else—and we all started laughing—that here I was, a male feminist, telling a female feminist what to think of her situation. As I gesticulated helplessly, hoping somehow to draw myself out of the abyss, someone called out, "Dick, stop shaking your fist at her." Whereupon I put my hand in my pocket—only to realize that there was no escape from the authority of a male-constructed body.[1]

The "Nausicaa" episode is important because it gives equal space to a man and a woman, because it explores male and female subjectivity, and because Bloom has been challenging the construction of male subjectivity as well as male ideology. But it is also important because it foregrounds the problems of gendered narrative and narrative dominance, and it invites us to compare the gendered positions of narrator and critic.

Philip Weinstein has shown that Bloom as well as Gerty has been constructed by the discourses of his society—and, more important, how Bloom's monologue has been naturalized, or seen as an unmediated and hence privileged form of expression. Certainly we see Bloom's weaknesses as well as his strengths. But we have accepted his views and judgments, if not his facts, partly because we have accepted the interior monologue as a direct representation of a character's inner thoughts. Of course we know that inner thoughts cannot be captured in logical sentences, but we read through the broken syntax. We know that inner thoughts are largely unconscious, emerging as disguised or displaced images, but we restore them to consciousness by working with image patterns and psychological models. What we have failed to recognize is that—while Joyce exposes the variety of social discourses mediating and shaping his characters' thoughts and identities in his playful use of free *indirect* discourse, or what Hugh Kenner calls the "Uncle Charles Principle"—he constructs interior monologue, at least of the male characters, as if it were *direct* discourse. It might be hard to follow Stephen's erudite and self-indulgent thoughts, but we feel that with some homework we can get to know the "real" young man thinking about the ineluctable modality of the visible. And it might be hard to follow Molly's thoughts but only, we confirm, because, being a woman, she is so illogical or confused or earthy or semiotic, or, like Gerty, so taken up with narcissism or so taken in by popular, commercial culture.

The contributors to *Molly Blooms: A Polylogue on "Penelope" and Cultural Studies* (which I edited) show that Molly's monologue is indeed mediated and that she negotiates the dominant discourses of her society through mockery, parody, mimicry, and appropriation. But they can do this because it has been easier to see Molly's thoughts as mediated than to see Bloom's that way. Molly's thoughts are easily related to ideas and products generated by the media of the day—newspapers, magazines, music halls, and the church. Moreover, the medium of Molly's unpunctuated interior monologue is far more visible than Bloom's. It is also gendered. Derek Attridge has shown that Molly's monologue is less erratic and more syntactically correct than Bloom's. But the visual image of unpunctuated, run-on, flowing, excessive thoughts is nonetheless coded as feminine. And it appears to be more mediated by images of popular culture than Bloom's or Stephen's, partly because the medium calls attention to itself and partly because popular culture is identified with women. (Tania Modleski takes Baudrillard to task for building on just this point [30–34].)

So it is only direct male thoughts that seem unmediated. And here I would like to bring in an analogy to voice-over narration in film. Kaja Silverman convincingly argues that in Hollywood cinema voice is "privileged to the degree that it *transcends the body*" (49). At one extreme is the disembodied voice-over of the male hero in film noir, which tells of his seduction and loss of innocence in a corrupt and irrational world. That voice issues from beyond the frame and is empowered by its distance in space and time. At the other extreme is the embodied voice-over of the transgressive and soon-to-be-repentant heroine in "women's films" of the forties, which issues from the figure of a woman on the screen, often addressing a male doctor or other male lis-

tener—and which "loses its power and authority with every corporeal encroachment, from a regional accent or idiosyncratic 'grain' to definitive lo-
calization, the point of full and complete embodiment" (49).

Applying Silverman's model to *Ulysses*, we can distinguish Molly's and
Gerty's monologues from Stephen's and Bloom's.[2] First, the men are barely located as they meander along the strand in "Nestor" and on the streets in
"Ithaca," while Molly is lying in bed or sitting on the pot and Gerty is sitting
on a rock. Second, though Stephen closes and opens his eyes, urinates or mas-
turbates, and picks his nose, and though Bloom unsticks himself, these are exceptional moments. Stephen's monologue is almost entirely abstract, and
Bloom's almost never calls attention to his body. And, third, though we can
distinguish Bloom's from Stephen's monologue by their rhythms and subject
matter, the language is literate, whereas Molly's is marked by its "idiosyncratic
'grain'"—bad grammar and spelling as well as malapropisms—and is embodied in its run-on sentences. Of course, Gerty's voice issues from a body made
more corporeal by her layers of clothing and her defect and is heavily ac-
cented by the style of women's romance.

Since Bloom's interior monologue is set against Gerty's, its power is monologic and controlling. Moreover, I will argue that our view of Gerty is largely
shaped, indeed constructed, by the discourses in which Bloom thinks—even
though his thoughts come after hers. But first let me introduce a complication.

Once we realize that interior monologue, like free indirect discourse (or
narrated monologue), is not transparent but opaque, we can also think of it as
a mirror. The discourses that mediate both Gerty's and Bloom's thoughts are
mirrors that throw back false images of the self as whole (to put it in Lacan's
terms). But Bloom sees himself and is reflected to us not only in the mirror of
his interior monologue. He also sees himself and is reflected to us in the mirror of Gerty MacDowell. To slightly revise Garry Leonard, Gerty and Bloom
mirror "'reality' for each other in their mutual masquerade"—Gerty composing herself as a "lovely seaside girl," and Bloom composing himself as her con-
sumer (58). The positions of these two mirrors, however, are not homologous;
the male gaze defines "the lovely seaside girl" and limits her position to that
of an object.

Early in his monologue, Bloom fantasizes "a dream of wellfilled hose . . .
Mutoscope pictures in Capel street: for men only" (*U-GP* 13:793–94). Bloom
has been physically and mentally gazing at women all day. He is a voyeur who
takes pleasure in looking at women from a distance and therefore establishes
himself as active subject and the woman as passive object. But Bloom's voyeurism is not simply a personal inclination; it is a position and posture constructed for men in general, in theaters, music halls, museums, shop windows,
the streets, and popular songs—as well as the books, magazines, and newspapers Bloom reads. Bloom takes pleasure in the pornographic books he brings
Molly, which in Victorian times were the mirror image of women's romance

(like Gerty's *Lamplighter*). Each provided a model for feminine display and masculine pleasure. He must also take pleasure in reading Molly's *Gentlewoman*, which, with a shift in class, is not that different from Gerty's *Lady's Pictorial*. And its pictures, as Garry Leonard points out, are different in degree but not in kind from those at the mutoscope (40). Of course, Bloom not only reads but composes and fantasizes newspaper ads, the most telling of which is "a transparent showcart with two smart girls sitting inside writing letters . . . catch the eye at once" (*U-GP* 8:132).

Moreover, Bloom writes, at least in his imagination, stories for *Titbits*. He thinks of following the nobleman who passes by but, identifying with him, reflects, "that would make him awkward like those newsboys me today. . . . See ourselves as others see us" (*U-GP* 13:105). Then he imagines himself writing a *Titbit* story, "The Mystery Man on the Beach." Given his identification with the nobleman, we could say that he imagines himself as the mysterious hero-lover, a "manly man with a strong quiet face who had not found his ideal, perhaps his hair slightly flecked with grey, and who would understand, who would take [Gerty] in his sheltering arms, strain her to him in all the strength of his deep passionate nature and comfort her with a long kiss" (*U-GP* 13:210–14).

But of course these are Gerty's lines. I have appropriated them to flesh out the implication of Bloom identifying with the mystery man on the beach—that is, to dramatize Bloom's thoughts as mediated by the discourse or mirror of women's romance, which he is complicit in constructing. I have also appropriated them to illuminate the logic of romance, like the mutoscope in Capel Street, which positions the woman as the passive object of male desire. And, I want to show how this logic turns her into a passive object—even after we give Gerty back her own lines and see them as her own assertion of imaginative desire. Most important, I have fleshed out Bloom's thoughts with Gerty's words to show how he implicitly author-izes Gerty's image of herself.

Let me recapitulate my argument so far. When we first read Gerty's section of "Nausicaa," not knowing that her mystery man on the beach is Bloom, we see her as a young woman imagining the object of her desire in the language— or mirror—of women's magazines and romance. We discover that the mystery man is Bloom exactly at the moment that Gerty's voice and view shift to Bloom's. Our image of Gerty changes, though we forget this on rereading the novel. While Bloom sees himself as the mystery man in the mirror of Gerty's image, he also helps construct that mirror—and not only historically, by the way women's romance evolved out of a patriarchal society, but through the power of his position in the narrative. Prudent, sensitive, trustworthy, and empowered by the Homeric parallel, no matter how parodic, Bloom has become the focal character in a male narrative. He has also been gazing at women, physically and mentally, since the beginning of the day. The mutoscope in Capel Street is a model for the discourses that dominate both Gerty's and Bloom's thoughts. And his monologue has the power of author-izing and limiting the image of Gerty—even though it comes after hers.

For, while the "namby pamby marmalady drawersy" style of her section might cause us to doubt Gerty's image of herself, Bloom establishes not only what we see but what we have seen: "Tight boots? No. She's lame!" (*U-GP* 13:771). Gerty, always seeing herself in and composing herself for the eyes of an ideal man, is always already lame—a defective product. But, despite the hint about her "one shortcoming," we don't realize this until we see her re-flected in Bloom's eyes. The impulse behind advertising as well as stories for women has always been to construct women as defective, in need of improve-ment—through soaps, cosmetics, perfumes, clothing, a husband, a lover, a male gaze—and, as Garry Leonard puts it, to define them as products for male consumption. Bloom has been complicit in constructing the mirror of adver-tising as well as romance and pornography. That is, he has been complicit in constructing the mirror in which Gerty sees herself and we see Gerty. And this mirror has the power to reflect Bloom himself, not only whole but, in the words of Virginia Woolf, "deliciously magnified" (35).

Which is not to say that Gerty doesn't look at Bloom as an object of her desire, no matter how mediated that desire is by male discourse. Nor do I mean to ignore Bloom's ability to think of women individually and em-pathetically. He sees that Gerty has been "left on the shelf" (*U-GP* 13:773) just as he has been "the last sardine of summer" (*U-GP* 11:1220–21), and he can empathize with Mrs. Duggan, with her "husband rolling in drunk, stink of pub off him like a pole cat" (*U-GP* 13:964), and he can feel for widows like Mrs. Dignam. Though his monologue has coercive, or monologic, power, it is also dialogic. It reflects a self beyond the self he sees through the eyes of the woman he's constructed to be his mirror. Indeed, it shifts from the position of the male gaze to that of the feminized empathetic look. It also shifts to the po-sition of the feminized gazed-at object, for he knows that Gerty has seen him and, moreover, has taken pleasure in seeing him. He is even reflected as the self-effacing object: "she must have been thinking of someone else all the time" (*U-GP* 13:884–85), as, we will learn, Molly did during the most mem-orable kiss of their lives. Moreover, prefiguring Hélène Cixous's "Laugh of the Medusa," he worries about the woman who gazes back: "See ourselves as oth-ers see us. So long as women don't mock what matter" (*U-GP* 13:1058–59).

And I should call attention to the shift in perspective at the end, when he writes a message for Gerty—or finally positions himself as the vulnerable ob-ject of her gaze—"I. AM. A." Indeed, as he effaces "the letters with his slow boot," he unconsciously identifies (or is identified) with Gerty's limp, ac-knowledging (or implying) that he too is a defective product. And finally he flings away "his wooden pen," which, ironically, sticks in the sand erect (*U-GP* 13:1258–64).

But I have to end with the questions of why, as a male feminist, I would prefer to argue that Bloom's monologue is dialogic rather than monologic, why I am disappointed by the negative image I have constructed of Bloom—in the chapter where he appears most pathetic—why I would like to vindicate Bloom, or celebrate the new womanly man, or show how he transcends the double mirrors he helped construct, or argue that he has negotiated as best he could the dominant discourses that make not only women but colonized Irishmen and wandering Jews defective.

The problem is that negotiation is only a step from navigation. And to take this step would bring him back into the Homeric paradigm, revised for middle-class consumption. It would relate him to Odysseus, traveling home to claim his paternity, his wife, his city, and his history. It would perpetuate the dualism of the male-female positions in the story of heroic romance. It would also ignore the fact that Gerty, who has played such an important role, is an absence, largely owing to his complicity in shaping the discourses that obscure her and to his perspective—disguised as natural and neutral—which dominates the episode. And it would ignore the fact that the wooden pen sticking up in the sand may be ironic, even parodic, but it is nonetheless the kind of humor that asserts phallic power.

I would like to think, though, that the mirrored mirrors of "Nausicaa" do not force us to choose either a happy ending that affirms Bloom or an ending that denies him, and that they may even take us beyond Fritz Senn's balanced acceptance of Bloom. The mirrored mirrors may force us to acknowledge and interrogate our gendered positions as readers. I can acknowledge that I want Bloom to transvalue the values of manliness (and provide an alternative to Iron John). But I have to acknowledge that this desire—given the Homeric superstructure of the novel and the present power structure of society—is a way of perpetuating male authority. This may be as far as I can go. But this may also be what a male feminist reader can do: see himself positioned dialogically in the mirrored mirror of the text.

I would like to end by generalizing, or theorizing, about what I have done in my reading of "Nausicaa"—which is to foreground not just my position as one male feminist, but the very notion of positionality. Linda Alcoff argues that positionality is the logical step for feminists to take after cultural feminism and poststructuralism. Cultural feminism celebrates, appropriates, and transvalues the devalued values of women's culture, so that passivity becomes a form of peacefulness, subjectivism and narcissism become ways of being in touch with oneself, and sentimentality becomes caring and nurturing. But cultural feminism tends towards essentialism, identifies women with their bodies, and perpetuates biological determinism. Poststructuralism, on the other hand, exposes "essence" and "femininity" as social and linguistic constructs. But in showing these constructs to be overdetermined by a wide range of social institutions and forces, it denies women agency, choice, and the possibility of change—and it renders gender invisible.

Teresa de Lauretis shows us a way out of the bind between cultural feminism and poststructural determinism by arguing that we are constructed through a continuous and ongoing interaction with the practices, discourses, and institutions that shape value, meaning, and feeling. Alcoff extends this to the notion of positionality. The self, rather than having an essence or being overdetermined, is a constellation of positions, formed by changing historical and personal relations. And agency is a matter of choosing to take this or that position or negotiating among them.

I would also like to argue that the notion of positionality opens the possibilities for male feminism beyond those discussed in Alice Jardine and Paul Smith's pessimistic *Men in Feminism,* which Stephen Heath opens by announcing, "Men's relation to feminism is an impossible one" (1). It is related to the ideas that for good reasons are more enacted than theorized in the diversity of Joseph Boone and Michael Cadden's *Engendering Men.* Male feminism may be a contradiction in terms or an oxymoron. But I would like to describe the conflict between "male" and "feminism" in terms of opposing positions within the same constellation. The position of the male feminist is not the same, but, as Joseph Boone says, is "an ever-present relation of contiguity with the originating politics of feminism" (23). It is potentially threatening, given the historical hegemony of male power and its propensity for cooptation. But that is only one in the constellation of positions, some of which have been chosen to deconstruct and destroy the hegemony, and some of which may be intersubjectively related to female positions. And we should recognize the multiplicity of male feminist positions that form along the axes of race, class, sexual preference, age, wellness, and so on.

Of course this is where I want my argument to end. But I also know that I have a stake in a happy ending, in proving that men can overcome the force of their historical positions. So I would include in my framing of positionality the need to foreground the problems, or to recognize that one does not choose a single position but a smaller constellation of positions, which includes some that need to be problematized and interrogated. This leaves the argument with an open end, but it does not preclude taking a stance.

NOTES

1. Our dialogue has been published as "Resisting 'the Dominance of the Professor': Gendered Teaching, Gendered Subjects." *National Women's Studies Association Journal* 4 (Summer 1992): 187–99.

2. We should consider the Gerty section as an interior monologue even though it is heavily mediated by free indirect discourse—or what Dorrit Cohn calls narrated monologue. In the first book on the stream of consciousness, Melvin Friedman recognized the section as a hybrid and called it an indirect interior monologue (236).

WORKS CITED

Alcoff, Linda. "Cultural Feminism versus Post-Structuralism: The Identity Crisis in Feminist Theory." *Signs: Journal of Women in Culture and Society* 13, no. 3 (1988): 405–36.

Attridge, Derek. "Molly's Flow: The Writing of 'Penelope' and the Question of Women's Language." *Modern Fiction Studies* 35, ed. Ellen Carol Jones (Autumn 1989): 543–65.

Boone, Joseph A., and Michael Cadden. *Engendering Men: The Question of Male Feminist Criticism.* New York and London: Routledge, 1990.

Caughie, Pamela, and Richard Pearce. "Resisting 'the Dominance of the Professor': Gendered Teaching, Gendered Subjects." *National Women's Studies Association Journal* 4 (Summer 1992): 187–99.

Cixous, Hélène. "The Laugh of the Medusa." *Signs* (Summer 1976): 39–54.

Cohn, Dorrit. *Transparent Minds.* Princeton, N.J.: Princeton University Press, 1978.

French, Marilyn. *The Book as World.* Cambridge, Mass.: Harvard University Press, 1975.

Friedman, Melvin. *Stream of Consciousness: A Study in Literary Method.* New Haven: Yale University Press, 1955.

Heath, Stephen. "Male Feminism." In *Men in Feminism,* ed. Alice Jardine and Paul Smith.

Jardine, Alice, and Paul Smith, eds. *Men in Feminism.* New York and London: Methuen, 1987.

Kenner, Hugh. *James Joyce.* London: Allen & Unwin, 1980.

Leonard, Garry M. "Women on the Market: Commodity Culture, 'Femininity,' and 'Those Lovely Seaside Girls.'" In *Joyce Studies Annual 1991,* ed. Thomas F. Staley. Austin: University of Texas Press, 1991.

Modleski, Tania. *Feminism without Women: Culture and Criticism in a "Postfeminist" Age.* New York and London: Routledge, 1991.

Pearce, Richard, ed. *Molly Blooms: A Polylogue on "Penelope" and Cultural Studies.* Madison: University of Wisconsin Press, 1994.

Senn, Fritz. "Nausicaa." In *James Joyce's "Ulysses": Critical Essays,* ed. Clive Hart and David Hayman. Berkeley and Los Angeles: University of California Press, 1974.

Silverman, Kaja. *The Acoustic Mirror: The Female Voice in Psychoanalysis and Cinema.* Bloomington: Indiana University Press, 1988.

Woolf, Virginia. *A Room of One's Own.* 1929. New York: Harcourt, Brace, Jovanovich, 1957.

For Gerty Had Her Dreams that No-one Knew Of

Philip Weinstein

A feminist account of "Nausicaa" might begin by noting that, until the 1980s, it has been read—canonically and with gender indifference—as a comic exposure of Gerty's dreams of her own uniqueness. Thanks to Joyce's liberating techniques, her entrapping dreams have been precisely what we all know about. This widely shared reading polarizes Joyce's stylistic flexibility against Gerty's rigidity by splitting the chapter into the gazed-upon antics of Gerty versus the unco-opted thoughts of Bloom. As Patrick McGee has warned, however, this reading naturalizes and hierarchizes opposing styles, genders, genres. I'd like to probe Gerty's "dreams that no-one knew of" in two ways: first, by analyzing the cultural activity that produces such dreams, and second, by destabilizing the polarity between Gerty as caught and Bloom as free. As Eve Sedgwick has argued with respect to Proust, the highlighting of one closet—one arena that is being exposed—often implies the strategic concealing of another, this one less amenable to assessment. I'll try to identify that other, concealed closet.

Gerty's foolishness was always highlighted, but, beginning with Suzette Henke a decade ago, we've begun to analyze her more precisely as a creature of her culture. Modern advertising has generated the lineaments of her subjectivity. Her body has been relentlessly trained to accede to her society's gender directives: iron-jelloids, Widow Welch's female pills, lemon juice, queen of ointments, Mme Vera Verity, Princess Novelette, Clery's summer sales, "eyebrowleine," the newest thing in footwear. . . . The list is long and familiar. Gerty is wholly tracked within a narrative of ersatz satisfactions that will apparently make up for—but actually energize forever—the class- and gender-caused poverty of her life. In Althusser's terms, she has been interpellated—

"Hey you!" the ads have proclaimed, and by responding "Me? You mean, Me?" she has defined herself as a woman with "dreams no-one knew of" and been defined as a woman in thrall to those same culturally dispensed dreams. Subjectivity and ideology are mutually constitutive terms; in Gerty we see their virtually formulaic fusion.

Twenty years ago Gerty's clichés were an easy target. Cliché itself was a safely delimited term, for the text seemed effectively to distinguish between its own free language on the one hand and Gerty's entrapping language on the other. There was little attempt to see what it might mean more generally to speak other peoples' language. (We of course spoke our own—this went without saying.) Since then, Bakhtin and Foucault have shown us the sense in which we always speak other peoples' language, that the social/ideological aspect of being in language is irresistible. "The ideological becoming of a human being . . . is the process of selectively assimilating the word of others" Bakhtin writes in "Discourse in the Novel" (341). To speak is to enact group affiliation; selfhood is inalienably social, an affair of others.

Foucault has argued further, in *Discipline and Punish*, that the body is socially programmed at all times, and that this programming is consensual, not inflicted. "The body becomes a useful force only if it is both a productive body and a subjected body," he writes (26). Subjected and subjectified as well, so that inscription and desire are no longer opposed but welded: "and her face was suffused with a divine, an entrancing blush . . . and he could see her other things too, nainsook knickers, the fabric that caresses the skin, better than those other pettiwidth, the green, four and eleven, on account of being white and she let him" (*U-GP* 13:723–26). In the midst of this erotic flow comes the price of the garments, and that phrase—"the fabric that caresses the skin"—that registers simultaneously the ad Gerty has ingested and the flush that she feels as it does its promised job. This fetishized object, like those others clustered in Gerty's "girlish treasure trove" (*U-GP* 13:638–39), reifies Gerty into an assortment of culturally validated icons of self-worth. These mirror back to her where she has come from ("her child of Mary badge"), where she is going (to capture a man), and how she will do it: by guising herself in guaranteed apparel.

This Foucault/Althusser reading might close by noting that men at every point pace and inflect Gerty's erotic narrative: it is Father Conroy who "told her that time when she told him about that in confession . . . not to be troubled because that was only the voice of nature and we were all subject to nature's laws, he said, in this life and that that was no sin because that came from the nature of woman instituted by God, he said, and that Our Blessed Lady herself said to the archangel Gabriel be it done unto me according to Thy Word" (*U-GP* 13:453–59). The male-dispensed Catholic narrative concedes and contains female sexuality by not naming it. Menstruation's studied referent is "that" and Gerty is not to worry because God has instituted "that." Through the triply masculine filters of God, Gabriel, and Father Conroy, Gerty receives her sexual message: that it will be done unto her in the appropriate ways, and that the vicissitudes of desire itself—which she knows only as sensation on the skin and the scalp, and which she can refer to only as "this" or as "a thing like that," certainly distinct from "the other thing," which you weren't supposed to do—have been foreseen and mapped by the Church. Gerty's lexical vagueness here is destiny itself: the words "that," "this," and "thing" are forced to do duty for crucial distinctions—menstruation, lust, masturbation, intercourse—for which it is of the first importance to have differential language in order to access them, interrelate them, and generate out of their differences a minimally liberated sexual identity.

Gerty has hardly a clue as to her problem. Power acts upon her molecularly, not coercively. Her social inscription registers precisely at those unselfconscious moments when she punctuates her narrative by proclaiming who she "instinctively" is. The word "instinct" (or its cognates) occurs as noun, adjective, or adverb four times in her narrative, at each point naturalizing her sense of self and revealing to us the nodes of her social construction: "Gerty was dressed simply but with the instinctive taste of a votary of Dame Fashion" (*U-GP* 13:148), "because she felt instinctively that he was like no-one else" (*U-GP* 13:428), "her woman's instinct told her that she had raised the devil in him" (*U-GP* 13:517), "from everything in the least indelicate her finebred nature instinctively recoiled" (*U-GP* 13:660–61). In these instances we find the bedrock word—instinct—employed to guarantee the inbred (rather than trained) quality of her clothing choices, the natural (rather than gender-taught) character of her desire for Bloom, and the morally immaculate tenor of her otherwise dubious sexual escapade. In these ways her vocabulary legitimates her behavior, confirms her unique identity, and arrests her in mystification.

This reading of Gerty seems to me unanswerable, but there has recently emerged a feminist counterreading that proposes a Gerty MacDowell who is not simply victimized. Embodying desire and revealing under closer scrutiny a complex erotic agenda, this Gerty MacDowell does not serve as a passive mirror for male sexual affirmation. Rather, the mirror moves on its own, using the gazing male as the stimulant for its own reflexive pleasures, neatly reversing the paradigm. Kimberly Devlin makes this feminist and Lacanian argument, proposing a Gerty who manages, in a male-defined culture, to achieve *jouissance* on condition that it escape the Catholic censor; a Gerty viewed as the site of linguistic disturbance rather than a fixed and silly figure. There remains one further dimension to the resurrection of Gerty, perhaps the most suggestive of all, for it refuses the high culture/low culture binary that has condescendingly subtended our treatment of this chapter. I am thinking of Margot Norris's work on "Nausicaa" and even more of Jennifer Wicke's analysis of the place of advertising in modern culture. Showing that the subject's absorption of advertising enables a metempsychotic journey—"in and through

117

consumption, in all its array, a transmigration of subjectivity is enacted into objects and back again" (U-GP 13:761)—Wicke argues for a Molly Bloom actively, coherently, invested in the work of consuming, not idly or passively victimized by it. In similar manner, Gerty MacDowall *lives* her cultural furnishing: "the fabric that caresses the skin" does indeed caress it, and she has cogently decked herself out in the garb, manners, thoughts, and feelings—all culturally proposed—that permit her sexual release. I realize this low-cultural analysis of everyday viability is in tension with the high-cultural one that bemoans her victimization; both make sense to me. Rather than explore either further, I turn instead to Bloom.

It is here, with Bloom, that our commentary has altered the least. Put otherwise, what imaginary arrangements are we still protecting through this preserved reading? Joyce's prose for him is so welcome after Gerty's sticky rhetoric that even if we grant that stream of consciousness now emerges (after four chapters without it) as a style—rather than as nature itself—even so, we have tended to let him run away with the chapter. I'd like to begin a reading of Bloom that is more aware of his gendered optic.

First, consider his focus on menstruation: "near her monthlies, I expect, makes them feel ticklish" (U-GP 13:777–78), "How many women in Dublin have it today?" (U-GP 13:781–82), "Devils they are when that's coming on them" (822), "Wonder if it's bad to go with them then. Safe in one way. Turns milk, makes fiddlestrings snap" (U-GP 13:825–26), "Some women, instance, warn you off when they have their period. Come near. Then get a hogo you could hang your hat on" (U-GP 13:1031–32). Granted, these speculations live among hundreds of others about the strange smells and behavior of fish, bats, dogs, and other creatures. The point is that women are inexhaustibly strange for Bloom—other, arousing, disturbing, creaturely—and their difference from men (which he seems to construe as natural—"Who did you learn that from? Nobody. . . . O don't they know!" [U-GP 13:924–25]) ceaselessly interests him.

Women are routinely referred to in his narrative in the plural. His text abounds with generalizations about what "they" do. "Because they want it themselves. Their natural craving" (U-GP 13:790–91), "Excites them also when they're. I'm all clean come and dirty me. And they like dressing one another for the sacrifice" (U-GP 13:797–98), and perhaps most succinctly this tableau: "*Tableau!* O, look who it is for the love of God! How are you at all? What have you been doing with yourself? Kiss and delighted to, kiss, to see you. Picking holes in each other's appearance. You're looking splendid. Sister souls. Showing their teeth at one another. How many have you left? Wouldn't lend each other a pinch of salt" (U-GP 13:815–20). Tableau indeed: the picture that emerges here is as saturated in a culture's gender assumptions as Gerty's pictures were. Only here the bias is subtler, diffused within the shapelessness of stream of consciousness and widely shared by the text's male readership. Women fawn upon each other, vie with each other for attractive males,

are deceitful, selfish, and as free from guilt as cats. Their narcissism is hyp-
notic. Bloom has no hesitancy in so categorizing them, and no interest in the
social forces that may have produced this kind of behavior. His narrative for
women is as dependent upon instinct terms as Gerty's was: "Where do they
get that? Typist going up Roger Greene's stairs two at a time to show her un-
derstandings. Handed down from father to, mother to daughter, I mean. Bred
in the bone" (*U-GP* 13:916–18).

Bred in the bone. We understand that today to mean so deeply trained into
us that it passes as nature, is invisible. And Bloom's portion in "Nausicaa" has
likewise passed as largely invisible, from a gender perspective. I suggest that this
has occurred because the text rises out of and speaks to a male imaginary for
whom the female is both innocent and arousing, erotic yet receptive: "all the
dirty things I made her say" (*U-GP* 13:868). If the exposed closet in the first
half of "Nausicaa" is Gerty's "dreams that no-one knew of," then the concealed
one is Bloom's own sexual imaginary, one that much of Joyce's readership
seems to share, an imaginary that we would indulge in, yet have no one know
about, a set of dreams we have no intention of spotlighting as cultural script.

Gerty's fantasies are laid open for symbolic assessment; Bloom's are imagi-
narily shared, in secret. She is there for our delectation: first, the precoital
spectacle of her being aroused by Bloom, then the postcoital dignity of Bloom's
wide-ranging thoughts. This arrangement too is gender shaped—the opening
up of the female's excitement, the private voyeurism of the male's detumes-
cence—for when we finally enter Bloom's mind his thoughts "cap" hers and
he is already, so to speak, safely zipped. The "we" parading throughout these
last paragraphs is, of course, male. But many females have participated within
its confines, we now can say, for it takes a feminist stance to nudge biological
differences out of a pregiven polar opposition and to reveal gender positions
as culturally produced.

I want to close by touching briefly on the question of male feminism itself.
Stephen Heath's arresting claim—"men's relation to feminism is an impossible
one"—seems to me both irrefutable and unacceptable (1). Irrefutable, because men just are the problem of feminism, the source—embodied locally
and operative systemically—of the injustice women suffer from. After dismantling Freud's claim that anatomy is destiny, feminists have retaught us the
vicious ways in which it still is destiny. Men grow up differently, encounter social structures shaped preferentially for them, enjoy a time-and-power curve
the reverse of women's.

But Heath's argument is also unacceptable, inasmuch as men (once they
see the light) cannot but attempt (Heath included) to be feminists. Patrick
McGee rightly claims that this attempt on our part is more than a matter of
choice, by which I think he means that in involuntary ways we remain complicit in a male structure of privilege; but this attempt is also not simply a
choice, inasmuch as we must be feminists—as we must oppose racism and

write against it, even though, if we are white, we are also complicit. Maleness (biological and cultural) is and is not our destiny: insofar as it is not we struggle to inhabit our maleness in a feminist way, revising our take on matters we had misread. I think we must be off-balance, unauthoritative, seeking neither to cash in on the central work done by women feminists nor to posture masochistically as hopelessly at fault and out of place on this terrain.

The two more radical alternative positions I know of are even less tenable: to assume in advance that our maleness invalidates any feminist stance we might articulate, or to envisage a wholesale dismantling of male and female altogether. A different way of being male, intent upon a more generous spectrum of relations to the female—this seems to me to be a worthwhile goal for any male feminist whose aim is to undo privilege, not to remove difference (including the eroticism of difference). Nausicaan comedy delights in the dialogic interplay (rather than melodramatic opposition) of norm and subversion, commodification and desire, containment and release, erotics male and female. Our own maleness neither licenses a special insight into Joyce's writing of gender in "Nausicaa" nor condemns us in advance to irrelevance. The best we can do may be to keep at it in our mix of good and bad faith, useful both in our critique of the postures we identify and in our being demonstrably caught up in them nevertheless.

WORKS CITED

Althusser, Louis. "Ideology and Ideological State Apparatuses." In *Lenin and Philosophy, and Other Essays*. London: New Left Books, 1971.

Bakhtin, Mikhail. "Discourse in the Novel." In *The Dialogic Imagination*, trans. Caryl Emerson and Michael Holquist. Austin: University of Texas Press, 1981.

Devlin, Kimberly. "The Female Eye: Joyce's Voyeuristic Narcissists." In *New Alliances in Joyce Studies*, ed. Bonnie K. Scott. Newark: University of Delaware Press, 1988.

———."The Romance Heroine Exposed: 'Nausicaa' and *The Lamplighter*." *James Joyce Quarterly* 22 (1985): 383–96.

Foucault, Michel. *Discipline and Punish*. Trans. Alan Sheridan. New York: Random House, 1979.

Heath, Stephen. "Male Feminism." In *Men in Feminism*, ed. Alice Jardine and Paul Smith. New York and London: Methuen, 1987.

Henke, Suzette. "Gerty MacDowell: Joyce's Sentimental Heroine." In *Women in Joyce*, ed. Suzette Henke and Elaine Unkeless. Urbana: University of Illinois Press, 1982.

McGee, Patrick. *Paperspace: Style as Ideology in Joyce's "Ulysses."* Lincoln: University of Nebraska Press, 1988.

Norris, Margot. "Modernism, Myth, and Desire in 'Nausicaa.'" *James Joyce Quarterly* 26 (1988): 37–50.

Sedgwick, Eve K. "The Epistemology of the Closet II." *Raritan* 8 (1988): 102–30.

Wicke, Jennifer. *Advertising Fictions.* New York: Columbia University Press, 1988.

———"'Who's She When She's at Home?' Molly Bloom and the Work of Consumption." *James Joyce Quarterly* 28 (1991): 749–63. A longer version appears in *Molly Blooms: A Polylogue on "Penelope" and Cultural Studies,* ed. Richard Pearce. Madison: University of Wisconsin Press, 1994.

When Is a Man Not a Man?
or,
The Male Feminist
Approaches "Nausicaa"

Patrick McGee

The choice of the "Nausicaa" episode as the focus of a discussion of male feminism seems to me both appropriate and bizarre. Appropriate because this episode is about the social construction of sexual identity; bizarre because it is difficult to imagine an approach to this episode by someone constructed as a male that would be truly feminist. Perhaps we can say that a male feminist is a biological male who engages in a feminist discourse or activity. I am not altogether happy with this formulation, however. What happens to the cultural determinations that we call "male" when the biological male decides to be a feminist? The answer to this question is commonplace. There is often a contradiction or at least a conflict between the "feminist" part and the "male" part of the male feminist. Ironically, it could be very "male" to produce a feminist accent in one's work in order to incorporate the authority of an established feminism. But before we condemn men for their opportunism we have to admit that women can also be opportunists: not to recognize this would be to accept the old gender essentialism that feminism has taught us to question. One is not born a feminist, and the decision to be a feminist, even for a biological woman, is not reducible to natural interests.

Briefly, I have another question relevant to the present context. What kind of a man has the choice to call himself a "male feminist"? Certainly, if one goes by the men who are writing for this volume, one would have to admit that male feminists are usually privileged males; I mean that they wouldn't be writing on this topic if they were not empowered by an education that is not accessible to everyone. They are more privileged than other males in a system that privileges males over females.

In the "Nausicaa" episode, while Bloom may be more privileged than Gerty MacDowell, I agree with Kimberly Devlin (136–40) and others that Gerty gets her own back from Bloom. She has her own gaze and takes her own pleasure from the exchange of looks and of objects to be looked at. Gerty's being has not only been invaded by the commodity culture of patriarchal capitalism, she embraces that culture and turns it into the instrument of her own pleasure in the other. She transforms herself into a commodity in order to manipulate the gaze of another. As she looks at Bloom, we read; "Whitehot passion was in that face, passion silent as the grave, and it made her his" (13:691–92/365).[1] But, let's face it, in another way, it makes him hers. Gerty has the power to control Bloom's body through his gaze, to make it do what she wants it to do so that she can see what she wants to see. Gerty knows what she wants from a man—that he be "a man among men" and "a manly man" (13:207, 210/351), "a real man" (13:439/358). Gerty knows what she wants to be for a man: "a womanly woman" and "his ownest girlie" (13:435, 440/358). Gerty is able to raise the devil in Bloom, not by showing him what she is but by showing him what covers what she is, making her sexual identity ambivalent. Bloom's body is also covered, which enables him, whether he knows it or not, to be what Gerty wants him to be: "a man of inflexible honour to his fingertips" (13:694/365). What those fingertips are doing is no secret to Gerty; but when she finally comes, she forgets about Bloom's body in the thought of what she must look like to him and what it cost her to look that way.

I agree with Philip Weinstein that Bloom is just as programmed by the ideology of gender as Gerty is. Bloom subscribes to Gerty's interpellation by commodity culture: "Fashion part of their charm" (13:804/368), he says, and later adds, "Must have the stage setting, the rouge, costume, position, music" (13:855–56/370). On the other hand, Bloom probably does not recognize to what extent he has been interpellated by Gerty's gaze as "her beau ideal" (13:209/351), though he does say to himself, "She must have been thinking of someone else all the time" (13:884–85/371). In *Ulysses* Joyce implies that, when it comes to sex, one is always thinking of someone else, as Bloom thinks of Molly by looking at other women. Penelope herself is not the unmediated object of desire since she is veiled by the commodified image of Calypso.

There is a curious moment in Bloom's section of "Nausicaa" that links this episode back to several others. Bloom gazes upon some "nightclouds" that "look like a phantom ship." Then he thinks, "Trees are they? An optical illusion. Mirage. Land of the setting sun this. Homerule sun setting in the southeast. My native land, goodnight" (13:1077–80/376). The phantom ship and the trees echo the last sentence of "Proteus": "Moving through the air high spars of a threemaster, her sails brailed up on the crosstrees, homing, upstream, silently moving, a silent ship" (3:503–5/51). Stephen sees this ship, just as he turns to see if there is anyone looking at him, on the same Sandymount Strand where Bloom later looks at Gerty. As in "Circe," Bloom and Stephen seem to be united by an imaginary gaze that makes it difficult to distinguish the real from the unreal. In "Calypso," the episode after Stephen's walk on the beach, Bloom first recalls Arthur Griffith's joke about the *Freeman's Journal* after he daydreams about the Orient, which has to be associated with Molly and Calypso. Arthur Griffith made fun of the sunburst over the Bank of Ireland in the headpiece of the *Freeman* because it put the sunrise in the northwest and thus reduced the *Freeman's* moderate-conservative support of Home Rule to the status of a mirage. The motto of the journal, "Ireland a Nation," recalls the subject of the "Cyclops" episode, in which Bloom's own national identity as an Irishman is called into question. When John Wyse Nolan asks him to say what a nation means, Bloom responds, "The same people living in the same place." Ned Lambert responds that he must be a nation since he has been "living in the same place for the past five years." So Bloom adds to his definition, "Or also living in different places." "That covers my case," says Joe Hynes. The Citizen finally puts it to Bloom to say what his nation is, and Bloom answers, "Ireland. . . . I was born here" (12:1431/331).

My point is that the mirage effects that derive from sexual identity in "Nausicaa" have to be situated in the series of imaginary identifications that dominate the political representations in *Ulysses*. Gerty's femininity is inseparable from the commodity culture that constructs her identity as the phantasm of masculine desire. In "Cyclops" Bloom's masculinity is as easily called into question as his nationality; and so in the next episode, "Nausicaa," he tries to regain what he has lost by becoming the "manly man" Gerty dreams of, thus reminding us that Gerty does not dream alone but participates in the collective symbolizations of the cultural hegemony. Perhaps Bloom has the edge over Gerty, in that he knows that his masculinity, like his nationality, is a mirage. During the course of his day, the real continually disrupts Bloom's daydreaming with the reminders of what he has lost and what he may yet lose. This gives him the power to project his own fear of symbolic castration onto Gerty and to take pleasure from the sexual ambivalence that makes the exchange of fantasies possible. For Gerty also projects onto Bloom the very identity he lacks: "She could see at once by his dark eyes and his pale intellectual face that he was a foreigner, the image of the photo she had of Martin Harvey, the matinee idol" (13:417/357). Sir John Martin-Harvey, a British actor/producer, helped to occasion a riot in 1910 when he staged *Richard III* in Dublin and offended the aesthetic sensibilities of certain Irish Nationalists (Gifford 390).

In other words, Gerty associates masculine sexuality with British cultural power and projects both onto Bloom. (Of course, as Jennifer Levine notes in detail, one should not read cultural signifiers like the name "Martin Harvey" as transparent with respect to the historical context. As an actor, Martin-

Harvey may well have been an emblem of the exotic in the same tradition that would later produce Rudolph Valentino and Errol Flynn in America. Nevertheless, he represents a popular and romantic construction of masculinity that is inseparable from the hegemonic constructions of British imperialism. The important point is not that Martin-Harvey was English but that he is able to embody a normative masculine principle even when he signifies cultural difference itself by playing the exotic. After all, the exotic is the imperialist representation of cultural difference par excellence.) In Gerty's discourse, Bloom is made to anticipate the patriarch of *Finnegans Wake*, H.C.E., who is also a foreign imperialist and whose sexual passion is indistinguishable from his passion for conquest. As the washerwomen on the Liffey recount the story of Anna Livia's courtship, it sounds like the invasion of Ireland: "I heard he dug good tin with his doll, delvan first and duvlin after, when he raped her home, Sabrine asthore, in a parakeet's cage, by dredgerous lands and devious delts, playing catched and mythed with the gleam of her shadda" (*Finnegans Wake* 197). Bloom makes reasonably good money or "tin" himself, and this is one advantage he has over the historical Gerty MacDowell, who would have limited economic opportunities. Bloom may not rape Gerty, but his passion is grave and loveless as he plays catch with her gaze and creates a myth for himself in the fetishistic gleam of her shadowy undergarments. Still, Gerty is no more innocent than the young women ALP sends in to please her husband after teaching them how "to shake their benders and the dainty how to bring to mind the gladdest undergarments out of sight and all the way of a maid with a man" (*Finnegans Wake* 200).

I am trying to suggest that in *Ulysses* and *Finnegans Wake* it is impossible to separate the question of gender politics from the question of imperialism. This does not mean that gender relations can be reduced to and dismissed as a subcategory of imperialist social relations, but rather that sexual, national, and class identity all operate within a system of hegemonic representations that reproduce the same inequitable distribution of power and autonomy. I use Gramsci's concept of hegemony to emphasize the fact that what we are talking about here is not the direct and unmediated domination of one subject by another but a system of values that must take into account, as Gramsci put it, "the interests and the tendencies of the groups over which hegemony is to be exercised" (216). Gerty MacDowell is not the innocent victim; for she is able to manipulate the system of sexual values, to employ its symbols and discursive practices, to achieve her own pleasure. Bloom is not the master of the situation, since his construction as a male is not reducible to a simple choice; like Gerty, he gives his consent quite unconsciously to those values that seem matters of common sense. Of course, one cannot ignore the fact that Bloom's masturbating in front of a young woman on a public beach is a transgression; but it is one of those social transgressions that proves the rule and establishes the boundaries that are not to be crossed.

In "Nausicaa" Bloom wants to be a man just as in "Cyclops" he wanted to be an Irishman. There is no question that Bloom, in comparison with Gerty, possesses more social autonomy, in part because of the cultural and economic privileges that accrue to him as a white European male. There is also no question that the Citizen and his Nationalist compatriots in "Cyclops," however victimized they may be by British imperialism, have the power to exclude Bloom from the homosocial bond of Irish Nationalism that to some extent, as David Lloyd has argued, mirrors the imperialism it opposes.[2] Everyone in "Cyclops" is the butt of a joke, but Bloom becomes the scapegoat of the group and undergoes the most severe ridicule. In "Nausicaa" Gerty as the subject of a discourse determined by romance conventions is more imaginary than Bloom, because Bloom has more irony in his voice. By irony I mean those self-conscious verbal abruptions in Bloom's discourse in which he seems to recognize the limits of his own language and thus registers the real as that which resists symbolization. There is a kind of irony in Gerty's voice, but it is a dramatic irony that registers the author function more than Gerty's self-conscious relation to the language she speaks; whereas Bloom is identified with those doubling effects in his discourse that keep him at a distance from the imaginary constructions occasioned by his desire. Not to recognize this difference between them—a difference of degree—is to remain blind to the social determinations of patriarchy and capitalism that result in the inequitable distribution of both symbolic and economic capital according to gender and class.

Male feminism must be subjected to the same scrutiny we would apply to Bloom's gaze in "Nausicaa." I don't mean that men who become feminists are automatically voyeurs or cross-dressers, but I am suggesting that becoming a feminist is more than a matter of choice. There is no reason why a biological male cannot be a feminist, but feminism as a critical discourse must call into question the social construction of the male as it exists in the present social system. Before Bloom can look at Gerty and see more than the fetishistic representation of his desire, he must change the symbolic structure of his eye/I (in both senses and spellings), that is, his visual apparatus as governed by his subjectivity. In my opinion, for a man to become a feminist, he must critically subvert his own construction as a man. Such a subversion cannot restrict itself to the question of gender only. It should entail a critique of the social and economic system within which gender relations are constructed. Masculinity is not only a sexual identity but a position of political and economic power. A critique of what it means to be male should not fail to investigate the ways in which gender interacts with class and race in the overall system of hegemony. Of course, women who choose to be feminists should not avoid these questions either. If gender is understood not as a natural but as a social construction, then the difference between men and women is not a matter of essence but of context.

In *Finnegans Wake*, Shem dictates to his brothers and sisters "the first riddle of the universe": "when is a man not a man?" The answer is, when he's a "Sham" (170). It seems to me that this is the risk that "male" or any other feminism necessarily takes: it is possible that the difference we propose for ourselves is only a sham. But then it is also possible to rephrase the question to say, when is a sham not a sham? My answer would be, when it is no longer necessary or profitable for a man to be a man.

NOTES

1. References to *Ulysses* are to the 1986 Gabler (*U-GP*) and the 1961 (*U*) editions, in that order.

2. Chap. 2 of Lloyd's *Nationalism and Minor Literature*, especially his conclusions on pp. 76–77, is relevant to this discussion.

WORKS CITED

Devlin, Kimberly J. *Wandering and Return in "Finnegans Wake": An Integrative Approach to Joyce's Fictions.* Princeton: Princeton University Press, 1991.

Gifford, Don, with Robert J. Seidman. *"Ulysses" Annotated: Notes for James Joyce's "Ulysses."* 2nd ed. Berkeley: University of California Press, 1988.

Gramsci, Antonio. *An Antonio Gramsci Reader: Selected Writings, 1916–1935.* New York: Schocken, 1988.

Joyce, James. *Finnegans Wake.* New York: Viking Press, 1959.

Lloyd, David. *Nationalism and Minor Literature: James Clarence Mangan and the Emergence of Irish Cultural Nationalism.* Berkeley: University of California Press, 1987.

"Nausicaa": For [Wo]men Only?

Jennifer Levine

I derive two general points from the essays in this section: first, a healthy self-consciousness about the "we" that writes (and teaches) and about the way gender quite literally makes a difference in the way we read; second, a sense that while it is impossible to separate the question of gender from questions of class, nationality, race, and religion, that does not make it a mere subcategory in a more "properly" political analysis. I am essentially in agreement with both these arguments.

I see a third assumption in play: that the inevitable focus for the reader of "Nausicaa" is Gerty MacDowell and Leopold Bloom—or rather, Gerty *with* Bloom, but I am interested here less in these two (and in the privileging of the couple that that implies) than in some of the other relationships "Nausicaa" is alert to. After all, this is the chapter in which a woman is positioned not just in relation to a man but also to two other women and to three little children. As the woman on the panel on "male feminisms" at the Symposium, I have tried to look at, and to make visible, the places in the text where the man is not.

❧ ❧ ❧

My first questions come from the opening pages in "Nausicaa." What is going on between the big sisters and the three male infants in their care? We watch and (not only here at the beginning but at various points in the chapter) we see the work of social reproduction, in particular the engendering of language, as Cissy Caffrey and Edy Boardman repeatedly lure the children into talk—or frame them into embarrassed silence. *Ulysses* provides a political context for this scene, since one of the stories unfolding in the background on June 16 is the debate over a forgotten, or never-learned, mother tongue. The Citizen's demand for news makes the links clear (though his terms, unlike those of

"Nausicaa," leave no space for women): "What did those tinkers in the city hall at their caucus meeting decide about the Irish language? . . . It's on the march. . . . To hell with the bloody brutal Sassenachs and their *patois*. . . . Tonguetied sons of bastards' ghosts" (U-GP 12:1180–1201). In general, too, the text is fascinated by verbal calisthenics, by the games we ask our tongues to play, mouthing nonsense sentences in order to master language. Thus, in "Scylla and Charybdis," "Peter Piper picked a peck of pick of peck of pickled peppers" (U-GP 9:276), or in "Eumaeus," "*Roberto ruba roba sua*" (U-GP 16:883), and in "Nausicaa," Bloom practicing Spanish: "*Buenas noches, señorita. El hombre ama la muchacha hermosa*" (U-GP 13:1208–9). The first words spoken in the chapter are the following:

—Now, baby, Cissy Caffrey said. Say out big, big. I want a drink of water.
And baby prattled after her:
—A jink a jink a jawbo.

The preceding narrative frames the interchange: Cissy Caffrey "cuddled the wee chap," "always with a laugh in her gipsylike eyes. . . . And Edy Boardman laughed too at the quaint language of little brother" (U-GP 13:29, 36–39). Note how the young child is being squeezed between two demands: that he is or should be a big man, and do big things; that he is a little, little boy. "O, he was a man already, was little Tommy Caffrey" (U-GP 13:249). The diminutive spreads like wildfire in this chapter, leaving all kinds of objects and people, but particularly women and children, be-littled in its wake: simultaneously condescended to and fondly caressed. And although Bloom also uses it, the word *little* functions as a particularly feminine way of negotiating the world, a way of "matronizing" it into place.

This opening scene goes on to suggest a certain affinity between learning the "mother tongue" and the child's position in a gendered world: we see how it is being teased into sexual difference. Or, put another way, it shows us how "it" is socialized into a little "he" by the older girls in charge. The lesson is overlaid on Jacky's need to pee and his inability to make his needs known. Like women, children lack a language by which to speak their bodies.

—Come here, Tommy, his sister called imperatively. At once! . . .
She put an arm round the little mariner and coaxed winningly:
—What's your name? Butter and cream?
—Tell us who is your sweetheart, spoke Edy Boardman. Is Cissy your sweetheart?
—Nao, tearful Tommy said.
—Is Edy Boardman your sweetheart? Cissy queried.
—Nao, Tommy said.
—I know, Edy Boardman said. . . . I know who is Tommy's sweetheart. Gerty is Tommy's sweetheart.
—Nao, Tommy said on the verge of tears.

Cissy's quick motherwit guessed what was amiss and she whispered to Edy
Boardman to take him there behind the pushcar where the gentleman
couldn't see him and to mind he didn't wet his new tan shoes.
But who was Gerty? (*U-GP* 13:51, 64–78)

"Nausicaa" brings us to Gerty and to Bloom by first putting women and children on the map. Its initial move is to highlight both speaking and silence: what can be spoken; where, when, and by whom; and how language is formative in constructing gender. Bloom is also a language teacher, though not, as he ruefully admits, a very successful one. Still, having taken gender for granted, he goes on to the next lesson, in which learning language is equivalent to learning sex. "Girl in Meath Street that night [he remembers]. All the dirty things I made her say. All wrong of course. My arks she called it" (*U-GP* 13: 867–69).

Taking my cue from a recently published interview with Toni Morrison, I am interested also in what happens among Gerty, Cissy, and Edy: "the three friends." I quote Morrison: "The real healing is often women talking to women. Hester Prynne now or Madame Bovary: they needed a good girl friend to come along and say, 'Honey, you did *what*? With *him*?' . . . But these women were written by men, so they didn't have girlfriends to confess to, or laugh with. Laughter is a way of taking the reins into your own hands."[1] There is surely some of this friendship in play between Miss Kennedy and Miss Douce, whose laughter in "Sirens" sets up self-protecting boundaries. "Watch out," it says, "we laugh: at you." (The "you" in "Sirens" is clearly gendered as male.) But Gerty, like Molly, is isolated, seemingly by her own hostility to other women. Much of her half of the narrative, as Philip Weinstein points out, is "saturated in a given culture's gender assumptions" that continually inscribe bitchiness in the place of friendship. Dick Pearce is right to say that this construction of "woman" hides behind the apparent shapelessness, or "naturalness," of the style, and since *Ulysses* is teaching us to be wary of such transparency elsewhere in the text we should not take it at face value here. Ergo: *Ulysses* itself (or even Joyce himself) is not complicit in the inscription. I think that, at some gut level, this is what a feminist who loves this book wants to hear. However, while I want to resist a reading that looks always for the woman in the text, that needs to find positive representations of female experience, it is important to acknowledge that *Ulysses* represents an intensely homosocial world where the primary bonds are between men. And yet, if *Ulysses* has so little to say about women's friendship, indeed, barely imagines it, it does insinuate how the *lack* of friendship operates in the construction of gender, in the female's setting herself aside, making herself available to the male. It may be that I am contorting myself into Joyce-saving knots. But I do not think so, because I do not believe that *Ulysses*, or any literary text, simply contains feminist—or antifeminist—meanings. Instead, paraphrasing Lévi-Strauss on culture, I read Joyce's work as goods (and good) to think with.[2]

What then to make of Gerty's isolation—so ready to take offence at her girlfriends, and not just unengaged, but deeply irritated by the demands of children? The question offers a vantage point from which to read her engagement with Bloom and with romance. I will briefly outline how such a reading might go. It would, in the first place, be very much indebted to the work of Janice Radway on popular romance and, through her, to Nancy Chodorow's account of how the female subject negotiates the Oedipal stage to define herself, eventually, as a woman.[3] It would also keep in mind Radway's useful distinction between the meaning of the act of reading (a demand, essentially, for a room of one's own, with no one else in it—particularly husbands and children), and the meaning of the romance as read (a search for the tender, nurturing figure who—because the world is constituted as heterosexual—must be male, must be, finally, a husband). That Gerty essentially says "leave me alone"; that she is fascinated by Bloom's apparent neediness and seems quite prepared to mother *him*; that she, in turn, wants to be taken in his "sheltering" arms, "comforted" with a long kiss; that she recodes the possibility of male violence into the signs of passionately fierce nurturing; that, for her, he is like no one else; that "he coloured like a girl," and that that is also part of the attraction; and that if we pick the story up again in "Circe" we see Gerty's manly man giving birth: all these elements cohere around a theory of reading the romance that understands this women's genre as a mechanism whereby the reader translates her search for the lost mother into the discovery of an ideal suitor: the manly man made perfect by his capacity to mother. All this is in shorthand, I know, but such an argument might go some way to explaining why female readers, on the whole, are so much less discomfited by Bloom than male ones. Even male feminists! (I am thinking here of Dick Pearce's rueful question as to why he would want to vindicate Bloom, or celebrate the new womanly man. Why not?)

❧   ❧   ❧

And so I come at last to the question of male feminism, which I will pose in a more personal way. What am *I* doing here? I want to start, somewhat perversely, by sidestepping for the moment my status as the female feminist.

I am here in part, too, to represent national variety: and while I doubt that my argument today has been substantially not-American, let alone essentially Canadian, I take my position as a reminder of the various kinds of difference—of nation, race, class—that inflect questions of gender, and vice versa. Dick Pearce has already alerted us to this when he argues that the dominant discourses make "not only women but [also] colonized Irishmen and wandering Jews defective." This general point is also crucial for Pat McGee, who links

131

gender politics to the history of British imperialism. These are important issues. I want to respond here, though, to part of Pat McGee's reading. It is simply too neat to say that when Gerty constructs Bloom as her ideal man, seeing him as the matinee idol Martin Harvey, she projects onto him a masculine sexuality *identical* to British cultural power.

The allure of Martin Harvey is a complicated foreignness, not just Englishness. Molly has dreamed some of the same dreams as Gerty has and has chosen Bloom for similar reasons: to escape the binary oppositions (Irish/English, Catholic/Protestant, maybe even male/female) that construct her world. "I always thought I'd marry a lord or a rich gentleman coming with a private yacht. . . . [she has confided, and Bloom asks back:] Why me? Because you were so foreign from the others" (*U-GP* 13:1207–10). And Gerty too: "she wanted him because she felt instinctively that he was like no-one else" (*U-GP* 13:429–30). I know, of course, that Gerty's dream of absolute originality is an absolutely mass-produced idea, but still, Martin Harvey is an interesting case.[4] Yes, in 1910 Irish Nationalists did object to his mounting an English play about an English king on the Dublin stage. But for Gerty in 1904, and for theatre audiences long after, the actor would have been known for his role as Sidney Carton in an adaptation of A *Tale of Two Cities:* the other man, the uncanny double of a man who is himself already double— the Frenchman/ Englishman, Jacques Darnay. In subsequent roles, too, Martin Harvey more often played the foreigner or at least the outsider than the Englishman. And in 1918, in a play by Maeterlinck, again he played the substitute, the man who puts himself, self-sacrificingly, in the place of another. An 1888 portrait shows a dark-eyed, dark-haired man who looks more Black Irish, or more like a Welshman (which he was, on his mother's side), or even perhaps a Jew than like a representative son of Albion. It is not without irony, I think, that just after the identification with Martin Harvey Gerty adds that she "could not see whether he [Bloom] had an aquiline nose or a slightly retrousse from where he was sitting" (*U-GP* 13:420–21). In this episode obsessed with noses (and it is: neither Gerty nor Bloom can stop themselves from noticing) Gerty has missed the signifier par excellence, the one that might have marked Bloom's foreignness as beyond the pale. Or rather, too much within the Pale. Martin Harvey was married to and performed with an actress whose name was so flamboyantly not-English that it reiterates my sense of what his name is doing here. She was called Angelita Helena Margarita de Silva, recalling another wife, Lunita Laredo, and Molly's Spanish connection. I do not want to disagree entirely with Pat McGee's point about Martin Harvey because to a large extent the actor's foreignness is an effect of representation, and of representations sanctioned by British cultural power. I do, however, want to complicate, or show how complicated is the notion of the manly man in *Ulysses.* I do this because I also want to argue that the notion of woman must be kept similarly complicated and various. In spite of his marked inclination to generalize about them, even Bloom has to acknowledge the question of difference: "But then why don't all women menstruate at the same time with the same moon, I mean? Depends on the time they were born I suppose. Or [and here is a mind-boggling possibility: perhaps they] all start [from] scratch then get out of step" (*U-GP* 13:783–85).

This brings me to say that, as a woman and a feminist, I do not represent some homogeneous, and therefore nonexistent, female feminism. A number of the questions that arise from the conjunction of "male" and "feminism" have already been explored in the preceding essays. I certainly am not here to play Cissy Caffrey, the big sister who already knows how to talk, whose job it is to teach the boys but who might very well, in the process, need to giggle at their "quaint language" and the "slight altercation" between them. Male feminists are not little feminists, though I think they are engaged in an enterprise that may not come as easily as it does to women. Why? Because, by its very nature, feminism entails a critique of structures that, to quote Pat McGee, still make it "profitable" to be a man.

Let me conclude by saying that what I especially value in these essays is their coming at the concerns of feminism in a particular way: by their authors' recognition that they live in the world as males. This seems to me a productive and honest starting point. The current move to read woman as a metaphor (as in "ecriture feminine," "reading as a woman," or Jonathan Culler's hypothesis of a woman reader), has a certain heuristic value. It allows us to name an alternate possibility for reading and writing, beyond phallogocentric closure. But such notions are worth a closer and more skeptical look. They strike me sometimes as a kind of "genderfication," a refurbishing or dressing up in the metaphors of woman. I agree with Teresa de Lauretis when she says that "to make gender synonymous with discursive difference(s), differences that are effects of language or positions in discourse, and thus indeed independent of the reader's gender," means that we lose the category of the actual female reader (22). It also means that concrete political and historical differences are set aside, massaged away by the metaphor. Her critique of this tendency is incisive.

So it is that, by displacing the question of gender onto an ahistorical, purely textual figure of femininity (Derrida); or by shifting the sexual basis of gender quite beyond sexual difference, onto a body of diffuse pleasures (Foucault) and libidinally invested surfaces (Lyotard), or a body-site of undifferentiated affectivity, and hence a subject freed from (self-)representation and the constraints of identity (Deleuze); and finally by displacing the ideology, but also the reality—the historicity—of gender onto this diffuse, decentered, or deconstructed (but certainly not female) subject—so it is that, paradoxically again, these theories make their appeal to women, naming the process of such displacing with the term *becoming woman (devenir-femme)*. (24)

"Male feminist" strikes me as a far more plausible conjunction than (what in this context might be called) "male female" or "male feminine." I am not convinced that we need figurative sex-change operations, particularly when the figures (both our metaphors and our bodies) are taken for granted. We do need to acknowledge who we are, and to listen to each other.

NOTES

1. *Globe and Mail* (Toronto), 5 May 1992, sec. C, p. 1.
2. For a general discussion, see "The Science of the Concrete," in Lévi-Strauss, 1–33.
3. See Radway's *Reading the Romance*, and Chodorow's *The Reproduction of Mothering*.
4. *Dictionary of National Biography, 1941–50*; *Encyclopaedia Britannica, Micropaedia*, 5th ed., 5:734; *McGraw-Hill Encyclopedia of World Drama*, 5:309.

WORKS CITED

Chodorow, Nancy. *The Reproduction of Mothering: Psychoanalysis and the Sociology of Gender.* Berkeley: University of California Press, 1976.

de Lauretis, Teresa. *Technologies of Gender: Essays on Theory, Film, and Fiction.* Bloomington: Indiana University Press, 1987.

Lévi-Strauss, Claude. *The Savage Mind.* Chicago: University of Chicago Press, 1966.

McGraw-Hill Encyclopedia of World Drama. Ed. Stanley Hochman. 5 vols. New York: McGraw-Hill, 1984.

Radway, Janice. *Reading the Romance: Reading, Patriarchy, and Popular Literature.* Chapel Hill: University of North Carolina Press, 1991.

The Shorter Works

All Things Come in Threes: Ménage à Trois in *Dubliners*

Zack Bowen

Father Flynn's confessional mirth has been the subject of critical speculation for as long as I can remember. It's one of those ambiguous questions that we all decide really can't be explicitly answered because to do so would somehow invalidate the universal ambiguity of modern literature, life, or whatever existentialism the modern age glories in suffering. Whatever "something" that *they* decide has gone wrong with him, we smugly suppose is what is wrong with *them*. They can't see it because they have been conditioned not to, while we, possessing post-Reaganite insight, know that the undefinable has the only chance at providing meaning. In this brief essay I am not going to try to change that thinking, but simply to reorder it, and to provide a new structure for the formless hopelessness that confronts the characters of these short stories. Since our panel topic dealt with competing groups of three, and the number didn't do Dante any harm, I would like to propose that Joyce had a similar numerical affinity, one that was destined to lead him to outbursts of childish jealousy at Nora's supposed affairs, and one that permeates all of the rivalries among his characters from *Chamber Music* to *Finnegans Wake*.

My reading will posit "The Sisters" as the introduction to the entire collection, with Flynn as a spiritual Cassandra, or an ecclesiastical Nestor, his laughter in the confessional stemming from his insight into the entrapped lives of the characters who grace the ensuing pages of the volume. His position as an annointed representative of the church is a constant reminder that the problems of Dublin's citizenry originate with their inescapable bondage to Irish Roman Catholicism, which frames the parameters of their servitude and their isolation.

The three stories forming the initial bildungsroman sequence constitute the growing awareness of the increasingly mature narrator(s). The first is a half-understood general lesson and a prediction of inescapable systematic bondage, the realization of which causes Flynn himself to be reduced to an intellectual invalid in the eyes of the other priests and the sisters. The boy, rebellious but willing to learn the art of priesthood, verbal or religious, refuses to listen to the sage wisdom of the misguided populace (old Cotter and his female companions) just as he refuses to join in the ritual speeches for the dead and to take cookie communions and the like, but is instead reminded of a three-word catechistic explanation for the experiences of the living: paralysis, simony, and gnomon, a formula for the crowd in limbo who populate *Dubliners*. They are caught in the simoniac implications of doctrinal corruption that produce a grubby, meretricious society, paralyzed physically and psychologically by poverty, inaction, and religious sanction, and they sell the freedom of their lives and souls for survival even while they compete in hopeless and misguided three-way rivalries for what meager crumbs of existence remain.

The third term of the structural blueprint the boy introduces for *Dubliners*, gnomon, resembles Joyce's introduction of the word *parallax* in *Ulysses* to explain the multiplicity of images for the same object, a kind of physical-science consubstantality in which the objects seen are both single and multiple, depending on their situation in regard to the observer. Gnomon is the shell of a parallelogram left when an equally proportioned part of it is removed. Its identity depends upon the presence of absence of the removed segment, and it is defined physically and spatially by its loss. The absence of the defining segment is nowhere clearer than in the defining presence of Michael Furey's absence in "The Dead," but it is also the vital missing segment in every one of the *Dubliner's* stories, the geometrical equivalent of the Holy Ghost in the Trinitarian view of completeness.

Let us apply this trinity of terms to the three-sided rivalries of the individual stories. The rivalry between Cotter and Flynn for the boy's soul is mitigated by the Flynn sisters' simpleminded devotion and subservience. They are the living dead, good-hearted, obedient, and accepting. Old Cotter, rebellious enough to challenge the motives and authority of a member of the clergy, speaks for prudence and the unexamined, the acceptance of another, socially acceptable, paralysis of development. Flynn, in his own way, opens the gates to doubt, even as he gleefully goes through the artificial minutia of catechistic interpretation, the very embellishments that establish the authority of the church. We take what comfort we can in the boy's refusal of the cream-cracker communion, but are left with only the sense of the boy's service in providing a measure of absolution to Flynn as the priest's own confessor. Is Flynn's sense of guilt the legacy he leaves both to the boy and the Dubliners who follow? The boy is still far from being free from his bondage to the all-enveloping church; he is merely playing an unaccustomed role, but one that will take hold and eventually characterize Stephen Dedalus and Shem in later works.

"An Encounter" will focus on the "unnatural" aspects of Flynn's surrogate, the Old Josser, as he engages in a rivalry over the boy—resumed from the first story—between Flynn/Josser's exotic otherness and the socially accepted, healthy, young, brainless normalcy of boyhood in the person of Mahony. The narrator's recognition of his own similarities to the Old Josser are frightening enough to drive the boy to Mahony for momentary comfort and the final recognition that intellectual freedom may well bring abhorant deviation. To be different or *other* implies risks that almost make paralysis welcome. The gnomon-shadow of the priest, the presence of his absence, like an obscene Holy Ghost, hangs over the spiritual journey to light, as the implications of the boy's wish for difference are made manifest in the concluding epiphany.

Flynn is reincarnated again in his surrogate's picture hanging on the wall, as the spiritual journey takes on the sexual overtones of a courtly love grail search in "Araby." The boy envelops his journeys through Dublin's shops and finally the fair itself in ecclesiastical terminology as he projects his quest in religious rather than sexual terms. His "praying hands" murmurings cast Mangan's sister as a Blessed Virgin Mary image, but his brief discussion with the attendant girl at the stall, crudely mirroring the confessional with her coquettish interchange ("But you did." "But I didn't") with the young Englishmen, deflates the sacredness of the boy's own sexual aspirations. The rivalry here is again with the world of the normal, the ardent young men whose approach is profane rather than sacred. Faced with the impossibility of his quest in monetary terms and in his devalued dreams, the boy clinks his remaining coins together and is reminded of the simoniac counting of collection coins after the service as he makes another involuntary surrender of his childish fantasies to the realities of simony and paralysis.

The life of abused drudge providing for her drunken father and the comic-opera fantasy life of freedom as a bohemian girl/Cinderella in Argentina offered by Frank are presented as the only alternatives in their rivalry for Eveline. The grim socially acceptable norm of spinster-daughter, for all its impending paralysis, is more an inescapable religious legacy than a viable choice. A romantic elopement seems to represent an alternative to a full-blown Dublin wedding with parental consent, the publishing of the banns, and so on, but the risk in going with Frank is that he might not marry her at all, and perhaps she would have to live in a spiritual hell even more confining than the one she would have to abandon in Dublin. Frank's last vision of Eveline as a caged animal contrasts with hers as a helpless drowning victim, paralyzed either way.

"After the Race" is a simoniac's dream come true. The prevalent metaphoric motif is money, mentioned over and over again in terms of commerce and the totem-animal imagery of the pagans. Betrayal of country by the elder Doyle, whose trade with the RIC stifled his Nationalistic zeal, is coupled with his firm belief that France and its cars will provide the monetary salvation of Ireland. As Jimmy loses heavily in a Nationalistic game, way beyond his means,

Joyce extends his vision of paralysis to the middle classes and their pig-pushing merchant princes.

To remain single and sexually active in Dublin is, however, nearly as hard as either married victimization or spinsterhood. The rivals of "Two Gallants," the slavey and Lenehan, vie for the affection of the walking phallus, Corley. The principal irony here is not the seduction of a slavey or its metaphoric counterpart in the monetary abuse of the female figure carved on the Irish harp, so much as the trick of lulling the reader into thinking that the climax of the story was to be a sexual one rather than a divine revelation in terms of the all-prevailing simony of Dublin's lovers. The crucifixion and betrayal metaphors at the end of the story turn Corley into a sexual suffering servant giving his body to provide a gold coin for his betraying disciple. No wonder Flynn found the whole business so funny.

Not all Dubliners operate against the prevailing religious grain. The rivalry between Doran and Mrs. Mooney regarding Polly is based on a set of ecclesiastical standards as unequivocal as a chop from the family butcher's ax. With guilt reinforced by confession and priestly admonishment, as well as Jack's fists, Doran sees through his steamed glasses darkly. The game is again money, the profaning of sacred rights for the top dollar—marriage. Mrs. Mooney is in many respects the ideal Dubliner, at home and comforted by her religion, just as she observes its dictates. Is there any question that she will make short twelve at Marlboro Street? Doran's fondest wish might well have been for precoital paralysis, something that never appeared in Mrs. Mooney's Tarot deck.

Little Chandler's rivals are two: Ignatius Gallaher and Chandler's son, Little Little Chandler. Together Gallaher and the infant form an axis to keep the dreamer in his literary and social place. While Gallaher's reputed triumph with assorted women in the fleshpots of the Continent apparently assures him a higher graduation place in the university of life, the child's wailing is superior to his father's self-pitying helplessness in the competition for baby-of-the-year demands for attention. Never one to leave any religious rock unturned, Joyce paints Annie's picture as a perverse little madonna, whose devotion is to the divine child rather than her husband, a forgotten cuckold in his own carpentry shop.

"Counterparts" explores a series of ménange à trois rivalry situations between Farrington and Mr. Alleyne, Farrington and Weathers, and Farrington and his son. The female components of each vary from Mrs. Delacourt in the office, through the exotic English woman in the bar, to that old staple, the BVM, at home. Farrington is always competing at a disadvantage: in the inferiority of his office position, in his aging muscles in the bar, and in his bullying unchristian behavior at home. While Farrington's principal weakness lies in his need for liquor, the wrath of the whole church establishment is summoned up against him in the boy's pleas at home. Alleyne's Protestant superiority, Weathers's English strength, and the BVM's ecclesiastical muscle all outweigh anything Farrington's wrath can produce. The absence of meaning-ful psychological or physical strength forms the gnomon of this paralysis of meaningful action, supported by the grubby world of the legal scrivener and interspersed with shops sporting snugs for surreptitious daytime drinking.

The triangular symmetry of the three bowls with ring, prayerbook, and water—all representing rival career choices for Maria in "Clay"—is disturbed by the addition of a fourth bowl, containing clay, by the next-door girls. Even though they were responsible for organizing the games, the next-door young-sters were playing with far more realistic rules than those appropriate to sweet, aging virgins on All Hallows Eve. In many ways the opposite of the self-centered and self-pitying Duffy of the next story, Maria's obliviousness to her own grim situation is her ultimate defense. If she chooses death's symbol, she merely understands that "it was wrong that time and so she had to do it over again." Her fantasy rivals for her affections—the tipsy gentleman in the tram and the knights on bended knee in her song—replace the absence of any real ones in her DisneyWorld of sweetness and light, music, and nostalgia. It's a small world after all, as Joe tearfully realizes while he searches for the corkscrew.

The lack of any emotional rival to Mrs. Sinico's unsolicited affections is the basis of Mr. Duffy's spiritually and emotionally impoverished dilemma. Duffy's life in suspiciously monklike surroundings is underscored by his substitution of an anticlerical, self-aggrandizing version of socialism for religious devotion. His antisexual beliefs are the dissenting counterpart of the holy orders fol-lowed by his rivals in the church. The newspaper article is itself little more than a creed of disavowal of blame for the social order embodied in the rail-road and the legal system in general. The irony of "no blame attach[ing] to anyone" is that the testimony was rigged to fault Mrs. Sinico's intemperance for her own demise, while Duffy's lengthy epiphany on reading the story is an extended ego trip in which he attaches the blame for her bibulous habits on his own fatal attraction for and subsequent rejection of her, even though two years passed between their association and the beginning of Mrs. Sinico's drinking. The grubbiness of Duffy's self-blame is rivaled only by the cupidity of a railway that claims she had been hit and dragged fifty feet by a train that had started from a dead stop at Sydney Parade Station, and was "brought . . . to rest" "a second or two afterwards," according to James Lennon, the engi-neer. The story concludes with Duffy's going through a brief period of self-in-crimination until he finally arrives at self-pity. The connection of the story to the church is that it is an allegory of the perversity of sexual denial. Sinico's fleeting gesture, which so horrified Duffy, is compounded by the furtive lovers by the Magazine wall. No Zarathustrian feats of rationalization can counter the phalluslike train-worm laboriously winding its way down the track with its little light blinking into the twin darknesses of the vagina and death.

"Ivy Day in the Committee Room" is built upon the gnomonlike presence of Parnell's absence. His defeat and death at the hands of his simoniac associates

141

informs the entire rainy afternoon in the committee room like the one where Parnell's downfall was earlier brought about. The clergy's surreptitious role in the Chief's demise takes the form of the dark figure of Father Keon, neither clergyman nor layman, there to meet the candidate on a little item of "business." The deferential attitude of the assembled political hacks underscores not only the role of the clergy in affairs in which they have no business but their influence on the denunciation of Parnell, whose redeeming value to the canvassers lies in his memory, soon dismissed if not forgotten. Their allegiance to the candidate and the Crown is easily bought with a few bottles of stout and the hollow promise of something more.

In "A Mother" Mrs. Kearney's rivalry with Hoppy Holohan over the musical services of her daughter, Kathleen, introduces simony to the performing arts and the arts into the service of the country. When Kathleen—who has not, after all, played for the number of performances that constituted the original bargain—insists on taking her full contractual award, she is theoretically impoverishing the Eire Abu Society by her meretriciousness while at the same time she degrades her art, at least in the eyes of Holohan, whose appeal for a final verdict goes not to the clergy but to the third estate's spokesman for the social order, O'Madden Burke, leaning on his augur's staff/umbrella. His final verdict in matters artistic (in which he has no credentials whatsoever) recapitulates the judgment of his counterpart, Crofton—equally unqualified in literary criticism—who bestows the final half-hearted approbation of Hynes's poem in "Ivy Day in the Committee Room."

"Grace," the original conclusion to *Dubliners*, is just the stuff that would have tickled Father Flynn's funny bone in the confessional. Kernan's trip to Paradiso, begun on the floor of the men's cellar-lavatory, is a journey through ecclesiastical misconception, in the company of a group of hard-drinking but devout comforters, to the illuminating hilarity of Purdon's misreading of holy scripture. Purdon's twisted Jesuitical logic equates the falsified books of the assembled mammonites to a spiritual accounting in which all the accounts are either balanced or are just about to be, the whole an exercise in simoniac comfort if there ever was one. Invoking in the words of Jesus, whose absence is hardly present, the church's rationalization for the bibulous spiritual impoverishment of Dublin, Purdon conveys the peaceful blessing of the church on the wasteland it has created.

The rivalry between Gabriel and Michael Furey for the love and soul of Gretta concludes the final story, which is fraught with all of the rivalries present in *Dubliners*. Three women vie for the role of most-likely-to-produce-flacidity: Lily, the abused servant; Miss Ivors, the nationalistic nag; and Gretta, whose all-encompassing fount of favors has been chilled by the snow and freezing rain fallen years before on Rahoon and now present all over Ireland. Gabriel's picturesque construction of the precipitation falling everywhere in this world and the next, which provides the book's concluding metaphor, turns emotional pain into artistic beauty and a country of misplaced allegiances into a puddle of sacrifice. Flynn's sisters come back to us as Gabriel's aunts, still devout but angered by the church's sexual misappropriation of their musical art, their talents no longer welcomed in the service of the church. The monks, who retire to coffins every evening—a walking-dead metaphor in their shuttle back and forth between life and death—prefigure the passion of Michael Furey, who died because the object of his love must go away to serve her convent penance. Gabriel, his limp upper fallen, has the life-sustaining artistic ability to turn his lament for his own unfulfilled condition into an ambiguous if pious linking of his rival's emotion with the peaceful serenity of falling snow, joining the dead with the living in a country inhabited by spirits shuffling between two worlds. It is Gabriel's self-proclaimed generosity and Joyce's genius for ambiguity that admit these concluding hints of redemption and peace to a most distressful condition depicted in *Dubliners*.

Duffy's Adventure: "A Painful Case" as Existential Text

James D. LeBlanc

There is an episode of *Dragnet* (*Dragnet*, by the way, is an American TV show, a crime drama that originally aired in the 1950s and late 1960s, in which a certain Sergeant Joe Friday, along with his sidekick, Officer Bill Gannon, investigate a wide array of felonies and misdemeanors, all allegedly based on real life incidents) . . . there is an episode of *Dragnet* in which a young, well-read factory worker with a powerfully inflated sense of intellectual and moral superiority murders two of his coworkers just to see what it feels like to kill someone. During the course of their investigation Friday and Gannon discover that their number-one suspect (who is, indeed, the murderer) is an "existentialist." Yes, the fellow's landlady informs the police, he's always reading Baudelaire— you know, "that fleurs d'mal stuff." And the local librarian, flagrantly defying the profession's code of ethics regarding the right to privacy, reveals to the two detectives that the suspect has been charging out a lot of Flaubert's works lately. The killer is, of course, brought to justice, and the TV audience is thus forewarned about the dangers of "existentialism"—and, apparently, the reading of French literature in general.

Existentialism has always been difficult to talk about. After all, it's a philosophy of existence: what could be more profound and universal? Or more trite? Popular culture's co-opting of the Sartrean enterprise during the late forties, the fifties, and on into the sixties resulted in a colorful but for the most part poorly grounded semiological corpus, the signatures of which were things such as goatees, long straight hair on women, dressing in black, jazz, and, of course, anything French, not to mention the pursuit of kicks— whether on Route 66 or through the committing of motiveless violent crimes. And let's face it, even in scholarly circles, any buzzword that can be made to encompass the work of Plato, Pascal, Kierkegaard, Dostoyevsky, Nietzsche, Sartre, Beauvoir, Camus, and Jack Kerouac . . . well, there's bound to be some slippage of the signified. Poststructuralism's entombment of existentialism (or, at least, its move to mothball its trendy predecessor) has not helped to clarify matters.

But what about Mr. Duffy? Now that I've crawled out onto what may be a perilously thin critical limb, rotten with potential misunderstanding and swaying in the stiff breeze of what is perhaps a well-warranted impatience that I get back to things Joycean, I shall take a moment to remind myself, perched up here in this Dublin tree, of one of Nietzsche's more pithy, gay-scientific dicta: "the secret for harvesting from existence the greatest fruitfulness and the greatest enjoyment is—to *live dangerously!*" (Nietzsche 228). Mr. Duffy would certainly know what I mean. Or would he?

Although seldom considered a writer of existentialist leanings, Joyce, in his "Painful Case," has presented us with a protagonist who is, in many ways, akin to Dostoyevsky's "underground" man, Nietzsche's "overman," and Sartre's "nauseated" man—a fellow who finds himself "outcast from life's feast" into a barren, lonely world of neurotic self-absorption. In the light of the reading of "A Painful Case" that I'll be sharing with you here, we might venture to label Mr. Duffy Joyce's "disembodied" man. What all these characters have in common, and what renders these texts existential, I would maintain, is the protagonists' realization—whether in moments of epiphany or during a longer, slower period of revelation—that their existence is not entirely understandable in empirical, idealistic, or socio-cultural terms, but that for every instant of their lives they are condemned to relentlessly choose the direction and nature of their becoming. They must create themselves in the face of an uncertain, contingent, and apparently purposeless world. It is this realization, which manifests itself through anxiety, suffering, and feelings of guilt, that is, in these texts, itself the "critical borderline situation"[1] that is often deemed to be an essential characteristic of existential literature, especially that of the *engagement* genre (Sartre's *Roads to Freedom*, Camus's *Plague*, etc.). The "adventure," therefore, in such texts as *Notes from Underground*, *Nausea*, and "A Painful Case" is an adventure in *being* for the "everyman," one who is not a soldier in wartime, a doctor in plague time, or, if you wish, a wacky afficionado of French letters in American prime time.

Let's take a closer look at the specifics of Duffy's situation and at the phenomeno-ontological parameters of what I am suggesting is his existential crisis.

Duffy likes to lead a neat, organized life, stripped of material and social frills, free from chaos. What's more, he takes this inclination to an extreme, as we know. He lives in a plain, somber, cheerless room, void of decoration and nearly empty of color. His books are arranged on white wooden bookshelves "from below upwards according to bulk" (*D67* 107)—that is, in an order. He has no friends, no faith, represses nearly every trace of emotion. He performs family social obligations "for old dignity' sake" (*D67* 109). He tells Mrs. Sinico that he ceased attending meetings of the Irish Socialist Party because "they [the workers] resented an *exactitude* which was the product of a leisure not within their reach" (*D67* 111; my emphasis). In short: "Mr. Duffy abhorred anything which betokened physical or mental disorder" (*D67* 108). He is a perfect paradigm of a compulsion neurotic, in Freudian terms.[2] Furthermore, and not surprisingly, James Duffy is a creature of habit. He rides the same streetcar to work every morning, eats the same frugal lunch at the same establishment each day (a small trayful of arrowroot biscuits and a bottle of beer) and dines at the same restaurant each evening. His life is free of "dissipations," with the exception of an occasional opera or concert, if works of Mozart are on the bill. He works as a bank clerk—hardly a dynamic profession—but then Duffy is not a fellow inclined to take risks, to seek adventure, nor, for that matter, to allow adventure to befall him. There is, however, one intriguing chink in his armor of negated possibilities, one highly suggestive fantasy: "He allowed himself to think that in certain circumstances he would rob his bank but, as these circumstances never arose, his life rolled out evenly—an adventureless tale" (*D67* 109). We are not told what the circumstances might be that would transform his lackluster, uneventful life into an "adventure" and, for the moment anyway, it is safe to say that whatever they are, they are certainly inoperative.

Clearly, Duffy is into control, but unlike those more colorful control freaks who spend their lives pushing the envelope (whether because of the force of circumstance or the sheer glee of existential chutzpah), Duffy's strategy is one of avoidance or, at least, of ontological stealth. He seeks a mode of being that will be stable: a life that is calmly rigid, not fluid, unassaulted, not relentlessly defended. He chooses freedom because he must, because he is condemned to be free, but the freedom he chooses is a freedom in confinement. He is in control because he shuns situations in which he might be confronted with adversity. He creates distances, not just between himself and others, but within himself as well: "He lived at a little distance from his body, regarding his own acts with doubtful side-glances. He had an odd autobiographical habit which led him to compose in his mind from time to time a short sentence about himself containing a subject in the third person and a predicate in the past tense" (*D67* 108). Duffy's flight from any real interpersonal interaction, his withdrawal into a life-of-the-mind-in-chosen-exile, and even the bland, orderly, habitual accoutrements of his everyday existence all reflect what Sartre would term Duffy's "fundamental project": to live without threat, without further choice, without existential free play.

There are two turning points in the story, both brought about by Duffy's relationship with Mrs. Sinico—a relationship that clearly *in itself* threatens to bring down the walls of Duffy's fundamental existential enterprise. The first occurs when Sinico takes his hand in a moment of passion and presses it to her cheek; the second, four years later, when after learning of the woman's sudden and tragic death, he imbibes two whisky punches at a public house.

Duffy meets Mrs. Sinico at a concert and they begin to keep company. Their affair is entirely platonic, but nonetheless there is an element of risk for both of them in the liaison: "Neither he nor she had had any such adventure before" (D67 110). For Sinico, there is the chance that her extramarital relationship will be misconstrued or that it will develop into something less innocent. Moreover, given the story's conclusion and the suggestion that her demise and death might be related to the failure of her romance with Duffy, this sense of "adventure"—a term that, at first glance, may have seemed a bit hyperbolic when applied to Sinico—appears, in the end, to have been on the mark. As far as Duffy is concerned, on the other hand, the element of adventure in this social intercourse is a bit more abstract but still potentially dangerous, for, as we have already noted, such a course of action for Duffy threatens to destabilize his very being.

At first, he does rather well walking this existential tightrope. He uses Sinico as a sympathetic mirror, confessing himself to her, lending her books, holding forth—and keeping his distance: "Sometimes he caught himself listening to the sound of his own voice. . . . He heard the strange impersonal voice which he recognised as his own, insisting on the soul's incurable loneliness. We cannot give ourselves, it said: we are our own" (D67 111). As we might expect, however, Sinico is not the perfect mirror. She shares *her* thoughts with Duffy, as well: "Little by little he entangled his thoughts with hers" (D67 110). And later: "Little by little, as their thoughts entangled, they spoke of subjects less remote" (D67 111). Finally: "[O]ne night during which she had shown every sign of unusual excitement, Mrs. Sinico caught up his hand passionately and pressed it to her cheek" (D67 111). End of affair—Duffy withdraws.

It is enough of a risk for Duffy, enough of an adventure, to allow himself cerebral "entanglement" with another, and even then, it is he who must call the intellectual shots. But a sensual, physical caress?! In *Being and Nothingness*, Sartre notes that: "my original attempt to get hold of the Other's free subjectivity through his objectivity-for-me is *sexual desire*" (497). Sinico's assault on Duffy's body (and this is unquestionably the way he experiences her caress) threatens to jeopardize the meticulously maintained, fragile sense of self that Duffy guards with such paranoid obsessiveness. What's more, it is by causing him to experience his body *as flesh*, as *his* flesh, this body from which he constantly tries to dissociate himself, that Mrs. Sinico insinuates her own being into Duffy's existential realm of ipseity. She might as well have speared him with a hot poker—Duffy runs for his life.

Four years pass, and little changes in Duffy's life. There are a few new pieces of music on the landlady's music stand, a couple of Nietzsche books on his white wooden shelves, his father dies (a rather unremarkable event, as far as Duffy is concerned), but his routine remains as it was in the days before he met Mrs. Sinico. But then one day, he reads the account of her death in the evening newspaper. She had become a drunkard and was killed by a train as she was crossing the tracks, or more precisely, she died of "shock and sudden failure of the heart's action" (*D67* 114). Did she die, at least indirectly, of a broken heart? Duffy's defenses go up. First, it's the journalistic prose of the newspaper article that upsets him: "The threadbare phrases, the inane expressions of sympathy, the cautious words of a reporter won over to conceal the details of a commonplace vulgar death attacked his stomach" (*D67* 115). Then, when this riposte fails, he takes a stab at the deceased woman: "Evidently she had been unfit to live, without any strength of purpose, an easy prey to habits [!], one of the wrecks on which civilisation has been reared" (*D67* 115). He finds a public house, enters and drinks a hot punch, then another. Now undoubtedly light-headed (the physical beginning to undermine the intellectual), he wanders into Phoenix Park: "He walked through the bleak alleys where they had walked four years before. She seemed to be near him in the darkness. At moments he seemed to *feel* her voice *touch his ear, her hand touch his*" (*D67* 117; my emphasis). She is touching him again and, like the onslaught of the returning repressed at the moment of the psychological trauma's repetition, this touch is existentially lethal: "He felt his moral nature falling to pieces" (*D67* 117). Soon the memory fades, the touch disappears, there is silence: "He felt he was alone" (*D67* 117). The walls of his emotionally self-sufficient bastion of being have crumbled. He now misses the company of others.

Duffy, until his epiphany, has ostensibly led a kind of "life of the mind." Living at a distance from himself, divorcing mind from body, even relegating certain moments of his life to an inert past experienced by another (recall his "odd autobiographical habit" of composing short sentences about himself in the third person and the past tense), Duffy condemns himself to failure unless he can somehow continue to believe in these sham virtues. And his existence *is* a sham: this self-insulated, cerebral posturing. He writes his autobiography only in his head; there is no suggestion that the writing materials that are "always on the desk" (*D67* 108) have ever been used for such an endeavor. His translation of Hauptmann remains, even after four years, only partially complete. His notebook of terse apothegms contains by his own admission little more than "Bile Beans." His shelves contain a complete Wordsworth, a catechism, and some Nietzsche, among other texts, but he has probably never read the Nietzsche, or at least never clearly understood or accepted even the most basic tenets of *Thus Spoke Zarathustra* and *The Gay Science* (the two works we know he owns). Duffy *never* laughs, either in a Zarathustrian fashion or otherwise: in fact he represses the Dionysian component of his existence. Although some critics have made Duffy out to be a would-be *Übermensch*,[3] he is actually a rather pitiful example of a Nietzschean misfit.

At the story's conclusion, however, Duffy is on the verge of undergoing a radical transformation. The eerie return of Mrs. Sinico's caress and the effects of the whisky have changed the way Duffy sees himself. Whether he will try to re-repress his disturbing discovery or whether this fresh insight will lead Duffy to completely reformulate his fundamental project we cannot know. But what if he opts for the latter? What if this pompous, withdrawn prig turns his previous lifestyle on its head? What a change! What adventure! Perhaps these are the circumstances in which this sociopathic clerk would rob his bank. After all, he already feels at least partly responsible for the death of Mrs. Sinico. Why not a life of crime? And what might we expect his landlady to say to the Dublin police, perhaps to the two agents who come to question her? "It's those Nietzsche books, y'know, that Zarathustra stuff!" Or maybe: "Say, d'ya think it was all that Wordsworth?"

NOTES

1. This phrase and some of the wording of the preceding sentence I owe to the definition of *existentialism* found in *Webster's New International Dictionary*, 2nd ed.

2. For further examination of this aspect of Duffy's persona from a psychoanalytic point of view, see Reid.

3. See, e.g., Magalener and Corrington.

WORKS CITED

Corrington, John William. "Isolation as Motif in 'A Painful Case.'" *James Joyce Quarterly* 3 (1966): 182–91.

Dragnet. Produced and directed by Jack Webb. NBC, 16 December 1951–6 September 1959; 12 January 1967–10 September 1970; syndicated thereafter.

Magalener, Marvin. "Joyce, Nietzsche, and Hauptmann in James Joyce's 'A Painful Case.'" *PMLA* 68 (1953): 95–102.

Nietzsche, Friedrich. *The Gay Science*. Trans. Walter Kaufmann. New York: Vintage Books, 1974.

Reid, Stephen. "'The Beast in the Jungle' and 'A Painful Case': Two Different Sufferings." *American Imago* 20 (1963): 221–39.

Sartre, Jean-Paul. *Being and Nothingness*. Trans. Hazel E. Barnes. New York: Pocket Books, 1966.

Dancing a Pas de Deux in *Exiles*'s Ménage à Quatre; or, How Many Triangles Can You Make Out of Four Characters If You Take Them Two at a Time?

Ruth Bauerle

Joyceans do not much like *Exiles*.[1] Few scholars have been as overtly antago-nistic as was Adaline Glasheen in the *Second Census to "Finnegans Wake,"* in which she described the play as "extremely boring."[2] Yet Joyceans have given the play scant attention. At the Thirteenth International Joyce Symposium, for example, Marilyn French addressed the theme of literature and domination, with reference to Joyce's works, without mentioning *Exiles*, where domination is a major theme.[3] Similarly, Robert Adams Day in his wide-ranging analysis "Joyce's AquaCities" made only brief reference to *Exiles*, though water is a major sexual image in the play, particularly in the second act.

We have neglected *Exiles* because we have largely misunderstood what Joyce was doing in the play. As Clive Hart pointed out, "Critics have often been troubled by *Exiles* . . . because the dialogue has been understood as an attempt at pure realism" (124).[4] For the experienced reader of Joyce, the contrasts of *Ulysses* and *Finnegans Wake* lie always in the background of this apparently conventional realism. These works draw all Joyceans by imaginative and cre-ative language, full of coinages and puns, and manipulated compositionally through a large number of motifs that are repeated with amusing variations.

Students of *Ulysses* and *Finnegans Wake* are also accustomed to structural experiments: episodes that represent a cave of winds, the growth of the human foetus, the musical form of a fugue or a catechism, prose representing a night's dreaming sleep or the flow of the river. Reading and re-reading we learn to recognize these as Joyce's serious jokes and our old friends. Indeed, some have argued that *Ulysses* and *Finnegans Wake* can never be read, but only re-read.

It is time now to re-read *Exiles* as the comedy Joyce intended, letting the language and the events on stage lead us into a correct understanding of the play's structure. Several points become evident:

1. Rather than a conventional triangle play of domestic passion, *Exiles* is a play of four triangles arranged in a regular tetrahedron, a form underlying the play's apparent rigidity.

2. *Exiles*'s tetrahedron is presented to the audience one edge at a time: we see only two characters on stage at one time, engaged in a series of duologues.

3. Each tetrahedral pair is in some sense opposite to each other tetrahedral pair, creating a set of thematic dualities that match the duologues.

4. The pair of characters on any edge of the tetrahedron are doubles of each other to some degree. So among the four major characters (excluding Brigid, the Fishwoman, and the child Archie) we have six pairs of character doubles.

5. Each character, viewing the other three from his or her apex of the tetrahedron, is therefore looking at three doubles of aspects of his/her personality.

6. This doubling of characters is achieved in large part by doubling of the language through echolalia.

If we re-read *Exiles* with these structural elements in mind, we become aware of familiar Joycean devices at work. There is, first of all, a good deal of language play, where a phrase or motif is doubled, sometimes repeatedly, through the play. There is also the kind of shifting character doubling we associate with *Finnegans Wake*. And there is additionally, amid the conventional three acts, an original, carefully arranged structure based on twos, threes, and fours, almost mathematical in form.

I. The triangles

Exiles is most usefully regarded as a drama of four people who, taken three at a time, give us four triangles (six if we include the "intimated" triangles), each of them one face of a regular tetrahedron. This can be represented in a small paper structure by photocopying figure 1, cutting out the copy, and folding it on the indicated lines (see also fig. 2). Each apex of the tetrahedron thus formed is one character from the play. Moreover, each edge of the tetrahedron represents the tensions between one pair of characters (Bauerle, *Word List* x); and the three edges reaching out from any apex represent the ties between that character and his/her mirror image in each of the other characters.

151

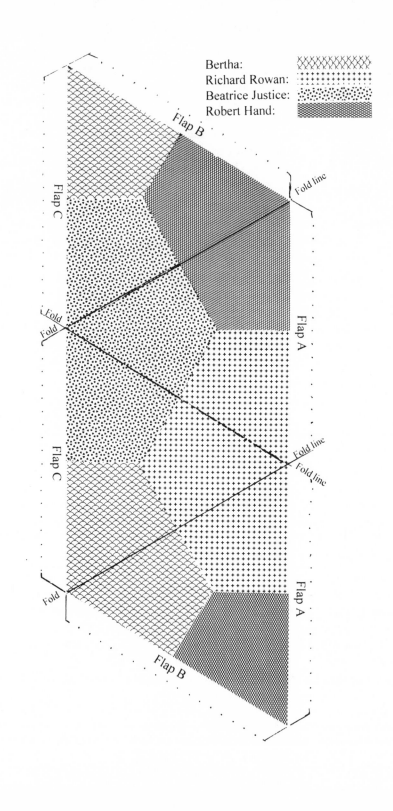

Bertha:
Richard Rowan:
Beatrice Justice:
Robert Hand:

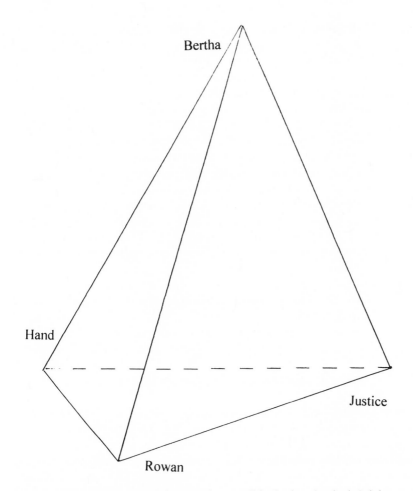

Bertha

Hand

Justice

Rowan

Figure 2 *(above)*. The tetrahedral pyramid as it will look when finished. Subdivisions on the flat sides have been omitted for clarity.

Figure 1 *(opposite)*. The Solid Geometry of *Exiles*. To construct the *Exiles* tetrahedral pyramid: 1. Photocopy figure 1, enlarging it if possible to fit legal-size paper. 2. Cut out the photocopy along the dotted lines, notching the edges at the points where the fold lines intersect. 3. Fold flaps A, B, and C back so they lie behind the parallelogram. 4. Fold the parallelogram backward along the three fold lines, to form four equilateral triangles. 5. As you bend the parallelogram backward on the fold lines, paste or staple the two flaps A together, and then the two flaps B. This will give you a paper tetrahedron with one open edge at flaps C. You may need to pull them outside to fasten them and close the pyramid. 6. Each point of the pyramid represents one character in *Exiles*. Each sharp edge of the figure represents a line of character doubling between the characters at opposite points of that edge. Each flat side of the figure represents one of the triangles of *Exiles*, where three characters interact.

Rowan/Bertha/Hand. The tangle of triangles in *Exiles* is, in a disorganized way, familiar to Joyce's readers. Dominating the play is the interrelationship of Richard Rowan, his mistress Bertha, and their mutual friend Robert Hand. On the surface this is a "conventional" struggle among husband, wife, and would-be lover. It is clear that Joyce also conceived this grouping as a linking of two men through their sexual experience with the same woman. This forms, from the same three characters, the first "intimated" triangle, hung like gauze or a scrim over the first, for Joyce is very delicate in his suggestion of homosexuality in the play. Though these first two triangles are composed of the same three characters they differ in their psychic energy and conflicts.

Rowan/Bertha/Justice. Another conventional triangle appears after the first: this time of a husband, wife, and the wicked other woman—if we apply those bourgeois titles to Rowan, Bertha, and Beatrice. This affair, lying mostly in Beatrice's yearnings and Bertha's suspicions, is nevertheless the source of tension for both women. Lacking intellectual endowments herself, Bertha has a powerful fear of the sexual attractiveness of Beatrice's intellect to the cerebrotonic Rowan. Conversely, Beatrice knows that whatever her intellectual attractions, her sexual endowments are inferior to Bertha's. Like our first triangle, this one also develops a shadow-self in the homosexual world, as Bertha and Beatrice, in act 3, begin to develop a friendship and a "glimmer of lesbianism" flickers on the stage. (*Exiles* 156) As before, the characters remain the same, but the emotional drama changes as the sexual nature changes.

Rowan/Justice/Hand. A subordinate triangle dates from nine years before the action of *Exiles*, when Robert Hand and Beatrice Justice were secretly engaged, thus frustrating Rowan's interest in Beatrice and hers in him. Richard and Beatrice have maintained contact, however; and, the engagement having quietly dried up without being broken, are renewing their acquaintanceship with (on her part at least) more than casual or intellectual interest.

Bertha/Justice/Hand. The final triangle, also quite conventional in terms of romance novels, is of two women (Bertha and Beatrice) pursued by the same suitor (Hand) who manages to betray both—Beatrice by his pursuit of Bertha, and Bertha by his denials to Rowan and (if we may believe Hand's story to Rowan) with the woman he picks up in a cab after the rendezvous at Ranelagh.

Those are the faces of the rigid tetrahedron—the most stable structural form and the first element in the "slowness" of *Exiles*. The second paralyzing element is Joyce's structure of the movement through duologues. Just as Buckminster Fuller chose the tetrahedron as the first structural element for his geodesic domes because the triangle could bear the greatest amount of tension along its edges,[5] so Joyce uses the tetrahedral edges to convey enormous tensions in the play.

154

II. The duologues

But Joyce disguises these edges by dividing the play into three acts that look "normal." If, however, we analyze the stage action in the play, we find a series of duologues. If two characters are on stage and a third enters, in most instances one of the previous pair exits almost at once. This can be seen most easily in a table of the "scenes" of *Exiles*. Of the play's 134 pages, only 17 present more than two characters; and of these, three seem insignificant to the play's action and characterization.

These duologues are Joyce's cue to the audience of *Exiles* that the play is dealing in pairs as well as in triangles. As Clive Hart pointed out in his excellent study, *Exiles* is built upon polarities that are reflected in repetitive dialogue. Hart identified "governing polarities" of "speech and silence, bondage and freedom, certainty and doubt" (125). To these we might add truth and falsehood, light and darkness, passion and intellect, courage and cowardice. Hart's analysis needs to be carried further. For at each end of each polarity in the play there is a double-image. Within the larger polarity of darkness and light, for example, both Beatrice and Robert represent darkness, while Bertha and Rowan represent light. Within the polarities of action and paralysis, it is Richard and Bertha who "do" things, Robert and Beatrice who remain paralyzed in Ireland. In the polarity of passion and intellect, Robert and Bertha represent warm passion, Richard and Beatrice cold intellect. But in this essay it is not the polarities of the play but the doubles of character we shall examine, with examples of their echolalia.

III. The tetrahedral edges and the doubles

Richard and Robert. The two males have alliterative given names, are both writers and intellectuals (though at differing levels) and university men. Each preaches freedom—Rowan of the spirit, Hand of the body. They shared a cottage at Ranelagh, have a shared pallid interest in Beatrice and a similar passion for Bertha. They also share a latent sexual interest in each other, unexpressed except for Richard's delicate remark to Bertha, "I cannot hate him since his arms have been around you" (96.3). Out of courtesy each held back, a decade earlier, in pursuing the other's woman friend; but each has been unfaithful to his fiancee/mistress, although they differ in that Rowan feels repentance for his carnal betrayal of Bertha (84.18–19, 88.28), while Hand concedes "no remorse of conscience" (48.29). They share one other important quality: both lie. Despite protestations of devotion to truth (Rowan at 84.14 and 87.20–21; Hand at 46.32, 139.7, .15), Hand repeatedly misrepresents his interest in Bertha (e.g., 75.5–6, 77.28–29), and Rowan lies to his son Archie about having Bertha's permission to accompany the milkman (71.11, .15) and incites a lie from Beatrice to cover his flight from an encounter with Hand (26.10).

Table 1
"Scene" sequence, *Exiles* (Penguin ed.)

Act no. and characters on stage	Page nos.
Act 1	
Brigid-BJ	13–14
BJ-RR	15–26
BJ-RH-Brigid	26–27 insignificant
BJ-RH	27–28
BJ-RH-A	28–30 kindness to Archie
BJ-RH-B-A	30–33 Beatrice lies; Robert speaks dismissively of her
RH-B	34–42
RH-B-RR	42 insignificant
RH-B	43
RH-B-RR	43 2 speeches show Hand's nerves
RH-RR	43–53
RH-RR-BJ-A-B	53–54 RH announces RR is coming home
RR-A	55–57
RR-B	57–70
RR-A	71
Act 2	
RH-RR	72–91
RR-B	91–96
B-RH	96–114
Act 3	
Brigid-B	115–117
Brigid-B-A	118–19 B wipes off A's smudges
Brigid-B	119–20
B-BJ	120–27
BJ-RR, w/Hand article	127–29 article constitutes 3rd voice
BJ-RR-B, w/Hand article	129 article is 4th voice
BJ-B	129–31
BJ-B-Brigid	131 B sends message to RH
BJ-B	131–32
B-RR	132–35
B-RH	135–38
B-RH-RR	138 insignificant
RH-RR-Fishwoman	139 significant mythic overtone
RH-RR	139–142
RR-RH-A	142–44
RR-RH-A-B, for 7 speeches	144 RH's "fairy godfather" speech
RR-B	144–47

Note: A = Archie, B = Bertha, BJ = Beatrice Justice, RH = Robert Hand, RR = Richard Rowan

Rowan and Hand share certain vocabulary and assertions within the play. Each urges others to "Believe me . . . Believe me" (Hand at 54.11 to Rowan; Rowan at 66.30 to Bertha). Rowan challenges Beatrice's and Bertha's courage (19.23, 65.20); Hand questions Rowan's courage (89.13–14). Both several times describe Hand as "common" (49.22–23, 63.30, 92.25, 107.19) and his wooing of Bertha as done "in the dark, secretly" (88.2–4, 89.13–14). Occasionally their echoic speech occurs with variations, as in the passage where Hand claims "the faith of a disciple in his master" (52.17–18) and Rowan turns the phrase to "the faith of a master in the disciple who will betray him" (52.26). The shift may be slighter but contradictory, as when Rowan answers Hand's "Then I am going" with his own peremptory "No. I am going" (90. 19–21). A similar echo occurs when to Hand's "Are you mad?," Rowan answers "Are you?" (74.6–8). Occasionally the variation is greater, as Hand's "our life-long friendship" (46.28) becomes Rowan's "Years, a whole life, of friendship" (77.10). The echo may be brief ("and I won." "Yes, you won" [47.25, .27]) or lengthy (Hand: "Is not this the language of your own youth?" Rowan: "Yes. It is the language of my youth" [89.29–35]). On occasion their common vocabulary is separated by many pages, as Rowan's "I have spoken always of my guilt" (88.28) repeats in Hand's "It was then that I was guilty" (109.22).

Bertha and Richard Rowan. Superficially these have less in common than Rowan and Hand, but they reflect similar values at a deeper level. They love each other deeply, even sacrificially. After nine years of life together they have a child whom they also love deeply. Both have the daring to be unconventional, to leave family and country to find something greater, to risk the opprobrium of returning with their bastard to parochial Ireland. They believe in sexual freedom for themselves and others, and act on that belief openly, knowing the risk. (Hand, by contrast, believes in sexual freedom but acts secretly.) They speak truth as they see it. As a result of their actions and others' reactions, both suffer deeply.

For this pair, too, the language supports the doubling of the characters. They are, for example, the only characters in the play who express fear on behalf of others (86.23, 87.5–13, 127.7) and anguish over their betrayal of another (86.30, 92.18). They repeat Richard's refusal to ask ("He refuses to ask me anything" 137.7; "Do not ask me, Bertha" 144.30), as well as his assertion of unknowingness ("But I will never know" 133.8; "He says he will never know" 137.7). They also make similar queries about belief: "What do you want me to believe?" (Bertha to Hand, 37.23) and "What then do you wish me to believe?" (Rowan to Hand, 141.24). Both parents are painfully aware of the contempt accorded Archie's bastard status in Ireland (24.26, 130.10–11), and, in their own relationship, of a degree of humility arising from personal shortcomings (88.8, .13; 133.5–6). Each urges the other to "believe me" (65.33, 66.30, 145.2), and fears blame (16.21–22, 70.24). Each, too, has a self-concept as a doer, one who acts, as Rowan asserts, "As I do, yes" (93.28), and Bertha reminds him, "I do things. But if I do one thing I can do two things" (95.15–16). In their passion and despair, both Rowan and Bertha become accusatory, denouncing the other for driving away friends and family (64.25, 129.26–27, 134.5–8). In their isolation, they also accuse others of hatred—Bertha expecting both Hand and Justice to be guilty of that wretched emotion, Rowan attributing it to Bertha's attitude toward Justice (97.21, 125.30, 126.31, 134.8).

Even when passions are cooler, however, Rowan and Bertha speak alike. Each offers the same "why not" to Hand's delicate query as to whether he may use Bertha's given name (51.32, 36.27). In a matter-of-fact tone each describes Rowan's dominating knowledge, Richard with a confident "He had no secrets from me" (20.23–24) and Bertha twice in "I could not keep things secret from Dick" (103.17–18) and "I could not deceive Dick. Never. In nothing" (103.5). Each adopts the instructional mode, Rowan to explain to Archie ("Do you understand what it is to give a thing?" 56.8) and Bertha to Beatrice ("You know what it means to hate a person?" 126.2). Amid the play's talk of nature and natural law, both Bertha and Rowan manage an ironic "naturally" (93.32, 122.15) before the action ends. More important than the rest, perhaps, is the suffering that pairs Rowan and Bertha, from his act 1 comment to Beatrice Justice, "O, if you knew how I am suffering at this moment" (22.26–27) to Bertha's cry, also to Beatrice, in act 3: "I am in such suffering" (130.26).

Bertha and Robert Hand. Strong as the connection is between Bertha and Richard, she is even closer in character and speech to his friend. Bertha and Robert are indeed so close in nature that Joyce has buried Bertha's name within Hand's: roBERT HAnd.[6] Among the four characters, this physical pair is somewhat more fleshy. Hand is described as "stout" (26.25), Bertha as "graceful" (30.10) but not, like Beatrice, "slender" (13.24). They are less intellectual than their opposites, creatures of passion, of nature rather than mind. Bertha's passion led her to follow Rowan into exile, giving up "everything for him—religion, family, my own peace" (129.26–27). Hand's passion leads him to invite the exiles back to Ireland and then to attempt betrayal of his lifelong friend by wooing Bertha right in Rowan's home. Perhaps because they are aware that they are sometimes foolhardy, each expresses fear. Yet each is extremely close to Rowan, so much so that each describes to Rowan lovemaking with another—Hand his kissing and secret engagement with Beatrice nine years ago (20.23–24; 20.31–32); Bertha, Hand's present advances to her (57.24–63.23). And they have a kind of humanity lacking in the others, for each is able to speak with Archie about a child's interests—swimming or the milkman's horse—whereas Rowan lectures Archie on the abstract concepts of giving and keeping, and Beatrice gives him piano lessons.

Robert and Bertha have less certitude than Richard has shown, which is why both say "I am afraid" (40.17; 97.10, .15, .23; 98.31; 101.20; 102.17). They also show their uncertainty in their dependence, to a degree, on what Rowan allows: Hand asks of Rowan, "Do you allow me?" in act 1, and "You allow me then?" in act 2 (51.29, 90.10). Bertha reminds Richard "you allowed me to go on" (59.24), and is reminded by him in return "I allowed you complete liberty—and allow you it still" (65.27–28). A similar uncertainty is displayed in their "Do you believe me" question—from Hand to Rowan (138.26, 139.15) and from Bertha to Rowan (144.27). This interrogative mode contrasts with the imperative "believe me" shared by Rowan and Bertha.

Both Bertha and Robert like to speak of what's natural (49.2, 64.28, 65.1–3), think the stone is beautiful (50.5, 50.8), and perceive an honesty in Hand (67.28, 83.6). In the best moments of their flirtation, both admit to physical excitement (60.30, 61.4–5), and both refer to the events in the cottage at Ranelagh as a "dream" (138.2, .5, .10).

There is a negative side to their flirtation as well. Each accuses the other of cruelty (98.22, 137.2); feels a fool (74.19, 92.18, 94.23) and indeed is called a fool by Rowan (63.30, 64.5, 93.23). Each likewise feels others have cause for hatred; Hand feels Richard will "hate me now for what I have done" (76.1) at the same time that Bertha fears Hand "hates me" (92.17, 93.1) and even asks him, "Do you hate me now?" (97.21). She also assumes Beatrice hates her (125.30). Both have endured being left alone by Rowan, for Robert recalls for Bertha that "you and he went away for your walk and I went along the street alone" (109.17),[7] just as she tells Richard that when he went walking in the rain in Rome, "I was alone, Dick, forgotten by you and by all" (145.27). It is perhaps this loneliness and poor sense of self that leads each to urge, "Listen" (103.4, 113.6); to exclaim "Tell me," as if being left out (70.20, 99.16); to ask "Do you believe" of Rowan (138.26, 139.15, 144.27).

Sometimes Bertha and Robert duplicate each other's language in a different tone. Both assure Richard "I will tell you the truth" (133.10, 139.7), and Robert emphasizes "I will tell you the whole truth" (46.32). Bertha's truth, however, rings true; whereas Robert's "whole truth" seems more false than his plain truth later. Likewise, when Robert avers "My life is finished—over" (40.31) after Bertha's kiss, we receive it as a melodramatic falsehood. Yet when Bertha tells Richard that, alone in Rome, she "felt my life was ended" (145.27), we accept it as a sincere portrayal of true feelings.

Even when they disagree, Bertha and Hand tend to echo each other. Each has a concept of love related to "nature," for instance, but Hand means sexual passion, whereas Bertha refers to the mother-child bond (49.2, 64.28, 65.1–3). Likewise, though Hand refers to Richard's love for Bertha, and whereas Bertha refers to Richard's presumed love for Beatrice, each tells Rowan he loves a woman ("You love her," 67.6; "You love this woman," 78.28). Most significantly, after Robert has twice compared a woman to a stone in his discourse with Richard (49.9, 49.13), Bertha (who has not heard his remark) demands of Beatrice "Do you think I am a stone?" (130.11).

Richard Rowan and Beatrice Justice are the intellectual pair, bookish, interested in writing (he writes, she reads it), and appear to be what psychologist William Sheldon termed *ectomorphs*—people living at the ends of their nerves. She is "slender." He is "tall." Each has an inner pride (though Beatrice admits her pride was joined with "loneliness" [19.27]). Despite their pride and their high ideals, both lie—he to Archie, as already noted, Beatrice at Rowan's behest, when she tells Hand, "He is gone to the post with some letters" (29.31) after Rowan has expressed his aversion to meeting Hand. Beatrice lies once more when she tells Bertha, "I just came for Archie's lesson" (31.17), though she has already admitted to Rowan that she has really come to see him.

As we would expect, Beatrice often speaks as Richard's echo. Rowan first uses "know" in the sense of understanding another person, after which Beatrice replies "It is hard to know anyone but oneself" (18.24). Richard first suggests that the reason Beatrice visits their house is "to give Archie lessons" (17.28), a line she echoes at 31.17. Likewise he first mentions his mother's "hardness of heart" (22.29) before Beatrice echoes the phrase three pages later (25.18). Richard first denies hatred to Robert (76.04) before Beatrice denies hating Bertha (126.05). Rowan has to repeat the most cruel line before Beatrice can say it even once, as he twice points out her inability to "give yourself freely and wholly" (22.8, 22.15), a gift she describes as "a terribly hard thing to do" (22.18).

Surprisingly, however, Richard echoes her almost as often as Beatrice echoes him. The lines Rowan repeats from Beatrice are equally important to the play. It is she, early in act 1, who refuses him: "I will not ask you" (17.7). At the end of act 3, it is Rowan who refuses to ask Bertha—not outright, but by implication:

Bertha
I will tell you if you ask me.

Richard
You will tell me. But I will never know. Never in this world.

(133.5–8)

In thus refusing to ask, Richard is also now echoing Beatrice's idea that it is hard—even impossible—to know another person or that person's actions. Another repetition is the "believe me" used by Beatrice to Richard early in act 1 and repeated by him to Bertha in act 2 (25.6, 65.33, 66.30), just as Beatrice's "you are free" to Richard (24.33) becomes his "You are free" to Bertha (70.26).

Some of the echoes of this pair are repeated for emphasis. As Richard repeats "You cannot give yourself freely and wholly," so Beatrice's explanation of her true reason for visiting the Rowans is spoken twice to Richard—in act 1

160

by Beatrice before he repeats it, and in act 3 by the noises on the strand, before he again repeats the line to her (18.8–11, 128.2).

Bertha and Beatrice, like Robert and Richard, have alliterative names and share the same sex. The two women also share their love for Rowan, their concern for Archie, and their rather tentative involvement with Hand. Their mutual affection for Rowan has led them to a mutual waiting—Beatrice for nine years in Ireland, hoping he would come back (while she urged her cousin to urge him to return); Bertha in Rome, while Rowan wandered in the rain and she, alone and lonely, waited with Archie for him. In a sense, she is waiting for him throughout the play—to leave his study and return to her bed; to tell her what to do about Hand; to become again "my strange wild lover" and "come back to me again" (147.18–19). By the end of *Exiles* the two women declare their friendship.

Echoic language links Bertha to Beatrice less strongly than to either Rowan or Hand, partly because Beatrice has so much less to say within the play. The correspondences are nevertheless close. Beatrice expresses early in act 1 the independence that "cannot say it. You yourself must ask me, Mr Rowan" (19.09). Bertha restates the position for herself in act 3: "I will tell you if you ask me" (133.6).[8] Each has a similar emotion when left by Rowan—Beatrice a "loneliness" in her heart when he leaves Ireland, Bertha that she was "sad" and "alone" when he went walking in Rome. From that loneliness comes the importuning of each woman for Rowan to "come back" (Beatrice at 123.30 and 124.3; Bertha at 124.17, .23—of his "coming back" to Ireland—and 145.8, 147.18–19—of his return, as lover, to her).

Given their shared loneliness, their resistance to being subjected to Rowan's inquisitions, and their sense of abandonment by all, it is unremarkable that both women lack peace, as Rowan points out to Beatrice (22.2) and Bertha says, again to Beatrice, of her sacrifices (129.26–27).

Beatrice Justice and Robert Hand are linked, first of all, by their cousinship. They share a pale, stale romance—a nine-year engagement that has seemingly been so lacking in interest to either of them that it is not even worth breaking off. Both are dark in coloring, emphasized by their dress—he in dark blue, dark green, and dark brown successively; she in dark blue with a black hat. Each has enough intellectualism to appreciate Richard Rowan's mind, though neither can match that mind in creativity or daring. After Rowan and Bertha flee Ireland, both Justice and Hand feel loneliness. Both urge Rowan's return for intellectual and personal reasons, and after the return, both are "intimate" in the house. Each of them is in love with at least one of the Rowans—perhaps with both.

Beatrice and her fiancé—or ex-fiancé—are linked early in the play by their lack of linguistic daring. Neither Beatrice speaking to Rowan (19.9, 19.18) nor Hand speaking to Bertha (34.7) "dares" to speak from the heart. In act 3 Hand once more echoes Beatrice, this time with "I cannot tell him" (137.19) to her "I cannot say it" (19.9).

If Beatrice cannot always say it, sometimes Hand has said it for her: he has described their betrothal kiss to Rowan (20.31–33), ungentlemanly behavior for which he is justly rewarded when Bertha describes Robert's kiss to Richard (59.33–60.31).

Robert's repetitions are occasionally quite innocent, as when he repeats Beatrice's white lie that Richard "is only gone to the post" (29.31, 30.2–3). Sometimes, however, Robert's echo of Beatrice adds an innuendo typical of his "common" character, as when she remarks of her travels that "my movements are not very interesting," and he replies suggestively, "A lady's movements are always interesting" (31.11–13). His heavy gallantry is probably painful for Beatrice, since her movements have, in fact, not been interesting enough to either Rowan or Hand for her emotional life to prosper. Finally, sometimes Robert and Beatrice are joined by another person's repeated speech, as when Bertha tells first Robert (101.24–25) and then Beatrice (122.26), "My nerves are all upset."

Summary

The tetrahedral structure and the six pairs of doubles in *Exiles* help explain both our dissatisfaction with the perceived slowness of the play and Joyce's insistence that it is a comedy. The triangles, coupled with the tensions of the doubled and redoubled characters and the echoic speech, make not for the usual passion of domestic infidelity but for a play with relatively little movement and a great deal of discussion. Moreover, the duplication of vocabulary deprives us of a delight all experienced Joyceans look forward to—the play of language, of inventive, original, witty diction that almost no other writer provides. Instead, Joyce gives us a relative verbal poverty.

Within that poverty, he *is* being playful, shifting a phrase from one character to another, sounding a series of motifs "sung" first by one character, then by another, in almost operatic fashion. Joyce also uses the repetitive language to provide a succession of mirrors reflecting doubles who are, nevertheless, not identical twins. In his own mind, Joyce was experimenting with the concepts of shifting, slippery counterparts that he would develop more fully in *Finnegans Wake*. By the time he wrote *Exiles* he had already established a world in which "everybody is somebody else."

NOTES

1. All references to the text of *Exiles* are to the Penguin edition as corrected in John MacNicholas, *James Joyce's "Exiles": A Textual Companion*. The play is cited in the text by page/line numbers in parentheses.

2. Glasheen, s.v. "Rowan, Richard."

3. When I asked afterward why she omitted *Exiles* from her discussion, French replied that she had read the play only once, hurriedly, and disliked it.

4. For a brief summary of reactions to *Exiles* see Ruth Bauerle, "Bertha's Role in *Exiles*," 108, 128–29 nn. 1–3.

5. R. Buckminster Fuller (1892–1983), was as innovative in the field of architecture as Joyce was in the field of literature. In his lectures at North Carolina State University in 1949–53, Fuller described his search for the architectural form to replace post-and-lintel construction—a form that would extend the tension-carrying ability of the structure to infinity and reduce the weight and compression factors as far as possible. His solution was the geodesic structure, of which the regular tetrahedron was one basic element.

6. Cf. Molly Bloom's comment in *Ulysses*, "whats the idea making us like that with a big hole in the middle of us" (*U-G* 18:151).

7. This sentence of Hand's seems an early version of the final sentence of *Finnegans Wake:* "away . . . along . . . alone" will become "A way a lone a last a loved a long the."

8. As Hart points out, Beatrice and Bertha are alike in rejecting language as well as inviting it (123, 125). Bertha admonishes Robert, "O don't speak like that now" (41.2), just as Beatrice has warned Richard, "O, do not speak like that!" (24.13).

WORKS CITED

Bauerle, Ruth. "Bertha's Role in *Exiles*." In *Women in Joyce*, ed. Suzette Henke and Elaine Unkeless. Urbana: University of Illinois Press, 1982.

———. *A Word List to Joyce's "Exiles."* New York: Garland Publishing, 1981.

Glasheen, Adaline. *A Second Census to "Finnegans Wake."* Evanston, Ill.: Northwestern University Press, 1963.

Hart, Clive. "The Language of *Exiles*." In *Coping with Joyce: Essays from the Copenhagen Symposium*, ed. Morris Beja and Shari Benstock. Columbus: Ohio State University Press, 1989.

Joyce, James. *Exiles*. New York and Harmondsworth: Penguin Books, 1973.

MacNicholas, John. *James Joyce's "Exiles": A Textual Companion*. New York: Garland Publishing, 1979.

The Wandering Gentile: Joyce's Emotional Odyssey in *Pomes Penyeach*

Adriaan van der Weel and Ruud Hisgen

The biographical links of the *Pomes Penyeach* have been documented and commented on by many critics. "Watching the Needleboats at San Sabba" was inspired by a rowing event in which Joyce watched his brother Stanislaus perform; "A Flower Given to My Daughter" is connected with the "affair" (whatever its nature) between Joyce and his pupil Amalia Popper; for "She Weeps over Rahoon" Joyce draws on a visit to the grave of Nora's childhood love Michael Bodkin; "On the Beach at Fontana" expresses Joyce's fatherly love for Giorgio; "Simples" was originally addressed to Lucia, who is the child of the poem; "Alone" recalls Joyce's evening walks along Lake Zurich; "A Memory of the Players at Midnight" uses Joyce's involvement in a performance by the English Players of a Browning play; "Bahnhofstrasse" describes Joyce's agony at a bad attack of glaucoma; "A Prayer" is obviously addressed to Nora, echoing in tone and subject matter the letters he wrote to her from Ireland in the course of 1909 (SL 157–95).

The only monograph on Joyce's poetry, Selwyn Jackson's *The Poems of James Joyce and the Use of Poems in His Novels,* also notices this biographical thread. Jackson writes: "It is characteristic of most of [the poems] that they describe personal feelings and stem from situations in Joyce's life that produced strong emotions in him" (15–16). But then he goes on to say that "in contrast to *Chamber Music* the poems in *Pomes Penyeach* are not in any sense a group or cycle. They are not united by a common theme or by a shared artistic purpose. They are simply the product of Joyce's spasmodic excursions into lyric poetry over a period of about twenty years" (16).

If one came to the poems without a knowledge of the life or the other work one would probably be very hard put to discover any such "shared artistic purpose." In fact, if one came to the poems without such knowledge one might not be inclined to spend a great deal of time on them at all, for they are not great poems, though some are quite interesting. As early as 1927 AE wrote in a review of *Pomes Penyeach*: "The book will have for many readers perhaps a greater psychological than poetic interest" (*Irish Statesman*, 23 July 1927; repr. in Deming 349). This appears to be precisely the situation today. However, we also know that "with Joyce all is intentional, premeditated, allegorical and—in the noble sense—calculated," as Marcel Brion wrote in another review of *Pomes Penyeach*, also from 1927 (*Les Nouvelles littéraires*, 15 October 1927; repr. in Deming 350). Unfortunately he fails to specify the way in which he suspected *Pomes Penyeach* to be intentional, premeditated or allegorical.

We should like to suggest that *Pomes Penyeach* is at least as intentional, premeditated, or allegorical as *Chamber Music*, and we should like to call *Pomes Penyeach* an odyssey of Joyce's emotional life. That is to say that Joyce's larger artistic purpose is to be found precisely in the emotional thread that runs through them. *Pomes Penyeach* is central to the personal myth that Joyce is devoted to creating—what Robert Adams Day has called "James Joyce as Everyman."

By the time he begins to write the first of the *Pomes Penyeach* in 1913,[1] Joyce has come to regard himself as a prose writer. He has not written any verse for some nine years, in fact since completing *Chamber Music* in 1904, with the sole exception of the broadside "Gas from a Burner" and possibly the poem that begins "The Flower I Gave Rejected Lies" (*Poems and Shorter Writings* 114). He has completed *Dubliners*, has almost finished reworking *Stephen Hero* as *A Portrait*, and is about to begin work on *Ulysses*. So Joyce's return to verse comes after a nine-year poetic silence. It also comes as somewhat of a surprise, after repeated disparaging comments he has made on his own earlier verse of *Chamber Music*. In one letter to Stanislaus he calls the verse "poor and trivial" (*SL* 121); in another he simply writes "I don't like the book" (*SL* 153). He also makes various statements to the effect that he will give up writing verse altogether, again to Stanislaus, who records them in *My Brother's Keeper* (247–49); in a letter to Stanislaus of December 1904 (*SL* 48); and in a letter to Molyneux Palmer of July 1909 (*SL* 155).

There are many reasons of course for his negative feelings about the verse he has produced so far. Frustrated desire underlies all of *Chamber Music*, a great but as yet unfulfilled longing for love, as *Stephen Hero* and *A Portrait* amply testify. But in 1904 real life intrudes. Nora in the flesh shows him to what extent *Chamber Music* was "a young man's book" (*SL* 153). He realizes that its verse is not "true," in the sense that it treats of a love that he did not actually experience. To Stanislaus he admitted as much: "It is not a book of love verses at all, I perceive" (*SL* 153)—a damning thing to say about verses that talk of nothing but love. But what Joyce meant was that they are based on nothing more than an imagined experience of love. In this regard one might call *Chamber Music* "A Portrait of the Young Man as an Aspiring Lover."

Incidentally, what lasting value and significance the *Chamber Music* verse had for Joyce it acquired long after its composition and even its publication, and probably unexpectedly. The cause was the crisis between Joyce and Nora in 1909. In the process of atoning for his false accusation of faithlessness Joyce almost convinced himself that he had actually written *Chamber Music* for Nora:

> When I wrote them I was a strange lonely boy, walking about by myself at night and thinking that some day a girl would love me. But I never could speak to the girls I used to meet at houses. Their false manners checked me at once. Then you came to me. You were not in a sense the girl for whom I had dreamed and written the verses which you find now so enchanting. She was perhaps (as I saw her in my imagination) a girl fashioned into a curious grave beauty by the culture of generations before her, the woman for whom I wrote poems like "Gentle lady" or "Thou leanest to the shell of night." But then I saw that the beauty of your soul outshone that of my verses. There was something in you higher than anything I had put into them. And so for this reason the book of verses is for you. It holds the desire of my youth and you, darling, were the fulfillment of that desire. (*SL* 161)

The fact that Nora found *Chamber Music* "so enchanting" gave the poems a new significance for Joyce and invested them with the emotional depth they originally lacked. *Chamber Music* always remained the one work by Joyce that Nora had actually read and approved of. The manuscript copy on parchment that Joyce made for her in that turbulent year became a material symbol of their love. It is questionable whether Joyce would have reprinted *Chamber Music* in his *Collected Poems* if it had not been for this unexpected new lease of life.

By the time he begins to write the *Pomes Penyeach* verses Joyce has said disparaging things about writing verse in his fiction, too. As early as 1904 he had written in *Stephen Hero* that Stephen's style was "over affectionate towards the antique and even the obsolete and too easily rhetorical" (27). In 1906 he wrote "A Little Cloud," in which he severely satirizes a character's poetic aspirations. Richard Ellmann does not think there is any reason to believe that Little Chandler owes anything to Joyce (*JJII* 220n). But what Joyce mocks in Little Chandler is precisely the sort of unfocused lyricism that pervades *Chamber Music*: "Could he write something original? He was not sure what idea he wished to express, but the thought that a poetic moment had touched him took life within him like an infant hope" (*D69* 73).[2] In 1913 Joyce is working on *A Portrait*, in which he mocks the verse-writing activities of his younger alter ego Stephen, especially the very tenuous connection between the emotions expressed in the verse and the experience on which it is supposed to be based (e.g., *P64* 71). One year later, in 1914, he begins *Ulysses*, in which we find Stephen still reeling from the crash of his fall back to earth after the unsuccessful attempt at flight in *A Portrait,* and writing a poem that is a direct imitation of one of Douglas Hyde's *Love Songs of Connacht.*[3] So in as far as Stephen is Joyce, we find Joyce mocking the derivative and untruthful nature of his own early verse in his fiction too.

If we add to this catalogue of Joyce's reservations about his youthful lyrics the remark to Stanislaus that a page of "A Little Cloud" gives him more pleasure than all his verses (*SL* 121)—and surely it is no coincidence that he chooses precisely this story to contrast with his verse—we cannot help concluding that Joyce no longer held his verse in quite the same esteem he did before 1904. The most positive assessment of *Chamber Music* Joyce can muster is that its verses "are not pretentious and have a certain grace" (*SL* 153) and even then he says this only because he feels that he has just attacked them a little too viciously.

In these circumstances it is surprising to find Joyce returning to poetry in 1913, especially since the first poems he writes breathe exactly the same archaic, Shelleyan, and Swinburnian atmosphere as the *Chamber Music* lyrics. Take for example:

> O hearts, O sighing grasses,
> Vainly your loveblown bannerets mourn!
> No more will the wild wind that passes
> Return, no more return.

Consciously or not, in these lines Joyce echoes Shelley's "A Lament": "When will return the glory of your prime? / No more—Oh, never more!" Or take such lines as

> Frail the white rose and frail are
> Her hands that gave
> Whose soul is sere and paler
> Than time's wan wave,

which eminently justify Ezra Pound's verdict that the verses were not worth printing: "They belong in the Bible or in the family album with the portraits" (*JJII* 591).

But whatever the similarities with *Chamber Music, Pomes Penyeach* shows a departure from the *Chamber Music* mode in at least one major respect. Joyce's main criticism of *Chamber Music* appears to be that his verse is not "true," in the sense that it is not based on feelings he had personally experienced. This, as we have seen, is obviously not true of *Pomes Penyeach,* with its strong autobiographical elements. However, though it is based on Joyce's personal experience, it is a heavily fictionalized version, with some aspects dramatized to receive greater weight and others expurgated for public consumption. The overall effect he is at pains to achieve is clearly to present an image of a complete and a good man—Joyce's odyssey is no less mythical than Homer's. Without study-ing the poems in great detail, we might still look at some of the ways in which *Pomes Penyeach* can be regarded as Joyce's personal emotional odyssey.

Like *Chamber Music*, *Pomes Penyeach* deals almost exclusively with love, though in a great many more guises. Its main concern is probably the chang-ing place of love and passion in a man's life as he grows older. The direct cause of Joyce's return to verse is the emotional upheaval that results from his infat-uation with Amalia Popper, which occurred in the period of roughly 1911–13. The bulk of the poems were written between 1913 and 1918 and thus cover the five-year period after the affair with Popper.

Disregarding for the time being "Tilly," which in its original form dates from 1903–4, the first poem Joyce wrote after his long silence was "Watching the Needleboats at San Sabba," in September 1913.[4] It is a poem about the end of passion: "No more will the wild wind that passes / Return, no more re-turn." The date places it shortly after the end of the affair with Popper, and it should obviously be read against that background. The affair has impressed on Joyce the inexorability of the aging process, and he is preoccupied with the consequences of that process for a man's emotional life. "Their young hearts" are the hearts of the rowers, who are young enough to have yet to experience love and passion. Though Joyce was not yet very old—barely over thirty[5]—he regarded himself as mature, however hard he found it in many ways to accept the consequences of that fact. In *Exiles* he has Bertha remark that "that time [of the passion of courtship] comes only once in a lifetime. The rest of life is good for nothing except to remember that time" (115/129/232).[6]

Many of the poems that follow return to this preoccupation with the con-sequences of aging. But there are other emotions. "A Flower Given to My Daughter" celebrates the mystery of a young girl's innocence. We know from *Giacomo Joyce* that the giver of the rose is Amalia Popper (GJ 3). If the poem remembers Popper's hands as "Rosefrail and fair," it describes her soul in con-siderably less flattering language. It is "sere and paler / Than time's wan wave." But ultimately Popper is hardly important to the poem. She all but disappears even in the passive voice of the title. More than anything the poem is an ex-pression of love for Joyce's daughter, Lucia:

> . . . —yet frailest
> A wonder wild
> In gentle eyes thou veilest,
> My blueveined child.

Joyce's summary dismissal of Popper strikes one as a rather sharp contrast with the mood of sentimental indulgence that characterizes *Giacomo Joyce*. If Ell-mann is right about the date of *Giacomo Joyce* (GJ x–xii), it was written at about the same time as the poem. The most likely explanation for the differ-ence is that the poem was written for publication whereas *Giacomo Joyce* was

not. Joyce could hardly recount in public his tender feelings for a young student in an affair that he was keeping a secret from the world. We always have
to remind ourselves that *Giacomo Joyce*, like, for example, the letters, which
we now regard as a natural part of Joyce's writings, did not belong to what he
himself regarded as his oeuvre.

"She Weeps over Rahoon" and "Tutto è Sciolto" were both inspired by
Joyce's visit to Oughterard and Rahoon in 1912.[7] The speaker in "She Weeps
over Rahoon" is a woman talking to her beloved about her dead lover, musing
that one day they too will be dead and buried. That the woman is Nora, the
dead lover Michael Bodkin, and the beloved James Joyce, there is no doubt.[8]
Joyce's jealousy of Bodkin is well documented, for example by Ellmann, but
also in Joyce's own fiction (cf. the notes for *Exiles* and the character of Gabriel
in "The Dead"). With almost masochistic perversion Joyce has Nora speak of
her "dark lover," the very words Joyce would have feared most to hear from her
mouth. The way to transcend this jealousy is to think of human love sub
specie aeternitatis, as he has Nora remind him. The poem's final impact is that
of a forceful memento mori, expressing Joyce's overriding concern with aging,
especially where the experience of love is concerned.

"Tutto è Sciolto" ("All Is Lost") is a companion piece to "She Weeps over
Rahoon." The place is again the west of Ireland (the same landscape, both
real and imagined, as evoked at the end of "The Dead"); the time, dusk; the
theme, the transience of love; the form, dramatic monologue. The title derives from the aria of that name in Bellini's *La sonnambula*, which also plays
an important part in *Ulysses*. For Joyce the central lines of the aria were:

All is lost now,
By all hope and joy am I forsaken,
Nevermore can love awaken
Past enchantment, no nevermore.[9]

In the "Sirens" episode the song is associated with Bloom's unhappiness about
the lost love between him and Molly, symbolized by her affair with Boylan. In
the poem there is a similar triangle. This time the voice is that of Joyce himself, addressing Michael Bodkin on the subject of his love for Nora. The
speaker has by now (Joyce has dated the poem a year later) transcended his
jealousy and writes from a sense of sympathy with that man, almost a boy, who
died for love. "Why then, remembering those shy / Sweet lures, repine" refers
to "his sad voice . . . ever calling" from Nora's poem. Joyce imagines Bodkin
remembering "love's time," and especially the "shy / Sweet lures" of the girl—
Nora—who was the object of that love:

The clear young eyes' soft look, the candid brow,
The fragrant hair,
Falling as through the silence falleth now
Dusk of the air.

The dusk falling from the air, of course, recalls Joyce's play—in chapter 5 of *A Portrait* (which dates from the same time)—with the line "Brightness falls from the air" from Nashe's contemplation of man's tenuous hold on life in his "Litany in Time of Plague." In Joyce's poem the phrase describes the scene for the character's musings, telling once again of his preoccupation with the onset of dark old age.

"On the Beach at Fontana" and "Simples" form another pair, expressing Joyce's parental love, tinged with anxiety, for Giorgio and Lucia respectively. The storm that rages in "On the Beach at Fontana" arouses Joyce's instinctive urge to protect his son from the powerful forces of nature that threaten to batter and buffet him as they have Joyce. "Simples," originally addressed to Lucia, breathes an atmosphere of magic, even ritual. It speaks of the poet's fear of his innocent young daughter growing into a woman under the influence of the moon. In Joyce's writings many references can be found to the power he attributes to the moon and its connection with woman. In "Ithaca," for example, Bloom perceives a long list of similarities between woman and the moon, such as: "her potency over effluent and refluent waters: her power to enamour, to mortify, to invest with beauty, to render insane" (*U-GP* 17.1163–65).

In *Chamber Music*, after number 11 has urged the beloved to "Bid adieu to girlish days," number 12 asks her what counsel the hooded moon has put in her heart. In the notes to *Exiles*, Joyce quotes a description of menstrual flow by Alfredo Oriana in *La rivolta ideale*: "*la malattia sacra che in un rituo lunare prepara la donna per il sacrificio*" [The sacred malady which, in a lunar rhythm, prepares a woman for the sacrifice] (147/163/343). The girl in "Simples" thus receives her initiation from the moon, a first step toward dark consciousness of her instincts and loss of innocence. Incidentally, the device used by the character is the same one Odysseus employs to shield his crew from the lures of the Sirens:

Be mine, I pray, a waxen ear
To shield me from her childish croon
And mine a shielded heart for her
Who gathers simples of the moon.

"The sated flood" swaying "the rockvine clusters" in "Flood" continues Joyce's contemplation of the moon's power. Like the moon, the movements of tide and waves that it causes form a powerful and inescapable natural force. The same theme returns in the "Proteus" episode of *Ulysses*, where the rock vine clusters ("weeds") are even more passive: "Under the upswelling tide he saw the writhing weeds lift languidly and sway reluctant arms, hising up their petticoats, in whispering water swaying and upturning coy silver fronds. Day by day: night by night: lifted, flooded and let fall" (*U* 49). As "Telemachus" and "Proteus" amply make clear, the sea with its tides and floods represents to Joyce an intractable force, at the same time to be feared and revered. "Love's full flood" is the force of life itself (the "grey sweet mother" of "Telemachus"), but like the anima within us it is an irrational force that cannot be checked or controlled by the (day)light of reason.[10] The poem enjoins the golden vine to let its clustered fruits participate in the full experience of life's passion—"love's full flood" in this poem, or the "flood of passion" in *Exiles* (111/125/228)—observed with disdain by the brooding angel of melancholy from Dürer's engraving and Milton's "L'Allegro" and "Il Penseroso."[11]

"Nightpiece" is associated in language with *Giacomo Joyce* (and thus Amalia Popper; see *GJ* 10) and Stephen's "Villanelle of the Temptress" in *A Portrait* (and thus Emma Clery). Both women are, in Joyce's view, temptresses, representing a frigid, almost sterile form of love: they attract men with their superficial beauty and feminity but are incapable of true female love. Where Popper is concerned, Joyce has already hinted at this in "A Flower Given to My Daughter" in his description of her as a girl "Whose soul is sere and paler / Than time's wan wave." The agent in "Nightpiece" is a woman who enlists the seraphim (who have fallen for her in Stephen's villanelle) to perform the task of awaking the lost hosts to her service—a service of adoration of herself. With the words "bleak," "void," and "waste" Joyce indicates the barrenness of this nocturnal travesty of love. The poem is the counterpart of "Flood" with its celebration of love's full flood.

"Alone" is a fantasy about a possibly imaginary other woman in the most vague and veiled terms. At the time of writing Joyce has not yet met Martha Fleischmann, but the theme fits the period of Joyce's life. As he confided to Frank Budgen, he felt that as an artist he had a need for the experience of an extramarital affair. The mere whisper of a female name is enough to cause a "swoon of shame" in the poet's soul: innocuous enough as a sexual fantasy.

In "A Memory of the Players in a Mirror at Midnight" and "Bahnhofstrasse," Joyce returns to his preoccupation—amounting almost to an obsession—with the aging process. The fear of physical as well as emotional aging is powerfully present in "A Memory of the Players in a Mirror at Midnight." The speaker in "A Memory" comments dejectedly on the gaunt and gray face he sees in a mirror, unfit for kissing. "The players" from the title are the English Players at Zurich founded by Joyce and Claud Sykes; the occasion was their performance of Browning's *In a Balcony*. The play's theme is precisely that of (physical) love belonging to youth. Joyce obviously compares his own experience with that of the Queen who, no longer young and beautiful, is painfully excluded from the domain of love. For one hopeful moment she thinks that Norbert has declared his love for her—that she is not too old after all and that she was wrong to believe the conventional view:

Men say—or do men say it? fancies say—
"Stop here, your life is set, you are grown old.
"Too late—no love for you, too late for love—
"Leave love to girls. Be queen: let Constance love." (365)

But her hope is presently dashed. Not only is old age unfit for love, it is envious of younger people's love.

In "Bahnhofstrasse" eye trouble again leads to a contemplation of the irreversibility of aging: "Highhearted youth comes not again," the speaker sighs, echoing Jan Pieterszoon. Sweelinck's "Mein junges Leben hat ein End." The personal significance to Joyce of the Sweelinck song is clear from its appearance in a key passage of *Giacomo Joyce*; it also occurs in Bloom's thoughts in the "Eumaeus" episode of *Ulysses* (see *GJ* 16 and xxvi n). Joyce wrote the poem shortly after he had experienced a bad attack of glaucoma in the Bahnhofstrasse (*JJII* 450), and he must have experienced it as objective confirmation of his notion of physical decline. What would have made the experience even more acute was yet another abortive illicit affair, this time with Martha Fleischmann.

That the poems cover exactly a twenty-year period, from 1904 to 1924, corresponding to the length of time Odysseus was away from home, may or may not be relevant. What is relevant is that Joyce appended the place of composition to each poem, evidence of his physical odyssey during those twenty years, from Dublin to Trieste to Zurich to Paris. Also, the bulk of *Pomes Penyeach* was written at the same time that Joyce was writing *Ulysses*, and Frank Budgen records Joyce's fascination with Odysseus, whom he admired as a complete all-round character (15–18). In the same way that he models Bloom on Odysseus, Joyce models himself on Odysseus in *Pomes Penyeach*. The collection presents Joyce as a son, father, husband, and lover, just as he perceived Odysseus.[12]

Unlike the poet of *Chamber Music*, the poet of *Pomes Penyeach* has lived, even if it has not been a spectacular life. His emotions are overridingly those of the fear and pain that every human being experiences. The resulting image is a tame, not to say bourgeois, version of a hero's life. Joyce's self-censorship in the Popper affair does not help (and leads one to surmise that he may have been reticent in other matters too). He has Robert in *Exiles* say: "All life is conquest, the victory of human passion over the commandment of cowardice" (88/99/201). But Joyce does not act on his character's conviction. The passivity of jealousy and cuckoldry sits more easily with Joyce than the activity of adultery. Joyce is masochistic, preferring to see himself as a sufferer and victim.

Looking at the dates of the poems in *Pomes Penyeach*, there are clearly three parts. "Tilly" (1904), the main middle section (1912–18), and "A Prayer" (1924). It is an obvious division by date, but also in another way. Though "Tilly" is dated 1904 and opens the collection, the final printed version almost certainly dates from as late as 1927, in other words from the time when Joyce was preparing the volume for the press. The main changes are to be found in the last stanza. As Robert Scholes convincingly demonstrates, the changes introduce the theme of exile and betrayal, the one important emotion from Joyce's life in the period covered by *Pomes Penyeach* missing in our discussion so far.[13] How important a theme it is for Joyce hardly needs stating.

In other words, Joyce rewrites "Tilly" in 1927 expressly to provide the point of departure from which he sets out on his emotional odyssey. That point of departure is Ireland 1904, the year he met Nora and the year he exiles himself from Ireland. It was the watershed in Joyce's emotional life as it was in his artistic development. However, in Joyce's perception, 1904 was also the year of betrayal. It is the year in which Cosgrave supposedly went out with Nora on alternate evenings from Joyce.

If "Tilly" provides the point of departure, the last poem of the collection, "A Prayer," provides the point of return, if not to the Ithaca of Dublin at least to Nora, his Penelope. The poem echoes Joyce's letters to Nora of 1909 in many ways: masochism, submission, the fusion of the experiences of love and religion.

> Nora, my "true love," you must really take me in hand. Why have you allowed me to get into this state? Will you, dearest, take me as I am with my sins and follies and shelter me from misery. If you do not I feel my life will go to pieces. Tonight I have an idea madder than usual. I feel I would like to be flogged by you. I would like to see your eyes blazing with anger.
>
> I wonder is there some madness in me. Or is love madness? One moment I see you like a virgin or madonna the next moment I see you shameless, insolent, half naked and obscene! . . .
>
> I remember the first night in Pola when in the tumult of our embraces you used a certain word. It was a word of provocation, of invitation and I can see your face over me (you were *over* me that night) as you murmured it. There was madness in *your* eyes too and as for me if hell had been waiting for me the moment after I could not have held back from you.
>
> Are you too, then, like me, one moment high as the stars, the next lower than the lowest wretches?
>
> I have *enormous* belief in the power of a simple honourable soul. You are that, are you not, Nora?
>
> I want you to say to yourself: Jim the poor fellow I love, is coming back. He is a poor weak impulsive man and he prays to me to defend him and make him strong. (SL 166–67)

His return to Nora at the end of his emotional odyssey is testimony to Joyce's indebtedness to her for the steadfastness of her love for him in the face of his own fickleness. On his twenty-year-long journey to her, James Joyce has found his way to the experience that he so much desired in *Chamber Music*. It is a long stretch from the unresponsive woman he once yearningly described in *A Portrait* as "a figure of the womanhood of her country, a bat-like soul waking to the consciousness of itself in darkness and secrecy and loneliness" (*P64* 221). In his endeavour to "recreate life out of life" he chose no longer to serve: "Non serviam." In "A Prayer" he celebrates his love for the woman who has not just accepted the fact that he has fallen but who is proud of his fall:

Bend deeper on me, threatening head,
Proud by my downfall, remembering, pitying
Him who is, him who was!

In another of his letters to Nora Joyce writes "I began this letter so quietly and yet I *must* end it in my own mad fashion" (*SL* 189). It is one of the last letters he writes in that extraordinary outburst of sexual candour in 1909. *Pomes Penyeach* also begins so quietly and ends in Joyce's "own mad fashion."

NOTES

1. The date 1912 is a late change (see *JJA* 1). We shall return to "Tilly" later, which dates from 1903–4—potentially in time for inclusion in *Chamber Music*.

2. Anderson (134) calls attention to the similarity.

3. In the "Proteus" and "Aeolus" episodes; see Jackson 75.

4. The dates Joyce chose to append to the poems when he first published them in 1927 are to a certain extent fictitious. We shall only mention discrepancies where they are directly relevant to our argument.

5. See p. xii of Richard Ellmann's introduction to *GJ* for the significance Joyce attached to his age.

6. Page references for *Exiles* are to the Granda, the Jonathan Cape, and the Penguin editions, respectively.

7. In *JJII* Ellmann connects "She Weeps over Rahoon" with Joyce's visit to the cemeteries (324–25). "Tutto à Sciolto" he connects tentatively with Amalia Popper (347), a connection that *Poems and Shorter Writings* (255) also makes.

8. Ellmann, *JJII* 324–25, cites the evidence from the notes to *Exiles*.

9. See Bowen 8 and 175–77.

10. We do not have to follow Tindall in the more notorious reaches of his reading of *Chamber Music* to agree that "maternal and therefore at once creative and dangerous, water is Joyce's principal symbol" (Tindall 222–23n).

11. See "L'Allegro" line 6 and "Il Penseroso" lines 75–76 for verbal echoes.

12. It is interesting to note in his 1912 essay on Blake (*CW*) how important Joyce thought the vicissitudes of Blake's emotional life were for a proper understanding of his work. Obviously regarding Blake as a kindred soul ("Like many other men of great genius, Blake was not attracted to cultured and refined women"), he talks of "the primitive goodness of his heart," commiserates with him for having had no children, and uses the rather odyssean metaphor "the bark of his married life . . . sailed among the usual rocks" when discussing his "mortal life."

13. See Scholes (263–66) for a discussion of the many literary allusions Joyce may have had in mind while rewriting "Tilly."

WORKS CITED

Anderson, Chester. "Joyce's Verses." In A Companion to Joyce Studies, ed. Zack Bowen and James F. Carens. Westport, Conn. and London: Greenwood Press, 1984.

Bowen, Zack. Musical Allusions in the Works of James Joyce. New York and Dublin, 1975.

Browning, Robert. Poems of Robert Browning. Oxford: Oxford University Press, 1919.

Budgen, Frank. James Joyce and the Making of "Ulysses." Bloomington: Indiana University Press, 1960.

Deming, Robert. James Joyce: The Critical Heritage. Vol. 1. London: Routledge & Kegan Paul, 1970.

Jackson, Selwyn. The Poems of James Joyce and the Use of Poems in His Novels. Frankfurt am Main: P. Lang, 1978.

Joyce, James. Exiles. London: Jonathan Cape, 1952; London: Granada, 1979.

———. Poems and "Exiles." Ed. J. C. C. Mays. London: Penguin, 1992.

———. Poems and Shorter Writings. Ed. Richard Ellmann, A. Walton Litz, and John Whittier-Ferguson. London: Faber & Faber, 1991.

Joyce, Stanislaus. My Brother's Keeper: James Joyce's Early Years. Ed. Richard Ellmann. New York: Viking Press, 1958; reprint, 1969.

Scholes, Robert. "James Joyce: Irish Poet." James Joyce Quarterly 2 (Summer 1965): 255–70.

Tindall, William York, ed. Chamber Music. New York: Columbia University Press, 1954; New York: Octagon Books, 1982.

"Aeolus" without Wind

Introduction

Derek Attridge

This sheaf of short essays is an echo—a silent echo—of an event that took place in the Physics Theatre of Newman House, Dublin, on Wednesday, 17 June 1992, and which was itself an echo—audible as well as visible—of an event that took place ten years and a day earlier in the basement of the same building. On that earlier occasion, eight young(ish) scholars, four from France and four from Britain, read papers on the subject "Sirens without Music" as part of the Eighth International James Joyce Symposium, thus responding to a series of events that did not take place in a nearby hotel exactly seventy-eight years before that.[1]

What the eight of us had in common was an admiration for Joyce's writing and an interest in the French developments in philosophy and literary theory that had come to be called—in Anglophone countries—poststructuralism. But our intention was far from programmatic: this was not to be an exposition of a body of "theory" and a demonstration of its "relevance" to Joyce (a genre of critical discourse that has become lamentably common in Joyce studies and elsewhere), but an engagement with a single chapter of *Ulysses* from our own perspectives, enriched as they had been by our reading of this new work. Literature, for us, was not the merely passive object of theorizing, but a discourse pre-empting and exceeding all theories. The panel title was a signal that we would start with no preconceptions about the interpretation of *Ulysses* of the kind installed by Stuart Gilbert's pioneering and "authorized" work, which in 1982 was still dominant in Joyce studies. And the (few) notes in the published papers evince no desire to insist on allegiances with fashionable "theorists": the references are to Ivan Fónagy, Roy K. Gottfried, Richard Ellmann, Freud, Plutarch, Blanchot, Gilbert, and Kafka.

Nevertheless, the panel seems in retrospect to offer itself as a benchmark: a solid wedge of "French theory" that by the time of the next International

James Joyce Symposium, held two years later in Frankfurt, had apparently become the dominant approach to Joyce's work.[2] More recently, we have heard calls for (and exemplifications of) other kinds of reading that were either overwhelmed by the wave of poststructuralism or that have been made possible by poststructuralism's advances. The essays that follow are the result of an invitation to mark the distance traveled by Joyce studies in the ten years between the two Dublin conferences by once more reading closely a chapter of *Ulysses*. What has the wind of theory wrought? What is there besides wind in the theoretical weather of the past decade? How does the Joycean text continue to challenge and subvert attempts to enclose it in the bag of theory?

The contributors to the panel included members of the original "Sirens" panel (Daniel Ferrer, Maud Ellmann, and myself as chair) and newcomers—such as Jennifer Levine, who might well have been included in the earlier panel had we looked across the Atlantic for readers of Joyce in tune with French developments, and Pascal Bataillard, who belongs to a new generation of Joyce critics for whom the 1982 Symposium is a matter of written history. (Bataillard's paper is not included in the selection that follows.) Maud Ellmann was obliged to fax her paper to Dublin, owing to examining duties at Cambridge; this had a certain appropriateness both to the substance of her paper and to the events of the chapter in question, in which the achievement of the great Gallaher that is celebrated is precisely the international transmission of graphic material by digital means. Robert Young, who was also unable to attend the Symposium owing to examining duties (in his case at Oxford), supplied the panel's title.

NOTES

1. The participants in the 1982 panel were Michael Beausang, Maud Ellmann, Derek Attridge, Robert Young, Colin MacCabe, Jean-Michel Rabaté, André Topia, and Daniel Ferrer. Six of the papers read were published in the conference volume (Beja, et al., 57–92).

2. See Benstock. It must be said that the conference program itself was less markedly influenced by "theory" than the volume of proceedings; though this is in itself of some historical and sociological significance.

WORKS CITED

Beja, Morris, et al., eds. *James Joyce: The Centennial Symposium.* Urbana: University of Illinois Press, 1986.

Benstock, Bernard, ed. *James Joyce: The Augmented Ninth.* Syracuse: Syracuse University Press, 1988.

A Brief Allegory of Readings: 1972–1992

Jennifer Levine

I take this occasion to reflect on what has been happening in Joyce studies in the last fifteen to twenty years and on the shifting allegiances we have forged with theory. Inevitably I am reminded of my own history as well, as measured by just a few of these Symposia. I remember hearing about the Paris conference in 1975, when the barricades between French Joyce and Anglo-American Joyce were so clearly set up. I had been a graduate student in England in the early 1970s and was much engaged with those structuralist and post-structuralist theories of narrative that had by then crossed the Channel. So although I had not actually been in Paris, I felt I knew which side of the barricade I was on. The first Joyce conference I attended was in Provincetown in 1983. Capital T theory was there, but only at the edges, whereas by the 1988 Symposium, in Venice, the polarization of interests and languages was obvious. By then, theoretical discourse had staked its legitimate claim. Yet I did not see much traffic between the old and the new. Last year in Vancouver seemed different. I was struck by how much real conversation was possible among readers coming to Joyce from very different perspectives. There are many reasons for this. The most obvious has been the recognition (and it has been inescapable) that full and detailed understanding of these texts can never belong to one person or to one mode of interpretation. We are necessarily engaged in a joint reading. I would argue that the place where we meet most productively, where all participants in the interchange can become temporary experts, is in the localized "close reading." That is essentially what I offer here.

I have been speaking about theory as if it were a single thing, whereas in fact it is a shifting terrain of questions and interests. If we rethink theory

181

along a chronological axis, its heterogeneous nature is even more obvious. I want to read a particular moment in "Aeolus" in order to represent a few key moments in the last two decades. First, I will briefly develop a linguistic and semiotic approach, informed by Saussure and the interest in arbitrary or shifting signifiers; then, I will move to a wider focus on language as a social interaction—recalling Bakhtin's heteroglossia, or other-voicedness; and finally, and very briefly (via feminism's taking gender and heterosexuality as starting points for analysis, not as answers), I will examine the work with an interest in homosocial relations—both as distinct from and as continuous with homosexual relations.[1] My serial reading implies that where we are now depends on where we have been. We do not renew ourselves, snakelike, by neatly shedding each old skin.

I must preface my comments by acknowledging a special affection for "Aeolus." It marked the place of my defeat when I first tried, as a teenager, to read *Ulysses* on my own. I got stuck there and left the book behind for at least two years. What I had discovered without knowing it was that *Ulysses* was changing the rules it had set up in the first six chapters: tracking the voices of Bloom or Stephen had brought me to a dead end. When I eventually came back to *Ulysses* and to "Aeolus," I was able to stand back from my expectations about character and point of view, about their centrality and consistency, and to shift my allegiance to the play of language itself. I had become more self-conscious, more interested in theorizing the text's resistance than in resolving it. This, in turn, allowed me to go forward.

∾   ∾   ∾

I have chosen to look at a rather unobtrusive bit: the story about the Phoenix Park murders, or rather the one about how that story got told—Ignatius Gallaher's journalistic scoop, recounted by Myles Crawford. It comes just after Crawford, the editor, asks Stephen to write something for *him*. What Crawford has in mind is something that will "paralyse Europe," as Gallaher (a Dublin hack who had gone off to work for Harmondsworth in London) was fond of saying. Indeed, Gallaher is presented as a model for Stephen. "That was a pressman for you," Crawford urges, "That was a pen" (*U-GP* 11:630). It is perfectly obvious that we are to take this with a grain of salt. Even Lenehan and O'Madden Burke are less than impressed. And, of course, after *Dubliners* "paralyse" is not an innocent word. Yet the story of the scoop, banal though it may seem, is worth considering.

The narrative moment is complex, for there is not merely the narration *of* a story, there is also narration *in* the story, and more than once, so that in effect we have three major narrative levels, each embedded within another. You might imagine a set of Chinese boxes, the innermost one being the story of the Phoenix Park murders, as reported to New York on 6 May 1881, the day they occurred, by Ignatius Gallaher. The story of his telling is subsequently boxed, or told, by Myles Crawford to the assembled gentlemen of the press on 16 June 1904. And Crawford's telling, as told in "Aeolus," is available to the readers of *Ulysses* whenever they take up the novel. Although the narratives are cunningly interlinked, I will separate them for the moment.

Gallaher in Dublin manages to cable an American newspaper, the *New York World*, with a description of the crime. But it is a rather particular account: not who, when, how, or why, but where. "Where it took place. . . . Where Skin the Goat drove the car. Whole route." (*U-GP* 11:639–40). Gallaher's telling is privileged because it gets through first, preempting all the other messages that are sent. In doing so he manages to speak or write what needs to be "seen"—to translate (as all acts of representation must do) one thing into another. More specifically, in this case he must translate a map into language, turning a set of static and spatial relationships into an inherently sequential code in which words follow each other in time. Of course a vocabulary of description already exists to do just that: cardinal points, angle, circumference, measurement, and so on. But Gallaher has to get his message through as quickly as possible, and the map he has in mind does not easily conform to Euclidian geometry. Why translate it into numbers or geometric relationships when he already "sees" it quite clearly? If he can just get the New York caller to "see" the same thing, he can jump ahead of the pack. As we know, he will find a text (the ad for Bransome's coffee) that his New York counterpart has access to as well and that he can then transcode so it takes on an entirely different meaning. Or, put another way, he treats the original ad ("buy Bransome's coffee") as though it were a coded message, meaning that he has pried the signifiers loose and, by announcing a different context, has grafted them onto an entirely new signified. Or, put yet another way (in terms that would at least make sense to Gallaher), he reads parts of words as though they were marks on a geometrized landscape. The B in *Bransome* becomes a signpost for the Parkgate; T, C, and K are each transformed into points on a Dublin map; and the route taken by Skin-the-Goat (Inchicore, Roundtown, Windy Arbour, Palmerston Park, Ranelagh) is perfectly described by a line joining a certain cluster of letters. As he cables New York, he translates a graphic image (the map of Dublin) into a linguistic message. He does so by way of an entirely unconnected message (the ad for coffee), treated in turn as if it were only a graphic image. And so, as Myles Crawford puts it, Gallaher serves the story to the New York paper "on a hot plate . . . the whole bloody history . . . out of an advertisement. . . . That's press. That's talent" (*U-GP* 11:676–77, 685–88). It is certainly astute, and a clever recognition of the signifier's potential to be transvalued, exploiting the fact that it can, and will, attach itself to whatever signified a teller and a listener agree to. Gallaher is a born semiotician. Clearly, the contract between teller and listener, which I shall return to, is central to the entire scene.

I want to pause for a moment to look at the new technology Gallaher is using.[2] When he sends his trans-Atlantic cable, his own text, too, and not just the Bransome ad, is dismantled. Dismantled in this sense: that the sound image and the graphic image, the two aspects of the signifier that seem naturally fused together and simultaneously present, are split apart. The process of cabling takes in the written message, which the sender would write on an official form, translates it into electrical impulses, which are heard as long or short tones. This alternation of silence and sound is emitted at the other end and eventually reconstituted as marks on a page—Morse code initially, which in turn is decoded into words at a later stage. The emitted message is literally disseminated and dispersed. The message received is, materially, entirely altered. We may read the story about Gallaher, then, as a narrative of transcoding text and "voice" as they play between eye and ear. At various points and in a number of ways, Ulysses replays the distinction between speech and writing. It does so most humorously, perhaps, in "Sirens," when Bloom responds to Martha Clifford, and, just as in Gallaher's scenario, one text (Bloom's letter back to her) is literally laid over and held within another (the newspaper whose ad Bloom pretends to answer). He speaks one letter but writes another. Bloom, however, unlike Gallaher, cannot get one of them to shut up. We read them jostling each other. "Bloom dipped, Bloo mur: dear sir. Dear Henry wrote: Dear Mady" (U-GP 11:860–61). "Bloom mur: best references. But Henry wrote: it will excite me" (U-GP 11:888).

$$\sim\!\!\!\sim \quad \sim\!\!\!\sim \quad \sim\!\!\!\sim$$

I turn now to Crawford's telling of the story. The narrative framework here is much more obvious, for Crawford, the teller, does not hesitate to point it out. "I'll tell you. . ." he says, "I'll show you. . . . I'll tell you" (U-GP 7:631, 633, 651). He claims the teller's privilege—control—and is furious when he does not get it. "Never mind Gumley" he snaps at Stephen, who breaks in with a question (U-GP 7:649). And a few minutes later, when Bloom telephones, "Tell him to go to hell, the editor said promptly. X is Davy's publichouse, see?" (U-GP 7:672–73). Like Gallaher, Crawford is determined to get his story through, despite the odds. But in his case there are different pressures on the transmission of the message. It is not the nature of the contact linking addresser and adressee that makes it difficult. (For Gallaher the distance is vast, and cabling imposes certain limits.) Nor is it the inevitable mediation of two codes, verbal and graphic. Rather it is the fact that other tellers and other stories also want their say. After all, Crawford's audience is right in front of him. This has its advantages. He can rely on the immediacy of his voice and gestures to represent Gallaher's original voice and gesture. And unlike the cabled message, what Crawford emits is what his audience receives, however they might choose to interpret it. Nevertheless, this immediacy is not without difficulties. Gallaher was able to superimpose his story of Skin-the-Goat on an ad for coffee that could not talk back, and he had a listener whose job it was to understand. If his triumph depends on and exploits a totally unequal relationship between sender and receiver, as between languages (in the sense that it shows one code colonizing and in effect erasing another), the story of Crawford's telling is exuberantly democratic. It allows listeners to become tellers. It does not resolve the clamor of competing discourses into a hierarchy. When Lenehan, for example, hears Crawford name Dick Adams, he merely takes that as his cue, bowing to a shape of air: "Madam, I'm Adam. And Able was I ere I saw Elba" (*U-GP* 683). For the reader, who has access to inner voices Crawford himself cannot hear, Stephen's interruption is just as discomposing. "The whole bloody history" that Gallaher serves up "on a hot plate" is transformed into the "nightmare from which you will never awake" (*U-GP* 678)—not quite what Crawford has in mind. His fate as storyteller is similar to Stephen's later in the episode, when the latter's parable of the plums is met not so much by blank incomprehension as by the eager substitution of other stories, conforming to the private agendas of his listeners. What fascinates Joyce in both scenes is the sea of language into which any single speech act falls and by which it is inevitably transformed. If the narration of Crawford's story is rambunctiously democratic, as I have just suggested, it is not because Crawford wants it that way. But Joyce does. He arranges things so that at exactly the right and the wrong moment the phone call coming into the newspaper office on 16 June 1904 cuts into the cabling transaction of 1881 that Crawford is struggling to recount. Right: because the rush to get the phone recreates the atmosphere of the original scene. Wrong in two ways: because it breaks Crawford's concentration and because it confuses our tidy sense of narrative levels.

Gallaher's story is framed by Crawford's, and Crawford's by Joyce's—the narratives are not only contained but also compromised. I have separated them out in order to show more clearly what *Ulysses* tells us about both the linguistic and the novelistic contracts. What I have had to say about Crawford's inability to impose himself and his discourse onto all the other languages clamoring for attention, and what I have winkled out of Gallaher's brief moment in the sun, could also be said of other moments in *Ulysses*. It seems to me, though, that the negotiation between languages that "Aeolus" places at the very center of its *represented* action (by showing us characters struggling for the floor and getting it but never being taken seriously or holding it for long) is subsequently internalized—most obviously in chapters like "Cyclops" and "Oxen of the Sun"—into an organizing principle of narration. What *Ulysses* stages, with increasing complexity, is the scene of novelistic writing, understood, as in Bakhtin, as the recognition that no language is privileged. This moment in "Aeolus" illustrates why readers of Joyce have found Bakhtin's account of the genre so compelling. We have been primed for notions like dialogism and heteroglossia.

However, since the Chinese-box effect is so clearly at play in this scene, why stop here? Why not reposition it in the most obvious intertextual frame, the *Dubliners* story, in which Ignatius Gallaher himself appears? The scoop that got him out of Dublin is never mentioned. Instead, there is a muffled sense of "some shady affair, some money transaction: at least, that was one version of his flight" (72). Like "Aeolus," "A Little Cloud" situates itself in an exclusively masculine circuit of journalistic hackwork, literary aspirations, and pub life. But the earlier narrative inflects its homosocial context in a more specific way. It brings the homosocial into painful collision with the domestic context of wife and child. More pointedly, it spirals around an unresolved and certainly repressed homosexual attachment.

Little Chandler's joy at seeing Gallaher again is intense, eroticized, in stark contrast to the sorry blankness of his married life. In this story the terrain of "for men only" relations—so central to Joyce's work—is complicated in all kinds of ways but particularly by a protagonist who invokes Atalanta and whose own attachments to gender and to sexuality are similarly troubled. Atalanta is the female child abandoned at birth precisely because she is not the longed-for boy but who nevertheless grows up to be as aggressively courageous and as adept at manly pursuits as any man. Although she is eventually matched by a suitor, with whom she has a son, her instinct is to flee from, and often to kill, any man who desires her. For Little Chandler she codes women as frighteningly unattainable and dangerous, but for the reader she is a reminder of Little Chandler's own ambiguous and frightened identity. The narrative says "he gave one the idea of being a little man" (70). It goes on to code him as both feminine and childlike, a combination common enough in the construction of "woman" but here disturbingly directed at a male protagonist. "His hands were white and small, his frame was fragile, his voice was quiet and his manners were refined. He took the greatest care of his fair silken hair and moustache and used perfume discreetly on his handkerchief. The half-moons of his nails were perfect and when he smiled you caught a glimpse of a row of childish white teeth" (70). Like a Victorian heroine, "he emerged from under the feudal arch of the King's Inns, a neat modest little figure" (71). Yet in spite of Little Chandler's blushes (72, 78, 79, 85), "immorality," "corruption," "vice" (77–78), and "other things, too" (75), are the subjects to which his conversation constantly returns. He longs for passion, for the agitation that threatens to overmaster him (74), but he is unable or unwilling to discover its true object. He hides himself from himself, just as he hides the poetry that contains and feeds his sadness. And so his self-disgust is projected onto "A horde of grimy children . . . [that] crawled . . . or squatted like mice . . . all that minute vermin-like life" (71). At the end, in a bitter reversal, he will be superseded and mirrored by his own infant. We come to see the child's pain, its wails and fear, as really belonging to the father. He is helpless before the pain because he cannot acknowledge it. He cannot mind it as his own. I say this not because I think "A Little Cloud" is "about" the punishment of its protagonist. It is about his pain—however compromised that may be by his sentimentality or his self-indulgence.

It is fascinating to watch Little Chandler watching Gallaher, taking him in as a physical presence, mesmerized in particular by his lips and mouth, and then to notice how Gallaher himself speaks of relationships with women, figuratively mouthing his contempt. (The story quite literally asks us to read its lips and to mark the contrasts among Annie's lips, "thin [and] tight" (82), Chandler's embarrassed gesture, "bit[ing] his lower lip with three childishly white front teeth" (79), and Gallaher's mouth, "very long and shapeless and colourless," (75) yet still somehow compelling to Little Chandler. Perhaps this last description translates to a sexualized plane what the story suggests in other ways: that to the disengaged reader there is nothing very attractive about the returning Dubliner.) "But tell me something about yourself" Gallaher says to Little Chandler. "Hogan told me you had . . . tasted the joys of connubial bliss" (78). For Gallaher himself marriage would mean putting his "head in the sack" (81); he would be like a tethered horse, no longer free to graze at will. The only women to consider are "rich Germans and Jews [like overripe fruit, perhaps], rotten with money" (81). As for tying himself up with one woman:

He imitated with his mouth the act of tasting and made a wry face.
—Must get a bit stale, I should think, he said. (82)

The misogyny is obvious, but that Joyce chooses not to motivate it in any explicit way allows us to see how continuous is the line between a possibly homosexual distaste and the socially sanctioned but exclusive solidarity of male bonding. Gallaher may be read as obliviously heterosexual, and as heterosexually oblivious to Little Chandler—or not. He turns down the invitation to a domestic evening with Chandler's wife and infant son in favor of "a little card party" with "another fellow, clever young chap" with whom he is traveling (79). In either case, "A Little Cloud" invites us to realign the scene in "Aeolus," to bring other things into focus—not just the exclusiveness of its homosocial relations (from which Bloom—Jew, cuckold, nondrinker—is deftly marginalized) but also the way in which, for example, in the Wildean subtext that runs through *Ulysses*, or later, more concentratedly in "Eumaeus," the homoerotic shades anxiously into view.[3] What I sense in *Ulysses* is both a flashing on and an enormous anxiety around this issue.

Indeed, reading backward from *A Portrait* and *Ulysses* it is difficult not to hear a reverse echo effect, not to notice how Stephen Dedalus is another, now self-conscious Little Chandler, and also perhaps how "James Joyce: literary persona" is constituted between these lines as well. "There was no doubt about it: if you wanted to succeed you had to go away. You could do nothing in Dublin. . . . He wondered whether he could write a poem to express his idea. . . . Could he write something original? . . . He would never be popular: he saw that. . . . but he might appeal to a little circle of kindred minds. . . . besides that, he would put in allusions" (73–74). If the overlaps between Little Chandler and his author have any force, they do suggest that the double question what does it mean to be an artist? and what does it mean to be a man? involves, for Joyce, an irresistible concern with (homo)sexuality.

◈   ◈   ◈

I began by saying that at a certain point thinking in terms of character and point of view had become a dead end for me. And yet I have been struck by the fact that the more I reread *Ulysses* the more I come back, and want to come back, to the human figures in the textual landscape. Certainly, I have just done so here. Crawford's hero is not entirely discontinuous with Little Chandler's, and Little Chandler's dreams gloss Stephen's. To think of them only as language-machines, or as sites for the investigation of language, is not enough. If I insist on their "life" as characters, have I merely come full circle? My answer today would be: not exactly, because history, as *Ulysses* tells us, repeats itself "with a difference" (U-GP 16:1525–26). Marxism and feminism in particular have changed our way of theorizing the personal with the political. That identity is socially and historically constructed (a polemical point not so long ago) now seems almost self-evident. This means, for example, that the categories of identity are not fixed. When we do think about figures like Gallaher and Little Chandler we are less likely to take for granted certain heterosexual and masculinist paradigms. I do so here not in order to find skeletons in Joyce's personal closet, but to shed some light on our own, collective closet: an ideological space that has so long excluded homosexual desire from the realm of what may be spoken, and done, between men.

NOTES

1. My general debt to Eve Kosofsky Sedgwick, *Between Men*, should be acknowledged here.
2. My discussion leaves out the political implications of the new media. I regret that I have only just learned about the important new research being done at the University of Dublin that establishes nineteenth-century Ireland as the first country to have been "covered" by national systems of communications, transportation, and policing: no one could get on or off a train anywhere in the country, for example, without hav-

ing his/her identity recorded. This conjunction of systems, of course, speaks to Ireland's subject (and potentially subversive) status. It also makes Ireland, in spite of its rural and nonindustrialized economy, a prototypically modern society. This in turn leads to further considerations of colonialism, combined and uneven development, and so on. Certainly, the relations among mass media, surveillance, and social control are ones that we are increasingly learning to understand, and about which Joyce may teach us a great deal.

3. On this issue I am indebted to two papers: Zack Bowen, "Wilde over Joyce" (at the Vancouver Joyce conference, 1991), showing how Stephen (surprisingly) plays Posey Douglas rather than Oscar Wilde to Mulligan; and Jean-Michel Rabaté's paper for a panel on Joyce and homosexuality at the 1992 Symposium. Through the letters, Rabaté traces Joyce's significantly shifting attitude to the homosexual artist, with whom—Rabaté suggests—Joyce came to see himself as complicit. For developments in "Eumaeus," see my "James Joyce, Tattoo Artist," in the special issue of the *James Joyce Quarterly*, "Joyce and Homosexuality," a volume that makes a very strong case for its subject.

WORKS CITED

Bakhtin, Michail. *The Dialogic Imagination*. Trans. Caryl Emerson and Michael Holquist. Austin: University of Texas Press, 1981.

Joyce, James. *Dubliners*. Harmondsworth: Penguin, 1981.

Levine, Jennifer. "James Joyce, Tattoo Artist: Tracing the Outlines of Homosocial Desire." *James Joyce Quarterly* 31 (Spring 1994): 277–99.

Sedgwick, Eve Kosofsky. *Between Men: English Literature and Male Homosocial Desire*. New York: Columbia University Press, 1985.

Between *Inventio* and *Memoria*:
Locations of "Aeolus"

Daniel Ferrer

"Imagination is memory"
—*Joyce to Frank Budgen*

The first part of my title might seem to be applicable to the event of the panel at the 1992 symposium rather than to "Aeolus." As Derek Attridge has pointed out, this was a commemorative panel: not only, like the whole Symposium, a commemoration of Joyce a hundred and ten years after his birth—in what happens to be, moreover, the very room where the funnel/tundish scene of the *Portrait* is supposed to have taken place—but also a commemoration of a panel that took place in Dublin ten years before, in 1982.

For reasons that are not immediately clear but that "Aeolus" may help us to understand later, coming back to a particular place is usually considered an appropriate occasion for taking stock of elapsed time. Accordingly, we decided to use the opportunity to reexamine the work done in 1982 and measure the changes in the critical landscape that occurred since then. Some may consider this an alarming symptom of the increasing reflexivity of recent Joyce studies. I am surprised myself and slightly worried when I am told that the published form of the 1982 panel is used as course material in some American universities. I wonder what may remain, in such a setting, of the tongue-in-cheek attitude that underlay the whole enterprise at that time. After all, it started with a joking title ("S without M") as a kind of challenge between friends: would it be possible to devote a whole panel to the "Sirens" while eschewing the musical question? It now seems rather odd that this playful tour de force should be considered a critical standard of the early eighties, against which present critical endeavours should be measured. But, after all, there is no reason why this new game shouldn't be as much fun as the old one.

Old and new, commemoration and fashion: the result of the exercise seems fairly predictable. It looks as if it was already inscribed in the composition of our panel: we supplemented a fair proportion of the original members of the "Sirens" panel with a suitable admixture of "new blood." Since we decided to commemorate what was the "new Joyce" of ten years before, we could hardly repudiate that Joyce completely. On the other hand, it would be difficult to acknowledge that nothing changed in ten years, that we had not moved at all. And yet we could hardly pretend that we invented anything new, anything that had not already been there ten years previously—we could hardly pretend that whatever we found has not been there all the time, at least since the publication of *Ulysses*.

I reread the published version of "Sirens without Music" for the preparation of this essay, and I do find that I would sign it again, except perhaps for a few mannerisms, a few quotations, which no longer seem to me necessary in this context. (Were they the wind that we decided to do without for the new panel?) Altogether, I would sign with pleasure, not just my own piece, but the whole 1982 panel. There is nothing to repudiate. But there would certainly be things to add. Incompleteness was inevitable: it was already announced in the *exclusive* title of the panel (i.e., *without* music). Jennifer Levine has pointed out some of the things that are now felt to be lacking. I will start by discussing a procedure: something I would *do* differently today.

The phrase "miss Douce's wet lips said, laughing in the sun" is the first passage from "Sirens" that is quoted in the published version of the 1982 panel (it subsequently recurs several times). It was used to illustrate the autonomy of the parts of the body and the disappearance or dissolution of the speaking subject. This is based on an implicit comparison with a "normal" sentence. The whole problem of a linguistic norm is such a difficult one, however, that I would prefer now, in order to make the same point, to compare the sentence with its earlier version in the Rosenbach manuscript, which was "miss Douce said, her wet lips laughing in the sun."

This is not just an easy way around a tricky corner. It is a matter of attitude toward the whole genetic dimension of the text: it was almost entirely absent from our field of investigation,[1] in a silent exclusion that paralleled the deliberate avoidance of music. The reasons for this exclusion of the writing process are ambiguous. Was this absolute privilege awarded to one particular stage (the ultimate published version of the text) based on social sanction or on author's intention? Paradoxically, one of the reasons why some of us were suspicious of the genetic point of view in those days was precisely the fear of a naive conception of intentionality associated with it, but I now feel that the exclusive concentration on the finished object is precisely based upon such a conception.

I will not attempt today a real genetic study of "Aeolus." This is partly for reasons of opportunity: a genetic study requires a precise analysis of documents much beyond the scope of this short paper, and partly because much of the work has already been magnificently done in Michael Groden's *"Ulysses" in Progress*, which includes a detailed chapter on "Aeolus." It is also for reasons of principle, which will be made clear later. But you will see that my remarks imply a genetic perspective, and even imply acceptance of the idea that the final text includes its earlier versions in its very structure, that it stands for what "Aeolus" would call the *akasic records* of its genesis.

We decided that each one of us was free to interpret the title of the 1992 panel in his or her own way. It seems to me that it contains implicitly two rhetorical figures (a metaphor and a parallelism) pointing toward the paradoxical meaning: "Aeolus" without rhetoric. But it is not possible to leave rhetoric entirely aside in this chapter in the same way that we left music aside in examining "Sirens." (It is impossible to leave rhetoric aside in any of the episodes—and saying that rhetoric is everywhere in *Ulysses* is just another way of saying that it cannot be the specificity of "Aeolus.") So I will restrict the restriction and simply attempt a displacement of emphasis within the realm of rhetoric.

Of the five traditional parts of rhetoric (*inventio, elocutio, dispositio, actio,* and *memoria*), two or three (certainly *elocutio* and *dispositio,* and perhaps *actio*) have been overemphasized in the study of "Aeolus." I will take these to be the *wind* of rhetoric. While the two remaining parts, *inventio* and *memoria* (the bag from which the wind is issued and into which it is stored again) seem much more promising. One could even go as far as suggesting that the central question of the chapter is the impossibility of making a distinction between the two.

A few quick reminders before going ahead. *Inventio* (from *invenire,* to find) should not be translated as "invention": it can be *re-*discovery as well as absolute discovery. Rhetoric organized a series of *places* (the "topics") where ideas could be found at hand. On the other hand, *memoria* is not a passive, natural faculty of reception, but an "artificial memory." The Greek, Roman, and Renaissance "arts of memory" were sophisticated processes of storage and retrieval of information, also based on the setting up of places (*loci memoriae*). Although *memoria* is traditionally the last part of rhetoric (because the memorization of the speech by the orator necessarily takes place after its elaboration?), it could very well take precedence. For the mode of extraction is clearly dependent on the mode of accumulation. In many respects, *inventio* and *memoria* can be considered two sides of a single system, two faces of the same grid.

To come back, for a moment, to the intermediary stages, the final organization (*dispositio*) cannot be independent of this dual preorganization: when Joyce said that the Jesuits had taught him "how to gather, how to order and how to present a given material," he clearly did not have three different operations in mind (but there would be much to say about the status of the "gift" here). Even *elocutio,* the ever growing list of rhetorical figures that features so prominently in most studies of this chapter can be shown to be related to this problem. Joycean critics have been contaminated by the "taxonomic frenzy" of rhetoric, its rage for naming and classifying thousands of figures, which Barthes explains as the result of "a true mirage," the attempt "*to code speech [parole]* and no longer language *[langue]*, i.e., the very space where, in principle, the code ceases" (85). Whether or not the irrepressible spontaneity of speech will always remain "unmasterable," the rhetorical project opens the possibility that every turn of speech, however unpredictable, will find its assigned place, the ideal inventiveness of discourse exhausting itself in the discovery that it is always prelocated in the rhetorical grid.

In "Aeolus" the systematic relation of *inventio* and *memoria* surfaces very concretely through questions of placing. Within the limits of this essay, however, we can only examine a few crude examples.

The first one seems to be easily explainable in terms of the simplest associative psychology. The remembering of a smell is immediately located, pinned down to an effect of spatial contiguity: "Heavy greasy smell there always is in those works. Lukewarm glue in Thom's next door when I was there" (U-GP 7:225). But the momentum of the metonymical process results in an immediate displacement ("next door") and to a new spatial reference. It is not, of course, a matter of indifference that this reference should be to Thom's, the place of origin of the directory that maps Dublin with the greatest precision— a book that can be considered as a kind of paper reduplication of Dublin and that Joyce's work reduplicates in several respects.[2]

The next example is openly a matter of *memoria artificialis*. In order to recall the telephone number of Keyes, Bloom uses a mnemotechnic system of his own, connecting it with a street number: "Number? Yes. Same as Citron's house. Twentyeight" (U-GP 7:220). To make the connections necessary to his trade, Bloom stores his telephone numbers on a map of Dublin, just as Ignatius Gallaher, to accomplish his feat of telecommunication, superimposed a map of Dublin on a newspaper advertisement—or just as Joyce himself, to write *Ulysses*, superimposed a map of Dublin on Homer's *Odyssey* (or superimposed the *Odyssey* on a map of Dublin), using the one as a *locus memoriae* to inscribe the other.

Now, if we start from the other end, from "literary creation," the same correlations are manifest. Stephen's stanza, written in "Proteus," is called up into this chapter (its first full appearance in the book) through its surface of inscription, the bottom of Deasy's letter, or rather through the absence of that surface, missing in its place:

Stephen handed over the typed sheets, pointing to the title and signature.
—Who? the editor asked.
Bit torn off.
—Mr Garret Deasy, Stephen said.
—That old pelters, the editor said. Who tore it? Was he short taken?

> On swift sail flaming
> From storm and south
> He comes, pale vampire
> Mouth to my mouth.

—Good day, Stephen, the professor said, coming to peer over their shoulders. Foot and mouth? Are you turned . . . ?
Bullockbefriending bard. [. . .]
—Good day, sir, Stephen answered blushing. The letter is not mine. Mr Garrett Deasy asked me to . . . (U-GP 7:521–25)

We may note here in passing the suggestion of an excremental model of writing ("Was he short taken?") as an evacuation of preprocessed, predigested, and a fortiori pre-existing matter, as opposed to an engendering or an organic growth. More important, however, is the close relationship that is established between the poem and the letter. When he tore the bottom of the sheet, Stephen seemed to be simply taking something away, a dishonest subtraction from someone else's property, perpetrated and presumably absolved in the name of art. Appropriating a piece of Deasy's letter is equivalent in that respect to the appropriation of library slips for similar purposes. But we discover that writing in the margin of his employer's epistle is not a neutral gesture—no more than writing on the back (endorsing?) or in the blanks of a library form. It confirms a relation of subordination to "Dominie Deasy," taking the exact form of the indenture, the written contract binding an apprentice to his master, which (like the *symbolon*) used to be divided in two so that each of the parties could prove the authenticity of the contract by a comparison of the torn edges.

The binding is so strong that it even leads to a relation of identification. The poem has been written on the bottom of the sheet, just after the formal ending (which happens to be dealing with the obligations entailed by insertion),[3] that is to say in the place reserved for the signature: the poem becomes a virtual cosignature of the letter, and by writing it the poet becomes, in spite of his repeated disavowals, the "bullockbefriending bard."

This relation of implication, of mutual inference between the poem and its locus of inscription sheds an interesting light on the so-called enthymemic technique of the episode. The enthymeme is a syllogism with implicit premises, an oratorical device lengthily analysed by Aristotle, but Voloshinov-Bakhtin has generalized the notion and shown that every utterance can be considered as an "objective and social enthymeme," because it is necessarily dependent on an implicit context that conditions its effectiveness. On the other hand, the "iterability" of any trace implies that it can be severed from its original context and intention—you will have recognized one of Derrida's most important themes. The whole of Joyce's writing (this becomes apparent with "Circe" and *Finnegans Wake*) is based on the complementary aspect of that principle: any text displaced, grafted in a foreign context, retains something of its origin and influences its new context accordingly.

It follows naturally that the earlier versions of the published text, the topology of its inscription on the successive layers of the "avant-texte," are active forces within the text. What we have just said about the relationship of Stephen's poem to the material circumstances of its composition exemplifies this in a small way—but the investigation must be pursued from the genesis of the poem as represented in the book to its genesis as we can reconstruct it from Joyce's manuscript. A study of the draft of "Proteus" and more specifically of page 15 of Buffalo MS. V. A. 3 is more rewarding than an internal study of that mediocre piece of verse. It is particularly illuminating to study the marginal inscription of the onomatopoeic variations on *moon* and *womb* in conjunction with Stephen's reflections about rhymes and paronomasia in "Aeolus" (*U-GP* 7:714–24). Seeing this page, it becomes obvious that the storage, the material location is not neutral: the spatial disposition of the writing on the page is a crucial factor for the interrelationships of its various elements. And even if these elements disappear from the surface of the printed page (*moombh*, the provisional choice, later became *moomb* and was then, perhaps mistakenly, replaced in the text by the simple *womb*), they remain active, and we can say that this *womb* is big with all the variations that preceded it.

But we are straying again from "Aeolus"—or are we? It is now becoming apparent why a genetic study of our episode is not only practically but even theoretically impossible within the limits of a separate paper; it cannot be isolated from the history of the whole book.

The same thing could be said of any chapter of *Ulysses*, even if it is truer of "Aeolus": Michael Groden has called it a miniature model of the composition of *Ulysses*, reflecting the various stages in the evolution of the whole book, with the late addition of the newspaper titles conspicuously changing the nature of the text, its fictional and enunciative structure, in relation with the development of the late chapters. But one could radicalize the assertion and suggest that the method of composition of *Ulysses* turns the whole text into a matrix of its own creation.

Again, we have to restrict ourselves to two rudimentary examples. Just after having recognized the smell of the printing works and compared them to the smell of Thom's, Bloom dabs his nose with his handkerchief and is surprised by another smell that he cannot "place" immediately: "Citronlemon?" (*U-GP* 7:226). The coinage (the invention of the portmanteau word) is connected with the earlier reminiscence, the use of Citron's house as a mnemonic aid, two paragraphs earlier. But there is also an interchapter connection: the word is first introduced in "Calypso" ("almonds or citrons" [*U-GP* 4:196]), where the link is soon established with Citron and his location ("Wonder is poor Citron still in Saint Kevin's Parade" [*U-GP* 4:205]). This becomes more interesting when we find that the "Aeolus" passage first read "Almonds" instead of "Citronlemon": the passage from "Calypso" has become a sort of didascalia, or script for the writing of "Aeolus"; the alternative that was "quoted" or "mentioned" within fiction, at best a parasitic status at the second remove according to speech act theorists, acquires a full performative value as an injunction to write.

The illocutionary force of the text proves to be even more powerful in our second example. The general problematization of memory in this chapter touches two extremes: the evanescence of oral speech ("scattered to the four winds") on the one hand and the parasitic inertia of print on the other. In relation with this, Bloom fantasizes about the presses getting out of hand: "Now if he got paralysed there and no-one knew how to stop them they'd clank on and on the same, print it over and over and up and back. Monkeydoodle the whole thing" (U-GP 7:102–4).

Three years after this had been written, the sentence which had remained for a long time the first of the chapter, "Grossbooted draymen rolled barrels dullthudding out of Prince's stores and bumped them up on the brewery float" (U-GP 7:21–23), was supplemented by an inverted repetition ("On the brewery float bumped dullthudding barrels rolled by grossbooted draymen out of Prince's stores"), inserted as a holograph addition on the typescript. This seems to be derived directly from a typographical error in the *Little Review* publication of the episode, where the sentence is repeated twice, verbatim (see Groden 70 n). The chiasmic structure was simply superimposed on the mechanic echo, compounding one kind of stereotyping with another.

Can we say that Joyce's text has generated the printer's mistake? Or that it had predicted it? We know, at least, that it contained it as one of the potentialities that it was ready to develop. The important point is the demonstration of the part played by the internal dynamics of successive places of inscription (whether or not they are materialized on paper)—of the constant interaction of *inventio* and *memoria*.

NOTES

1. Concerning, at least, the "Sirens" episode: most of us had already felt its necessity for the study of *Finnegans Wake*.

2. See Hart and Knuth; see also Kenner on the modern city and the printed book as analogous finding systems, "the deep congruity on which [Joyce's] whole art turned" (76).

3. "Thanking you for the hospitality" (3:405).

WORKS CITED

Barthes, Roland. "The Old Rhetoric: An Aide-mémoire." In *The Semiotic Challenge*, trans. R. Howard. New York: Hill & Wang, 1988.

Groden, Michael. *"Ulysses" in Progress*. Princeton: Princeton University Press, 1977.

Hart, Clive, and Leo Knuth. *A Topographical Guide to James Joyce's "Ulysses."* Colchester: A Wake Newslitter Press, 1975.

Kenner, Hugh. *The Mechanic Muse*. New York: Oxford University Press, 1987.

"Aeolus": Reading Backward

Maud Ellmann

"The ghost walks," Professor McHugh murmurs "biscuitfully" in the Aeolus episode of *Ulysses* (*U-GP* 7:237). What his expression means is that the treasury is full and that the wages will be paid, an important issue in a chapter so concerned with circulation and short-circuitry. The episode begins with a vision of the transportation system circulating Dubliners around the city; then the perspective shifts abruptly to the general post office, where "loudly flung sacks of letters, postcards, lettercards, parcels, insured and paid," are dispatched upon their sundry odysseys, "for local, provincial, British and overseas delivery" (*U-GP* 7:18–19). However, the word "ghost" is haunted by the shades of former meanings, and the central themes of Aeolus may be detected in its obsolete associations. For instance, "ghost" has been used to translate *spiritus* from Latin, meaning "breath" or "wind," both of which are dominant motifs of "Aeolus." In Homer's version of the episode, Aeolus speeds Odysseus on his homeward journey by giving him a wallet full of winds, instructing him to keep it firmly sealed; but the crew, suspecting hidden treasure, untie the silver thong, and the resulting tempest blows their vessel back to Aeolus's floating isle. In *Ulysses*, Joyce transforms these backward-blowing winds into the breath that the windbags of the chapter waste in bombast; the flatulence of Irish Nationalism and the wind that breaks out of the R.I.A. in mockery of the divine afflatus.

Yet if "ghost" suggests the breath of life, the living voice, it is also associated with the death that the voice, the transportation system, and the post can never overcome, because they owe their very presence to the absence that they strive to hold at bay. In "Aeolus" this absence erupts into the narrative itself, dismembering the speeches of the orators. Curiously, the word "ghost" signified dismemberment long before it came to be allied with breath, for it derives from a pre-Teutonic root meaning "to wound, to tear, to pull to pieces."

In "Aeolus" it is Bloom who is commissioned to enact this ghostly principle of laceration. Indeed, the first words that he utters in the episode are *"cut it out"* (*U-GP* 7:26). He is asking that the ad for Alexander Keyes be cut out of the *Evening Telegraph*, so that he can sport this "cutting" (a word that reverberates throughout the chapter) at the *Freeman's Journal*. Red Murray guillotines the page with chilling expertise: "Red Murray's long shears sliced out the advertisement from the newspaper in four clean strokes." Bloom, as he witnesses the amputation, muses: "scissors and paste" (*U-GP* 7:31–32). A telling phrase, for Bloom himself performs the role of scissors in this episode: he intrudes into the *Freeman's* office as a stranger, "a perverted jew," and thereby undermines the orators' attempts to forge a unitary national identity. In his role as interloper, he conspires with the headlines of the chapter to disrupt the voice of Irish Nationalism and to hollow out a "cleft" in speech (to borrow one of "Aeolus"'s stranger formulations [*U-GP* 7:860]). Being keyless, like Stephen, whom he fails to meet (in one of many missed encounters of the episode), and having also failed to place his ad for Keyes, Bloom stands for the castrative aesthetic of the newspaper, for the demonic "sllt" of a writing machine that "speaks in its own way" (*U-GP* 7:175–77), slitting through the phallic inflation of the voice, through all the bluster of the "GREAT DAILY ORGAN" (*U-GP* 7:84), and substituting for the art of rhetoric the blind mechanical effects of shock, which Walter Benjamin regarded as the hallmark of the Modernist aesthetic. The modern newspaper, for instance, by juxtaposing random fragments of events, disrupts the delusory coherence of experience, and thus subverts the very notion of a "Pisgah Sight" (*U-GP* 7:1057), of a central and commanding overview.

In "Aeolus" Bloom's task is to defy the voice of rhetoric, just as his task in "Sirens" is to overthrow the voice of music. These voices both belong almost exclusively to men. In either case, Bloom finds himself marooned, a floating island in a sea of sound, resisting the temptation to compete with men for vocal prowess. In "Sirens" the voice is equated with the penis, in that it violates the virgin sanctuary of the ear: "Sure, you'd burst the tympanum of her ear, man, with an organ like yours" (*U-GP* 11:536–37). In "Aeolus" voice is also associated with the masculine, proceeding "FROM THE FATHERS" (*U-GP* 7:841): this is the headline that titles the speech by John F. Taylor which relates the story of Moses, the father of the Jews, ascending Mount Sinai in order to receive the word of God the Father. Stephen mocks this fable of the apostolic succession of the voice from father to father, "from only begetter to only begotten" (*U-GP* 9:838–39), with his countervision of two "FRISKY FRUMPS" (*U-GP* 7:1070), who climb up Nelson's pillar to spill their plumseeds over the Hibernian metropolis, under the very "PROBOSCIS" of "the onehandled adulterer" (*U-GP* 7:1033, 1019).

Bloom is unconsciously in league with Stephen, but he sabotages voice in subtler ways. Just as he uses writing to elude the blandishments of song in

"Sirens," so he uses spelling to wind his way out of the winds of "Aeolus." Under the headline ORTHOGRAPHICAL (*U-GP* 7:164), Bloom proves that "PEN IS CHAMP" (*U-GP* 7:1034) by showing that the way a word is spelled can never be identified with how it sounds. What this means is that a residue of writing necessarily eludes the jurisdiction of the voice and opens up the possibility of new modalities. While the spoken word moves forward, like the favorable winds of "Aeolus," the written word moves backward: Bloom observes that the typesetter "reads backwards first" in order to be sure of his orthography. It is no accident, moreover, that the letters he is reading backward spell the name of the most impotent of all the dead or fallen fathers of *Ulysses*, "mangiD. kcirtaP," that is, Patrick Dignam. The backward reading of this *nom du père* launches Bloom himself upon a backward journey through the seas of memory, for he remembers how his own "poor papa" used to read the Hebrew Haggadah backward at the feast of Passover. "Dear, O dear," Bloom misremembers, "All that long business about that brought us out of the land of Egypt and into the house of bondage *alleluia*" (*U-GP* 7:208–9). Here Bloom sends the Jews back into the bondage they were trying to escape, just as Odysseus was driven back to Aeolus's floating island when his crewmen let the winds out of the bag. Reading backward could be seen as the textual equivalent of both of these Aeolian inverted odysseys. Indeed, the very layout of the page in "Aeolus" instructs us in the art of reading backward, "rere regardant" (*U-GP* 3:503), and undermines the teleology of speech. For example, the reference to the posterior in K.M.R.I.A. is only decodable a posteriori:

K.M.R.I.A.
—He can kiss my royal Irish arse, Myles Crawford cried loudly over his shoulder. Any time he likes, tell him. (*U-GP* 7:991–92)

Bloom's task in "Aeolus" is to reveal the mutinous orthography within the word that undermines the linearity of language and opens up a "cleft" within the father's voice, the father's name. It is therefore symptomatic that names are constantly mistaken or forgotten in *Ulysses*, particularly names associated with paternity. In "Hades" Bloom forgets the name of Father Coffey, partly because "his name is like a coffin," as he realizes when it resurfaces into his mind (*U-GP* 6:595). Similarly, Nannetti forgets the name of Monks the Dayfather in "Aeolus": "Where's what's his name?" he barks (*U-GP* 7:182). In "Lestrygonians" Bloom forgets the name of the "priesty-looking chap" Penrose, which reminds him of Nannetti's amnesia with regard to Monks: "Well, if he couldn't remember the dayfather's name that he sees every day . . ." (*U-GP* 8:179–80). The "dayfather" of a printing office performed the role of a shop steward; but the loaded term *father* (as well as the name Monks), probably contributes to Bloom's lapse of memory. Reading backward, we realize he forgets Penrose because the "rose" reminds him of his father's floral name and of his own.

Freud, in *The Psychopathology of Everyday Life,* devotes the whole of his first chapter to the forgetting of proper names; and he draws an eerie analogy between those forces that rob the mind of names and thieves who ambush their victims in the night:

> Let us suppose that I have been imprudent enough to go for a walk at night in a deserted quarter of the city, and have been attacked and robbed of my watch and purse. I report the matter at the nearest police station in the following words: "I was in such and such a street, and there *loneliness* and *darkness* took away my watch and purse." Although I should not have said anything in this statement that was not true, the wording of my report would put me in danger of being thought not quite right in the head. The state of affairs could only be described correctly by saying that *favoured* by the loneliness of the place and under the *shield* of darkness *unknown malefactors* robbed me of my valuables. Now the state of affairs in the forgetting of names need not be any different; favoured by tiredness, circulatory disturbances and intoxication, an unknown psychical force robs me of my access to the proper names belonging to my memory. (21–22)

What "Aeolus" reveals is that the loneliness and darkness that rob us of our speech are not reducible to the "unconscious," if the unconscious is conceived of as a secret self or a concealed intentionality. On the contrary, these forces represent the mindless and autonomous effects of writing, to which we are subjected as inexorably as the prisoners of Kafka's penal colony, whose legal sentences are drilled into their flesh by the needles of a monstrous printing press. It is writing that pounces on the voice, like a thief in the night, and strips the speaker of memory and consciousness. "Everything speaks in its own way," Bloom tells us (*U-GP* 7:177), and in "Aeolus" the voice of intention is supplanted by a writing machine—by the headlines, for example, whose styles are too multifarious to be ascribed to any single human consciousness. In "Aeolus" *it* speaks, not I, and it dismembers me in the very *sllt* by which it calls me into being. *Sllt.*

WORK CITED

Freud, Sigmund. *The Psychopathology of Everyday Life.* Vol. 6 of the *Standard Edition,* ed. James Strachey. London: Hogarth Press, 1901.

The Novels

Stephen Haunted by His Gender: The Uncanny *Portrait*

Sheldon Brivic

Stephen Dedalus is haunted. He feels the uncanny in every chapter of *A Portrait of the Artist,* and a ghost stalks him in *Ulysses.* Freud's use of *uncanny,* a dread connected to repressed memories, always involves uncertainty about what is real and what is imagined, what is external and what is internal, what is alive and what is dead, what is new and what is repeated. A person in the grip of the uncanny wants to separate these polarities and cannot, and fears that life is controlled by what is unreal, external, dead, and mechanical.

In using this theory of the uncanny to explain the haunting of Stephen in *Portrait,* I will try to supplement Freud's argument by presenting the uncanny as gender oriented. Lacan's analysis of genders as language systems allows me to link the forces in the unconscious to sexual difference. What frightens Stephen most chillingly is a sense that femininity may be obliterated by masculinity. There is also the fear of woman in the book, but the most uncanny moments, some of which have hardly been examined, seem to confront male threats and to compel a valorization of femininity. The uncanny object is the subject itself rendered as an object, so that object is woman insofar as she acts as mirror for the subject. The way for man to overcome the uncanny in Joyce is to strive to recover contact with woman as a real person, an independent being.

In E. T. A. Hoffmann's tale "The Sand-Man," Freud's main example of the uncanny, the student Nathaniel is haunted by a demonic Sandman from childhood, who reappears as the lawyer Coppelius and the optician Coppola. Freud identifies the sandman, who takes boys' eyes and kills Nathaniel's benevolent father, with the castrating aspect of the father: Freud points out that every time the sandman appears, he interferes with Nathaniel's love

("Uncanny" 231–32 n). Nathaniel is at first in love with Clara, but after Coppola gives him a spyglass, he uses it to see the exquisite Olympia. He falls obsessively in love with Olympia, but she turns out to be a doll, causing him to have a breakdown. At the end of the story Nathaniel recovers and returns to Clara. He is about to marry her when he looks through the spyglass and sees that Coppelius is back. This causes Nathaniel to go berserk and leap to his death. From a feminist perspective, the spyglass is the specularity of the male gaze that turns woman into a mere reflection.

The story expresses a fear that woman is inactive or even inanimate, that the father alone is real, that the agency of womanhood must disappear behind the inescapable power of masculinity. Olympia, the doll who attracts, is made by father figures, so that the feminine is enclosed by masculine construction. Olympia's eyes turn out to have been stolen from Nathaniel when he was a child, which suggests not only that his vision of her, through Coppola's spyglass, was controlled by paternal manipulation, but even that she is only Nathaniel's alienated feminine side. Coppelius also unscrewed the child Nathaniel's arms and legs, showing that the boy was a mechanical construction of the paternal isolated from the maternal. Freud concludes that Nathaniel illustrates how a "young man fixated upon his father by his castration complex becomes incapable of loving a woman" (232 n). This fits a view of Stephen that I have been expressing for many years now in a repetitious, if not uncanny way (see my Joyce between 17–83). Stephen keeps encountering male threats in Portrait, and in Ulysses he seems to be working out his problem with the father figure Bloom—or not working it out.

The obliteration of the feminine by the masculine that Stephen fears intensely may be described in linguistic terms through Lacan's theories. In Lacan femininity is a language system associated with change, the sliding of words into new meanings that Lacan calls the jouissance of the woman "which goes beyond" (145–47). Masculinity for Lacan is a language system involving fixity, words that stick to meanings. The distinction corresponds to Julia Kristeva's distinction between the semiotic, the feminine, rhythmic aspect of language, and the symbolic, its masculine, referential aspect (Revolution 24–27). The element of recurrence in the uncanny expresses fixity, entrapment in the past, the inability to shift into the feminine modality of change.

The distinction between feminine and masculine systems may also be described as one between feeling and the control of feeling. Freud says in Inhibitions, Symptoms and Anxiety, "There is no doubt that hysteria has a strong affinity with femininity, just as obsessional neurosis has with masculinity" (143). Insofar as this statement suggests that the genders consist of these neurotic configurations, it has the advantage of separating gender personality characteristics from any sense that they could be biologically inherent. Juliet Mitchell accepts Freud's distinction in Psychoanalysis and Feminism and expands on it: "At least in Western society, obsessionality is closely linked to excessive rationality, a quality that is valued—the description 'hysterical' is invariably derogatory" (112). Freud in fact describes hysteria as pure feeling: "A hysterical attack may be likened to a freshly constructed individual affect, and a normal affect to the expression of a general hysteria which has become a heritage" (*Inhibitions* 84). So hysteria is the flow of emotion before it has been made ordinary by symbolic ordering, by being put into comprehensible language. The Freudian theory thus supports Lacan's linkage of the feminine to the sliding of language and the masculine to its fixation and the repetition of compulsion.

Another way to approach the linguistic difference between genders is to say that femininity is excluded from the symbolic, the register of authoritative language that includes masculinity. Slavoj Žižek points out a significant contrast between Antigone and Hamlet's father, both of whom occupy a margin between death and life. Antigone is killed symbolically by being banished before she is killed physically, and the result of her exclusion from the symbolic is to make her sublime. Hamlet senior is killed physically before he is killed symbolically, and this makes him uncanny (Žižek 135). His claims for his name and position make him a pure embodiment of the symbolic, and the vastness of the patriarchal principle he expresses is a big factor in the terror he evokes.

The images that frighten Stephen most in *Portrait* center on the male authority of God and its exertion of control. The way this figure hangs over him is established in chapter 1 as he undresses, hurrying his trembling fingers because God will send him to hell if he doesn't get to bed before the gas is lowered: he "knelt trembling at his bedside and repeated his prayers quickly quickly, fearing that the gas would go down. He felt his shoulders shaking" (*P64* 18). Stephen does not realize that he shakes partly because he has a cold: the only cause he knows of for his agitation is the fear of God. It is an interesting reflection on the way gender systems can never really enclose individuals that Stephen seems more hysterical than obsessive here. Perhaps obsession is a way of controlling hysteria that women are not usually enabled to develop.

This scene is soon followed by the ghost of the marshal and other uncanny male images. One pattern established here is that uncanny images are liminal: they occur when Stephen goes to his room or goes to sleep. This not only indicates a fundamental fear of the dark, but it also involves Stephen approaching his feminine side, which calls forth a male threat. In Lacan, as in Freud, everyone includes both masculine and feminine and represses the gender (s)he is not supposed to have. When Stephen is alone he often dreams of his mother, and his thoughts often flow in ways that constitute femininity as a language system. When he goes to sleep, he enters a flux of shifting language, as we see when we follow his mind into sleep in the infirmary. The fire at the start of this passage is an actual fire, but the sea at the end is a dream:

The fire rose and fell on the wall. It was like waves. Someone had put coal on and he heard voices. They were talking. It was the voice of the waves. Or the waves were talking among themselves as they rose and fell.

He saw the sea of waves. . . . (*P64* 26)

The feminine flow of Stephen's interior corresponds to the novel's consistent references to his soul as female. He describes the creative core of his mind as "the virgin womb of the imagination" (*P64* 217). His fear of his own femininity, which relates to Kristeva's idea of abjection, brings out the dreaded paternal images of the uncanny.[1]

The next example occurs in chapter 2 after the episode of the school play, which ends with Stephen being disappointed that E——. C——. does not hail his performance. His bitterness about being unable to make contact with her seems to carry through to his depression on the train to Cork on the next page. The dread he feels on this ride may be related to the fact that it begins the only long period that he spends with his father. He falls asleep, and when he wakes next to the sleeping Simon, we are told that "the terror of sleep fascinated his mind," suggesting that what frightens him is a mystery of inwardness. "The neighbourhood of unseen sleepers filled him with strange dread as though they could harm him; and he prayed that the day might come quickly" (*P64* 87). His prayer, "addressed neither to God nor saint," trails off into "foolish words" that he makes "to fit the insistent rhythm of the train." The paragraph ends, "This furious music allayed his dread and, leaning against the windowledge, he let his eyelids close again" (*P64* 87). I suspect that the prayer is addressed to his mother, to whom he wrote an imaginary letter to relieve his anxiety in the infirmary in chapter 1. When he becomes religious, it is Mary (which is his mother's name) he prays to. The rhythmic language that relieves him and allows him to return to sleep corresponds to the maternal pulsative aspect of language that Kristeva calls the semiotic. He escapes his dread by projecting a personal version of his mother.

The chapter most dominated by the male language of authority is the third, and the most oppressive thing about Father Arnall's sermons may be not their gore but their logic. An elaborate system of categories subdivides the main division between physical and spiritual pains in hell. The four "last things," the faculties of the body, the phases of experience and memory, the worm of the triple sting, the pains of extension and intensity, and other components of psychology and morality are unfolded methodically to give a feeling that every possibility is accounted for. And all these layers of proof impress on the audience that the obsessive understanding behind this vision cannot be escaped because of its rigorous masculine rationality.

The most uncanny or scariest point in chapter 3 occurs when Stephen halts on the landing before his room and hears demonic voices speaking like bureaucrats:

> He waited still at the threshold as at the entrance to some dark cave. Faces
> were there; eyes: they waited and watched.
> —We knew perfectly well of course that although it was bound to come to
> the light he would find considerable difficulty in endeavouring to try to in-
> duce himself to try to endeavour to ascertain the spiritual plenipotentiary and
> so we knew of course perfectly well—(P64 136)

Evil people can be frightening, ghosts are worse, vampires are worse still,
demons are even worse than that, and then there are administrators. This demonic discourse embodies the compulsively methodical logic of the Church,
which has just hit Stephen with a mechanical exposition of the awfulness of
eternity. Here there are swarms of judgmental latinate phrases such as "perfectly well of course," "considerable difficulty," and "to endeavour to ascer-
tain." The confused repetition corresponds to the dreary repetition of the sermons, implying that this grinding system is really demented. The "it" that "was
bound to come to the light" is Stephen's sexual sin. This was described at the
end of chapter 2, not in phallic terms but in terms of being overwhelmed by
femininity. Therefore what the demons say is that they knew he would go on
seeking feminine release with prostitutes rather than recognizing the phallic
power of God, represented by the word *plenipotentiary*, which means full of
potency.

This moment of confrontation with ecclesiastical authority may be the
most frightening moment in *Portrait*. It forces Stephen's conversion, and is
followed by (and perhaps results in) his scatological dream of goatish creatures
in a field. On waking, he concludes that these excremental goats were his sins.
These sins may have been not only goatish but also excremental, yet the bi-
zarreness of that aspect is somewhat ameliorated by the fact that these sins
were extremely mental.

Calling the goats sins explains the obscenity and terror of the dream, veil-
ing it with religious terminology; and I think the reason the uncanny loses its
power after this in *Portrait* is that religion rationalizes it, making it understandable and manageable, a step forward for Stephen's consciousness. It may
be said in defense of religion that it gives people the ability to handle psychic
demons that might be there in some form before religion.

Joyce, however, concluded that the authority of the Church, which taught
him to regard it as patriarchal, and which decidedly frightened the shit out of
him, was so great that it could not be seen as giving much in relation to what
it took. Stephen says of a prostitute in *Ulysses*, "She is a bad merchant. She buys
dear and sells cheap" (U-GP 16:738). This not only describes one of the main
levels of relation that women have to the Church, but the relation of the soul,
which is always feminine (anima), to the divine paternal power to whom the
soul belongs or is sold by the Church. The idea that the Church prostitutes
the spirit is emphasized in Joyce's work from "Grace" to "Circe."

Yet the Church gives Stephen an important level of control over his mind.

Even after he leaves religion, he continues to explain frightening things systematically and intellectually; but now instead of demons, they come to represent the deadening powers of the religion and imperialism, of repression. I see this in the few traces of the uncanny in the fourth chapter: the Jesuit director who offers Stephen priesthood is described as a "spectre" (*P64* 155), and the boys he sees on the beach remind him "in what dread he stood of the mystery of his own body" (*P64* 168).

Dread of the mystery or interior of the body seems to be a common factor in all experiences of the uncanny in *Portrait*. It is associated with undressing, and as the beach scene suggests, the naked bodies that frighten him most on the conscious level are male, not female—perhaps because the attraction they have as bodies is coded as unnatural. There was the bath at Clongowes: "As he passed the door he remembered with a vague fear the warm turfcolored bogwater, the warm moist air, the noise of plunges, the smell of the towels, like medicine" (*P64* 22). In effect fear of his body is expressed as he rushes to get his trembling form under the covers before God can get it (*P64* 18). And this fear of the immanent as controlled by the transcendent is reflected in such forms as his terror of the inwardness of sleep (*P64* 87) and his fear that the pious demons know that his physical desires will come to light (*P64* 136).

The uncanniest passage in the last chapter may be an inexplicable dream in Stephen's diary that can be seen as following the lines I've developed. On this level, the first part of this dream represents the moribund rulers of tradition, while the second part shows the enslaved populace, which the diary has just referred to as "a race of clodhoppers!" (*P64* 249).

> A long curving gallery . . . peopled by the images of fabulous kings, set in stone. Their hands are folded upon their knees in token of weariness and their eyes are darkened for the errors of men go up before them for ever as dark vapours.
> Strange figures advance from a cave. They are not as tall as men. One does not seem to stand quite apart from another. Their faces are phosphorescent, with darker streaks. They peer at me and their eyes seem to ask me something. They do not speak. (*P64* 249–50)

Insofar as I can explain this dream by saying that the weary kings are the establishment and the stunted people who are not separated are the oppressed masses, the dream loses its uncanny quality and is less disturbing—and less interesting. But there is always a field behind the margin that can be explained. In this case, the dream reaches back to the ghosts at Clongowes in chapter 1, about whom Stephen thought, "What did they wish to say that their faces were so strange?" (*P64* 19). The figures in the second part of the dream (or second dream, for the diary entry refers to "dreams") have phosphorescent faces, suggesting that they are also ghosts, and the fact that "their eyes seem to ask me something" means that he wonders what they wish to say.

The inhabitants of Dublin may here be seen as walking dead, an idea developed explicitly in "The Dead." Stephen fears that it may be beyond his ability to save them, that he may end up like the established leaders, wearily gazing at their errors as dark vapors. Thus the dream also reaches forward, in that the mystery of these figures is that of the social world Stephen will encounter and struggle to understand and change.

In this sense the uncanny as the realm of uncertainty is a creative field, the area in which the disturbing unknown appears. All uncertainty includes a touch of fear, and there is virtually no creativity that does not pass through terror, which Stephen defines as the feeling that unites the mind with "the secret cause" of human suffering (*P64 204*). Such suffering, moreover, usually consists of the sensitive side of humanity, which is to say feminine feeling, subordinated to the brutal side that corresponds to male aggressiveness. Thus the language systems that constitute the genders articulate injustice, and so we return to the unnatural quality of the dominance of the phallic over the feminine.

The strongest version of the subordination of woman to the father in Stephen's life is the death of his mother, which logically follows the grinding oppression of her life, and which in *Ulysses* makes her a shadow in God's domain. When her ghost speaks in "Circe," it turns out to have no point of view of its own: it mechanically recites the threatening doctrines of the Father: "Beware! God's hand!" This destruction of womanhood corresponds to Stephen's vision in the last chapter of *Portrait* of the soul of Ireland as a "batlike" victimized woman with limited awareness of herself and a tendency to depend on the male "stranger" (183). She is the soul of Ireland in that the positioning of woman makes her the repository of sensitivity, so that, as the "Oxen of the Sun" episode suggests, the civilization of a nation may be measured by how much concern it shows for the feelings of its women (*U-GP* 14, p. 314). And if she is the soul of Ireland, then the pervasive vision of her subjugation will have to be made up for by the final focus on Molly as a woman whose mind is free of masculine control.

All of Joyce's novels move from masculine conflict to feminine release, as each chapter of *Portrait* ends with Stephen feeling he has freed himself by relating to a maternal image. The movement toward apprehending woman's position leads Stephen to realize on the last full page of *Portrait* that he was all wrong about E——. C——., as Gabriel Conroy realizes he was wrong about Gretta at the end of "The Dead." And Joyce's two main novels end with the unrestrained voices of women. This movement toward the feminine mind is motivated not only by desire but by dread. The male conflict that makes up the bulk of the typical unit of Joycean fiction will lead to abstraction and destruction unless feminine mentality relieves it.

Christine van Boheemen speaks in *The Novel as Family Romance* of a widespread tendency in Modernism to explore and promote feminine mentality, and she argues that the presentation of women in the works of male Modernists always serves male purposes (3, 38–42). What she says is true, but the involuntary nature of Joyce's drive toward contact with feminine subjectivity suggests that the need to dominate may not explain this compulsion adequately. Freud in fact says that one reason the phallus is valued by males is that it represents connection with mother (*Inhibitions* 139). Within his historic situation, Joyce made contributions to the portrayal and understanding of women, and a contribution that is also important to the development of the feminine side of man. He showed that the constitution of the genders is not natural, but is shaped by culture and driven by anxiety.

NOTE

1. Kristeva says that the abject, which involves confusion of identity with the mother, is "essentially different" from the uncanny, and more violent (*Powers* 5). But she also says that the abject causes "a massive and sudden emergence of uncanniness" (2). In Freudian terms, a woman's main conflict will tend to be with her mother, so it is appropriate that Kristeva's vision of horror centers on the mother's body. On the other hand, Freud, like Joyce, was preoccupied with father-son conflict.

WORKS CITED

Brivic, Sheldon. *Joyce between Freud and Jung.* Port Washington, N.Y.: Kennikat Press, 1980.

Freud, Sigmund. *Inhibitions, Symptoms and Anxiety.* In vol. 20 of the *Standard Edition,* ed. James Strachey. London: Hogarth Press, 1959.

———. "The 'Uncanny.'" In vol. 17 of the *Standard Edition,* ed. James Strachey. London: Hogarth Press, 1955.

Kristeva, Julia. *Powers of Horror: An Essay on Abjection.* Trans. Leon S. Roudiez. New York: Columbia University Press, 1982.

———. *Revolution in Poetic Language.* Trans. Margaret Waller. New York: Columbia University Press, 1984.

Lacan, Jacques, and the École freudienne. *Feminine Sexuality.* Ed. Juliet Mitchell and Jacqueline Rose, trans. Jacqueline Rose. New York: W. W. Norton, 1985.

Mitchell, Juliet. *Psychoanalysis and Feminism.* New York: Vintage Books, 1975.

Van Boheemen, Christine. *The Novel as Family Romance: Language, Gender, and Authority from Fielding to Joyce.* Ithaca: Cornell University Press, 1987.

Žižek, Slavoj. *The Sublime Object of Ideology.* London: Verso, 1989.

That Form Endearing: A Performance of Siren Songs; or, "I was only vamping, man"

Sebastian D. G. Knowles

The business at hand is to perform and discuss certain songs in and around the "Sirens" section of *Ulysses*, particularly Lionel's aria from Flotow's comic opera *Martha*, a German song sung by Simon Dedalus in English and known to Bloom by its Italian title, "M'Appari." A great deal has been written about this and other siren songs, and about their pertinence to Bloom's marital and extramarital situation, but by and large what has been written treats the songs as texts, not as pieces of music. This is generally true of "Sirens" criticism, which seems to be always searching for great codes. There was the gentleman from New Zealand who shoehorned the opening into *The Art of the Fugue*:[1]

The argument is intriguing, but the words don't fit. If Joyce had meant to set his words to this music, he would have omitted the extraneous "the," preserving in one neat excision both the semantic and the musical senses of the phrase. Neither does the overture act as a cryptogrammatic vehicle for musical notation, no matter how pleasant and plausible the resulting melodies may be (Rogers 15–18). It is perhaps worth leaving the false grail of fugal form

---

Notes from a Lecture/Recital given in Dublin on 17 June 1992, with Zack Bowen, page turner, songwriter, and occasional tenor.

213

aside for the present, and looking at the siren songs as pieces of music, to see how they work musically in the episode. "It was the only language" (*Ulysses* 278), Mr. Dedalus says to Ben; this, the music of what happens, is the language of what follows.

The first song sung in the Ormond Bar is sung a cappella by Lydia Douce. It's "The Shade of the Palm," a tenor aria from the musical *Floradora*. The line in *Ulysses* reads:

> Gaily Miss Douce polished a tumbler, trilling:
> —*O, Idolores, queen of the eastern seas!* (261)

This line establishes Lydia as a musical siren, with her trill, as a sexual siren, in her polishing off a tumbler, and as a singer of siren songs, for "queen of the eastern seas" recalls Cleopatra, a well-known siren, and Floradora is also a perfume, presumably containing some sort of man-luring pheromone. Here is "The Shade of the Palm," then, from the musical *Floradora*:

> There is a garden fair, set in an Eastern sea,
> There is a maid, keeping her tryst with me
> In the shade of the palm, with a lover's delight,
> Where 'tis ever the golden day, or a silvery night;
> How can I leave her alone in this dream of sweet Arcadia?
> How can I part from her for lands away?
> In this valley of Eden, fairest isle of the sea,
> Oh, my beloved, bid me to stay
> In this fair land of Eden, bid me, belov'd, to stay . . .
> Oh, my Dolores, Queen of the Eastern sea!
> Fair one of Eden, look to the West for me!
> My star will be shining, love,
> When you're in the moonlight calm,
> So be waiting for me by the Eastern sea,
> In the shade of the sheltering palm.[2]

Cleopatra is a snake in the grass throughout "Sirens": the seagreen drop-blind Lydia later lowers is associated with "*eau de Nil*" (268), the color of the viceroy's wife's dress, and Bloom echoes Enobarbus's celebration of Cleopatra with "The seat he sat on: warm" (264). *Antony and Cleopatra* is very much behind Joyce's use of this song, for "look to the West for me" is precisely what Antony would be saying to Cleopatra, and "fair one of Eden," the other half of the line, is transformed in "Sirens" to "fair one of Egypt" (266). It is worth observing that Miss Douce gets it wrong twice in the space of her one short line. It's not "Idolores," as she sings it, but "my Dolores"; neither is it "seas" but "sea."[3] With "Idolores," Joyce is preparing us for Bloom's thoughts of the croppy boy ("he dolores" [286]) and Molly ("shedolores" [275]).[4] That Bloom has not entered the bar as Lydia sings this little snatch of song and thus can have no idea that he later is mirroring her mistake is one of many fascinating narrative irregularities in "Sirens" that are perhaps worth developing in a footnote.[5]

The next song, the first one actually played on the Ormond Bar piano in "Sirens," is "Good Bye Sweetheart Good Bye." Before singing the song, Simon Dedalus raises the piano lid: "Upholding the lid he (who?) gazed in the coffin (coffin?) at the oblique triple (piano!) wires. He pressed (the same who pressed indulgently her hand), soft pedalling a triple of keys to see the thicknesses of felt advancing, to hear the muffled hammerfall in action" (263). A tuning fork, left by the piano tuner on the piano, is sounded: "From the saloon a call came, long in dying. That was a tuningfork the tuner had that he forgot that he now struck. A call again. That he now poised that it now throbbed. You hear? It throbbed, pure, purer, softly and softlier, its buzzing prongs. Longer in dying call" (264). The A from the stripling's fork is the tuning note of a con-certmaster, preparing the orchestra and the audience for the extraordinary performance to follow. And with Simon's preparatory actions a new narrative voice is set free, a voice that plays musical chairs with syntax, that rings the changes on all possible puns before proceeding. "Sirens" has many voices, all in different registers: the songs themselves, a voice with piano accompani-ment; Bloom's thoughts, a solo clarinet; the conversational voices, in the winds; the straight narrative, on strings; the trenchant syllables that shadow Bloom on his way to the bar ("With sadness . . . A man . . . But Bloom?" [258–59]), on the double basses; the leitmotivs, wandering in and out of the score like mislaid chords; and the sounds of keys, quoits, coins, knockers, tun-ing forks, garters, farts, bells, and whistles, all on percussion. This new voice, the quicksilver voice of musical language, released like music from a box with the opening of the piano lid, sounds in the highest, the merriest register of all, a glockenspiel played by a lunatic Mozart.

This Mozartean voice is also unerringly accurate in its musical renditions.[6] "Good Bye Sweetheart Good Bye" opens with four bars of triplet introduc-tion, described by the narrator as follows: "A duodene of birdnotes chirruped bright treble answer under sensitive hands. Brightly the keys, all twinkling, linked, all harpsichording, called to a voice to sing the strain of dewy morn, of youth, of love's leavetaking, life's, love's morn" (264). The performance of "Good Bye Sweetheart Good Bye" neatly circumscribes Boylan's brief ap-pearance at the bar. The first verse goes like this:

The bright stars fade, that morn is breaking,
The dew drops pearl each bud and leaf,
And I from thee my leave am taking,
With bliss too brief, *etc.*
How sinks my heart with fond alarms,
The tear is hiding in mine eye,
For time doth thrust me from thine arms;
Good bye sweet heart good bye! *etc.*

And then Bloom enters, hearing only the second verse. As Bloom enters, Boylan prepares to leave, and the mood of the song entirely switches. This is the second verse:

> The sun is up, the lark is soaring,
> Loud swells the song of chanticleer;
> The lev'ret bounds o'er earth's soft flooring,
> Yet I am here, *etc.*
> For since night's gems from heaven did fade,
> And morn to floral lips doth hie,
> I could not leave thee, tho' I said
> Good bye sweet heart good bye! *etc.*[7]

Bloom enters the bar in between the singer's reluctant decision to leave and his ecstatic decision to remain. Boylan leaves the bar not when the singer decides to leave but when the singer decides to stay:

> — . . . *Sweetheart, goodbye!*
> —I'm off, said Boylan with impatience. (267)

Boylan is off at the wrong time, leaving after the wrong verse. The song undercuts his intention, ironizing his departure.

The song's conclusion coincides with Lenehan's urging Lydia to *"Sonnezlacloche"* (266) as well as Boylan's departure, raising through the "smackable woman's warmhosed thigh" (266) the offstage presence of Molly Bloom. The associations with Molly here are narrative, as is a minor lexical adjustment to the lyrics of the song. The second verse, it will be universally acknowledged, has in it some of the worst lines in all of nineteenth-century drawing-room song. They serve Joyce's purpose well, however, for "the lev'ret" is not only a hare but figuratively a mistress (as exemplified in Shirley's *Gamester*: "Some wives will bid her husband's leverets welcome") and a spiritless person, thus combining in one word the harelike Boylan, the mistress Molly, and the spiritless Bloom. But the line "And morn to floral lips doth hie" is too horrible even for Joyce, and he changes "floral lips" to "Flora's lips":

> —Go on, pressed Lenehan. There's no-one. He never heard.
> — . . . *to Flora's lips did hie.*
> High, a high note, pealed in the treble, clear. (266)

This neat exchange from floral to Flora not only gives the moon a much more sensible place to hie to, it makes the association with Molly through the floral network that trails the Bloom family wherever it goes.[8]

I have had occasion to remark elsewhere that every song sung in the Ormond Bar is threaded with every other through common reference to the siren myth, and to Molly Bloom (Knowles 461). The next song, "Love and War," is no exception. The singer of "The Shade of the Palm" is dying to stay, the singer of "Good Bye Sweetheart Good Bye" cannot leave, and the soldier in "Love and War" sings *I care not foror the morrow"* (270). Molly is "Dolores shedolores" from "The Shade of the Palm" (275), Bloom knows where Boylan is off to after "Good Bye Sweetheart Good Bye" ("He's off. Light sob of breath Bloom sighed on the silent bluehued flowers" [268]), and "Love and War" reminds Bloom of Molly's reaction to Dollard's "belongings on show" (270) during its earlier performance. All the songs serve to underscore the centrality of Molly Bloom.

"Love and War" is a duet between a tenor, the lover, and a bass, the soldier, sung by Big Ben Dollard. Dollard begins with the tenor part by accident, with disastrous results:

> Over their voices Dollard bassooned attack, booming over bombarding chords:
> —*When love absorbs my ardent soul . . .* (270)

He is quickly corrected by Father Cowley—"War! War! cried Father Cowley. You're the warrior" (270)—and moves down to the bass part:

> —So I am, Ben Warrior laughed. I was thinking of your landlord. Love or money.
> He stopped. He wagged huge beard, huge face over his blunder huge.
> —Sure, you'd burst the tympanum of her ear, man, Mr. Dedalus said through smoke aroma, with an organ like yours.
> In bearded abundant laughter Dollard shook upon the keyboard. He would.
> —Not to mention another membrane, Father Cowley added. Half time, Ben. *Amoroso ma non troppo.* Let me there. (270)

Again, this song is afforded a sexual significance, and raises the question of what's taking place offstage. The broken tympanum announces the Virgin Mary, who, with Cleopatra, is one in the series of Bloom's sirens in the episode. Lydia will later have a "Blank face. Virgin should say: or fingered only" (285), and Mary loses the pin of her drawers again as Bloom writes to Martha (279). In "Lotus-Eaters" the Virgin Mary's church is revealed to have, like Farmer McGregor's lettuce, a dangerously soporific effect: "Safe in the arms of kingdom come. Lulls all pain. Wake this time next year" (81). Passing Bassi's blessed virgins in "Sirens," Bloom thinks:

> Bluerobed, white under, come to me. God they believe she is: or goddess. Those today. I could not see. [. . .] All comely virgins. That brings those rakes of fellows in: her white.
> By went his eyes. The sweets of sin. Sweet are the sweets.
> Of sin. (259–60)

"Sirens" is a closely woven text: the weave is never closer than it is here. The blue-robed Virgin Mary leads to the rear view of the statues (Venus Kallipyge), which leads to Raoul's mistress from *Sweets of Sin.* "I could not see" looks ahead to the blind stripling, and "Bluerobed, white under, come to me" brings us directly to the next siren song, the last words of which are, as Bloom anticipates here, "come to me."

As Cowley sings it to a painted siren on the wall:

—M'appari tutt amor:
Il mio sguardo l'incontr . . .
She waved, unhearing Cowley, her veil to one departing, dear one, to wind, love, speeding sail, return. (271)

And then Simon Dedalus has a go:

Mr Dedalus laid his pipe to rest beside the tuningfork and, sitting, touched the obedient keys.
—No, Simon, Father Cowley turned. Play it in the original. One flat.
The keys, obedient, rose higher, told, faltered, confessed, confused.
Up stage strode Father Cowley.
—Here Simon. I'll accompany you, he said. Get up. (271–72)

Cowley strides upstage, Dedalus rises, and the piece moves up three keys, from D-major, the traditional key in the English-Italian edition, to F-major, the original key for the German aria as it appeared in Flotow's Martha, "Ach so fromm." Cowley takes over the keyboard, and Dedalus sings:

When first I saw that form endearing,
Sorrow from me seem'd to depart:
Each gracefull look, each word so cheering
Charm'd my eye and won my heart.
Full of hope, and all delighted,
None could feel more blest than I;
All on Earth I then could wish for
Was near her to live and die:
But alas! 'twas idle dreaming,
And the dream too soon hath flown;
Not one ray of hope is gleaming;
I am lost, yes I am lost for she is gone.

When first I saw that form endearing
Sorrow from me seem'd to depart:
Each graceful look, each word so cheering
Charm'd my eye and won my heart.
Martha, Martha, I am sighing
I am weeping still; for thee;
Come thou lost one Come thou dear one,
Thou alone can'st comfort me:
Ah! Martha return! Come to me![9]

"M'Appari" is the central song of "Sirens"; it is the musical heart of Joyce's book. When Auguste Morel was translating "Sirens" into French, Joyce wrote to Harriet Shaw Weaver for the record: "I want the *Martha* one for Mr Morel."[10] While it is sung Bloom is most literally Odysseus, gyving himself fast with a rubber band around his fingers. When it is over Leopold and Simon are consumed into Siopold, Stephen has one father, and the book, which is about the search of father for son and vice versa, is given its impetus for the rest of the day. Lionel, the lover who sings the aria in Flotow's opera, was originally included in Siopold, according to Zack Bowen via Joseph Prescott via a Harvard proof sheet, which has the progression:

Lionel
    Leopold
        Simon
           Richie
              ~~Richsiopold~~
                Siopold[11]

After the song Bloom is "Lionel Leopold" (290) and Dedalus is "Simonlionel" (289), further tying them together through *Martha*. Mario sings *Martha* throughout *Ulysses*, he appears in "Circe" as Henry Flower, and Henry Flower sings "When first I saw," caressing on his breast a severed female head (522). Milly is "thou lost one" in "Oxen" (414), and Martha Clifford, the obvious Martha, calls Bloom "thou lost one" in "Circe" (456). But Molly is the one Bloom has lost, the one who will not "Come. To me, to him, to her, you too, me us" (276). Molly is at the center of all these songs.

Martha takes place in the Middle Ages, in the reign of good Queen Anne—according to Flotow, who obviously had no idea what he was talking about. It is the story of two women, Lady Harriet and her friend Nancy (note the authentic medieval names), who are bored and decide to go to the fair dressed as servants. There they are sold to be chambermaids for Lionel and Mr. Plunkett. In the *Odyssey*, it is Odysseus who disguises himself as a servant; in the German *Verkleidungskomödie* the cross-class-dresser is usually a woman.[12] Dressed as a maid, Lady Harriet sings "The Last Rose of Summer," a song also referred to in "Sirens":

> And *The last rose of summer* was a lovely song. Mina loved that song. Tankard loved the song that Mina.
>   'Tis the last rose of summer Dollard left Bloom felt wind wound round inside. (288)

"The Last Rose of Summer" begins "'Tis the last rose of summer, left blooming all alone" (Bauerle 383–85), and it is clear that Joyce knew about "blooming." The twenty-ninth note on the opening keyboard is "I feel so sad. P. S. So lonely blooming" (256). The fiftieth note is "Last rose Castille of summer left bloom I feel so sad alone" (257). But it is not clear how Flotow passed this song off as an original composition. The song was sung at his graveside; everyone seems to have assumed that he had composed it himself. It's lifted completely from Moore's *Irish Melodies of 1807*, where it was known as "The Young Man's Dream," "The Groves of Blarney," and by other titles. Its original history is extremely complicated: it was written either by a harper or a hedge schoolmaster in the early nineteenth century, possibly as a parody of yet another tune called "Castlehyde." Joyce had a copy of Moore's collection, and so must have Flotow, for in 1845 he beats the tune to death, scoring it for horns, for winds, for strings, for full orchestra in the overture, until you think you'll go mad if you hear it again. If you don't like the song, you're in for a terrible two hours. It's Sergeant Cuff's favorite song in *The Moonstone*; Molly reads *The Moonstone* and has a gynecologist called Collins.[13]

So "The Last Rose of Summer" is a false song, which is actually Irish, sung by a woman under a false name, disguised as a false servant, falsely contracted to Lionel in a false landscape, which is not really England. It's perfect for Joyce. Lionel falls in love with the illusion; Lady Harriet escapes, meets him hunting—"Got the horn or what?" (267)—and hounds him off to prison, where Lionel (and this is the interesting part)[14] has gone mad and doesn't recognize Lady Harriet. He only recognizes her as Martha, so she puts on peasant dress, and the opera ends with one more rousing chorus of "The Last Rose of Summer" with the illusion maintained.

Martha, then, is an unauthenticated transumption of something Irish, a cracked looking glass in which is pictured a servant, Martha and not-Martha. It is also, as Wilhelm Hübner has remarked, a comic opera obsessed with the music of language: "Der Stil des Stückes kennzeichnet sich vornehmlich durch eine besonders enge Verbindung zwischen Wort und Musik."[15] At one point in the opera, Tristan, the buffo aristocrat, opens the window and asks for "Luft," summoning a resounding blast from the wind instruments. An editor of Flotow has said that "there are many numbers in *Martha* which sound curiously like Sullivan."[16] A recent review of a performance of the opera in New York makes the same comparison: "Now, for the first time since 1944 City Opera has disinterred 'Martha' (revived is hardly the word) in what appears to be a similar attempt to pass the work off as Gilbert-less Sullivan."[17]

And there are also numbers in *Martha* that sound curiously like Joyce. One notorious example is the spinning scene, in which Harriet and Nancy, disguised as Martha and Julia, are forced to learn how to use the spinning wheel. "I can't spin" says Harriet. "Do it," says the evil Plunkett. "Like this," says the helpful Lionel, and Lady Harriet begins to enjoy it, trilling "Oh how lustig" over the grinding syncopation of the men singing "Brr, brr," imitating the sound of the rotating wheel. "Spin, spin," "Lick your finger," they cry, and Lady Harriet flies off the handle, reaching a high D, staccato in her excitement, "sending it flying with a will." They all pause for breath and Lionel asks "So now you know how?" She says yes, thanks, "here's a pass," and they're off again, laughing in exact time as Harriet rejoices at the "golden thread through my fingers," and everyone collapses in fits of helpless giggles on the floor.[18]

It's German comic romantic opera at its very worst, but it's also extremely Joycean in its overt sexuality, as coarse and comical as Lydia playing with the barpull. Sewing has represented sex since long before Bovary pricked her thumb and Gretchen sat by the spinning wheel worrying about her boyfriend,[19]

and let us not forget that *Faust* also has a quartet, which takes place in Martha's Garden,

that for Ellmann *Ulysses* is an Irish *Faust*, that Faust the University student has many connections with Dedalus,

that Gretchen's name for Faust is Heinrich, which is Bloom's assumed name when he courts his pen-pal,

who is called Martha, on whose letter he pricks his finger - no, the thread between spinning

and the eternal feminine begins, of course, with Penelope, weaving and unweaving her tapestry,

which brings us back, by a commodious vicus of recirculation, to Molly Bloom.

The spinning scene is like Gilbert and Sullivan in its wordplay—*Mädchen* rhymes with *Fädchen*, which rhymes with *Rädchen*—and Arthur Sullivan, in fact, edited the English-Italian edition of *Martha* that gave rise to the aria's popular name in the British Isles, "M'Appari." Hearing "M'Appari" sung, you notice, though Sullivan is not responsible for it, that the English translation turns the German into a patter song, especially at "full of hope and all delighted," and that the first four lines of the first verse are subtly different from the first four lines of the second—not textually, but in their emphasis. The first time the four lines are sung, you think he's with her. The second time, you know he's not. The "seemed" of "sorrow seemed to depart" cuts the illusion dead; "charmed my eye" becomes the false charm of a siren. It's a trick ending, as in "Good Bye Sweetheart Good Bye," except that here the twist is the other way, and the lover ends the second verse emphatically alone. Already within the song the impossibility of return is established. While Dedalus and Cowley are preparing to sing "M'Appari," Richie Goulding whistles "All Is Lost Now," from *La sonnambula*. This, too, parodies the Odyssean *nostos* in defeating the promise of return: "Thou lost one. All songs on that theme" (277). It has clear connections both with Molly and the siren network and acts as a prelude for Dedalus' more searing loss in "come to me," a distant accompaniment to the grander tragedy Bloom can only overhear.

During the singing of "M'Appari," Bloom thinks of his wife, of the song, of Lydia, of Martha, and back to his wife. At the end, his thoughts race toward a union with all of these, with his wife, with the song, and with the singer, as he becomes consumed by the final soaring phrase. What I would do now, if I had a piano, is play "M'Appari" again, singing only the lines of the song as they appear in Joyce's text. At the same time, I would read Bloom's thoughts, as they are recorded beside the lines of the song. The parallactic presentation of Joyce and Flotow establishes that Joyce has gone to some trouble to have Bloom's thoughts fit with the music that lies beneath his text.[20] Without a piano, I must resort to a written representation of what is essentially an aural analysis. It is not possible to reproduce here what is possible in performance, but the following gives a rough idea.[21] In what follows, the italicized lines from "M'Appari" are those also printed in *Ulysses*, quoted exactly as they appear in *Ulysses*. The rest of the song is in smaller roman type, in editorial brackets. Joycean text that is clearly attached to the music has been overlaid into the score. The rest of the text is found on pages 273–76 of the Vintage International edition. Here's how it works:

Piano again. Sounds better than last time I heard. Tuned probably.
Stopped again.[22]

harping chords of prelude

Dollard and Cowley still urged the lingering singer out with it.
—With it, Simon.
—It, Simon.
—Ladies and gentlemen, I am most deeply obliged by your kind solicitations.
—It, Simon.
—I have no money but if you will lend me your attention I shall endeavour
to sing to you of a heart bowed down.[23]

By the sandwichbell in screening shadow, Lydia her bronze and rose, a
lady's grace, gave and withheld: as in cool glaucous *eau de Nil* Mina to
tankards two her pinnacles of gold.
The harping chords of prelude closed. A chord longdrawn, expectant drew
a voice away.[24]

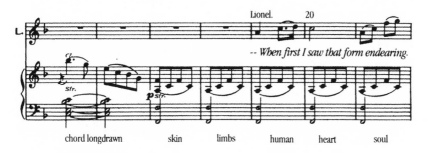

chord longdrawn   skin   limbs   human   heart   soul

Richie turned.
—Si Dedalus' voice, he said.
Braintipped, cheek touched with flame, they listened feeling that flow en-
dearing flow over skin limbs human heart soul spine.[25] Bloom signed to Pat,

bald Pat is a waiter hard of hearing, to set ajar the door of the bar. The door of the bar. So. That will do. Pat, waiter, waited, waiting to hear, for he was hard of hear by the door.

like leaves in murmur

-- *Sorrow from me seemed to depart*   Each gracefull look,

spine   like no voice of strings of reeds   troubled double

Through the hush of air a voice sang to them, low, not rain, not leaves in murmur,[26] like no voice of strings of reeds or whatdoyoucallthem dulcimers, touching their still ears with words, still hearts of their each his remembered lives. Good, good to hear: sorrow from them each seemed to from both depart when first they heard. When first they saw, lost Richie, Poldy, mercy of beauty, heard from a person wouldn't expect it in the least, her first merciful lovesoft oftloved word.

each word so cheering Charm'd my eye and won my heart .   -- *Full of hope and all delighted* . . .

in octave   Jingle all delighted

Love that is singing: love's old sweet song. Bloom unwound slowly the elastic band of his packet. Love's old sweet *sonnez la* gold.[27] Bloom wound a skein round four forkfingers, stretched it, relaxed, and wound it round his troubled double, fourfold, in octave, gyved them fast.

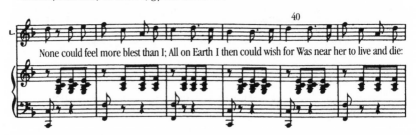

None could feel more blest than I; All on Earth I then could wish for Was near her to live and die:

Tenors get women by the score. Increase their flow. Throw flower at his feet when will we meet? My head it simply. Jingle all delighted. He can't sing for tall hats. Your head it simply swurls. Perfumed for him. What perfume does your wife? I want to know. Jing. Stop. Knock. Last look at mirror always before she answers the door. The hall. There? How do you? I do well. There? What? Or? Phila of cachous, kissing comfits, in her satchel. Yes? Hands felt for the opulent. Alas! The voice rose, sighing, changed: loud, full, shining, proud.

-- But alas, 'twas idle dreaming ... And the dream too soon hath flown; Not one –... *ray of hope* ...

Alas! The voice rose, singing, changed: loud, full, shining, proud.

Glorious tone he has still. Cork air softer also their brogue. Silly man! Could have made oceans of money. Singing wrong words. Wore out his wife: now sings. But hard to tell. Only the two themselves. If he doesn't break down. Keep a trot for the avenue. His hands and feet sing too. Drink. Nerves overstrung. Must be abstemious to sing. Jenny Lind soup: stock, sage, raw eggs, half pint of cream. For creamy dreamy.

Tenderness it welled: slow, swelling. Full it throbbed. That's the chat. Ha, give! Take! Throb, a throb, a pulsing proud erect.

Words? Music? No: it's what's behind.

Bloom looped, unlooped, noded, disnoded.

Bloom. Flood of warm jimjam lickitup secretness flowed to flow[28] in music out, in desire, dark to lick flow, invading. Tipping her tepping her tapping her topping her.[29] Tup. Pores to dilate dilating. Tup. The joy the feel the warm the.[30] Tup. To pour o'er sluices pouring gushes. Flood, gush, flow, joygush, tupthrop. Now! Language of love.

is gleaming; I am lost, yes, I am lost for she is gone. *Martha* it is.

Beaming Lydia for Lidwell squeak scarce- so la - the muse a ray Coincidence.

dimin.

- ly hear -dy like unsqueaked of hope Just going to write.

Beaming.[31] Lydia for Lidwell squeak scarcely hear so ladylike the muse un-squeaked a ray of hope.

Martha it is. Coincidence. Just going to write. Lionel's song. Lovely name you have. Can't write. Accept my little pres. Play on her heartstrings purse-strings too. She's a. I called you naughty boy. Still the name: Martha. How strange! Today.

Lionel's song.   How first he saw that form endearing,   how sorrow seemed to part,

The voice of Lionel returned, weaker but unwearied. It sang again to Richie Poldy Lydia Lidwell also sang to Pat open mouth ear waiting, to wait. How first he saw that form endearing, how sorrow seemed to part, how look, form, word charmed him Gould Lidwell, won Pat Bloom's heart.

Wish I could see his face, though. Explain better. Why the barber in Drago's always looked my face when I spoke his face in the glass. Still hear it better here than in the bar though farther.

Round and round slow.

First night when first I saw her at Mat Dillon's in Terenure. Yellow, black lace she wore. Musical chairs. We two the last. Fate. After her. Fate. Round and round slow. Quick round. We two. All looked. Halt. Down she sat. All ousted looked. Lips laughing. Yellow knees.

Singing. *Waiting* she sang. I turned her music. Full voice of perfume of what perfume does your lilactrees. Bosom I saw, both full, throat warbling. First I saw. She thanked me. Why did she me? Fate. Spanishy eyes. Under a peartree alone patio this hour in old Madrid one side in shadow Dolores she-dolores. At me. Luring. Ah, alluring.[32]

with deepening yet with rising chords of harmony.

Quitting all languor Lionel cried in grief, in cry of passion dominant to love to return with deepening yet with rising chords of harmony. In cry of li-onel loneliness[33] that she should know, must Martha feel. For only her he waited. Where? Here there try there here all try where. Somewhere.

dominant to love

Alone. One love. One hope. One comfort me. Martha, chestnote, return.

Martha return! - -*Come!*

chestnote, return.

It soared, a bird, it held its flight, a swift pure cry, soar silver orb it leaped serene, speeding, sustained, to come, don't spin it out too long long breath he breath long life, soaring high, high resplendent, aflame, crowned, high in the effulgence symbolistic, high, of the ethereal bosom, high, of the high vast irradiation everywhere all soaring all around about the all, the endlessnessnessness . . .

Siopold! Consumed.

- -To me!

più animato

Come. Well sung. All clapped. She ought to. Come. To me, to him, to her, you too, me us.

—Bravo! Clapclap. Goodman, Simon. Clappyclapclap. Encore! Clapclipclap. Sound as a bell. Bravo, Simon! Clapclopclap. Encore, enclap, said, cried, clapped all, Ben Dollard, Lydia Douce, George Lidwell, Pat, Mina, two gentlemen with two tankards, Cowley, first gent with tank and bronze Miss Douce and gold Miss Mina. (276)

"Words? Music? No: it's what's behind." And behind this heady and beautifully timed sunburst are two important words, "spin," as in "don't spin it out too long," which clearly ties the note back to Flotow's spinning-wheel scene, and "Come." "Come" appears in many forms in "Sirens": "Come on, Simon," "I'm coming," Dollard's "come down," Molly's "kissing comfits," "Elijah is com." It is sung in "Comfort me," "See the conquering hero comes," "Comes love's sweet song," and so on. "Come" presents an unexpected crux in the versions of its broken form in "Aeolus" and "Sirens." Mario sings in "Aeolus":

Co-ome thou lost one,
Co-ome thou dear one. (117)

but Dedalus sings in "Sirens":

—*Co-me, thou lost one!*
Co-me thou dear one! (275)

The exclamation marks in "Sirens" can be taken as indications of a greater emotional commitment on Dedalus's part, but how to explain the added comma and the lost *o* s? The music clearly requires some sort of separation between the syllables, but which form, "Co-me" or "Co-ome," is correct? Joyce's division of the glowworm's lamp from "The Young May Moon" in "Lestrygonians" supports the "Aeolus" reading: "Glowworm's la-amp is gleaming, love" (167).[34] The "Aeolus" reading also has the virtue of consistency through the text's various genetic transformations, having begun in manuscript as "Co-ome" and continued that way throughout the process of transcription.

The "Sirens" reading of the last phrases of "M'Appari," on the other hand, began as follows:

—*Co-ome, thou lost one!*
Co-ome, thou dear one!
Alone. One love. One hope. One comfort me. Martha, [^chestnote], re-turn!
—*Come* ⁺ . . .!
It soared, a bird, it held its flight, a swift pure cry, soar silver orb it leaped serene, to come, dont spin it out too long long breath he breath long life, soaring high, high resplendent, crowned, aflame, high in the effulgence [^symbolistic], high, of the etherial bosom, high of the vast irradiation, high, everywhere all soaring all around about the all, the endlessnessnessness.
—*To me!*[35]

In the typescript the comma of the second line was dropped for good, leaving the first comma to dangle by itself all the way into the 1990 edition. The four dots were removed from "*Come. . . . !*" and seven dots were added after "end-lessnessnessness," of which now only three remain.[36] By the first version of the page proofs, in September 1921, the second *o* of "Co-ome" had been lost; it was not until the second version of the proofs approximately a month later that "Siopold!" was added between "—*To me!*" and "Consumed" (*Ulysses: Facsimile Page Proofs* 192, 208–9).

At the same time, in October 1921, Joyce made two significant alterations to the paragraph just before "*Co-me, thou lost one!*": "Quitting all langour Lionel cried in grief, in cry of passion [^dominant] to love to return with deepening yet with rising chords chords of harmony. In cry of lionel loneliness that she should know, must martha feel. For only her he waited. Where? [^Here there try there here all try where.] Somewhere."[37] These two changes, marked here by editorial brackets, are musical, tied directly to the music of "M'Appari."[38] The phrase is amended to read "dominant to love," and the music moves smartly into the dominant at that moment (see bar 76). "Here there try there here all try where" fits exactly with the deepening yet rising chords of harmony underneath the voice (see bars 69–77). As the *io* of Siopold is not just an *i* from Simon and an *o* from Leopold but also the *io* of Lionel and an Italian *I*, so at the same time that he writes in this all-consuming word Joyce is strengthening the link between his text and Flotow's, between language and music. It is no accident that it takes as long for me to say the paragraph between "—*Come!*" and "—*To me!*" as it does for my page turner to sing the line.

Gabler, it is worth noting, chooses to keep the second *o*, both commas, three of the four dots after "—*Come!*", and all seven of the dots after "endlessnessnessness."[39] It is not clear that the "Aeolus" reading is to be preferred over the "Sirens" one, since "Co-me" is a sufficient indication to a singer to separate the word into two distinct parts, one for each of two notes, and "Co-ome" both takes the sense of the word away by misspelling it and overdetermines the sense of the word by raising the slag heap, Coombe Hill, and the sluts in the Coombe singing "*O, Mary lost the pin of her drawers.*"[40] What is clear is that Joyce is uncharacteristically precise in his musical effects at this point in "Sirens." Having sloppily mistranscribed lines from "The Shade of the Palm," "Good Bye Sweetheart Good Bye," and other half-remembered songs, he takes a certain amount of trouble to make the words and music fit. This kind of precision, it may be added, invalidates the practice of taking the final "Come!" up to the fifth, from B-flat to C, as certain tenors have allowed themselves the liberty of doing. The absence of a hyphen within the word clearly establishes unequivocally that the note is to be held and not raised.

Leopold Bloom can never return to his wife, and his desire for return to Molly is the message of "come to me." Molly is behind all these songs. She is the queen of the Eastern seas, the last rose of summer, the sweetheart in "Good Bye Sweetheart Good Bye." She is the flower of the mountain, Floradora, the Flora of "Flora's lips." Her husband's penname is Henry Flower, or Enrique de la Flor, his real name is Bloom, his member is a languid floating flower, she kisses him among the rhododendrons, she will wear a white rose, she's the Yorkshire Girl, "Rose, Rose, Rose." It *is* entirely a coincidence, however, that when "M'Appari" appeared as a jazz tune some fifteen years after *Ulysses* was published it was called "Flowers for Madame."

"Sirens" is a tremendously funny episode; it is also unbearably sad. Listening to "The Croppy Boy," the next song sung at the bar, Bloom realizes that his son Rudy is dead, that his daughter Milly is in love with a Gentile, and that he cannot have another child: "I too, last my race. Milly young student. Well, my fault perhaps. No son. Rudy. Too late now. Or if not? If not? If still?" (285). This hope, this very false and painful hope of "If not? If still?", the desire for love, a true father, a true wife, a true son, is all compressed into "The Croppy

Boy." The boy is Bloom, the last of his race; is Stephen, omitting to pray for his mother; and is the blind stripling, tapping his way to the Ormond Bar during the singing of the song, on his way back to pick up the tuning fork he left on the lid of the piano. The connections with Molly are obvious: thoughts of Molly are raging in Bloom's head as he listens to the song, the tap of the blind stripling's cane is the cockcarra on the door of 7 Eccles Street, the tap of the barpull Lydia caresses, and the phonetic link to tip/top/tup, all established as sexually descriptive verbs during "M'Appari." The betrayal of the false priest is Molly's, and the loneliness of the croppy boy is Bloom's.

While all this is going on in the bar, Molly is keeping her assignation with Blazes Boylan. It's a musical appointment as well, and presumably the songs Molly will take with her on the concert tour are rehearsed before or after anything else takes place, if anything does. Two songs lined up for the concert are the duet "La Ci Darem" and "Love's Old Sweet Song." "La Ci Darem" is, curiously, a nonstarter in "Sirens": Bloom, though he is obsessed with the correct words of the song throughout the day, never wonders about that *voglio* in the Ormond Bar. Cowley does play the *Don Giovanni* minuet before "The Croppy Boy," which would have been as good a moment as any for Bloom to think of Zerlina. But for "La Ci Darem" to appear in an episode about maids and sirens and music would perhaps be overkill: this may be a rare instance of Joycean restraint, a delicate resistance of the temptation to pile it on. In any case, the omission of Bloom's pedantic insistence on the correct words to a song is particularly interesting, given Joyce's blatant disregard of actual song lyrics throughout most of the episode.

The final piece on Molly's program, "Love's Old Sweet Song," is really, if any song is, Molly's song. Bloom thinks of it as he hears "M'Appari": "Love that is singing: love's old sweet song" (274). It should be sung at twilight, for obvious reasons, and it has to be sung at the end:

> Once in the dear dead days beyond recall,
> When on the world the mists began to fall,
> Out of the dreams that rose in happy throng
> Low to our hearts Love sung an old sweet song;
> And in the dusk where fell the firelight gleam,
> Softly it wove itself into our dream.
> Just a song at twilight, when the lights are low,
> And the flick'ring shadows softly come and go,
> Though the heart be weary, sad the day and long,
> Still to us at twilight, comes Love's old song,
> Comes Love's old sweet song.
>
> Even today we hear Love's song of yore,
> Deep in our hearts it dwells for evermore
> Footsteps may falter, weary grow the way,
> Still we can hear it at the close of day,

So till the end, when life's dim shadows fall,
Love will be found the sweetest song of all.
Just a song at twilight. . . .[41]

NOTES

1. Lees 47. The example is as printed in the *James Joyce Quarterly*. The article does usefully point out, however, that "Sirens" originally opened with an acrostic that ana-grammatizes the name of *The Art of the Fugue*'s composer. Bronze, Chips, Horrid, And (47). The new line given to "Imperthnthn thnthnthn" in the Gabler text bitches up this argument. "Wandering Rocks" also has an acrostic *(SWAM)* as Stephen envisions his mother drowning *(Ulysses* 243).

2. Leslie Stuart, "The Shade of the Palm," in Bauerle 358–61. Only the first verse is printed here. Bauerle's invaluable collection is the source for all of the song lyrics printed in these pages.

3. The dropped *h* from "Oh" we will give her, as a scribal error, since it is not aspi-rated. For more on Dolores, and on her possible connections with Swinburne, see Crumb, 239–45.

4. "Shedolores" is more likely to be Bloom's voice than the narrator's, while "he dolores" could be either narrative or indirect discourse. See below for more on this blurred distinction.

5. Bloom and the narrator do maintain a kind of counterpoint in their overlapping voices, especially in the sections describing Bloom's progress to the Ormond Bar. It is, for instance, impossible to determine whether Bloom or the narrator thinks of *Sweets of Sin* in the following passage: "Hair streaming: lovelorn. For some man. For Raoul. He eyed and saw afar on Essex bridge a gay hat riding on a jauntingcar" (263). At the beginning, the voice is clearly Bloom's and at the end it is clearly the narrator's, but "For Raoul" can be taken as either. If it is Bloom's association, it reveals Bloom's aware-ness of Boylan's role as Raoul; if it is the narrator's, it mimics Bloom's syntax to un-dercut Bloom with a reference to Boylan's correlative. The one reading is sympathetic, the other sardonic, and both occur at exactly the same time. See Knowles 447–63.

6. Though not in its attention to song lyrics, about which Joyce is strikingly cavalier.

7. John Hatton, "Good Bye Sweetheart Good Bye," in Bauerle 363–65.

8. "Doth" is also switched for "did," like "seas" for "sea" in "The Shade of the Palm," one of the many trivial adjustments Joyce makes to his song texts in "Sirens."

9. Friedrich von Flotow, "M'Appari," *Martha*, in Bauerle 395–403. English words by Charles Jeffrys. There are as many different versions of the words as there are edi-tions; this text is particularly corrupt, with variant spellings of "graceful," and what can only be described as singer's punctuation.

10. Letter to Harriet Shaw Weaver, 1 May 1925, in *Letters III* 120. Morel translated "Sirens" four years earlier: on 3 April 1921 Joyce wrote to Weaver that "about a week ago Mr Auguste Morel took *The Sirens* to translate for a French review" (*Letters I* 161). Nevertheless, Ellmann writes that the late request was "Presumably to help Morel with the translation of the *Sirens* episode" (*Letters III* 120 n).

11. Joseph Prescott, "James Joyce's *Ulysses* as a Work in Progress," quoted in Bowen

354. It is surely irrelevant that the name of a third tenor, the lead singer of the "Commodores," is also concealed in this progression.

12. Shades of Mrs. Bellingham and Mary Driscoll. The counterassaulting chambermaid ("I had more respect for the scouringbrush, so I had" [461]) is connected to Bellingham not only by virtue of appearing with her at Bloom's trial, but also by vice of originally appearing in nineteenth-century sadomasochistic soft pornography: Bellingham as *Venus in Furs* (466) and Driscoll in *The Way of a Man with a Maid*. Bloom refers to this latter book in "Sirens" ("Better give way only half way the way of a man with a maid" [288]), after the discussion of "The Last Rose of Summer."

13. Who, it should be said, is not primarily modeled on Wilkie but on Dr. Joseph Collins, author of *The Doctor Looks at Literature*.

14. Almost worth waiting for. . . . It will not have escaped students of Michael Flanders that this gambit, like many others in this essay, is lifted from *A Drop of a Hat*. Any parallels between the stately Flanders & his diffident accompanist Donald Swann and Bowen & Knowles are purely superficial.

15. Hübner 619. Hübner speaks particularly of occasions when the musical rhythm serves to underscore the dramatic situation, listing examples as follows: "'Vornehme Langeweile' (wiegendwohlklingende, einförmige 6/8-Melodie); der eitle Nichtstuer Lord Tristran (bombastisch grotesker Marsch); 'Spinnrad' (schnurrendes Motiv); das hurtige Treiben und das Durcheinanderschnattern der Mägde auf dem Markt (Jagdmusik); die 'Verlobung' des Buffopaares (mit einer altväterlich gezierten Gavotte beginnend) und vieles andere" (619).

16. Dent xvi. Dent even suggests that one song in the English-Italian edition edited by Sullivan, not found in the original, may actually have been written by Sullivan.

17. Oestreich. This was not, needless to say, a rave review: set in a seaside carnival, the production "postured interminably," "pander[ed] to current American sitcom sensibilities," and ultimately "resembled nothing so much as a televised beer commercial."

18. Flotow, act 2, Spinning Quartet. The translation is by Natalia Macfarren.

19. Schubert, "Gretchen am Spinnrade," words by Johann Wolfgang von Goethe, in *Goethe-Lieder*, 12–21. What Hübner calls the "schnurrendes Motiv" is a familiar trope for female sexuality—the magic web of the Lady of Shalott is worth recalling here. Roland Barthes remarks of Schubert's song in *The Responsibility of Forms* that "this first great song, Gretchen at the Spinning Wheel, utters the tumult of absence, the hallucination of return" (289). The hallucination of return is precisely the tumult at the heart of Rudy's reappearance, the return of Stephen's mother and Bloom's father, and the botched and thwarted reunion between the three protagonists at the book's close. Barthes is more clearly Joycean, in Howard's translation, when discussing Gretchen in *A Lover's Discourse:* "The Spinning Songs express both immobility (by the hum of the wheel) and absence (far away, rhythms of travel, sea surges, cavalcades)" (14). The only other place where cavalcades and sea surges go side by side is "Sirens," which expresses both immobility (Bloom is unable to return to 7 Eccles Street during the episode) and absence ("Sirens" acts as a cover for *Ulysses'* most absent scene).

20. The score is from Flotow, act 3. This musical text differs from Glover's version, printed in *The James Joyce Songbook*, in several respects. First, it is in F, the actual key of the performance, rather than D, the key Dedalus first plays the song in. Second, it is a piano reduction of the full orchestral score rather than an arrangement for drawing-

room piano. Flotow's introduction foreshadows the modulation in "But, alas 'twas idle dreaming," and has a long-drawn line on solo winds that Glover replaces with a breathless pause. Glover's version is the one heard on most recordings of the piece made for Joycean purposes, perhaps because it is easier to sing. I have amended the syllabification of the text printed here in order to bring it into line with the English translation. The English translation is as printed earlier (see no. 9 for variant spellings).

21. Murray Beja reminds me of the possibly apocryphal Syrian pastry chef, who, despairing of being able to properly describe the complicated steps required in the preparation of a particular pastry, simply printed her phone number in the cookbook and asked curious readers to call her. (614) 292–6065.

22. "Piano again" is a reprise: just before Dedalus is urged to perform Bloom thinks "Piano again. Cowley it is" (271). "Stopped again" similarly recalls Cowley's truncated performance of "Love and War": "Bad breath he has, poor chap. Stopped" (270). "Tuned probably" anticipates the blind stripling, and "than last time I heard" is an advance warning of the coming song. The narrator scavenges this line twenty-two bars into the song with "sorrow from them each seemed to from both depart when first they heard" (273).

23. If Cowley is playing during the persuading of Dedalus, then Simon's speech can be usefully considered a form of recitative. And Cowley presumably knows that is easier to convince reluctant singers with the music rolling. "If you will lend me your attention" is probably a gloss on "If you give me your attention I will tell you what I am," King Gama's song in Gilbert and Sullivan's *Princess Ida*. If so, this is the only identified reference to *Princess Ida* in Joyce's works.

24. "Harping" presumably refers to the arpeggiated accompaniment in the strings, played by the left hand in bars 1–7, and the right hand from bar 17. The "chord long-drawn," broken off in Glover's version, is the C^7 chord held in bars 15–16.

25. I take "human" here as a noun rather than an adjective, allowing all six to be represented in the six times repeated F-major chord.

26. The leaves can be heard falling in the melody in bars 23–24.

27. This elastic band, lashing Odysseus to the mast next to the deaf waiter, establishes "M'Appari" as the central siren song.

28. Note the anagram ("to flow") of the composer here. This flow is flower ("language of flow" [263]), the flow of language, the sexual flow in this paragraph, and Flotow himself.

29. Mabel Worthington says that this may possibly be an allusion to the fairies "Tripping hither, tripping thither" in *Iolanthe*, but it isn't. See Worthington 212.

30. Cf. "A way a lone a last a loved a long the" (*FW* 628). Love, music, and language discover each other in this paragraph; they become—what shall I call them?—the Three Graces of the Joycean world. *Finnegans Wake* continues their dance.

31. The word in the song is "gleaming." Having criticized Dedalus for "singing wrong words," Bloom is getting them wrong himself. In performance, the transition from the sung "ray of hope" to the spoken "Beaming" is an enormous fall.

32. In the next line of Joyce's text, *"Martha! Ah, Martha!"*, the "Ah" is wrong. It is a compound borrowed from "Ah, alluring." It didn't take an eon for this plastic voice to become pleonastic.

33. Lionelness is an anagram of loneliness. Note also the use of the dominant in bar 76, and the deepening/rising chord progression of bars 69–77.

34. What the glowworm possessed was, in manuscript, "laamp," then typed as "lamp," then corrected by the typist to "laamp," then returned to "lamp" for the placards, and finally corrected by Joyce in the placards to "la-amp," as it reads in the 1990 edition. The added hyphen in the placards may in this case be evidence of nothing more than frustration.

35. *Ulysses: A Facsimile*, vol. 1, P 264–65/L 355–56/N 275–76. The carets indicate insertions made in the manuscript. Note that the two insertions in the manuscript, "chestnote" and "symbolistic," are directly linked to the music: one a directive to the tenor to sing with his diaphragm, the other a comment on the nature of music in literature. The exclamation point after the unbroken "Come" is struck through, as printed here.

36. *Ulysses: Facsimile and Typescripts* 71. Other changes made in the typescript, all retained in all editions, are as follows:

dont	—>	don't
return!	—>	return.
crowned, aflame,	—>	aflame, crowned,
the vast irradiation	—>	the high vast irradiation

37. *Ulysses: Facsimile Page Proofs* 208. "In cry of passion" is reinserted by hand, since the phrase was accidentally dropped in preparing this second version of the page proofs.

38. Interestingly, this was the case with the two manuscript insertions as well.

39. *U-GP* 11:740–50. The Gabler edition also restores the original "etherial," silently corrected to "ethereal" in other editions.

40. *Ulysses* 78. Overdetermination, however, is never a bad thing; Bloom thinks of the song the sluts sing as he writes to Martha Clifford in "Sirens": "You naughty too? O, Mairy lost the pin of her" (279).

41. J. L. Molloy, "Love's Old Sweet Song," words by G. Clifton Bingham, in Bauerle 243–47.

WORKS CITED

Barthes, Roland. *A Lover's Discourse.* Trans. Richard Howard. New York: Farrar, Straus & Giroux, 1978.

———. *The Responsibility of Forms: Critical Essays on Music, Art, and Representation.* Trans. Richard Howard. Los Angeles: University of California Press, 1985.

Bauerle, Ruth, ed. *The James Joyce Songbook.* New York: Garland Publishing, 1982.

Bowen, Zack. *Musical Allusions in the Works of James Joyce.* Albany: State University of New York Press, 1974.

Crumb, Michael. "'Sweets of Sin': Joyce's *Ulysses* and Swinburne's 'Dolores.'" *James Joyce Quarterly* 28 (Fall 1990): 239–45.

Dent, Edward. Introduction to *Martha*, by Friedrich von Flotow. London: Oxford University Press, 1941.

Flotow, Friedrich von. *Martha.* Ed. Edward Dent. New York: Schirmer, 1901.

Hübner, Wilhelm. "Martha, Martha, Komm Doch Wieder!" *Musick und Gesellschaft* 13 (1963): 619.

Joyce, James. *Ulysses*. New York: Vintage International Edition, 1990.

———. *Ulysses, A Facsimile of Page Proofs for Episodes 10 and 11*. New York: Garland Publishing, 1978.

———. *Ulysses, A Facsimile of the Manuscript*. New York: Octagon Books, 1975.

———. *Ulysses, A Facsimile of the Manuscripts and Typescripts for Episodes 10–13*. New York: Garland Publishing, 1977.

Knowles, Sebastian. "The Substructure of 'Sirens': Molly as *Nexus Omnia Ligans*." *James Joyce Quarterly* 23 (Summer 1986): 447–63.

Lees, Heath. "The Introduction to 'Sirens' and the *Fuga per Canonem*." *James Joyce Quarterly* 22 (Fall 1984): 39–54.

Oestreich, James. "A Lady-in-Waiting Goes Slumming." Review of *Martha*. *New York Times*, 15 October 1990.

Rogers, Margaret. "Decoding the Fugue in 'Sirens.'" *James Joyce Literary Supplement* 4 (Spring 1990): 15–18.

Schubert, Franz. *Goethe-Lieder*. Kassel: Bärenreiter, 1971.

Worthington, Mabel. "Gilbert and Sullivan in the Works of James Joyce." *Hartford Studies in Literature* 1 (1969): 209–18.

Cribs in the Countinghouse: Plagiarism, Proliferation, and Labor in "Oxen of the Sun"

Mark Osteen

The "Oxen of the Sun" episode of Joyce's *Ulysses* presents, on several levels, a debate about human proliferation and its effects on the political economy and on the quality of life. Depicting the painful and prolonged delivery of a child to Mina and Theodore Purefoy by means of a capsule history of English prose style, the episode first confronts the inescapable fact of literary debtorship and then demonstrates how Joyce both acknowledges the debts to his predecessors and makes literary capital from them. The episode's two thematic planes intersect in Joyce's borrowings from nineteenth-century writers, particularly John Ruskin, whose writings on value, labor, and political economy reveal the same conflicts displayed in the *Ulysses* episode. Like the "Scylla and Charybdis" episode that anticipates it, "Oxen of the Sun" uses homologies between physical and artistic generation to translate the debate about human proliferation into a self-reflexive questioning of Joyce's own artistic practice. As it explores parallels between Mr. Purefoy's work in a bank and Joyce's management of the intertextual economy, the episode also discloses relationships between the Purefoys' prolific childbearing and Joyce's prolixity and textual extravagance. By pairing the intertextual and political economies, "Oxen" ultimately illustrates how Joyce privileges artistic labor—an Irish labor of excess that emerges from debt—over both the female labor of childbearing and the male labor of physical and financial begetting.

"Oxen of the Sun" is merely the most extreme example of a typical Joycean strategy that Richard Ellmann has called "inspired cribbing" (xv). The dual meanings in the word *crib*—it signifies both plagiarism and a baby's bed—

237

punningly embody Joyce's achievement in "Oxen." An instance of what Michael Riffaterre calls syllepsis (a pun that combines different etymological levels and that may incorporate opposite meanings), *crib* denotes both licit and illicit creation, and forms of it are used in both senses in the episode. In the "Ruskin" section it describes the bed of the Christ child (*U-GP* 14:1283); later Mulligan comments that Stephen's sardonic telegram ("the sentimentalist is he who would enjoy without incurring the immense debtorship for a thing done") has been "cribbed out of Meredith" (*U-GP* 14:1486). Joyce's cribbing is more systematic than Stephen's; throughout the episode, in fact, he kidnaps the literary offspring of his forebears and places them in his own textual crib. Since he borrows not only their stylistic mannerisms but also many of their words, Joyce's strategy in "Oxen" may be seen as bold plagiarism. The latter term also befits the episode's concern with offspring, since *plagiary* was originally a word for kidnapping a child.[1] By appropriating others' textual progeny and becoming their foster father, Joyce aims to beget his own literary progenitors in a manner similar to the one Stephen describes in "Scylla and Charybdis" (see *U-GP* 9:866–70).

These syllepses on *crib* and *plagiary* more generally invoke the problem of intertextuality, two versions of which have gained prominence in literary theory since the 1960s. The first and most radical depicts an infinite citationality that affects not only texts but also the consciousnesses of authors and readers. Jacques Derrida, among others who have developed the notion, employs another syllepsis, iterability, to define the linguistic condition in which repetition and alterity operate simultaneously; for him this means that "every sign . . . can be cited . . . thereby it can break with every given context, and engender infinitely new contexts in an absolutely nonsaturatable fashion" (Derrida 315). An "iterable" text is thus an original tissue of citations. To search for specific sources is precisely to miss the point: the intertextual citing (and siting) of a text in relation to the discourses of others is both ongoing and irrecoverable. In one sense "Oxen of the Sun" seems to exemplify iterability, as it undermines barriers between text and context by enveloping within its frame precisely those historical discourses that have produced the conditions for reading it. It deconstructs the difference between borrowing and originality by making the latter a function of the citationality of the text: an original author is one who cribs successfully and extravagantly. According to this reading, Joyce announces himself as artistic criminal and heretic, a plunderer of copyrights and archives, a Shem-like forger armed with a "pelagiarist pen" (*FW* 182.3) who means to "utter an epical forged cheque on the public for his own private profit" (*FW* 181.15–17). In addition to challenging legal definitions of words as property and shattering the linear version of literary history that depends upon tracing influences, such extravagant cribbing violates the author-reader contract, in which the reader's labor is rewarded with original artistic currency. If Joyce commits a "crime against [literary] fecundity" (*Letters I* 139) by stealing words and reneging on his contract, he cannot be prosecuted, since all authors are guilty of plagiary. Some are just better at it than others. Indeed, according to this theory there *are* no authors, only circulating and recirculating texts.

The other school of intertextuality argues, by contrast, that tracing specific textual debts is not only helpful but, according to Riffaterre, its most systematic theorist, compulsory. For him the intertext consists only of those texts the reader "may legitimately connect with the one before his eyes" ("Syllepsis" 626). His use of "legitimately" is telling: Riffaterre's intertextuality seeks to sanction authorial power and ownership—the same functions overturned by general citationality—by recognizing the author's ingenuity and by restoring intertexts to their rightful "owners." Riffaterre regards the intertextual stock as a kind of fund, and the author's role as resembling that of bank manager or notary. For him an author is a "guarantor, witness to a verbal contract. Intertextuality is to the hypogram [i.e., the precursor text] and its palimpsest what escrow is to the lender and the borrower" (*Semiotics* 85–86). The writer may take interest on these deposits by borrowing the words of others, but this operation, like financial usury, is subject to regulations.

Where does "Oxen" fit into these competing schemas? Although the episode seems to exemplify infinite citationality, it also bears the stylistic signatures of its originals: Joyce wants his readers to recognize his specific intertextual sources (he named them to certain friends) and invites us to try to recover the historical conditions of the discourses he imitates. But we cannot truly recover them. Instead, the borrowed styles impose upon the events a moral discourse alien to them, as for example in the famous "Bunyan" passage, in which the episode's characters are transformed into allegorical figures such as "Young Boasthard," "Cautious Calmer," "Mr Sometimes Godly," and so on (see *U-GP* 14:429–73). The styles thus demonstrate the irrecoverability not of sources but of the sociohistorical framework within which each style operates; though a style may be imitated, such imitation cannot restore to power the ideology that begets and is begotten by that style.

This fact suggests that we must further historicize plagiarism and intertextuality. When we do, we learn that plagiarism as literary theft was seldom recognized until the late sixteenth century, when economic factors (the ability for writers to live by the pen) and aesthetic movements (the new premium on originality) led writers to view words as individual property (Mallon 2, 39). Obviously, the "crime against fecundity" we call plagiarism became a "crime" only after it was perceived to be violating a law. In a sense, then, texts begin to have authors only when, as Foucault states, "authors became subject to punishment" for illicit appropriation (148). That is, the "crime" of plagiarism defines the modern notion of authorship as much as authorship defines plagiarism. Only when texts are implicated in the "circuit of ownership" or "system of property" do they become subject to legal and economic regulation (Foucault 148–49).

Thus, everything preceding the "Milton-Taylor-Hooker" passage (about line 333 in "Oxen") is public domain, since the "authors" of this passage would not have conceived of themselves as authors (owners) in the modern sense. The earlier passages represent, rather than a signed investment, a kind of collective fund of circulating capital available to all later linguistic workers.[2]

In "Oxen," then, plagiarism and originality are the poles around which the intertextual economy circulates. To be true to the historical definitions of authorship, however, we must see the episode's words as both (or first) freely circulating in a general economy of citation and (or then) manifesting the restricted economy of ownership that generated the concept of authorship. "Oxen" invokes both versions of intertextuality and in so doing weaves and unweaves itself, its catalogue of plagiarized authors at once constructing the system of authority and tearing it down. "Oxen" thus invites us to examine the economic and legal foundations of authorship, and thereby reveals what both models of intertextuality share: the recognition that authors are readers before they are writers. In foregrounding the relationship between authorship and the appropriations necessary to reading, "Oxen" valorizes the labor of reading by suggesting that readers are cocreators. The redefinition and redistribution of authorship Joyce performs here thus undermines the ideology that grounds plagiarism even as it seems to canonize those who have created it. The cataloguing of the "fathers" of English prose style actually deconstructs the models upon which such lists are based by implying that original authorship and cribbing are themselves historical constructs. In its place it proffers a paradoxical intertextual economy in which originality and authority are functions of the proliferation of plagiarism.

This leads us to my second, related topic. That the overt subject of "Oxen" is human proliferation is both stated and illustrated in the opening Latinate paragraphs, which announce that "by no exterior splendour is the prosperity of a nation more efficaciously asserted than by the measure . . . of its solicitude for . . . proliferent continuance" (*U-GP* 14:12–15). Thus all should "be fruitful and multiply." But because the passage embodies its content, its periphrastic style and tortured syntax exemplify the dangers of verbal proliferation, thus by analogy undercutting its praise for physical proliferation. Mere abundance enhances neither the quality of life nor the clarity of style. It seems, then, that the subject of "proliferent continuance" refers both to reproduction and literary production (as Robert Bell has recently noted [150]).

The tensions in the episode's treatment of proliferation are made manifest through a pun on "labor," which I want to develop a bit later. In any case, the early paragraphs seem to offer unqualified praise for proliferation, using the Purefoy family as exemplars and the idle and drunken medical students (and their cronies) as antagonists. The latter are repeatedly associated with poverty and infertility, as if to suggest negatively the connection between proliferation and prosperity. For example, the leech Lenehan is "mean in fortunes" and fraternizes with con-men and criminals (*U-GP* 14:535–37). Therefore both his purse and his scrotum are merely "bare testers" (*U-GP* 14:542–43). Similarly, "donought" Costello (*U-GP* 14:554), though he has conspired to commit plagiary ("kidnapping a squire's heir"), has only "naked pockets" to show for his criminal enterprises (*U-GP* 14:562–64).

The debate about reproduction is most apparent, however, in the passages adopted from nineteenth-century writers. This foregrounding is historically appropriate since, as Mary Lowe-Evans has shown in detail, nineteenth-century society was preoccupied with issues of population and reproduction. Both passages in question describe the Purefoys and seem to applaud their fecundity. The first announces the birth of the baby in a parody of Dickens's *David Copperfield*. It lauds mother Mina for "manfully" helping, congratulates father Theodore (Doady) and ends with "well done, thou good and faithful servant" (*U-GP* 14:1313–43). Of course, "Doady" is not here to help his wife endure her pain; moreover, the ironies of describing Mina's labor as "manful" or "helping" are excruciating. "Dickens" represses Mina's agony while aggrandizing Theodore's labor, but it is difficult to see what the latter has done that is so worthy of praise. The narrator's articulation of patriarchal values emerges plainly in his ventriloquism of the voice of Christ as master in the final lines, which are quoted from the parable of the talents. In it a master praises his good servants for multiplying what they have been given, while condemning the bad servant for failing to increase his store by trade or usury (Matthew 25:14–30). When we consider that the Dickens passage also reveals that Purefoy works as the "conscientious second accountant of the Ulster bank" (*U-GP* 14:1324), Joyce's multiple intertexts converge brilliantly: like the good servants in the parable, Purefoy's labor is to earn interest, to multiply what he has been given. Like Shakespeare's Shylock, he breeds money as well as children, but unlike the good servants and Shakespeare's merchant, he gains nothing from his chrematistic generation.[3] The new baby will be christened Mortimer, "after the influential cousin of Mr Purefoy in the Treasury Remembrancer's office, Dublin castle" (*U-GP* 14:1334–35). The parents will use this baby—like many of his siblings, named for British nobility or members of the Anglo-Protestant elite—to ingratiate themselves with wealthier relatives. This mercenary motive collides with the cloying tone of the passage; indeed, it implies that the Purefoys have used their children as currency, as ladders to class mobility. Ironically, however, by having more children than they can easily provide for, their efforts produce the opposite result.

The last of the historical pastiches (and the only one out of chronological order) mimics another nineteenth-century writer, Thomas Carlyle. Praising Mr. Purefoy for doing a "doughty deed," it names him "the remarkablest progenitor . . . in this chaffering allincluding most farraginous chronicle" (*U-GP* 14:1410–12). Since I will be discussing the passage in some detail, it is worth quoting at length:

Let scholarment and all Malthusiasts go hang. Thou art all their daddies,
Theodore. Art drooping under thy load, bemoiled with butcher's bills at home
and ingots (not thine!) in the countinghouse? Head up! For every newbegot-
ten thou shalt gather thy homer of ripe wheat. See, thy fleece is drenched. . . .
Copulation without population! No, say I! Herod's slaughter of the innocents
were the truer name. . . . She is a hoary pandemonium of ills, enlarged glands,
mumps, quinsy, bunions, hayfever, bedsores, ringworm, floating kidney, Der-
byshire neck, warts, bilious attacks, gallstones, cold feet, varicose veins. . . .
Twenty years of it, regret them not. . . . Thou sawest thy America, thy lifetask,
and didst charge to cover like the transpontine bison. (*U-GP* 14:1415–31)

"Malthusiasts" are accused of encouraging "copulation without population,"
and thus of sterilizing the act of coition. A discussion of Malthusian doctrines
is outside of my scope here; but it is clear that in "Oxen" Joyce has borrowed
Malthus's implication that "economic laws of commercial production have an
allegorical relation to the economics of human (sexual) production," a relation in which "production and reproduction contradict each other."[4]

More pertinent perhaps are the Carlylean intertexts that circulate here.
Robert Janusko (99, 126–27, 155) shows that Joyce's primary stylistic model
for the passage was Carlyle's *Past and Present* (also a fitting title for the
episode). I would suggest that Joyce has adopted some of the content as well
as the style. For example, *Past and Present* condemns in turn the gospels of
Mammonism and dilettantism, both of which are on display in "Oxen": the
Purefoys (unsuccessfully) practice the former, while the medicals exemplify
the latter. But unlike Joyce's "Carlyle," the real Carlyle criticized laissez-faire
economics for leading precisely to what Malthus predicted: "such world ends,
and by Law of Nature must end, in 'over-population'; in howling universal
famine, 'impossibility,' and suicidal madness" (179).

Borrowing Carlyle's style, Joyce inverts his views on political economy.
Carlyle's remedy for such misguided credos is, of course, labor, which he praises
indiscriminately and redundantly, especially in the section called "Labour,"
which, I submit, was Joyce's primary Carlylean intertext for the pastiche. One
excerpt from the section typifies both the real Carlyle's style and his ideology:
"Doubt, Desire, Sorrow, Remorse, Indignation, Despair itself, all these like hell-
dogs lie beleaguering the soul of the poor dayworker . . . but he bends himself
with free valour against his task and all these are stilled".[5] Ironically, Joyce's
"Carlyle," unlike his evangelical original, praises as "man's work" only Theodore's labor of sexual intercourse, not his banking job; but though her labor is
virtually ignored, it is Mina who is tortured by sorrow and pain. At any rate,
for the original Carlyle, the value of labor is limitless: "labor is life" (191).

The Joycean Carlyle's words, however, owe more to Ruskin's economic
ideas than to the real Carlyle's. Joyce's familiarity with Ruskin has been well
documented, and it appears initially that he borrowed Ruskin's definitions of
value and labor as the cornerstones of the episode's anticontraceptive preach-

ments.[6] In *Unto This Last* (1862) Ruskin defines value as that which "avails toward life" (17:84). This enables him to divide labor into positive and negative kinds: "the positive, that which produces life; the negative, that which produces death; the most directly negative labour being murder, and the most directly positive, the bearing and rearing of children" (17:97). Rebutting Malthusians, he asserts instead that "the final outcome and consummation of all wealth is in the producing as many as possible full-breathed, bright-eyed, and happy-hearted human creatures" (17:56). In sum, he boldly states, "THERE IS NO WEALTH BUT LIFE" (17:105).

However, Ruskin's definitions of key terms, particularly *labor* and *life*, complicate these straightforward axioms. He immediately qualifies his distinction between positive and negative labor by noting that he means "rearing not begetting," and implies that a person is not truly created until he or she is grown up (17:97). Merely begetting a child is not particularly worthy of praise. In *Munera Pulveris* (1866) he further refines his definition of *life*. Now advocating increasing the population only "so far as that increase is consistent with their happiness" (17:148), he defines the goal of political economy as "the multiplication of human life at the highest standard" (17:150). Dunned by the butcher, "drooping" under their load of children and work, and with Mina chronically ill, the Purefoys have surpassed the number of children that Ruskin would find consistent with their happiness.

As for labor, Ruskin believed that its most unpleasant aspects were "what is mechanical about it" (Anthony 157). If, as Leopold Bloom earlier observes, the Purefoys produce "hardy annuals," mechanically and methodically making children as a factory manufactures goods, then for Ruskin their methods sap their labor of its positive qualities (*U-GP* 8:358–65). As the "Carlyle" passage implies, Theodore works in the "countinghouse" to multiply the "ingots" (i.e., money) of others; thus his principal labor is generating interest. Drawing from Aristotle and the Bible, Ruskin condemned all taking of interest as illicit (see 34:417); according to him, then, Theodore's bank job would be negative labor and would offset the positive aspects of his reproductive "work." Indeed, the Purefoys turn their house into a countinghouse by attempting to generate wealth through reproduction. Theodore's generation of financial and physical offspring are thus homologous: both are excessive and chrematistic. A kind of inverse Shylock who equates ducats and daughters, Purefoy breeds more of the latter than of the former. In "Calypso" Bloom makes his own deposits into what he calls his "countinghouse": the jakes (*U-GP* 4:499). This connection between the outhouse and the countinghouse further suggests that the Purefoy children, used as "ingots" by their parents, are little more than excremental deposits, at once precious and worthless. Thus Bloom consistently confuses the Purefoys with hack writer Philip Beaufoy, whose "prize titbit" literary productions become toilet paper in Bloom's "countinghouse." Since the family's energy is directed toward the purgation of birth rather than toward provision, the Purefoy children, their parents' prize titbits, may seem as superfluous as Beaufoy's productions.

But what of Mina's labor? It is certainly arduous enough: even the "Carlyle" passage acknowledges her suffering on the way to dismissing it. Upon first hearing about Mina's protracted labor from his ex-paramour, Josie Breen, Bloom is led to think of childbirth as "life with hard labour" (U-GP 8:378), as if it were a prison sentence. Similarly in "Oxen" Crotthers comments ironically on "women workers subjected to heavy labours in the workshop" (U-GP 14:1258). Indeed, this birth is not only the most difficult that Mina has endured; it is the most difficult even that the experienced nurse Callan has ever witnessed (U-GP 14:116). Thus she may be forgiven if her attitude toward this pregnancy is rather less joyful than the "Carlyle" narrator's. In any case, Mina Purefoy's "job"—bearing babies—is labor. In this respect Ruskin's definition of *labor* is highly pertinent: it is "the quantity of 'Lapse,' loss, or failure of human life, caused by any effort. . . . Labour is the suffering in effort. . . . In brief, it is 'that quantity of our toil which we die in'" (17:182). For Ruskin, labor is not life-preserving, as it is for Carlyle, but rather life "spending" (17:184). Mina Purefoy's childbearing labor, which has turned her into a living encyclopedia of disease, exemplifies Ruskin's negative definition of labor. Joyce's own views about contraception are as problematic as Ruskin's views about labor. In this regard, it is worth noting, as Lowe-Evans does, that James Joyce had observed the effects of excessive childbearing on his own mother, a woman who died at the age of forty-five, in part from exhaustion brought on by seventeen pregnancies (Lowe-Evans 26; see also *Letters II* 48). Mrs. Purefoy's labor in fact resembles Marx's description of the worker in capitalist production, who owns "only [the] capacity for depletion . . . because the capitalist has purchased his [or her] capacity for production".[7] Mr. Purefoy's juggernaut of procreation begets babies as a capitalist creates surplus value—at the cost of the laborer, who in this case is also the "factory." For Mrs. Purefoy the result of this "inversion of fertilities" (Goux 233) is not wealth but, to use another of Ruskin's coinages, "illth" (17:89).

Of course, *Ulysses* elsewhere criticizes the Purefoys' proliferation, through Bloom, primarily, but also by casting Mina in the role of sacrificial victim in the Black Mass staged in the Nighttown episode. Ironically, the activity of reproduction, which ostensibly leads to prosperity and life, may, when performed to excess, "sterilize the act of coition" by robbing it of its life-enhancing sacredness. By producing more and more children without increasing their provisions or considering the mother's suffering, the Purefoys subject the act of coition to a mechanization that imitates the depredations of capitalism. As in monetary inflation, so in physical proliferation: there are more lives, but less value in each. The intertextual and textual evidence in "Oxen" thus collaborate to undermine the episode's apparent praise for proliferation by exposing the economic, physical, and spiritual effects it brings upon laborers, both male and female. And just as the episode appears to sanction (male) definitions of authority and authorship but actually challenges them by plagiaristic prolifer-ation, so it appears to applaud the patriarchal values behind excessive repro-duction (in which more children equal more possessions and greater proof of male ownership) but actually subverts them.

The relevance of these issues for the labor of artistic creation may not be immediately apparent. But we must remember that the homologies between artistic and physical generation were introduced in "Scylla and Charybdis" by Stephen Dedalus, another (would-be) writer who appears in the "Oxen" cav-alcade. These homologies therefore apply to him. Unfortunately, Stephen's lit-erary offspring so far consist of the vampire poem he scribbles in "Proteus" and the parable of the plums he narrates in "Aeolus." His problem is not excessive proliferation but its opposite, artistic contraception. He *has* spent money: en-tering the hospital with £2 19s of his £3 12s wages (*U-GP* 14:286–88), he buys two more rounds of drinks for himself and his cronies, and he enters Night-town with about £2 14s 7d.[8] He will spend another pound at Bella Cohen's brothel. Unlike Joyce's, however, Stephen's expenditures remain financial rather than literary or "spiritual." The episode's extravagant marshaling of En-glish literary history thus merely highlights Stephen's artistic paralysis and suggests that his debts to these "fathers" are yet another "net" preventing his flight. Unlike Joyce, he has not learned to make interest out of his forebears' lit-erary capital nor to pay those debts by weaving them into his own currency, nor to incorporate the female principle he describes at such length. Stephen's artistic identity is thus captured in the word he utters at the end of the Ruskin passage—"Burke's!" (*U-GP* 14:1390). Another syllepsis, the word *burke* (in addition to being the name of a Dublin pub owner) was derived from a famous nineteenth-century graverobber and strangler and was later expanded to de-note all kinds of smothering or suppression, but especially that of a book be-fore publication (*OED*). Stephen's artistic birth is indeed burked, his idleness starkly contrasting with both the arduous labor of Mina Purefoy, and, I now want to argue, with the labor of James Joyce.

I have argued elsewhere that we may conceive of Joyce's extravagant meth-ods of composition as a kind of excess expenditure of words that parallels the "spendthrift habits" he believed he had inherited from his father (*Letters II* 48; see my "Narrative Gifts"). If so, then in one way Joyce resembles Stephen. The major difference lies in the fact of labor: unlike Stephen's, Joyce's expendi-tures themselves constitute labor. Indeed, in another sense Joyce's labor re-sembles Theodore's: in "Oxen" he treats English literary history as a kind of vault, an "immense repository" or clearinghouse from which he may draw at will (Lawrence 143). In storing, then borrowing from and expending this hoard, Joyce both increases his own stock and augments the value of his forebears' deposits. Laboring in his linguistic countinghouse, Joyce generates interest from his debts and begets his own "fathers," who have now become offspring. His labor also resembles and valorizes Mina's; it must, or it would merely duplicate the patriarchal ideology that the episode critiques, and thereby commit a "crime against fecundity." Joyce's and Mina's labor have in common an economy of excess. Joyce estimated that "Oxen" cost him "1000 hours of work" (*Letters II* 465)—less than Mina's nine months (multiplied by nine children) but an enormous expenditure nonetheless. At times Joyce, too, felt abused by this labor, writing that he worked at "Oxen" "like a galley-slave, an ass, a brute" (*Letters I* 146)—"like a very bandog" (*U-GP* 14.1414–15). Just as the delivery of baby Mortimer is the most difficult labor Mina has ever endured, so "Oxen" was for Joyce "the most difficult episode" to execute (*SL* 249). We recall that Stephen ends his description of the creative process in "Scylla and Charybdis" with an image of "weaving and unweaving" (*U-GP* 9:376–78), actions associated with Homer's Penelope and therefore with femininity. Similarly, in "Oxen" Joyce mimics what Stephen calls the "economy of heaven" in which the author, an androgynous angel, is simultaneously male usurer and female laborer (*U-GP* 9:1051–52); in revolutionizing the economy of gender and thereby becoming "a wife unto himself," Joyce brings forth his text from the intertextual economy. Joyce's delivery of the episode mimics Mina's difficult delivery of the baby; like hers, his labor is excessive, and his offspring—all the authors that he now adopts as parts of his own identity—numerous. Moreover, by legitimizing cribbing as artistic labor, the episode at once unweaves Joyce's "image" as original author and reweaves it as a female principle of collective, antiauthoritarian authority.

The debate about proliferation and economy dramatized in the episode is in fact staged on another level throughout the second half of *Ulysses*, which offers many examples of Joycean verbal proliferation (for example, the lists in "Cyclops," or the water hymn in "Ithaca"). Thus, although "Oxen" critiques the excessive proliferation of families like the Purefoys and Dedaluses (and the Joyces), its own compositional economy imitates that proliferative excess. If, as Foucault writes, "author" is the word we give to "the principle of thrift in the proliferation of meaning" (159), then Joyce redefines the nature of authorship by violating that principle. Challenging the fear of proliferation that Foucault describes as the function of authorship, Joyce instead authorizes textual excess. His banking on signs thus deconstructs the Jamesian sublime economy of art—an economy that "saves, hoards and 'banks'" (James vi)—with one of splendid expenditure. In short, "Oxen" satirizes the economy of proliferation on one level only to reinstate it on another as a principle of artistic composition. Hence, the textual economy of "Oxen" reinscribes the conflict between control and expenditure, between miser and spendthrift, that Joyce's economic habits betray again and again.

Throughout Joyce's writings Dublin and Ireland are depicted as dominated by indebtedness; his characters respond to their colonized condition by a variety of economic stratagems, most of which defy the bourgeois economy of balance and acquisition by versions of excess and illegitimacy—gift exchange, gambling, extravagant expenditures. In redefining authorship as plagiarism, as proliferation and expenditure, Joyce similarly defies the principles of bourgeois artistic economy, employing instead an economy of excess that adapts Irish economic behavior as a compositional principle. "Oxen" exemplifies and valorizes this excess, whether we conceive of it as labor or as expenditure. Extravagantly rewriting male English literary history, Joyce appropriates it for those excluded from that history: the female, the Irish. Joyce's economy of excess is thus also political, because it identifies his art as Irish labor. Moreover, if the catalogue of styles in "Oxen" shows that all authors are readers before they are writers, then it also encourages—even demands—a Joycean expenditure of labor on the reader's part. The reader of "Oxen" must revise his or her relationship to the textual and intertextual economies; we too must perform "heavy labour" in the textual and intertextual countinghouse in order to bring forth *Ulysses*. The reader, too, must labor and spend in excess; the reader too must become more Irish, more female. The labor of reading thus collaborates with the labor of writing, enabling readers to become coauthors. It is this extravagant, arduous and proliferating labor of reading and writing—Irish labor—that "Oxen" ultimately affirms.

NOTES

1. Mallon 6. The two meanings of the word were both in currency in the seventeenth century. The first use of the word in its contemporary sense is attributed by the *OED* to Ben Jonson and dates to 1601; as a term for kidnapping the word was still in use for much of that century. Other early users of the word to mean literary theft include Browne, one of Joyce's models in "Oxen." Curiously, Sterne, another of Joyce's intertexts here, was himself accused of plagiarizing Burton's *Anatomy of Melancholy* (see Mallon 12–14).

2. I am adapting the terms "linguistic capital" and "linguistic work" from Rossi-Landi 146–58 and 39–54, respectively.

3. These remarks depend upon a Greek pun on *tokos*—meaning both "interest" and "offspring"—which I have developed, along with the notion of literary usury, in my essay "Intertextual Economy."

4. Heinzelman 92. One entry in the *"Ulysses" Notesheets* establishes Joyce's familiarity with Malthusian ideas: "Malthus in Irel. food decreases arithm population incre geometrically" (282). It is also a misreading of Malthus, who did not claim that subsistence decreases, but only that it increases more slowly than population.

5. Carlyle 190. The "Labour" chapter contains not only the sentence just quoted but also an allusion to Gideon's fleece, which is used as a metaphor for the rewards gained by the "man of nature" (192). This is the same biblical passage alluded to in the "Oxen" Carlyle pastiche. At the end of "Labour" Carlyle also exhorts his readers to make the world bear them to "new Americas" (193), a metaphor also employed in the "Oxen" passage.

6. Joyce acknowledged his debt to Ruskin in a letter to Stanislaus, in which he ad-

mitted that he had been educated "by Father Meagher and Ruskin" (*Letters II* 108). According to Stanislaus, when Ruskin died, Joyce wrote a "studious imitation" of him called "A Crown of Wild Olive" (89).

7. Heinzelman 175. Similarly, Jean-Joseph Goux writes: "The position of labor within the capitalist 'act of production' reproduces in its specific domain the position of female reproductive labor within a paterialist [i.e., patriarchal and philosophically idealist] reproduction. The value of produced (children, goods), is a lost positivity, a 'surplus' that becomes estranged from the producer. The relation between mother and offspring, under the father's control, is like that between worker and product under capitalist domination. There is an *inversion of fertilities*" (233; emphasis his).

8. Stephen buys two rounds of drinks in "Oxen." The first costs him 2s 1d ("two bar and a wing" [*U-GP* 14:1502–3]) and the second about 2s 4d, for a total of 4s 5d. I have arrived at the price for the second round by calculating how many half crowns his pocket holds at the beginning of "Eumaeus," before he lends one to Corley (*U-GP* 16:195–96); the text does not specify how many, but it is probably three. I have also assumed that the expenditures must all be subtracted from £2 19s. Efforts to determine exact expenditures must remain inconclusive, however, since we never know how much money Stephen has at the end of the day, nor whether the (indeterminate number of) half crowns in "Eumaeus" are part of the total.

WORKS CITED

Anthony, P. D. *John Ruskin's Labour.* Cambridge: Cambridge University Press, 1983.

Bell, Robert H. *Jocoserious Joyce: The Fate of Folly in "Ulysses."* Ithaca: Cornell University Press, 1991.

Carlyle, Thomas. *Past and Present.* New York: Frank F. Lovell, n.d.

Derrida, Jacques. *Margins of Philosophy.* Trans. Alan Bass. Chicago: University of Chicago Press, 1982.

Ellmann, Richard. Introduction to *My Brother's Keeper,* by Stanislaus Joyce.

Foucault, Michel. "What Is an Author?" In *Textual Strategies: Perspectives in Post-Structuralist Criticism,* ed. Josue V. Harari. Ithaca: Cornell University Press, 1979.

Goux, Jean-Joseph. *Symbolic Economies: After Marx and Freud.* Trans. Jennifer Curtiss Gage. Ithaca: Cornell University Press, 1990.

Heinzelman, Kurt. *The Economics of the Imagination.* Amherst: University of Massachusetts Press, 1980.

James, Henry. *The Spoils of Poynton.* New York: Scribner's, 1908.

Janusko, Robert. *Sources and Structures of James Joyce's "Oxen."* Ann Arbor: UMI Research Press, 1983.

Joyce, James. *Joyce's "Ulysses" Notesheets in the British Museum.* Ed. Philip F. Herring. Charlottesville: University Press of Virginia, 1972.

Joyce, Stanislaus. *My Brother's Keeper: James Joyce's Early Years.* Ed. Richard Ellmann. New York: Viking Press, 1958.

Lawrence, Karen. *The Odyssey of Style in "Ulysses".* Princeton: Princeton University Press, 1981.

Lowe-Evans, Mary. *Crimes against Fecundity: Joyce and Population Control.* Syracuse: Syracuse University Press, 1989.

Mallon, Thomas. *Stolen Words: Forays into the Origins and Ravages of Plagiarism.* New York: Ticknor & Fields, 1989.

Osteen, Mark. "The Intertextual Economy in 'Scylla and Charybdis.'" *James Joyce Quarterly* 28 (1990): 197–208.

———."Narrative Gifts: 'Cyclops' and the Economy of Excess." In *Joyce Studies Annual 1990,* ed. Thomas F. Staley. Austin: University of Texas Press, 1990.

Riffaterre, Michael. *Semiotics of Poetry.* Bloomington: Indiana University Press, 1978.

———"Syllepsis." *Critical Inquiry* 6 (1980): 625–38.

Rossi-Landi, Ferruccio. *Linguistics and Economics.* The Hague: Mouton, 1975.

Ruskin, John. *The Library Edition of the Works of John Ruskin.* Ed. E. T. Cook and Alexander Wedderburn. 39 vols. London: George Allen, 1903–12.

The Irish Undergrounds of Joyce and Heaney

John S. Rickard

"Out of sight, out of mind," Leopold Bloom thinks hopefully to himself as Paddy Dignam is buried in the "Hades" episode of *Ulysses* (*U-GP* 6:872), but in *Ulysses*, what goes down must come up, and in the course of the novel we see or imagine drowned corpses popping to the surface of Dublin Bay, dead mothers and sons returned to visit the living, and even the ghost of poor Paddy Dignam himself come back for some buttermilk to soothe his stomach. Foxes, dogs, and rats scuttle through the text, digging up and "vulturing the dead" (*U-GP* 3:363–64). Even the pragmatic Bloom can't help but get nervous as he thinks of ghouls "scraping up the earth at night with a lantern . . . to get at fresh buried females. . . . Give you the creeps after a bit. I will appear to you after death. You will see my ghost after death. My ghost will haunt you after death. There is another world after death named hell" (*U-GP* 6:998–1002). Joyce's Dublin is a city of memories, of doors into the dark, "where dwell the vast hosts of the dead" that Gabriel senses at the end of "The Dead" (*D67* 223).

James Joyce and Seamus Heaney are both fascinated by the persistence of memory, especially the memory of the dead. Despite differences created by their choices of literary genre and the urban versus rural natures of their visions, both writers are particularly fascinated by the notion of an underworld of memory, a repository connected to and triggered by place, by a landscape, or, in Joyce's case, cityscape, loaded with the significance of the past and of memory.

The world of memory and the past—whether personal or cultural—is a world conceived of as in some ways *other* and *under*—a world buried, in the case of each individual, under all the moments and events that have followed it and, in the case of a culture, under all of the interpretations and retellings that stand between the original events and the present. This underworld is often accessible, as are the underworlds of Homer, Virgil, and Dante, through the landscape of the present, by finding the right *place* in our world. Whether it be across "the stream of Ocean" in Homer or through Dante's "dark wood," the imaginative landscape of the present always contains the links, triggers, and doorways that open the underworld to the writer and, consequently, the reader.

Heaney and Joyce are highly conscious of the interconnectedness of place and memory, highly aware of the presence of the dead, both in terms of our personal lives and the ghosts that haunt them, and the hovering, shaping, and directing presences of literary ancestors. Perhaps the best way to compare their visions of place, memory, and underworld is to look at the ways in which each of them appropriates Dante when constructing an underworld. Both Joyce and Heaney have paid homage to Dante, highlighting their connections and debts to the author of *The Divine Comedy*. Joyce compared his own situation as an artist most fully to Dante while writing *Ulysses*, writing to Martha Fleischmann in 1918, "I am 35. It is the age at which Shakespeare conceived his dolorous passion for the 'dark lady.' It is the age at which Dante entered the night of his being" (Ellmann's translation from the Italian, *SL* 234). Just as Joyce observed that he was "nel mezzo del cammin di nostra vita" when he composed *Ulysses*, so Stephen Dedalus describes Shakespeare in the "Scylla and Charybdis" episode, "with thirtyfive years of life, *nel mezzo del cammin di nostra vita*" (*U-GP* 9:830–31). Just so, Heaney sees himself at the start of "September Song" in *Field Work*, published when Heaney was forty years old, "In the middle of the way / under the wet of late September" (43).

What interests me here is the way in which each writer appropriates Dante, the ways in which *The Divine Comedy*—especially the *Inferno* and the *Purgatorio*—is used as a model for the presentation of the dead. The best model for carrying out this comparison is one set up by Heaney himself in his 1985 essay "Envies and Identifications: Dante and the Modern Poet." In this important and graceful essay, which appeared in the same year as *Station Island*, Heaney argues that "when poets turn to the great masters of the past, they turn to an image of their own creation, one which is likely to be a reflection of their own imaginative needs, their own artistic inclinations and procedures" (5). Briefly summarized, "Envies and Identifications" looks closely at the very different ways in which T. S. Eliot and Osip Mandelstam have constructed Dante as a literary predecessor, each poet serving the needs of his own career. Heaney argues that "Eliot's work is haunted by the shade of Dante" (as Heaney's own work seems more and more to be), and he goes on to examine the style and tone of "Little Gidding" in order to determine what it was that Eliot needed from Dante and how he went about setting up a Dante who fit those needs, a "universal" poet who writes in a language close to the "universal Latin" of the late middle ages, a poet above the frays and decay of the waste land, an "illusion of oracular authority," to use Heaney's words (9). Eliot's Dante allowed him to escape from the local, the trivial, and the particular into "an absolute and purely delineated world of wisdom and beauty," a repository of "images free from the rag-and-bone-shop reek of time and place" (9). As Heaney points out, Eliot's "Little Gidding" emulates these supposed qualities of Dante's writing, tending "to eschew the local, the intimate, the word which reeks of particular cultural attachments" (9). Eliot, then, envies and identifies with Dante's classicism, certitude, coherence, and solid anchoring in tradition, turning him into "the figure of the poet as expresser of a universal myth that could unify the abundance of the inner world and the confusion of the outer" (14).

Heaney contrasts Eliot's stately, austere Dante with Osip Mandelstam's Dante, an experimental writer closer to Rimbaud than to Virgil, an "eager" and "approachable" fellow who, in Mandelstam's words, "shakes up meaning and destroys the integrity of the image" (quoted in Heaney, "Envies" 15–16). While Eliot needed a Dante who would anchor and sustain him amid the instability and aridity of the modern waste land, Mandelstam needed a Dante who could help him liberate himself imaginatively from the constricting, suffocating didacticism of the Stalinist vision of art. Like Joyce, Mandelstam craved liberation from the confining political and artistic requirements of his culture; unlike Joyce, unfortunately, he could not flee. Naturally, however, his Dante is a figure who, in Heaney's words, "wears no official badge, enforces no party line, does not write paraphrases of Aquinas or commentaries on the classical authors" (18).

Perhaps we can turn the tables on Heaney and ask the same questions about his own appropriation of Dante, comparing it to Joyce's by focusing especially on the different ways in which each of these Irish writers constructs an "underworld" under the influence of the author of The Divine Comedy. Joyce's method of appropriation and incorporation of other authors is most often ironic and oblique. Although, as Mary Reynolds has capably demonstrated, Joyce was drawn to the grandeur of Dante's design, using it as one of the paradigms or shadow structures that underlie such books as Dubliners and Ulysses, generally his literary appropriation of Dante, seen especially in the kind of psychic underworld he creates in Ulysses, is not a translation or a veneration, but an ironic and parodic transfiguration. Joyce's ghosts are almost always personal, almost always incoherent, often ironic, and always ambiguous. Where Heaney's underworld is fundamentally Jungian and Modernist, setting up an imaginative refuge, a repository of useful information, a sounding board for the poet's own thoughts and needs, Joyce's underworld, especially as manifested in "Circe," is more Freudian than Jungian, more postmodernist than Modernist, and as much Homeric as it is Dantean. It is useful to recall that in the Odyssey, the voyage to Hades is not necessarily a journey down or underground to another world, but rather a voyage to a vague and ambiguous zone somewhere very close to our own world, a vision more compatible in some ways with the ways in which memory and the dead remain always connected to the present world of the trivial and mundane in Joyce's work: Bloom's mother's memory is attached to a potato, for example, while Stephen's vision of his mother's ghost is involuntarily provoked by a series of seemingly random and trivial events, rather than consciously summoned.

Thus, though Joyce may pattern his Dublin in part on Dante's *Divine Comedy*, his intertextuality is always ironic, deliberately confused, a little warped. For example, the passage in *Ulysses* most often compared with Dante's interviews with the dead in *The Divine Comedy* is Bloom's vision of his grandfather Lipoti Virag. Mary Reynolds has called this "a pastiche of Dante's Cacciaguida episode" from the *Paradiso*, but notes that this is mixed with "descriptive details from two cantos of the *Inferno*, the highly coloured episode of the Malebranche." "The result," Reynolds argues, "is a grotesque parody of a grandfather" (70). Bloom's progenitor is a colorful but ridiculous figure, walking, when he first appears, "on gawky pink stilts" and "sausaged into several overcoats" (*U-GP* 15:2305–6). And what sort of wisdom does grandfather Virag bring back from the world of the dead? When he is not talking nonsense or leering at prostitutes or metamorphosing wildly from a man to a weasel to pig to parrot and so on, he speaks, as Dante's and Heaney's dead spirits do, in the imperative, advising Bloom, "Never put on you tomorrow what you can wear today" and telling him to "Stop twirling your thumbs and have a good old thunk. . . . Exercise your mnemotechnic" (*U-GP* 15:2383–85). While we are free to decide that this advice is useful to Bloom in some way—that he might indeed benefit from exercising his mnemotechnic—the appearance and decorum of the speaker are a far cry from the generally dignified and decorous ghosts of *Station Island* or *Seeing Things*. Similarly, when Paddy Dignam is briefly resurrected from the dead, he is "putrid," "ghouleaten," and "mutilated" (*U-GP* 15:1204–14). Stephen's mother, May Goulding, is more of a figment of Stephen's own neurotic imagination, a ghoul compounded of guilt, fear, and sorrow, than a Dantean spirit from purgatory. She arises, "emaciated," "her face worn and noseless, green with gravemould," not in order to bring her son useful information or salvation but to berate him for not saying his prayers. "Get Dilly to make you that boiled rice every night after your brainwork," she adds (*U-GP* 15:4202–3).

More elevated figures from the cultural memory do not fare any better in Joyce's underworld; in the "Circe" episode, for example, Bloom and Stephen look into a mirror together and see reflected there the face of Shakespeare. Yet here again, Joyce opts for a fractured Danteism, a vision of Shakespeare "beardless . . . rigid in facial paralysis," who speaks nonsense "with paralytic rage" (*U-GP* 15:3821–29). Specters from the Irish Nationalist past are similarly incapacitated, as we see when absurd representations of the Croppy Boy and Old Gummy Granny arise before Stephen near the end of the "Circe" episode. These are not the weighty ghosts that Eliot's Dante would deliver, full of important information and advice to help the modern writer anchor himself in the world of the present after his return from the world of the dead; Joyce's ghosts in *Ulysses* seem more akin to the creations of Mandelstam's Dante: unstable, batlike souls with little coherence, more comic than tragic, creatures drawn more from the Freudian unconscious than from the depths of hell or the terraces of purgatory.

As Heaney's career has developed, so have his ghosts, the voices of the dead that he incorporates into his poetry. In the earlier verse up through the "bog poems," the dominant metaphor for memory is "digging" or archaeology, a stripping away of the layers of time to (literally) discover or uncover the buried dead and the significances they hold for modern Ireland. Often passive and powerless, like the bog people in such poems as "Bog Queen" and "The Grauballe Man" who rise from what Heaney has called the "memory bank" of the bog (quoted in Stallworthy 167), these awakened victims speak only haltingly, if at all, depending on the poet to interpret their experience, their significance, and, especially, their relevance to the political situation in Northern Ireland, as in "Punishment" or "Kinship." The landscape of Heaney's earlier work is a cache of cultural memory in the sense that it contains the dead themselves, ready to be exhumed, examined, and explained. In these earlier poems, the lessons the dead teach us are often inscribed on their buried bodies in the form of punishments—nooses, blindfolds, and the like—and depend on the voice of the poet for their articulation. Heaney's more recent poetry, however, relies increasingly on a more traditional, more formal method for managing the literary encounter with the dead—the *nekyia* or *katabasis*, a descent into the underworld, a summoning of the dead. The significance of what Heaney's dead have to tell us has not diminished—on the contrary, his spirits now speak more directly to the poet and the reader, and are fuller than ever of wisdom and advice about the proper role of the poet.

Heaney's turn toward Dante begins in *Field Work*, after he has moved away from the archaeological metaphors of the bog poems in *North*. Neil Corcoran has remarked that "the major poetic presence in *Field Work*, and in much of Heaney's subsequent work, is . . . Dante" (*Seamus* 129). Much has been made of Dante's influence (especially the *Purgatorio*) on "The Strand at Lough Beg" and "Station Island," and Heaney has written that he turned to Dante partly (as Mandelstam might have) for "the local intensity," the "vehemence," and the "personal realism" of Dante's writing; however, he is also attracted to Dante in a way that is closer to Eliot's reading, for he admires "the way in which Dante could place himself in an historical world yet submit that world to scrutiny from a perspective *beyond history*, the way he could accommodate the political *and the transcendent*" (18; my italics). In *Field Work* Heaney's allusions to *The Divine Comedy* tend to deploy Dante in a more violent and political manner than in his more recent verse: in "Leavings," for example, the speaker imagines Dante's hell as the appropriate place for Thomas Cromwell, despoiler of tradition, breaker of statues ("Which circle does he tread, / scalding on cobbles, / each one a broken statue's head"); in "The Strand at Lough Beg" he appropriates Virgil's cleansing gesture at the beginning of the *Purgatorio* into an elegy for a cousin murdered in sectarian violence, and he gives us the first of his translations from classical *nekyia* in his "Ugolino," a short translation from the *Inferno* that again indirectly conjures the violence in Northern Ireland and images of hunger strikers. The tone in these poems is serious and stately, as befits their subjects—a far cry from Joyce's gibbering ghouls in *Ulysses*.

The most telling sign that Heaney was attracted to Eliot's manner of appropriating Dante by the time he wrote "Station Island" is his choice of Eliot's "Little Gidding" as a model for the final section of the poem. The Dantean overtones of "Station Island" have been thoroughly discussed; the point I wish to make here concerns the nature of the ghosts in this poem—the way they talk, the things they have to say. Some of these familiar ghosts are ordinary people—a tinker, a teacher, a missionary—while others are writers—Carleton, Kavanagh, and, of course, Joyce. This combination of ordinary folks and exalted predecessors in his craft reflects in part Heaney's perhaps unconscious ambivalence about his use of Dante; to some extent he wants to evoke the pungent, local tones that Mandelstam heard in Dante's *Inferno* and *Purgatory*, while on the other hand, he seeks coherent and useful answers to important questions he needs to ask about the direction of his art and its relation to matters Irish. In "Station Island" Heaney's underworld (or, more accurately, purgatory) is full of ghosts who deliver important advice, telling the poet what he needs to hear about his own art. Like Eliot, Heaney uses Dante as a model in this poem to help himself find coherence and stability, a link with a tradition that forms itself in the course of the poem, a lineage of writers who have found their own voices despite the various nets Ireland has thrown at them. In the already famous final section of the poem, Joyce advises the poet to "swim out on your own," to forget his anxieties about the use of English rather than Irish, the need for "infantile" pilgrimages, all the "dead fires" that now constitute the ashes of "that subject people stuff" (93). Heaney's evocation of Joyce's spectral presence here consciously echoes Dante through its overt allusions to Eliot's "Little Gidding"; in fact, as Lucy McDiarmid has noted in her thorough investigation of Joyce's presence in "Station Island," this final section of that poem was "originally published under the title 'A Familiar Ghost' in the *Irish Times* on Joyce's hundredth birthday" (131). In choosing Eliot as his link to Joyce, Heaney constructs a Joyce who, while perhaps seeming a bit peevish, bears the most serious, important, and potentially liberating advice for Heaney as a poet. While the difference in genre is to some extent the determining factor here, Joyce's terse and useful words for Heaney present a marked contrast to the indecipherable ramblings of the cuckolded Shakespeare of *Ulysses*, who crows "'Tis the loud laugh bespeaks the vacant mind. . . . Iagogo! How my Oldfellow chokit his Thursdaymornun. Iagogogo!" (*U-GP* 15:3826–29). In this revealing series of apparitions of literary ancestors, Heaney chooses the more coherent, traditional model provided by Eliot (and, indirectly, by Eliot's appropriation of Dante) rather than the troubling and unstable Joycean paradigm, presumably because Heaney, like Eliot, requires an "illusion of oracular authority" to justify his own poetic needs and choices.

Heaney's volume *Seeing Things* announces itself as a *nekyia*, or descent to the underworld, by beginning with a translation of a passage from book 6 of the *Aeneid*, in which Aeneas learns of the golden bough that will provide access to the underworld, and ending with a translation from canto 3 of the *Inferno*, in which the flesh-and-blood poet journeys across the river Acheron in Charon's boat. Heaney thus sets his latest volume up as a book of memory, a summoning of the dead in which he calls forth numerous dead friends and relatives, most significantly his father. The collection announces itself with the Virgilian phrase,

the way down to Avernus is easy.
Day and night black Pluto's door stands open.
But to retrace your steps and get back to upper air,
This is the real task and the real undertaking. (*Seeing* 4)

The poet here seeks to strengthen his contact with his predecessors and his memories, both personal and literary, rather than return to the troubled upper world of present-day Ireland.

Heaney seems to be using the trope of the underworld as one way to follow Joyce's advice in "Station Island," to swim out into the watery world of memory (and *Seeing Things* is full of water, rivers, and boats), finding his subject matter primarily in his childhood memories, in the objects and activities of everyday life, and in his relationships with the dead that he remembers. The matter of Ireland can be deflected or mystified by this technique: for example, in one of the poems in the "Crossings" sequence, the speaker remembers "Those open-ended, canvas-covered trucks / Full of soldiers" that he used to see "year after year" in Ulster. "They still mean business in the here and now," he thinks, but the poem ends in an aestheticized infernal image of "a speeded-up / Meltdown of souls from the straw-flecked ice of hell" (80). In the last of the "Crossings" poems, the memory of a peace march in Northern Ireland is cast in terms of a "Scene from Dante, made more memorable / By one of his head-clearing similes"; the marchers, herded to their cars by police, resemble the shades on the bank of the Acheron in Hades, while their parked car "gave when we got in / Like Charon's boat under the faring poets" (90).

The title poem of the volume, "Seeing Things," represents the peace and coherence Heaney seems to find in the reassuring presence of Dante that hovers over the volume. The three-part poem begins with a boat ride to "Inishbofin on a Sunday morning" reminiscent of Dante's crossings in the *Inferno*, in which "our ferryman / Swayed for balance" as they sailed "evenly across / The deep, still, seeable-down-into water" (18). In the final section of the poem the speaker recalls his father, "his ghosthood immanent," after a farm accident involving a cart that "went over into a deep / Whirlpool, hoof, chains, shafts, cartwheels, barrel / And tackle, all tumbling off the world"; the disorder of the circumstance is resolved, however, by the epiphany it produces between father and son:

> That afternoon
> I saw him face to face, he came to me
> With his damp footprints out of the river,
> And there was nothing between us there
> That might not still be happily ever after. (20)

The rivers of Dante's hell become the waters of memory in *Seeing Things*, a clear, "seeable-down-into" medium that enables meaning to be retrieved from the past, a past which might seem irredeemably muddied had Heaney adopted Joyce's (or Mandelstam's) more radical construction of Dante.

Heaney's allusions to Dante in *Station Island* and *Seeing Things* enable him to create a space where, like Mandelstam, he is able to contemplate the local, the everyday, and the personal in his own language and on his own terms. More important, however, is his appropriation of Dante as a means of continuing to "swim out on his own," a technique for distancing himself from the unstable upper world of Ireland, for giving a stateliness, meaning, and coherence to his experience, his memories and his poetry. Heaney's traditional, decorous translations and adaptations of Dante allow him to create the stability Eliot sought in Dante, rather than the experimental freedom Joyce and Mandelstam found in their Dantes. The descent into an underworld populated primarily with benign spirits, objects, and memories from his own personal and artistic past allows him to confer on himself, in Neil Corcoran's words, "a wily neutrality—alert, unsubmissive, refusing declaration but implying the election of new alignments" ("Heaney's" 45). Corcoran wrote this before *Seeing Things* was published but added presciently that Heaney's recent tendency toward "poetry in translation" heightens the move toward—for want of better words—the abstract or cosmopolitan or "universal" in his work, toward what Heaney called, in an interview with Dennis O'Driscoll, his desire "to discover a sure, confident voice, born out of a particular history . . . that will be able to walk out of its colonial circumstances and be a universal voice" (13).

Neil Corcoran has suggested that Heaney's encounter with the shade of Joyce in *Station Island* is a response to his "potential embarrassment" at taking on the mantle of Catholic Nationalist poet, "visibly and publicly serving," Corcoran writes, "the position against which Joyce had uttered his 'non serviam' sixty years earlier" ("Heaney's" 42–43). Heaney's sense of having a re-

257

sponsibility as a spokesperson and yet wanting at times to evade that responsibility may explain his attraction both to Joyce as cultural icon and to the sort of Dantean voice and Dantean underworld that he describes Eliot being attracted to—a European, not insular, voice of universality, tradition, significance, and calm amid chaos—rather than Mandelstam's destabilizing Dante, a position we more readily associate with Joyce's writing.[1] We can see this concern reflected in many of Heaney's prose writings on place and literature: discussions of Kavanagh, Montague, Hardy, and John Crowe Ransom explore the tension between writers tied to the local, national, and colloquial versus those committed to the creation of a broader, more widely European or universal culture, which Heaney at one point labels "a kind of pseudo-past which can absorb the prescribed local present" ("Place" 47).

For Joyce, then, the underworld is always mixed up with the world of everyday objects, trivial events, and familiar places—a world no less confusing, chaotic, and ambiguous than our own. It perhaps contains no more than the garbled contents of our own experiences: memories that don't behave, that won't hold still or stand and deliver. In Heaney's recent verse, the underworld has become more and more of a place apart, a parallel world that serves, in some poems at least (particularly the translations that begin and end *Seeing Things*) as a sanctuary in which coherence, continuity, and tradition can be preserved. In an interview with Rand Brandes, Heaney describes the more abstract style of his recent verse as "like pseudo-translations from some unspecified middle European language" (18). For Heaney, crossing the river into the underworld is one way to escape into a world of relative peace and coherence, where the poet can "re-enter the swim, riding or quelling / The very currents memory is composed of" (*Seeing* 95).

Joyce, like Mandelstam, sought to escape what he saw as a stifling, authoritarian, paralyzed culture partly by constructing an art that ironizes, undercuts, and destabilizes tradition and thus liberates the artist and the reader; his appropriation of Dante as one source of inspiration for his psychic underworld is part of this larger strategy. Heaney, seeking like Eliot to construct a stable place to stand and speak from, has created a more coherent, classical Dantean underworld in his recent work in which "Running water never disappointed. / Crossing water always furthered something. / Stepping stones were stations of the soul." "It steadies me," Heaney writes, "to tell these things" (*Seeing* 86).

NOTE

1. In commenting on the manner in which Heaney positions himself between Joyce, Eliot, and Dante in the final section of *Station Island* in order to align himself with "Tradition with a big *T*," Lucy McDiarmid notes the poem's "determination not to be insular" and its consequent orientation "outward to a European literary tradi-

tion" (137). She argues, as I do above, that "to use Eliot with respect and admiration, as Heaney's poem does, is to get beyond provincial antagonisms to that larger Tradition which Eliot himself reverenced so much" (137–38).

WORKS CITED

Corcoran, Neil. "Heaney's Joyce, Eliot's Yeats." *Agenda* 27 (Spring 1989): 37–47.

———. *Seamus Heaney*. London: Faber & Faber, 1986.

Heaney, Seamus. "Envies and Identifications: Dante and the Modern Poet." *Irish University Review* 15 (Spring 1985): 5–19.

———. *Field Work*. London: Faber & Faber, 1979.

———. "An Interview with Seamus Heaney." With Rand Brandes. *Salmagundi* 80 (Fall 1988): 4–21.

———. *North*. London: Faber & Faber, 1975.

———. "Place, Pastness, Poems: A Triptych." *Salmagundi* 68–69 (Fall/Winter 1985–86): 30–47.

———. *Seeing Things*. New York: Farrar, Straus & Giroux, 1991.

———. *Station Island*. New York: Farrar, Straus & Giroux, 1985.

McDiarmid, Lucy. "Joyce, Heaney, and 'that subject people stuff.'" In *James Joyce and His Contemporaries*, ed. Diana A. Ben-Merre and Maureen Murphy. Westport, Conn.: Greenwood Press, 1989.

O'Driscoll, Dennis. "In the Mid-Course of His Life." *Hibernia*, 11 Oct. 1979, 13.

Reynolds, Mary T. *Joyce and Dante: The Shaping Imagination*. Princeton: Princeton University Press, 1981.

Stallworthy, Jon. "The Poet as Archaeologist: W. B. Yeats and Seamus Heaney." *Review of English Studies*, n.s., 33, no. 130 (1982): 158–74.

Cinema Fakes:
Film and Joycean Fantasy

Thomas L. Burkdall

> The act which in the ordinary theater would go on in our mind alone is . . . in
> the photoplay projected into the pictures themselves. It is as if reality has lost
> its own continuous shape and become shaped by the demands of our soul.
> —Hügo Munsterburg

As Joyce laid aside the beginnings of Ulysses to compose Exiles in 1915, one
of the first American studies of the cinema appeared. The relationship between Joyce and Vachel Lindsay's eccentric book on the photoplay, The Art of
the Moving Picture, was first noted by Austin Briggs at the Copenhagen symposium and published in the proceedings. Lindsay's book, as Briggs suggests,
bears particular relevance to the more fantastic aspects of Joyce's cinematic
techniques and aesthetics: the representation of dreams, visions, and hallucinations. Briggs also considers the similarity of these protosurrealist portions
of Joyce's fiction to the filmic fantasy of Georges Méliès. Other movie magi-
cians such as Leopoldo Fregoli, who on stage and film entertained audiences
by swiftly transforming himself into a succession of different characters seemingly instantaneously, and Billy Bitzer, later renowned as D. W. Griffith's
cinematographer, toyed with comparable techniques in their work. These
fantastic, but seemingly real, elements of the early trick film are frequently
spliced between the psychic and physical realism of Joyce's novels.[1]
  As a point of departure, one cannot help but acknowledge the convention-
ality of the dreams and visions in the early fiction—no matter how effective
they may be, the phantasms of the night and the imagination in Dubliners follow traditional paths; the events of the dreams seem little different from day-
light activities. In "The Sisters" the boy envisions the deceased Father Flynn
in his bedroom in great detail. The next day, however, the boy no longer recalls so many particulars from the dream—it has slipped back into the re-

cesses of the unconscious, never to be fully experienced by the reader, as are the more painstakingly re-created and vividly described dreams in Joyce's later works. Likewise, Gabriel's shade-filled reverie at the close of "The Dead," though specific, somber, and heart-rending, assumes a conventional, almost mundane, form. Gabriel's description of the afterlife contains nearly as many clichés as his toast to Irish hospitality after his aunts' dinner. Even Stephen's fevered prophetic visions of Parnell's funeral procession as the youngster languishes in the infirmary in the first chapter of A Portrait represent a relatively tame dream sequence.

Only in Stephen's vision of hell do we begin to receive a sense of a dream logic and the personae of the unconscious, of the fantasy that is to come in the later novels. His satyrs augur beings in the nightmare of "Circe," the goats dressed and speaking as humans reminding one of the talking animals and props of that episode. Combining sin and guilt in an archetypal form, clad in tatters, their tails covered with feces, these creatures suggest a compression of imagery resembling the logic of a dream and the techniques of Finnegans Wake: the symbolic personification of lust in its mythical avatar and those fallen beings clothed in the shabby but soiled respectability of humanity suggest the animism of sexuality and the shame frequently connected with the body. The topoi and motifs of this guilt-induced vision have been kindled by Father Arnall's fire and brimstone sermons, which, in turn, invoke centuries of Catholic imagery depicting the fates of the damned. The content of dreams and visions calls on the collective unconscious of Irish and Western culture, but it also includes the more personal mythology of the character/dreamer.

Joyce himself realized the connection between "Circe" and the cinema; if unaware of the affinity at the time of composition, it certainly became clear to him later. In the "Circe" section of his notebook for Finnegans Wake, Scribbledehobble, he writes: "Cinema fakes, drown, state of sea, tank, steeplejack, steeple on floor, camera above; jumps 10 feet, 1 foot camera in 6 foot pit" (119). The notebook entry itself suggests a staged drowning, in a tank made to look like the sea. A crewman perches on a steeple with the camera above aiming down; it may look as though an actor jumps ten feet, but it's probably just a camera in a deeper hole that creates the illusion. Such an entry not only demonstrates Joyce's awareness of cinema tricks but also that he believed film to be related to "Circe" in the context of the workbook and the technique of the episode.

The genre of the trick film may have provided Joyce with an apt model for his literary representations of dreams and fantasies. Robert Ryf tantalizes us by informing us that Georges Méliès exhibited his films near Joyce's residence in Paris in 1904.[2] The cinematic creativity of Méliès evokes apparitions and hallucinations similar to those in Ulysses and Finnegans Wake, which move toward a more fluid and transforming literature. A magician turned director, Méliès fully exploited the cinema's potential for illusion. As Gerald Mast explains, Méliès discerned "that the camera's ability to stop and start again brought the magician's two greatest arts to perfection—disappearance and conversion. Anything could be converted into anything else; anything could vanish" (38). The fluidity of change implicit here anticipates the nonlogical, free-associational style favored by surrealism, creating a prototype of this art movement which, while closely yoked with the dream world, makes use of strikingly realistic images. Typical of this genre is Méliès's 1898 film *Four Troublesome Heads*, in which the filmmaker portrays a magician who "removes his head three times over, strikes up a song with the resulting chorus, and then causes the extra heads to disappear by smashing them with a banjo" (Wakeman 752). Or one might think of Billy Bitzer's *A Pipe Dream*, a 1905 Biograph production; the *Biograph Bulletin* provides the following synopsis of the company's trick film: "A novel picture showing a young woman smoking a cigarette and dreamily blowing the smoke over the palm of her hand. As she watches the smoke the figure of a young man appears kneeling on her hand and addressing her in passionate terms. The image seems to amuse her greatly, and she tries to catch it. It vanishes as her hand goes to seize it" (Barnouw 100). Lindsay suggested that "the possible charm in a so-called trick picture is in eliminating the tricks, giving them dignity till they are no longer such, but thoughts in motion and made visible" (142).

Much of *Ulysses*, especially "Circe" and the stream-of-consciousness passages, can be discussed using the terms that Lindsay employs to analyze the potential of the inchoate form, then often referred to as the photoplay, especially the type which he calls the "picture of Fairy Splendor." In the "Photoplay of Splendor," according to Lindsay, "the camera has a kind of Hallowe'en witch power" (59). This category includes a number of subcategories, including the picture of Fairy Splendor, by which he means the "highly imaginative fairy-tale" with its attendant trick scenes, those primitive forerunners to today's special effects (62). With the motion-picture camera's ability to create sudden appearances and disappearances, transformations and other cinematic legerdemain, one can call up the dark spirits and macabre mood of Halloween and summon the type of supernatural and magical powers traditionally attributed to witches and warlocks. Lindsay might have been referring to films like Méliès's *The Vanishing Lady*, in which not only does a woman disappear from a chair (as she did on stage at the Robert-Houdin Theater), but also, with camera stops, a skeleton assumes her place. Finally, the skeleton, too, disappears and the woman reappears seated in the chair. Or perhaps he had in mind a film such as *The Devil and the Statue*, in which Satan, played by Méliès, "reaches giant proportions before a terrified Shakespearean Juliet and then, through the intercession of the Virgin Mary, shrinks to the size of a dwarf and disappears" (Wakeman 750, 754). Such techniques and events have parallels both in the supernatural world of "Circe," in which images of Bloom's grandfather and son as well as Stephen's mother return from the grave, and in many of the macabre stream-of-consciousness passages that occur to Bloom in "Hades." Among a number of possibilities, consider the mental transformations of this passage in "Lestrygonians," in which Bloom ruminates upon some ideas of advertising campaigns for Wisdom Hely, the stationer:

> I suggested . . . a transparent showcart with two smart girls sitting inside writing letters, copybooks, envelopes, blotting paper. I bet that would have caught on. Smart girls writing something catch the eye at once. Everyone dying to know what she's writing. Get twenty of them round you if you stare at nothing. Have a finger in the pie. Women too. Curiosity. Pillar of salt. Wouldn't have it of course because he didn't think of it himself first. Or the inkbottle I suggested with a false stain of black celluloid. His ideas for ads like Plumtree's potted under the obituaries, cold meat department. (*U-GP* 8:131–45)

Such grim collocations of curiosity, which led to the gruesome saline death of Lot's wife, alongside the horrific linkage of potted meat with corpses indicate the potentially macabre splicing of ideas made possible with a stream-of-consciousness that creates swift transmogrifications, with an apparent ease reminiscent of a stop-motion sequence.

As Briggs has suggested, this sorcerous power and its potentially horrifying emotional tenor manifests itself most obviously in the "Circe" episode. The stage directions of the episode indicate this from the outset:

> (*The Mabbot street entrance of nighttown, before which stretches an uncobbled tramsiding set with skeleton tracks, red and green will-o'-the-wisps and danger signals. Rows of grimy houses with gaping doors. Rare lamps with faint rainbow fans. Round Rabaiotti's halted ice gondola stunted men and women squabble. They grab wafers between which are wedged lumps of coral and copper snow. Sucking, they scatter slowly, children. The swancomb of the gondola, highreared, forges on through the murk, white and blue under a lighthouse. Whistles call and answer.*) (*U-GP* 15:1–9)

The metaphoric skeletons, the stunted figures of children, the danger, and the darkness all contribute to the disturbing atmosphere. The whistles at first appear also to be a part of this squalid district of ill repute; however, these sounds are seemingly embodied as the Call and the Answer who speak the first words of this hallucinatory drama.

A significant element of the visions in "Circe" can be linked to the type of animism that often occurs in the cinema, what Lindsay calls, in a wonderful phrase, a "yearning for personality in furniture," an aspect that "begins to be crudely worked upon in the so-called trick scenes" (61). Lindsay mentions as a "typical . . . comedy of this sort" a film titled *Moving Day*, in which the furniture and possessions of a household march by themselves from one domicile to another, relocating the family in short order. He might also have mentioned an early Dewar's whiskey advertisement of Méliès: during the film, the solemn "family portraits descend from their frames to sample" the scotch being served

(Barnouw 101). Other, later examples include Oscar Fischinger's animated advertisements during the 1930s, some of which featured armies of marching Muratti cigarettes. Similarly, inanimate objects are imbued with personality, including the power of speech, in the Circean psychodrama. The legion of furnishings, animals, elements, and even actions that (or who) exhibit personality range from the wreaths of cigarette smoke to the kisses for Bloom, from the bleats of Staggering Bob, "a whitepolled calf," to the "bright cascade" of the Poulaphouca waterfall of the upper Liffey. Each is given voice and identity by the stage directions and dialogue in the episode, the calf and the waterfall possibly having been witnesses to a masturbatory indiscretion of the young Leopold Bloom. (Perhaps they saw; evidence in "Circe" can hardly be relied upon.)

While these animated apparitions may surprise the reader, comments in earlier episodes prefigure them. In "Lestrygonians" Mrs. Breen tells Bloom of her husband Denis's nightmare in which "the ace of spades was walking up the stairs" (U-GP 8:253). And both Stephen and Bloom remark upon the often ignored voices of the inanimate world: in "Proteus," the young poet-aesthete listens to the "fourworded wavespeech" (U-GP 3:456–60). The more practical Bloom notes in "Aeolus" that machines and objects speak: "Sllt. The nethermost deck of the first machine jogged forward its flyboard with sllt the first batch of quirefolded papers. Sllt. Almost human the way it sllt to call attention. Doing its level best to speak. That door too still creaking, asking to be shut. Everything speaks in its own way. Sllt" (U-GP 7:174–177). Each of these passages is more than the onomatopoeia of Joyce's earlier work, like the sound of the cricket bats in *Portrait*—"pick, pack, pock, puck"; they represent nonhuman speech as interpreted by these two observers, individuals who attempt to discern the personality of the world about them.

Lindsay also suggests that in "all photoplays . . . human beings tend to become dolls and mechanisms, and dolls and mechanisms tend to become human" (53). He anticipates what André Bazin would later consider the cinema's "specific illusion": "to make of a revolver or of a face the very center of the universe" (1:105). One of the most human aspects of mechanisms—speech—has already been considered in Joyce's work. However, in many of the episodes of *Ulysses* Joyce also imbues humans with apparently mechanical qualities, as other critics such as Alan Spiegel have noted: reminding one of the machinelike antics of silent film stars such as Max Linder, Charlie Chaplin, or Harold Lloyd. The characters in "Wandering Rocks" resemble automatons, comprising the moving parts of a Dublin machine; in "Sirens" the humans are frequently reduced to their musical equivalents; while in "Oxen of the Sun" Bloom, Stephen, and the medical students all find themselves subjected to the ventriloquism of the author's chronological/gestational obsession; finally, in "Circe" Bloom's stiff walk turns his movements into mechanical ones.[3]

But perhaps more importantly, Joyce does attain the potential that Lindsay foresees in the photoplay of fairy splendor, "the possible charm in a so-called trick picture," by re-creating "thoughts in motion," literally embodying ideas and emotions (Lindsay 142). "Circe" represents the character's consciousness in motion, rendering the ideas and emotions of Stephen and Bloom apparent to the reader, not through the usual novelistic means of description or even by entering their streams of consciousness, a device readers of Joyce have become quite accustomed to much earlier in the novel.[4] Fantasies and thoughts are given shape and substance; the mind is projected as a dreamlike representation. For example, Bloom's trial for a catalogue of numerous and varied sex crimes—a fantasy that starts shortly after he finds himself confronted with this graffiti in nighttown: "*a scrawled chalk legend* Wet Dream *and a phallic design*" (U-GP 15:649–50)—objectifies and projects his most secret desires baldly for all readers to see and hear, to follow unequivocally, while at the same time demonstrating his own guilt concerning these longings. The apparition of Shakespeare as cuckold is similarly evocative of many buried themes:

LYNCH
(*points*) The mirror up to nature. (*he laughs*) Hu hu hu hu hu!

(*Stephen and Bloom gaze in the mirror. The face of William Shakespeare, beardless, appears there, rigid in facial paralysis, crowned by the reflection of the reindeer antlered hatrack in the hall.*)

SHAKESPEARE
(*in dignified ventriloquy*) 'Tis the loud laugh bespeaks the vacant mind. (*to Bloom*) Thou thoughtest as how thou wastest invisible. Gaze. (*he crows with a black capon's laugh*) Iagogo! How my Oldfellow chokit his Thursdaymornun. Iagogogo!

BLOOM
(*smiles yellowly at the three whores*) When will I hear the joke? (U-GP 15:3819–31)

Through the logic of dreams and the unconscious, one finds here a cinematic representation of issues and themes related to important motifs in the novel. With his allusion, one of those "chance words" that evoke memories, Lynch calls forth the bard and the question of artistic creation. Shakespeare first mouths words that actually are a variation from Oliver Goldsmith's *The Deserted Village*, raising the issue of artistry and plagiarism. Yet before Shakespeare even speaks, his appearance as antlered cuckold in the mirror brings to mind the displacement of both Bloom and Stephen. Like Bloom, Stephen has of course been denied by a usurper, although not to the joys of the marriage bed but of access to his castle-home in Sandycove. Furthermore, the vision of Shakespeare taunts Bloom's hope that his transgressions would not be found out and derides him with the laughter of a black (hence ostracized, like the Moor) castrated rooster. Bloom doubts his own masculinity through this apparition, who further mocks him with the punning variations of Othello and Desdemona—Oldfellow and Thursdaymornun—reminding him both of the waning of sexual prowess and the morning when he said nothing ("chokit") to prevent the adulterous liaison of his wife. With this densely layered passage, foreshadowing both the themes and the sort of encoding ubiquitous in *Finnegans Wake*, we certainly have moved beyond the tricks of the cinema to the dignity and artistry of thoughts in motion.

Certainly this passage and others like it suggest, as Lindsay comments, "how much more quickly than on the stage the borderline of All Saints' Day and Hallowe'en can be crossed. Note how easily memories are called up, and appear in the midst of the room. In any [photo-]plays whatever, you will find these apparitions and recollections. . . . The dullest hero is given glorious visualizing power" (65–66). In his chapter "Furniture, Trappings, and Inventions in Motion," Lindsay provides a lengthy summary and analysis of a Griffith film, *The Avenging Conscience*, a collage of macabre scenes in homage to and in imitation of Edgar Allan Poe. In this film, Griffith effortlessly enters into the world of dreams and horror, giving the audience filmic entree to the mind of the protagonist/poet of the tale and allowing them to experience the frightening rearrangements of his daily life into nightmares of murder and persecution. Likewise, using cinematic means, Joyce can easily take the reader into the depths of Bloom's and Stephen's personal Halloweens, their particular houses of horrors. We traverse the boundaries between saints and sinners, moving from All Hallow's Eve to All Saints' Day quite readily; in "Circe," the voice of all the blessed follows hard on the voice of all the damned—the difference between "the Lord God Omnipotent" and "Tnetopinmo Dog Drol eht" (as His name is rendered backwards by the chorus of the damned) is only six short lines (see *U-GP* 15:4700–720). As Lindsay suggests may occur in film, memories are called up throughout *Ulysses*—a passage from "Oxen of the Sun" explains the explosion of repressed occurrences and secret reflections in "Circe." In the voice of Cardinal Newman, the book informs us:

There are sins or (let us call them as the world calls them) evil memories which are hidden away by man in the darkest places of the heart but they abide there and wait. He may suffer their memory to grow dim, let them be as though they had not been and all but persuade himself that they were not or at least were otherwise. Yet a chance word will call them forth suddenly and they will rise up to confront him in the most various circumstances, a vision or a dream, or while timbrel and harp soothe his senses or amid the cool silver tranquility of the evening or at the feast, at midnight, when he is now filled with wine. (*U-GP* 14:1344–55)

A chance word evokes memories in "Circe," but such stimuli also bring up memories in other episodes: in "Calypso" reminiscences of earlier life with Molly arise; in "Proteus" Stephen remembers the Paris of Kevin Egan; and in "Nestor" Stephen's student Sargent triggers recollections of his own school days at Clongowes. Through Joyce's tricks that parallel those of the cinema, Bloom, our dullest hero, is given glorious, if sometimes frightening, visualizing power in many episodes of the novel, but especially in the phantasmagoria of "Circe."

Of course, "Circe" represents a stunning departure from what we previously expected of a novel; not much more than a generation ago even such an astute critic as Vladimir Nabokov could comment, "I do not know of any commentator who has correctly understood this chapter" (350). Due to its unusual qualities, critics often search for literary precedents. The list of sources that they generally offer as potential models for "Circe" includes the *Walpurgisnacht* section of Goethe's *Faust*, Flaubert's *The Temptation of St. Anthony*, and Strindberg's *A Dream Play*. Yet the common element between these works seems to be their use of words and descriptions to create the type of illusions readily achievable by the magic of the cinema. If Joyce was not actually inspired by trick films, at the very least he borrowed literary techniques from earlier attempts at what could be considered a cinematic form.

The form, tone, and technique of the episode can certainly be traced to these sources that Joyce undoubtedly knew. Goethe's *Walpurgisnacht*, that magic-filled and demonic orgy of spring, with its talking will-o'-the-wisp, its choruses of witches and wizards, and its disembodied voices, clearly offers one precedent and influences the nightmarish tone of the episode. Flaubert's *The Temptation of St. Anthony* provided a model for both the content and the appearance of "Circe." The crowded hallucinations, though peopled with folk from the ancient world rather than Dubliners, the layout incorporating various typographical devices to indicate the action and description of the hallucinations, and the magic of scenes in which buildings and their decorations sway, while the heads of the crowd become waves—all these qualities predict the form and substance of "Circe" and could only be aptly represented and convincingly performed in film. In the winter of 1898–99, Méliès filmed a version of *The Temptation of St. Anthony*, suggesting the cinematic magic inherent in the story. In his version, as you may recall, he utilizes the tricks of the camera to create a scene which Joyce certainly would have appreciated: "the camera-stop is used to transform a statue of Christ on the cross into a seductive woman" (Wakeman 752).

However, Strindberg's *A Dream Play* may be the most important source. In a preface to this work, the author defines this new genre: in it, he attempts

> to imitate the inconsequent yet transparently logical shape of a dream. Everything can happen, everything is possible and probable. Time and place do not exist; on an insignificant basis of reality, the imagination spins, weaving new

patterns; a mixture of memories, experiences, free fancies, incongruities and improvisations. The characters split, double, multiply, evaporate, condense, disperse, assemble. But one consciousness rules over them all, that of the dreamer, for him there are no secrets, no illogicalities, no scruples, no laws. He neither acquits nor condemns, but merely relates; and just as a dream is often more painful than happy, so an undertone of melancholy and of pity for all mortal beings accompanies this *flickering* tale. (175, my emphasis)

Even the set of *A Dream Play* could only be realistically represented through the magic of the cinema's special effects. Within three pages, and without a pause for the substitution of props nor time to allow for the striking of the set, a lime tree transforms from the barrenness of autumn to the green of spring again and the nearly withered monkshood blossoms anew (196–98). The audience of the play might suspend their disbelief and accept a change of lighting to represent the seasonal transformations, but to follow the stage directions literally, to relate such a "flickering tale," would require the magic of the movies.

Such magic also suggests the relationship of the movies to *Finnegans Wake*, a work in which the magic is even more complex, the changes quicker. Complex meanings emerge in a multilayered fashion from a single word or phrase from the *Wake;* at the level of a scene or a speech from the work, ambiguities and possible interpretations run nearly rampant. Tricks abound and can be used to tell the recurring stories of the human fall and the cycles of history told and retold in *Finnegans Wake*—but a complete examination of the relationship between Joyce's last complex work and the cinema is a subject for future study. These hints and the notebook's explicit connection with "Circe," however, further strengthen the case that Joyce's interest in the cinema was far from an idle pastime: with their technical wizardry, movies represent an ideal model for a literary means to re-create the dreams and fancies of Leopold Bloom and Stephen Dedalus, as well as those multiply exposed visions seen by the sleeping Humphrey Chimpden Earwicker and related to us in the montage narrative of the *Wake*. The illusions of the trick film also share affinities with the personalized but inanimate world of "Aeolus," the psychological drama of "Circe," and the streams of consciousness that Joyce presents to the reader throughout *Ulysses*.

NOTES

1. Briggs's short essay not only makes mention of Lindsay's work, it also discusses the conditions in which early cinema was shown and audience reaction to it, as well as describing the mutoscopes which Bloom mentions in "Nausicaa," and identifying the production that Bloom recalls in the phrase "Willy's hat and what the girls did with it" (*U-GP* 13:795), all within nine pages. I am grateful that his work led me to further research on Lindsay, which inspired this essay.

2. Méliès is also the most recognizable of the many early cineastes who had roots in the world of magic. See Erik Barnouw's *The Magician and the Cinema*.

3. Mary Parr, in her obsessional study, *James Joyce: The Poetry of Conscience, A Study of "Ulysses,"* links Chaplin to Bloom's stiff-walk in "Circe."

4. Whether, as Vladimir Nabokov and others have maintained, "Circe" represents *Ulysses* itself dreaming, the thoughts are still motivated—in the etymological sense of the word.

WORKS CITED

Barnouw, Erik. *The Magician and the Cinema*. New York: Oxford University Press, 1981.

Bazin, André. *What Is Cinema?* 2 vols. Ed. and trans. Hugh Gray. Berkeley: University of California Press, 1971.

Briggs, Austin. "'Roll Away the Reel World, the Reel World': 'Circe' and Cinema." In *Coping With Joyce: Essays from the Copenhagen Symposium*, ed. Morris Beja and Shari Benstock. Columbus: Ohio State University Press, 1989.

Flaubert, Gustave. *The Temptation of Saint Anthony*. Trans. Kitty Mrosovsky. Ithaca: Cornell University Press, 1981.

Gifford, Don, with Robert J. Seidman. *"Ulysses" Annotated: Notes for James Joyce's "Ulysses."* 2nd ed. Berkeley: University of California Press, 1988.

Goethe, Johann Wolfgang von. *"Faust": Part One and Sections from Part Two*. Trans. Walter Kaufmann. New York: Anchor Doubleday, 1961.

Joyce, James. *James Joyce's Scribbledehobble: The Ur-Workbook for "Finnegans Wake."* Ed. with notes and introduction by Thomas E. Connolly. [Evanston, Ill.]: Northwestern University Press, 1961.

Lindsay, Vachel. *The Art of the Moving Picture*. 1922 Rev. ed. Reprint, New York: Liveright, 1970.

Mast, Gerald. *A Short History of the Movies*. 2nd ed. Indianapolis: Bobbs, 1976.

Nabokov, Vladimir. *Lectures on Literature*. Ed. Fredson Bowers. New York: Harcourt Brace, 1980.

Parr, Mary. *James Joyce: The Poetry of Conscience, A Study of "Ulysses."* Milwaukee: Inland Press, 1961.

Strindberg, August. *Plays: Two*. Trans. with an introduction by Michael Meyer. London: Methuen, 1982.

Wakeman, John, ed. *World Film Directors*. Vol. 1: 1890–1945. New York: H. W. Wilson, 1987.

Mulligan and Molly: The Beginning and the End

Ralph W. Rader

Mulligan and Molly are clearly the literal beginning and end of *Ulysses*, as the book presents each in central focus, *solus*, at the outset and close respectively, no Stephen or Bloom in sight; and yet we are not inclined to see them as an interimplicit alpha and omega because there seems too little connection between them to give their initiating and concluding positions significance. Neither knows or is aware of the other, and by the time Molly looms into view, Mulligan has faded out of the book's awareness.[1] Mulligan, if not Molly, would apparently seem just a piece of contingency drawn into the book from Joyce's real world of bitter memory but then forgotten as the book takes its predominantly Bloomian course. But this apparent authorial lapse, I will claim, is deeply part of the book's design, so that the disconnection of Mulligan and Molly is a manifestation of their differential but structurally interrelated functions within its unity.

The apparent disjunction of the two characters is strikingly manifest in the nearly absolute contrast in their provenience and presentation. Mulligan, we know, is a transcription of Joyce's memory of the very real Oliver St. John Gogarty, as the denomination of Buck as "Malachi Roland St John Mulligan" makes internally clear (*U-GP* 14:1213). This quasi-identification is the book's most explicit indication of the pervasive interpenetration within it of the real world of the author and the supposedly autonomous realm of fiction, a fact that notably violates both old New Critical and current poststructuralist doctrinal proclamations of the separation of the factual and textual realms.

But Molly, strikingly enough in this connection and in sharp contrast to the factual Mulligan, is unquestionably and totally fictional/textual in that, much as Joyce may have derived her mentality from his observation of Nora, she can in principle have no true model in the external world, since no person in the real world can experience another person as we experience Molly, wholly from the inside, without any external anchoring perspective. In polar contrast, Mulligan is given wholly in external transcription, as befits his status as deriving from a real memory of the author, who does not presume accordingly to give us any interior view of him. The reader has no access at all to Mulligan's mind, whereas, lost in Molly's mind, he has no access to anything else. The apparently radical inconsistency of technical "point of view" presentation here, considered in the canonical terms of the traditional standard novel, would seem an extraordinary discordance in this most celebrated of all novels. But that there is consistency behind the inconsistency is suggested by Joyce's choice of names for these two characters with transposed initials: Buck (Malachi) Mulligan, Molly (Marion) Bloom.

I have argued elsewhere that Joyce's intention in *Ulysses* is in fact to reconstruct and recompose remembered contingent factualities from his real remembered life into a structure of artistic permanence, or, as Stephen more tersely and beautifully puts it, to build eternity's mansions out of time's ruins. The logic of this constructive process involved Joyce in an extraordinary spiritual journey, in the course of which he sequentially imagines his real remembered self from the outside, projects himself into Bloom's inside from an outside perspective, and then yields up that anchor as he melds fully with Molly's inner otherness, so that the whole book records, as I have put it, his "long creative passage from May Dedalus to Marion Bloom, from the dream of the time-and-tomb-bound body of the real mother from whose womb he came, to incorporation, through his experience of Nora, with the word-borne everliving body of Molly, the woman who never was" ("Exodus" 168).

I suggest now that Mulligan/Gogarty is also to be understood as a reference point, a beginning, of Stephen/Joyce's journey from the pregiven world of the real to its fictional culmination in Molly by way of Bloom. *Ulysses* is centered on the pivotal event of Joyce's life—his seduction by Nora on 16 June 1904—an event that (in his own phrase) made him a man and freed him from the memory of his mother's death and the imprisoning past to which it was connected, and left the future open to new, self-directed development. On that day, as represented in *Ulysses*, Nora is, as I have suggested elsewhere, a strongly implicit offstage presence ("Why Stephen's Hand Hurts"), but during the period of Joyce's life in the Martello tower, he was already involved with her and in fact seems to have asked her to go away with him into exile on the subsequent night (Maddox 43). Before his commitment to Nora, who was to be his psychic center and stay the rest of his life, he had found provisional spiritual support in a series of brothers/male companions—his brother Stanislaus, John F. Byrne, Vincent Cosgrave, and Gogarty, each of whom may be considered as his rival for a mother-figure woman (see Schechner 34ff)—Stanislaus the younger brother literally with their mother and later perhaps with Nora; Byrne with Mary Sheehy (as suggested by E——. C——.'s attraction to Cranly in *Portrait*);[2] and Cosgrave with Nora in 1904 (as Joyce was horrifically convinced for a few traumatic days in 1909), with Gogarty a co-conspirator, as Joyce came to believe. In *Ulysses*, however, Nora is an implicit, impending presence, Mulligan/Gogarty's rival and replacement, as she was in life.

In *Ulysses* the literal brother who was Joyce's companion-confidant, Boswell, and keeper during his youth and the early years of his exile is reduced to a single textual reference in a passage articulating the series just mentioned: "Where is your brother? Apothecaries' hall. My whetstone. Him, then Cranly, Mulligan" (*U-GP* 9:977–78).[3] Cranly/Byrne has no place in *Ulysses* except in Stephen's memory, as in the passage just quoted and, more importantly, in his earlier thought in "Telemachus," after Mulligan links arms with him, of "Cranly's arm. His arm" (*U-GP* 1:159).

In the remembered scene in *Portrait*, in which Cranly seizes and presses Stephen's arm, Stephen is "thrilled" by his touch. Just before this (*P64* 244–45) Stephen had registered Cranly's "strange smile," his "large dark eyes," "handsome" face, and "strong and hard" body.[4] Stephen nevertheless feels that the "friendship was coming to an end" as he moves toward a solitary creative life of "unfettered freedom" (*P64* 246). Stephen is subsequently unmoved when Cranly seems to offer an implicitly homosexual friendship as an anodyne against loneliness:

> —Alone, quite alone. You have no fear of that. And you know what that word means? Not only to be separate from all others but to have not even one friend.
> —I will take the risk, said Stephen.
> —And not to have any one person, Cranly said, who would be more than a friend, even more than the noblest and truest friend a man ever had.
> His words seemed to have struck some deep chord in his own nature. . . .
> —Of whom are you speaking? Stephen asked at length.
> Cranly did not answer. (*P64* 247)

In "Telemachus," despite Stephen's association of Mulligan's linkage of arms with Cranly's parallel action, there is no suggested consciousness of homosexual feeling, but there is, as with Cranly, a sense of alienation and estrangement. Stephen views the gay and witty Mulligan with disdain as a sacrilegious mocker, a weaver of the wind to whom nothing is truly serious and worthy of commitment. The threadbare Stephen bitterly resents his class inferiority to the well-fed Mulligan, who, despite his seeming to make a common intellectual cause with Stephen, obviously feels social solidarity with Haines, "stinking with money," who thinks Stephen is "not a gentleman" (*U-GP* 1:156–57).[5] Mulligan's alliance with Haines is all the more troubling because of the threat of violence implicit in the latter's strange conduct of the night before, "raving and moaning to himself about shooting a black panther"

(*U-GP* 1:61–62). In this situation Mulligan's insistence on having the key to the tower suggests that he and Haines may plan to lock Stephen out, prompting Stephen's parting epithet, "Usurper" (*U-GP* 1:744).

But Stephen's further thoughts in "Proteus" are more psychologically complex: "Staunch friend, a brother soul: Wilde's love that dare not speak its name. His arm: Cranly's arm. He now will leave me. And the blame? As I am. As I am. All or not at all" (*U-GP* 3:451–52). Now the linked arms take on an overt homosexual association in his mind, and Mulligan is seen, at least in possibility, as staunch friend and brother soul; but what will sunder them is ambiguous. "He now will leave me" carries a note almost of lingering regretful attraction, as well as abandonment and betrayal, but assigns responsibility for the break to Mulligan; Stephen, however, has previously himself decided that "he has the key. I will not sleep there when this night comes" (*U-GP* 3:276). Both the emphasis on the possession of the key and Stephen's insistence on maintaining his absolute spiritual autonomy seem to express a fear—and rejection—of a domination that homosexual attraction would seem to involve for him.[6]

But Stephen's resistance to such an attraction, which would limit his autonomy while providing companionship, is strengthened by his more urgent current longing for the consoling touch of a woman: "Touch me. Soft eyes. Soft soft soft hand. I am lonely here. O, touch me soon, now. . . . I am quiet here alone. Sad too. Touch, touch me" (*U-GP* 3:434–36).[7]

Later, in "Scylla and Charybdis," Stephen returns to and hardens his rejection of Mulligan, as he now attributes homosexual orientation and awareness solely to him. "Lovely! Buck Mulligan suspired amorously," as he recalls Edward Dowden's conversation; "I asked him what he thought of the charge of pederasty brought against the bard. He lifted his hands and said: All we can say is that life ran very high in those days. Lovely!" This prompts in Stephen the contemptuous one-word judgment, "Catamite" (*U-GP* 9:731–34).

Just before this we are given Mulligan's presumptive judgment of Bloom as homosexual: "I found him over in the museum where I went to hail the foamborn Aphrodite. . . . He knows you. He knows your old fellow. O, I fear me, he is Greeker than the Greeks. His pale Galilean eyes were upon her mesial groove" (*U-GP* 9:609–15). Mulligan renews his tendentious imputation at the end of the episode when, after Bloom passes out between them, he warns Stephen of Bloom's homosexual threat: "He looked upon you to lust after you. I fear thee, ancient mariner. O, Kinch, thou art in peril. Get thee a breechpad" (*U-GP* 9:1210–11).

Joyce's formal purposes here seem discernible beneath the dramatically compelling presentation: Mulligan's confident assertions appear on inspection insufficiently grounded—how would he know that Bloom knows Stephen's father, and how probable is it that he would leap to his inference about Bloom's lustful designs on the basis of a glance? But the remarks serve to shift the onus of homosexual preoccupation from Stephen to Mulligan at the same time that they transfer narrative focus from Mulligan's potential homosexual relationship with Stephen to the latter's potential homosexual relationship with Bloom. Further, they foretell developments yet to come this day of which neither Mulligan nor Stephen has any idea but which are foreshadowed here, and connected with Haines' dream of a black panther, by the narrative reference at this point to Bloom's gait as the "step of a pard" (U-GP 9:1214) and to Stephen's thought of his own dream of a "street of harlots" and a "creamfruit melon" to be held out to him (U-GP 9:1207–8).

The latter reference is to be understood, I have elsewhere argued, as prefiguring not Stephen's literal destiny this day but Joyce's self-created artistic destiny as he re-enters his earlier life through Bloom via his memory of the Alfred Hunter who picked him up after a fight and took him home. In this projected identity he could make the quasi-homosexual gesture of offering Molly to Stephen,[8] an offer not accepted in the book but, I have suggested, taken up and realized by Joyce as he passes imaginatively through Bloom's and Molly's melons into full immergence with Molly's body. Thus, Joyce resolves in high androgynous art his ambivalent sexuality, according to the rationale indicated in Stephen's account in "Oxen of the Sun," with a cross-reference to Mulligan/Dowson, of the love arrangements of Beaumont and Fletcher: "they had but the one doxy between them and she of the stews to make shift with in delights amorous for life ran very high in those days and the custom of the country approved with it. Greater love than this, he said, no man hath that a man lay down his wife for his friend" (U-GP 14:358–63).

Immediately after this, however, Stephen gives voice to a bitter denunciation of Mulligan in terms that clearly suggest a homosexual betrayal with Haines that nothing earlier in the book has prepared for: "Bring a stranger within thy tower it will go hard but thou wilt have the secondbest bed. . . . Remember, Erin, thy generations and thy days of old, how thou settedst little by me and by my word and broughtedst in a stranger to my gates to commit fornication in my sight and to wax fat and to kick like Jeshurum. . . . Why hast thou done this abomination before me that thou didst spurn me for a merchant of jalaps?"[9] Aesthetic objectification of a fiercely projected sexual jealousy is barely achieved here through the comic deployment of the parodic Biblical idiom.

The rejection of Mulligan as imputed homosexual culminates in our last glimpse of his "grey bare hairy buttocks between which a carrot is stuck" (U-GP 15:4705–6). Obviously, this turning back upon Mulligan of the fate he had predicted for Stephen is Joyce's final aggressive rejection of Gogarty's implicit threat to his own masculinity, but this blends in more largely with the treatment of Mulligan's proposed role as "Fertilizer and Incubator,"[10] a role somewhat undercut by Mulligan's later humorous assertion that "the supremest object of desire [is] a nice clean old man" (U-GP 14:999–1000). This gratuitous perversity serves to infuse his identity as "Le Fecondateur" (U-GP 14:778) with suggestions of spiritual sterility—suggestions that lead beyond any narrow sexual issues into larger ones of spiritual fruitfulness and creativity.

Others have noted that Mulligan's proposal that he and Stephen "do something for the island. Hellenise it" (U-GP 1:158) can be taken as a prediction of the creation of Ulysses. Stephen's telegram to Mulligan ("*The sentimentalist is he who would enjoy without incurring the immense debtorship for a thing done*" [U-GP 9:550–51]) implicitly asserts that Mulligan, unlike Stephen/Joyce, does not have the gifts and commitment to "do something"—to conceive and bring to fruition such a regenerative project, whereas Stephen's dedication to the Shakespearean thought that he shares with Bloom—"Do. But do" (U-GP 9:653, 11:908)—is manifested in the "thing done" of the book that we find ourselves reading.

Similarly, the mass that Mulligan mockingly celebrates at the beginning may be understood as reprised, transposed, and transfigured in a book that is the outcome of the author's sacrificial eucharistic projection of his life and body in order to redeem the ruins of time. After our last view of Mulligan in "Circe" we have further knowledge of and reference to him only through Bloom, who, as already indicated, is his psychic replacement, as Joyce becomes not only his own father, mother, and son but his own sexually ambiguous brother as well. Joyce seems to mark the Mulligan/Bloom continuity in a number of ways, first in giving a retrospectively colored view of Mulligan's relationship with Stephen through what seems Bloom's somewhat improbable knowledge of and insight on the basis of so slight an acquaintance, just as he had given a prospectively colored view of Stephen's relationship with Bloom improbably to Mulligan.[11] In both cases the seam where fact is welded to fiction is not completely concealed, in a way that clearly reveals Joyce's constructive intention.

But there seem to be further deliberate signs in the book by which Joyce apparently meant to call attention to the Mulligan/Bloom continuity. Both are referred to as Stephen's "fidus Achates," Mulligan by Simon Dedalus, Bloom by the narrator of Eumaeus,[12] while Lenehan in "Wandering Rocks" refers to Bloom as a "cultured allroundman" (U-GP 10:581–82) in parallel with Bloom in "Eumaeus" referring to Mulligan as a "versatile allround man" (U-GP 6:288). Most salient, perhaps, is the fact that at the end of "Eumaeus" Bloom links arms with Stephen just as Cranly and Stephen had ("Accordingly he [Bloom] passed his left arm in Stephen's right and led him on accordingly" [U-GP 16:1721–22]), just before Bloom recommends that Stephen "sever his connection with a certain budding practitioner" (U-GP 16:1868).[13]

Finally it may be that the present line of thought illuminates one of the continuing minor mysteries of Ulysses, the "two strong whistles" that, on the first page of the book, answer through the calm to Mulligan's "long slow whistle of call." Some see these unexplained whistles as functionally appropriate in

Mulligan's mass (see Boyle 127), while one recent commentator takes them as Buck's interchange with his friends in the forty-foot below, and another, emphasizing their openness to interpretation, suggests that the two answering whistles come from a passing mailboat (Benstock and Benstock 20). Undoubtedly they must have some naturalistic referent in the book, but they may also have a metaphysical echo when in "Eumaeus" Bloom hails a cab for himself and the just-rescued Stephen by "emitting a kind of a whistle, holding his arms arched over his head, twice" (*U-GP* 16:30).

In any event, we can see from all this that Joyce, in rejecting and leaving behind his contingent friend Gogarty, also managed, willy-nilly, to gather him, along with his creatures Bloom and Molly, into the artifice of his eternity.

NOTES

1. James F. Carens notes that "Mulligan pretty well departs from the novel as an actual presence in Chapter 14; and he figures very little in the more than three hundred pages that follow" (30).

2. In his recent biography, Peter Costello provides substantial evidence that the primary original of E——. C——. was not Mary Sheehy but probably Mary Elizabeth Cleary (185ff). Cleary was (annoyedly) aware of Joyce's interest in her and confided to her daughter-in-law that he had once been "keen on her," whereas Sheehy told Richard Ellmann that she had not been at all aware of Joyce's interest in her (*SL* 162 n.). Costello's rejection (191–92) of Stanislaus Joyce's identification of E——. C——. with Mary Sheehy does not really discredit the account Stanislaus gives of the relationship (149–50), but clearly room is left for the Cleary relationship as the possible basis of some of the E——. C——. episodes in the novels—episodes that Ellmann has to think of, given Mary Sheehy's ignorance of Joyce's feelings toward her, as (very uncharacteristically) "invented" (*JJII* 51). Byrne himself notes, in an obscure and little noted sentence in passing, that one of the four Sheehy sisters "is referred to by Joyce in *The Portrait of the Artist*" (146). E——. C——. is the only candidate for the reference, which seems to indicate that, in Byrne's clearly informed view, her original was a Sheehy sister (undoubtedly Mary); but the rigidly chivalrous Byrne does not elaborate on the passing reference or comment on his own represented relationship in the book to this figure.

3. A later reference to Lynch as "Whetstone!" (*U-GP* 15:2101) seems to acknowledge Cosgrave's place in the series, but of course the latter's role as rival for Nora is entirely left out of the book along with Nora herself, though it is forcefully implicit perhaps in Stephen's assigning him the role of Judas.

4. In *Silent Years* Byrne notes that, as the time of their college friendship, he was two years older than Joyce, which, he notes, "meant a lot, at least in physical and muscular equipment." And he continues, "Moreover, I was unusually strong, much stronger than anyone would have thought from my appearance, whereas Joyce was thin, light and weak. Due to this, my attitude toward him became, and to a great degree remained, protective" (40).

5. Richard Ellmann notes the relevance in this connection of Joyce's identification of Gogarty in 'The Holy Office' as "'. . . him whose conduct seems to own / His preference for a man of "tone"'" (*James Joyce's Tower* 19). Despite Simon Dedalus's scornful reference to Mulligan as "a counter-jumper's son" (*U-GP* 6:70), Gogarty was of course the son of a prominent doctor and member of a prosperous and privileged family, as is suggested by his matriculation at Trinity College and later study at Oxford. Gogarty's preference for the privileged life was marked in later years, as his success as a surgeon brought him Rolls Royces and a country estate (see Ulick O'Connor, *Oliver St. John Gogarty*).

6. As with Cranly, Stephen may register Mulligan's strong physical presence as covertly attractive and therefore threatening. Joanne Rea calls attention to the activity of cutting consistently associated with Mulligan in "Telemachus" and interrelates several notations of Mulligan's physical self-exposure as constituting implicitly registered sexual aggression ("Joyce's 'Beastly' Bitch Motif"). Bernard Benstock sees the calf-faced Clive Kempthorne, in the ragging scene in which he is vividly visualized by Stephen fleeing Ades of Magdalen's shirttail snipping shears, as standing in parodically as sacrificial calf for Stephen, "the 'Bous Stephanoumenos, Bous Stephaneforos' of *A Portrait*" ("Telemachus" 11).

7. Joyce, who described himself at the corresponding time of his life as "a strange lonely boy, walking about by myself at night and thinking that some day a girl would love me" (*Letters II* 161), twice uses the word "touched" in describing Nora's seductive masturbation of him, an action that very possibly occurred on 16 June 1904 (see *SL* 182). In a letter to *James Joyce Quarterly* Richard Craig argues against Brenda Maddox's assertion that the seduction took place on the 16th, the day the couple first walked out together, correctly pointing out that Joyce's letter does not specifically refer it to that occasion; but in the same issue of *JJQ* (in my "Why Stephen's Hand Hurts"), I note that Joyce's description of Nora's act is echoed in his description in *Ulysses* of both Shakespeare's seduction of Adonis and Molly's of Mulvey—a congruence that suggests that his memory of this "sacrament" (*Letters II* 49) by which Nora "made him a man" (*Letters II* 233) was central to his structural sense of the book, which he chose to set on the now famous date of the 16th. Date and act need not have coincided for both to be deployed in the book, but it makes cogent sense to link them.

8. Hunter's original encounter with Joyce would seem to have had the character of a homosexual pickup and may actually have had such coloring. Costello gives new information about Hunter (231).

9. *U-GP* 14:367–73. We have learned earlier that Haines's "old fellow made his tin by selling jalap to Zulus or some bloody swindle or other" (*U-GP* 1:156–57). Ellmann notes that the reference to the "secondbest bed" may memorialize the fact that Joyce had to give up his bed to Trench when the latter moved into the tower (*Joyce's Tower* 17).

10. Under this title Mulligan proposes to set up "a national fertilizing farm to be named *Omphalos* with an obelisk hewn and erected after the fashion of Egypt and to offer his yeoman services for the fecundation of any female of what grade of life soever who should there direct to him with the desire of fulfilling the functions of her natural" (*U-GP* 14:684–88).

11. It may be that this is one of those cases where quasi-autonomous character is "endowed with knowledge by his creator" (*U-GP* 9:470).

12. Kathleen Hancock pointed this double reference out to me.

13. Bloom goes on: "who, he noticed, was prone to disparage and even to a slight extent with some hilarious pretext when not present, deprecate him, or whatever you like to call it which in Bloom's humble opinion threw a nasty sidelight on that side of a person's character, no pun intended" (U-GP 16:1869–73).

WORKS CITED

Benstock, Bernard. "Telemachus." In James Joyce's "Ulysses": Critical Essays, ed. Clive Hart and David Hayman. Berkeley: University of California Press, 1974.

Benstock, Bernard, and Shari Benstock. "The Benstock Principle." In The Seventh of Joyce, ed. Bernard Benstock. Bloomington: Indiana University Press, 1982.

Boyle, Robert. "Joyce's Consubstantiality: Woman as Creator." In Light Rays: James Joyce and Modernism, ed. Heyward Ehrlich. New York: New Horizon Press, 1984.

Byrne, J. F. Silent Years: An Autobiography with Memoirs of James Joyce and Our Ireland. New York: Farrar, Straus & Young, 1953.

Carens, James F. "Joyce and Gogarty." In New Light on Joyce, ed. Fritz Senn. Bloomington: Indiana University Press, 1973.

Costello, Peter. James Joyce: The Years of Growth, 1882–1915. Cork: Roberts Rinehart, 1992.

Craig, Richard. Letter. James Joyce Quarterly 26 (Spring 1989): 469–470.

Ellmann, Richard. James Joyce's Tower. Dun Laoghaire: Eastern Regional Tourism, 1969.

Joyce, Stanislaus. My Brother's Keeper: James Joyce's Early Years. Ed. Richard Ellmann. New York: Viking Press, 1958.

Maddox, Brenda. Nora: The Real Life of Molly Bloom. Boston: Houghton Mifflin, 1988.

O'Connor, Ulick. Oliver St. John Gogarty. 1964. Reprint, London: Mandarin Paperbacks, 1990.

Rader, Ralph W. "Exodus and Return: Joyce's Ulysses and the Fiction of the Actual." University of Toronto Quarterly 48 (Winter 1978–79): 149–71.

———. "The Logic of Ulysses, or Why Molly Had to Live in Gibraltar." Critical Inquiry 10 (June 1984): 567–78.

———. "Why Stephen's Hand Hurts: Joyce as Narcissus in Ulysses." James Joyce Quarterly 26 (Spring 1989): 440–45.

Rea, Joanne. "Joyce's 'Beastly' Bitch Motif: Sadic Castration Threat and Separation Anxiety." Journal of Evolutionary Psychology 7 (March 1986): 28–33.

Schechner, Mark. Joyce in Nighttown. Berkeley: University of California Press, 1974.

Finnegans Wake: The Obliquity of Trans-lations

Laurent Milesi

1. THE GLOSSIC/LALIC VEINS IN *FINNEGANS WAKE*

One can easily imagine the lack of understanding that must have prevailed after the confusion of tongues at Babel, which, until the remedy of translation, made an unintelligible babble of each post-Babelian parlance. This lalic (from Greek *lalein:* to babble) relationship that languages bore to one another may be compared with the ecstatic manifestations in the Biblical charisma of glossolalia, also called the gift of tongues in allusion to Pentecost, with which it has often been assimilated by Biblical exegesis, especially in the Pentecostal view.[1] However, an operative distinction must be kept between these various linguistic events. Whereas the glossolalic utterance in the Corinthian experience as described by Paul is unintelligible and its communality spells division and disunity (Mills 104–5), every one Galilaean spoke intelligibly in a foreign, previously unknown tongue, according to the Lucan account of the Pentecostal miracle (Acts 2:6–8ff.), an act made possible by the intercession of the Holy Spirit. Pentecost is therefore a manifestation of what is now more technically referred to as xenoglossia, while the gift of tongues, or glossolalia proper, cannot be likened to any known idiom (despite various inconclusive attempts) on account of its semantic unintelligibility.[2] Although glossolalia also bears some basic features of existing languages (such as recurrent phonic patterns, which it emphasizes artificially) and children's secret talk (Samarin esp. 140; see also McHugh), its foregrounding of the phonological apparatus on which there is no need to impose a semantic system (Samarin 127) and its ultimate lack of (grammatical) rules place it outside the scope of meaning— hence outside the sphere of languages, which are the vehicle for meaning and any ideology that language users might wish to encode. This extralinguistic phenomenon could be the model on which God had planned to undo the language of a sinful ideology so as to revert it to its former state as the innocent language of infancy. However, Antoine Compagnon's remark that "parler en langue ou en langues, cela revient au même, à l'unique dans la diversité" (826) may be used to point to the convergences between speaking in tongues (glossolalia proper), speaking in existing alien(ated) tongues (what one could call post-Babelian xenolalia), and speaking in reconciled idioms (Pentecostal xenoglossia) as overlapping currents in the *Wake*.

At first sight, *Finnegans Wake* is run through by post-Babelian xenolalia; its opaque, foreign-sounding, alien-looking texture causes the signifier to be foregrounded and deprives the written trace of spontaneous semantic intelligibility, and the (temporary) disruption of the link between signifier and signified leaves the reader/decipherer in a maze of arcane sounds.

The gift of tongues or glossolalia also appears in the *Wake* in all its best known recurrent features (alliterative, vocalic, and other truly lalic phenomena), especially when "Wakese" becomes ecstatically self-conscious of its rhythmic and phonic patterns (e.g., *FW* 186.20–21). If the *Wake's* post-Babelian xenolalia is the outcome of edification, Saint Paul reminds us that the gift of tongues has more to do with self-edification (1 Corinthians 14:2–4). In a passage that invites comparison with the unbelievers' equation of the Pentecostal tongues with libation in Acts 2:13 (for which see *FW* 624.34–35), the *Wake* describes HCE in his cups, blubbering and self-edifiying, as "thruming through all to himself with diversed tonguesed through his old tears and his ould plaised drawl."[3] This double lalic vein turns the theme of misunderstanding and the quizzes (*FW* 1.6) and riddles often left unguessed into structural elements. Both currents would intersect in Nimrod's much-glossed infernal glossolalic babbling as rendered by Dante in *Inferno* XXXI 67 (Baranski 130) and in Jacques Lacan's view of Joyce's linguistic elation or *élangues* (see Aubert 37).

Then, as a child who gradually acquires a language, the reader finds his/her way through the musical ballet of words and sentences; hears, sees/understands,[4] that is, invests them with stratified layers of reassuring meanings by reducing them to isolatable (recurrent) elements. Thus, s/he may eventually hope to account for the proliferation of languages by an overall problematic that would offer the promise of their reconciliation (Milesi esp. 174–75, 177–78). Within Joyce's linguistic melting pot, a basically Irish family, like the Galilaeans, is made to speak in foreign idioms unknown to them before.

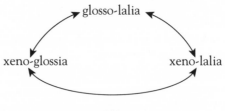

The various idioms confused in the babel of *Finnegans Wake* remain glossolalic and xenolalic to one another, as long as mediation between linguistic elements is not established, until the advent of Pentecost (divine forgiveness) or translation (the human remedy bypassing the need for Pentecostal atonement). From Babel to divine Pentecost (as the restoration of tradition) or from Babel to human translation there is only a double step, a duality of readings in which the linguistic war between God and wo/man is inscribed, between *traditio* and *traductio,* human duplicity and treason *(traditio)* or wo/man's refusal to expiate. God's Pentecostal forgiveness must be felt as imminent but forever deferred in order to perpetuate the linguistic struggle against him, the lability (Latin *labi,* past participle *lapsus:* to slip) of the Wakean "lapsus langways" (FW 484.25) and the *felix culpa* of its cyclically renewed creative falls. It is in that sense of a struggle against the Holy Word that one should understand the contract of translation that, in their effort to unite, men must draw up, so as to establish a passage (Latin *translatus,* past participle of *transferre:* to carry across, transfer, translate) from one language to another, between "nativeness" and "foreignness," and restore semantic intelligibility and communication out of the babel of inarticulate utterances. Attempting to fight against the horizontal dimension of language(s), a consequence of their dissemination after Babel, without the possibility of re-creating the verticality of an originary erection of language, the use of translation can appropriately be described as an oblique makeshift, the human alternative to God's creation but also to divine leniency.[5]

2. THE TWO WAYS OF TRANS-LATION[6]

If we consider the sur-vival of a text that is a legacy, the narrative or the myth of the tower of Babel, it does not constitute just one figure among others. Telling at least of the inadequation of one language to another . . . of language to itself and to meaning . . . it also tells of the need for figuration, for myths, for tropes, for twists and turns, for translation inadequate to compensate for that which multiplicity denies us. In that sense it would be the myth of the origin of myth, the metaphor of metaphor, the narrative of narrative, the translation of translation, and so on. It would not be the only structure hollowing itself out like that, but it would do so in its own way (itself *almost* untranslatable, like a proper name), and its idiom would have to be saved.[7]

The presence of interpreters (FW 91.3–4, 478.8, 479.9, etc.) mediating between various characters emphasizes the role of translation in the linguistic fabric of *Finnegans Wake,* not to mention the numerous generic references (FW 152.12–13, 215.26–27, 276.F6, 419.24–25, etc.). But the subtler impact on the work's writing, especially on the unfolding of the polysemic sentence, is achieved in what Atherton aptly described as the "trope of translation"

(203): in "drim and drumming on her back" (*FW* 223.10) the Irish *druim/drom* is translated into English "back" whereas a shift in signifiers ("drumming") twists, turns, tropes, trans-lates, or meta-phorises, the first element into the first link of a second semantic chain. The break from monosemy is thus obtained by variations on the paradigmatic axis (the vertical dimension of the portmanteau word as a concretion of signifiers and signifieds) as well as syntagmatically (the horizontal dimension of various linear readings), breaking down the barrier between intralingual and interlingual translation through a constant switch between the phonic and the graphic poles of language. As such, these plural readings are in need of the reader's singularly oblique intervention. In the light of this tropic use of translation to establish narrative polysemy, one can see how the inbuilt vein of intralinear translation is coupled with a status of untranslatability. The exploration of the passage between languages in the *Wake* precludes a later passage of the whole work from the source parent language into any other language without disrupting its tightly knit polyglottal mosaic: the Wakean creation partly preprograms the defeat of its filial re-creations.[8]

The untranslatability of Joyce's Babelian work bears the inscription of God's real project motivating the confusion of tongues if we adopt Derrida's account of the Tower of Babel episode. For Derrida in "Des Tours de Babel," God compelled wo/man to translate Babel, the proper noun born with the Father's will, into a common name; that is, God set humankind the necessary as well as impossible and forbidden task of translating what by nature can only be transferred and not translated, since a proper noun is beyond the scope of all existing languages.[9] The untranslatable nature of proper names is also developed by Hélène Cixous in conjunction with Stephen's efforts in A *Portrait* to think of God's names "in all the different languages in the world," efforts that reveal the mystery of the difference and identity of being in its relation to language (Cixous 261).

This detour through God's name, the logos responsible for Babel or the confusion of language, shows how translation means identity in difference/difference in identity, an essential feature of the language altered by humans as early as Adam in paradise.[10] However, these interpretations must be confronted with the more classical view of translation as wo/man's own palliative for the loss of the universal language, which thus stands in opposition to the idea of a divine retaliation. The human way aims not only at doing away with the Pentecostal forgiveness, hence with the filial debt to the Redeemer, but also at giving a secular, debased version of God's project, an immanent reduplication immediately frustrating the design of the transcendent Being. The translation of the nameable and translatable would thus be superposed on the divine wish to set wo/man to translate the unnameable and untranslatable. This opposition shows through the texture of *Finnegans Wake*, a medley of Babelian languages bonded together in part by translation and thus equally bearing the scars of a partial structural untranslatability imposed by the Law of the Word, and of the entropy of translation caused by the differences in what languages must convey, according to Roman Jakobson in "On Linguistic Aspects of Translation." Predraft compilation of linguistic elements from several languages, belonging to the same semantic field (linguistic interferences across the whole range of the Buffalo notebooks) or related by theme and motif (and often in indexes or clusters), gives better evidence of the impact of (inter/intralingual) translation on the polyglottal fabric of the *Wake* than the final text, in which Joyce's compact research is diluted and made less visible by the adjunction of several other linguistic layers. Here are a few examples scattered throughout the work:

"Achdung! Pozor! Attenshune!" (*FW* 100.05); German *Achtung!* = Slavonic *pozor!* = French *attention!*: be careful!

"Byfall. Upploud!" (*FW* 257.29–30); German *Beifall:* applaud, which somehow means "up loud." This follows the sixth thunderword, semantically unified around the notion of closing the door.

"Comme bien, Comme bien! Feefeel! Feefeel!" (*FW* 420.12–13); French *combien?* = German *wieviel?*: how much?

This simple version (from Latin *vertere:* to turn) of the trope of translation discussed above helps to highlight the Wakean reformulation of intralinear translation, which sets aside the historical developments of national languages and groups them together following Joyce's own associative decisions so as to reestablish a creative passage between sound and sense, if not a lost universal concord. We are not far from the approach of Walter Benjamin in "The Task of the Translator," which Derrida's "Des Tours de Babel" analyzes after preliminary "framing" reflections on the Babel episode in Genesis. For Benjamin the intralinear version of the sacred text is the model founding the possibility of translation in general; translation makes tangible the active presence of a universal language and "ultimately serves the purpose of expressing the central reciprocal relationship between languages . . . [which are] not strangers to one another, but are, a priori and apart from all historical relationships, interrelated in what they want to express."[11]

This anhistorical practice counteracts the consequences of Babel insofar as exhausting the possibilities of combinations between languages also goes against the symbolic choice of one fragmentary linguistic medium for each oral and textual utterance, a choice that was made necessary by the division of the whole linguistic community after Babel. While subverting linguistic parentage, already inscribed in a narrative of filial betrayal and trans-lation of paternity,[12] it also points towards the originally plural dimension of Wakese as a mode of linguistic displacement, the ontological loss of the unicity that the myth of Babel had placed at the "origin" and had established as being proper to the Father only.[13] The original language of *Finnegans Wake* is already

derived by the effects of these various modes and appropriations of translation. Derrida further notes that the original is a priori indebted to transla-
tion(s) insofar as it owes its survival to the scission of languages, which
enables its proliferation by rewritings in other idioms ("Des Tours de Babel"
178–79; and McDonald 121ff.). Taking his cue from Walter Benjamin's notion
of the *Überleben* and *Fortleben* of the original in translation, Derrida also
writes in "Living On—Border Lines" that it is the mixed status of (un)trans-
latability that enables the text to live on (102), a paradox that he and De Man
had pointed out in the ambivalent title of Walter Benjamin's essay: *Aufgabe*
(task) also means "giving up."[14] (One may add that the sense of "giving up"
and "surrender" is precisely contained in the Latin *traditio* seen above.) In this
double bind one may register the linguistic war between Father and sons,
since a parallel may be established with the debt that binds God, the original
creator, to his human creatures, whose mission on earth is to promote his adoration, first in one language then in the various post-Babelian tongues through
God's deed of translation. (The divine punishment seems therefore a desire
to strengthen the filial bonds within the human race by reenacting the secre-
tion or scission of the origin—God multiplying his substance in humankind—in a linguistic scene in order to ensure for veneration of his Law and
Word in a multitude of languages.)But in return the origin of language(s) is
indebted to those who perpetuate it/them from generation to generation. In
Joyce's work the English substratum stands for the derived original logos, the
traditional law of language already displaced in the first drafts, which was
gradually revitalised by the multilayered grafting of foreign vocables but which
never ceased to impose its grammatical constructions as substructure for the
literal translation of foreign parts of speech:[15]

> "agentlike . . . thundersday" (*FW* 5.13); German *eigentlich:* really, where *-lich* is
> equivalent to English *-like*, and German *Donnerstag:* lit. "thundersday," i.e.
> Thursday.
>
> "cubehouse" (*FW* 5.14); literal translation of Arabic *Ka'aba*, the Black Stone
> at Mecca, the centre of Islam.
>
> "cowrieosity" (*FW* 14.2–3); the context also invites "cowrie" since an informal
> name for it in French is *pucelage*, which also means "maidenhood."
>
> "clearobscure" (*FW* 247.24); "chiaroscuro," of Italian origin, rendered
> literally.[16]

Finnegans Wake is traversed by a dialectical tension between the amalga-
mation or naturalization of foreign imports and the alienation or "foreigniza-
tion" of the source parent tongue. In Shaun's satirical portrait of his mixed
brother Shem the Penman, the "outlex" (*FW* 169.3), outside the law (or beyond the pale) of normative English and using "several lingua" (see entry in
Buffalo Notebook VI.B.17 36), but also an "inlaw" (*FW* 169.4) destroying the
language within its limits, is said to wage a linguistic-ideological war against

the law of the English language: "he would wipe alley english spooker, multa-phoniaksically[17] spuking, off the face of the erse" (*FW* 178.6–7). The loss of the capital *E* in "english" may be seen as Shem's desire to debase the English Word, though like any act of profanation, his desecration implicitly depends on a prior recognition of the Law.

The translation of Joyce's work cannot be envisaged as a faithful rendering of meaning into another language, nor even into "deforeignized" English, pre-cisely because of the English substratum on which the *Wake* is ineradicably grounded and which is yet already displaced. (Likewise, in the *Convivio,* I viii 14, Dante mentions the impossibility of transposing the tightly knit musical fabric of an artistic creation into another language without disrupting it.) To recognize this level of (un)translatability, a true dimension of any literary work, which the *Wake* fully exploits, let alone when it is itself already somehow a translation,[18] is to forgo in part the meaning imparted by the language of the Law and to experience a lalic *jouissance* from the babelization of writing. The reduplication of original English vocables in the process of translation dispos-sesses them partly of their semantic-ideological value as they become en-meshed with new coinages in new fictions, giving another orientation to the new text. One must recall at this stage the extracts from "Anna Livia" that Joyce recast into French (in 1930) and Italian (in 1937) with the help of sev-eral collaborators, each time transposing a tangential part of the original in order to adapt it to the new linguistic context, where the language was allowed to be "powerfully affected by the foreign tongue."[19] Since meaning is the re-sult of the negative estrangement of language from its referential field, its evac-uation points the way to the recapture of the original, universal language in which words and things tallied and therefore meaning did not exist . . . but nor did humankind's subversive ideology! *Finnegans Wake* is full of undecidables or structural hesitencies. Its (un)translatable nature, that of the proper noun Babel, itself a metaphor, acquired despite the intralinear human translation born of the interplay between the seventy-odd Wakean languages, anchors in writing the ceaselessly renewed opposition between the son and the Father, the jubilation in the fall into languages serving in part to undo paternal su-premacy, to which the Wakean hero will however try either to cling or to ac-cede. The trans-lation between languages and meta-phorical passage from generation to generation stop where the covers of the book meet and we enter the derived (*FW* 3.1: "riverrun") realm of the untranslatable possible transla-tions of the original Wakean struggle between the creator and the created.

NOTES

1. *La Bible de Jérusalem* 1573 n. g, 1659 n. f; and Samarin 16. Mills (esp. 101–5) maps out several exegetical links between the theophany at Mount Sinai and the

Tower of Babel story in the Old Testament and the Pauline and Lucan texts in the New Testament (the book also has an abundant bibliography on glossolalia). Finally, one cannot fail to mention Borst's monumental study (1:224) for another connection between the episode on Mount Sinai (esp. Exodus 19:16ff.) and Pentecost.

2. However, aligning himself with the Pentecostal position, Michel de Certeau understands the mystery of the Pentecost as another ecstatic utterance, which the Apostles explained according to the hermeneutics of meaning and intelligibility (30). I wish to take a more "literal" view of this crucial passage, which I regard as the actual, however allegorized, restoration of communication between estranged peoples and languages. For a further synthesis of contrastive positions on glossolalia and xenoglossia, see, e.g., Samarin 109–15 and Williams 25ff.

3. *FW* 381.19–21. Of interest for *Wake* readers is Samarin's account of the glossolalic outburst of a psychoanalysand who had recently been involved in Pentecostalist religion, in connection with his guilt feelings about certain sexual acts (90ff.). A decoding of his talk could proceed along associational lines not unlike the linguistic mechanisms of the *Wake*'s dream techniques.

4. For an account of exegetical emphasis on hearing as opposed to speaking in the Pentecostal narrative, see Mills 60–61. The Pentecostal tongues of fire may also be regarded as a visual translation of the voice heard on Mount Sinai (Schlossman 157).

5. For a similar post-Saussurean view of translation as both a diachronic (vertical) and synchronic (horizontal) process through time and space—and despite my reservations about how he chooses to consider the "vertical" and "horizontal"—see Steiner 31.

6. Fritz Senn's admirable readings of creative issues of intralinear translation in Joyce's oeuvre, in between the "so familiar and so foreign" of Joyce's English, must be recalled here (see e.g. *Nichts gegen Joyce* 207–77; his other cited works are pertinent in their entirety). See also Bosinelli for a recent discussion of some implications of translation as writing and reading process in *Finnegans Wake*.

7. Jacques Derrida, "Des Tours de Babel" 165. That Derrida's brilliant opening tells the inadequation of translation can be checked against the corresponding original fragment (209).

8. For similar arguments, see Heath, "Ambiviolences" 35 (curtailed English version in Heath, "Joyce in Language"), and Risset 58–59, who quotes from the French translation of Walter Benjamin's essay on translation, to which we shall come back.

9. Derrida, "Des Tours de Babel" 170ff. See also Derrida in the roundtable discussion on translation (in McDonald, esp. 101–2); also Derrida "The Post Card" 165; and of course the whole of his reading of "he war" (in "Two Words"). The Derridean double bind of writing and translation is taken up in Benstock, "Letter of the Law" 174 and "Apostrophizing the Feminine" 590.

10. For instance, in *Paradiso* XXVI 133–36, Dante uses Adam himself to recant his earlier doctrine of the immutability of the Adamic language expressed in *De Vulgari Eloquentia*, especially in connection with its original essence, the divine name. Adam had accounted for the lability inherent in human language even before Nimrod's generation, by man's fallible desire, as found at lines 124–32. For Dante's constant rewritings of earlier positions, including his conflicting views on the loss of a man-made or God-given original language, see Tambling, esp. 129–63.

11. Walter Benjamin 72. Benjamin further adds that "all suprahistorical kinship of languages rests in the intention underlying each language as a whole—an intention, however, which no single language can attain by itself but which is realised only by the totality of their intentions supplementing each other: pure language" (73).

12. "[Joyce] confronts the problem of parenthood, as well as the problem of translation and betrayal, on the level of language itself, not merely on the level of language-as-narrative" (Deane 52).

13. Derrida, "Des Tours de Babel" 174. For the bearing of our argument on Walter Benjamin's text, see also Andrew Benjamin 100, and De Man.

14. De Man 80. In the case of Derrida, this indication is given only in the French version of "Des Tours de Babel," later collected in *Psyché: Inventions de l'autre* (212).

15. It would take another study to unravel the metaphorical web and thematic complexities tying together mother tongue and the fathering law of language in *Finnegans Wake*. Such an analysis would have to consider relations of parentage and filiation between English, Irish, and Anglo-Irish as these are implemented in Joyce's text and might take as a starting point Heidegger's insight into the notions of idiom and dialect (*Mundart*) as the language of the mother but also, in the first instance, the mother of language, as well as starting from Derrida's observation in "Le retrait de la métaphore" that "langue maternelle ne serait pas une métaphore pour déterminer le sens de la langue mais le tour essentiel pour comprendre ce que 'la mère' veut dire" (*Psyché* 76).

16. For *FW* 450.20–21, 22, see Gilbert 72 and my "Italian Studies" 125ff.

17. Note the intrusion of the Finnish translative ending *-ksi*, which registers the impending process of transformation (see my "L'Idiome babélieu" 204).

18. "Translations . . . prove to be untranslatable not because of any inherent difficulty, but because of the looseness with which meaning attaches to them" (Walter Benjamin 81).

19. Walter Benjamin 81, quoting from Rudolf Pannwitz's *Die Krisis der europäischen Kultur*. Or "a translation touches the original lightly and only at the infinitely small point of the sense, thereupon pursuing its own course according to the laws of fidelity in the freedom of linguistic flux" (Walter Benjamin 80) and "the translation must be one with the original in the form of the interlinear version, in which literalness and freedom are united" (82).

WORKS CITED

Atherton, James S. *The Books at the "Wake": A Study of Literary Allusions in James Joyce's "Finnegans Wake."* 1959. Mamaroneck, N.Y.: Paul Appel, 1974.

Aubert, Jacques, ed. *Joyce avec Lacan.* Foreword by Jacques-Alain Miller. Paris: Navarin, 1987.

Baranski, Zygmunt G. "Dante's Biblical Linguistics." *Lectura Dantis* 5 (1989): 105–43.

Benjamin, Andrew. *Translation and the Nature of Philosophy: A New Theory of Words.* London: Routledge, 1989.

Benjamin, Walter. "The Task of the Translator: An Introduction to the Translation of

Baudelaire's *Tableaux parisiens.*" In *Illuminations,* ed. Hannah Arendt. Trans. Harry Zohn. London: Jonathan Cape, 1970.

Benstock, Shari. "The Letter of the Law: *La carte postale* in *Finnegans Wake.*" *Philological Quarterly* 63, no. 2 (1984): 163–85.

———. "Apostrophizing the Feminine in *Finnegans Wake.*" *Modern Fiction Studies* 35, no. 3, ed. Ellen Carol Jones (1989): 587–614.

La Bible de Jérusalem. Revised ed. Paris: Cerf, 1978.

Borst, Arno. *Der Turmbau von Babel: Geschichte der Meinungen über Ursprung und Vielfalt der Sprachen und Völker.* 6 vols. Stuttgart: Anton Hierseman, 1957–63.

Bosinelli, Rosa-Maria. "Beyond Translation: Italian Re-writings of *Finnegans Wake.*" In *Joyce Studies Annual,* ed. Thomas F. Staley. Austin: University of Texas Press, 1990.

Cixous, Hélène. *Prénoms de personne.* Paris: Seuil, 1974.

Compagnon, Antoine. "La glossolalie: Une affaire sans histoire?" *Critique* 35, nos. 387–88 (1979): 824–38.

Dante Alighieri. *La Commedia secondo l'antica vulgate.* Ed. Giorgio Petrocchi. *Le Opere di Dante Alighieri.* Edizione nazionale a cura della Società Dantesca Italiana. Vol. 7. Milan: Mondadori, 1966.

———. *Il Convivio.* 2nd ed. 2 vols. Florence: Le Monnier, 1964.

———. *De vulgari eloquentia.* Florence: Le Monnier, 1957.

Deane, Seamus. "Joyce the Irishman." In *The Cambridge Companion to James Joyce,* ed. Derek Attridge. Cambridge: Cambridge University Press, 1990.

de Certeau, Michel. "Utopies vocales: Glossolalies." *Traverses,* no. 20, *La voix, l'écoute* (1980): 26–37.

De Man, Paul. *The Resistance to Theory.* Manchester: Manchester University Press, 1986.

Derrida, Jacques. "Des Tours de Babel." Trans. Joseph F. Graham. In *Difference in Translation,* ed. Joseph F. Graham. Ithaca and London: Cornell University Press, 1985. (bilingual text)

———. "Living On—Border Lines." Trans. James Hulbert. In *Deconstruction and Criticism,* ed. Harold Bloom, et al. London: Routledge & Kegan Paul, 1979.

———. *The Post Card: From Socrates to Freud and Beyond.* Trans. Alan Bass. Chicago and London: University of Chicago Press, 1987.

———. *Psyché: Inventions de l'autre.* Paris: Galilée, 1987.

———. "Two Words for Joyce." Trans. Geoff Bennington. In *Post-structuralist Joyce: Essays from the French,* ed. Derek Attridge and Daniel Ferrer. Cambridge: Cambridge University Press, 1984.

Gilbert, Stuart. "Prolegomena to *Work in Progress.*" In *Our Examination Round His Factification for Incamination of "Work in Progress,"* by Samuel Beckett et al. 1929. Reprint, London: Faber & Faber, 1972.

Heath, Stephen. "Ambiviolences: Notes pour la lecture de Joyce." *Tel Quel,* no. 50 (1972): 22–43.

————. "Joyce in Language." In *James Joyce: New Perspectives,* ed. Colin MacCabe. Sussex: Harvester Press; Bloomington: Indiana University Press, 1982.

Jakobson, Roman. "On Linguistic Aspects of Translation." In *On Translation,* ed. Reuben A. Brower. Cambridge, Mass.: Harvard University Press, 1959.

McDonald, Christie, ed. *The Ear of the Other: Otobiography, Transference, Translation: Texts and Discussions with Jacques Derrida.* Trans. Peggy Kamuf and Avital Ronell. Lincoln and London: University of Nebraska Press, 1985.

McHugh, Roland. "Jespersen's *Language* in Notebooks VI.B.2 and VI.C.2." *A Finnegans Wake Circular,* 2, no. 4 (1987): 61–71.

Milesi, Laurent. "L'idiome babélien de *Finnegans Wake:* Recherches thématiques dans une perspective génétique." In *Genèse de Babel: Joyce et la création,* ed. Claude Jacquet. Paris: CNRS, 1985.

————. "Italian Studies in Musical Grammar." In *James Joyce 3, "Scribble" 3: Joyce et l'Italie,* ed. Claude Jacquet and Jean-Michel Rabaté. Paris: Lettres Modernes, 1994.

Mills, Watson E. *A Theological/Exegetical Approach to Glossolalia.* Lanham, Md.: University Presses of America, 1985.

Risset, Jacqueline. "Joyce traduit par Joyce." *Tel Quel,* no. 55 (1973): 47–58.

Samarin, William J. *Tongues of Men and Angels: The Religious Language of Pentecostalism.* New York: Macmillan; London: Collier-Macmillan, 1972.

Schlossman, Beryl. *Joyce's Catholic Comedy of Language.* Madison: University of Wisconsin Press, 1985.

Senn, Fritz. "Foreign Readings." In *Work in Progress: Joyce Centenary Essays,* ed. Robert F. Peterson, Alan M. Cohn, and Edmund L. Epstein. Carbondale: Southern Illinois University Press, 1983.

————. "Joycean Translatitudes: Aspects of Translation." In *Litters from Aloft: Papers Delivered at the Second Canadian James Joyce Seminar,* ed. Ronald Bates and Henry J. Pollock. University of Tulsa Monograph Series, no. 13. Tulsa: University of Tulsa, 1971.

————. *Joyce's Dislocutions: Essays on Reading as Translation.* Ed. John Paul Riquelme. Baltimore: Johns Hopkins University Press, 1984.

————. *Nichts gegen Joyce: Joyce versus Nothing, Aufsätze 1959–1983.* Ed. Franz Cavigelli. Zurich: Haffmans Verlag, 1983.

Steiner, George. *After Babel: Aspects of Language and Translation.* London: Oxford University Press, 1975.

Tambling, Jeremy. *Dante and Difference: Writing in the "Commedia."* Cambridge: Cambridge University Press, 1988.

Williams, Cyril G. *Tongues of the Spirit: A Study of Pentecostal Glossolalia and Related Phenomena.* Cardiff: University of Wales Press, 1981.

Countlessness of Livestories: Narrativity in *Finnegans Wake*

Derek Attridge

Most readers of *Finnegans Wake* would probably hesitate to call it a novel, and one of the reasons for this reluctance is that it lacks anything that could unproblematically be called a *narrative*, something which even such exceptional texts as *Tristram Shandy* and *Ulysses*, for all their oddity, can be said to possess. Yet narrative is hardly absent from the *Wake*; indeed, in the words of the text itself, at one of its many auto-descriptive moments, "Countlessness of livestories have netherfallen by this plage, flick as flowflakes, litters from aloft, like a waast wizzard all of whirlworlds" (*FW* 17.26–29). *Finnegans Wake* is a great mound of stories, a gigantic accumulation of the world's narratives, but it seems that it is not one of them.

To explore this paradox, it will help to establish a working definition of narrative. Let us say that it is a linear (though often multileveled) account of recognizable characters and events, engaging with the reader's pre-existing mental schemata to arouse expectations and to modify, complicate, defeat, or partially satisfy those expectations, arriving at full satisfaction—or something like it—only at the end (thereby constituting it as the end). Individual narratives work in different ways to produce pleasure and perhaps some form of understanding or insight, but what they all have in common is the condition of being narratives, of engaging with the world and the mind in the specific manner of narrative. I propose to call this quality *narrativity*, and my suggestion is that narrativity, so defined, is a crucial element in our enjoyment of any narrative *as* a narrative. The word *narrativity* is not recognized by the second edition of the *Oxford English Dictionary*, but it does appear in the titles of a few books and in the work of some narratologists. Gerald Prince, for instance, defines it as "The set of properties characterizing narrative and distinguishing it from nonnarrative; the formal and contextual features making a narrative more or less narrative, as it were" (64). Though the final phrase reveals Prince's uncertainty about his own definition, this remains a more technical (and perhaps emptier) employment of the term than the one I'm suggesting; my interest is not so much in a "set of properties" as in a quality or timbre, inseparable from the operation of readerly desires and satisfactions, that is precisely not reducible to any objectively ennumerable features or rules.

Narrativity, that is to say, has everything to do with the reader's performance of the text as he or she reads it (which is a strange kind of performance, since it involves being performed by the text as well). Our consciousness that we are experiencing not a series of events as they might unfold "in the real world" but a dynamic structure built out of inherited cultural materials according to (but also in deviance from) known codes, a series of events possessing a certain phantasmal quality, is not a hindrance to our full enjoyment of the narrative but on the contrary a precondition of it; and our appreciation of a skillfully deployed narrative sequence in a literary text is in part a savoring of this quality of narrativity as it is foregrounded and exploited.

Among the many other things they do with narrative, Joyce's first three books of fictional prose all practice a certain stretching of it, to produce an experience of controlled exiguousness. To take one example from *Dubliners*, "The Sisters" arouses a host of expectations as it encourages its readers to recall familiar plots involving youthful induction into the mysteries of the adult world (of knowledge, of sin, of death), yet it ends with those expectations unfulfilled, with an awkward silence whose awkwardness is not just that of social intercourse brought up against a deeply embarrassing event but also that of a structural closure that fails to satisfy narrative norms. A *Portrait* offers more in the way of accepted narrative satisfactions than *Dubliners*, but has many sequences that stretch—and thereby raise for a kind of questioning—narrativity itself; the extended recitation of Father Arnall's sermons would be one example. Moreover, the central narrative of A *Portrait*—the familiar story of the growth of the artist through obstacles and false starts to maturity—is one that is constantly ironized by other forces in the book, questioning Stephen Dedalus's own exploitation of that narrative as a guide to life even as it questions Joyce's exploitation of it as a novelistic schema. *Ulysses* plays at extraordinary length with the familiar narrative patterns of sundering and union, departure and homecoming, trust and betrayal, and in that extraordinary length it too foregrounds narrativity itself: we do, it is true, experience a certain traditional kind of tension as Bloom continues to find more and more ways of postponing his return home, and we're aware of rising expectations of conventional resolution as his and Stephen's paths converge more and more closely, but to read *Ulysses* for its narrative tensions and resolutions (or nonresolutions) would be like reading *Middlemarch* for its eroticism. The sequence of tensions and resolutions do constitute, however, an essential cord

291

on which everything else is strung, a cord stretched almost to breaking point without actually snapping. And the final word of the novel does somehow manage to release the multiple tensions built up throughout the book's extraordinary length.

In *Finnegans Wake* the connecting cord is gone. The broad scheme of day (perhaps), evening, night, and morning that structures the text is not a *narrative* scheme at all; it arouses no tension (we aren't asking "Will night fall?" "Will morning come?"), it hooks onto no pre-existing narrative formulae, it offers no enigma to be solved or human crisis to be resolved. Heroic and ingenious efforts have been made to derive from the multifarious and ambiguous episodes an overarching narrative—for instance, the story of a publican who dreams epic dreams after a hard day's work, waking only in the penultimate book to make somewhat unfelicitous love to his wife—but apart from its thinness as it is spread over several hundred dense pages, any such derived sequence of events fails to engage with the traditional resources of narrative, and hence lacks momentum or drive.[1] What is more, this kind of simple linearity hardly corresponds to the experience of reading the text of *Finnegans Wake*, page by page, sentence by sentence. This is not to deny the sense of a beginning at the beginning and the sense of an end at the end (which are not overridden by the syntax that links—fairly weakly, I would argue—unfinished end and uninitiated beginning); but my argument is that these are *structural*, not narrative, features of the book.

On the other hand, *narrativity* abounds in *Finnegans Wake*; the book's very texture is a tightly woven web of stories. Through his extraordinary development of the portmanteau technique, Joyce found a way of interweaving narrative possibilities at several levels simultaneously: a paragraph, a sentence, a phrase, or even a word can offer a mininarrative to the reader. Linearity—a crucial feature of narrative—goes out the window. There are two requirements for this technique to work successfully: (1) most of the narratives must be familiar ones, so they can be triggered by the smallest fragment or allusion (and we might note in connection with this that among the books Joyce owned in Trieste was Georges Polti's *Thirty-Six Dramatic Situations*, which claimed to derive all the world's narratives from thirty-six basic situations);[2] (2) the book must be a long one, so that it can produce its own multiply reiterated versions of familiar plots (the sin in the park, the captain and the tailor's daughter, Buckley and the Russian General, and so on), and set up its own complex network of allusions and easily triggered associations. The result is a certain emptiness of narrative—the stories are not new ones, and they keep coming back again and again—and a fullness of narrativity, a rich layering of stories allowing narrative echoes to fly back and forth among holy scripture, ribald joke, national history, pantomime, literary masterpiece, nursery rhyme. I'm reminded of the opening of Barthes's "Introduction to the Structural Analysis of Narratives":

Numberless are the world's narratives. First of all in a prodigious variety of genres, themselves distributed among different substances, as if any material were appropriate for man to entrust his stories to it: narrative can be supported by articulated speech, oral or written, by image, fixed or moving, by gesture, and by the organized mixture of all these substances; it is present in myth, legend, fable, tragedy, comedy, epic, history, pantomime, painting . . . , stained-glass window, cinema, comic book, news item, conversation. (95)

Of course, the *Wake* for the most part uses one substance, the verbal (though there are visual and musical narrative effects too); but it can certainly be said to be "an organized mixture" of all these sources of narrative—there isn't one in Barthes's list that's not mined by Joyce.

The effect of this excess of narrativity over narrative could be described as a *staging* or *performing* of narrative, a putting it into play, a testing of its limits.[3] (In a similar fashion, one might say that the *Wake* has an excess of, for instance, referentiality over reference, metaphoricity over metaphor, descriptivity over description, ethicity over ethics, that results in a kind of staging of reference, metaphor, description, and ethics.) A single sentence, chosen more or less at random, will help clarify my argument:

Fudder and lighting for ally looty, any filly in a fog, for O'Cronione lags acrumbling in his sands but his sunsunsuns still tumble on. (FW 415.20–22)

Different narratives of death and succession intermingle here: Cronos succeeded by his son Zeus; John Brown's body moldering while his soul lives on to inspire his followers; the topos of monumental statuary (Ozymandias, perhaps?) crumbling into the sand while humanity persists regardless of individual claims to greatness. Two of these stories—Cronos and Ozymandias—entail disrespect for patriarchal authority, and the carnivalesque scene after the death of the father is depicted also in "Fudder and lighting for ally looty"—food (or fodder) and illumination made available for everyone (*für alle leute*), with a suggestion of "loot" as well—and in the (male) sexual promiscuity of "any filly in a fog." But there's a story of authoritarian rage here as well, in the initial thunder and lightning; and perhaps one of circumnavigation (reinforced by the immediate context of this sentence) in the tumbling suns and in the allusion to Phileas Fogg, whose voyage around the world in eighty days is another one of our culture's recycling and recycled narratives, going back, of course, to the *Odyssey* itself.

Within the context of the whole book the narrative texture of this sentence is even richer, since other stories of fathers and sons, parental anger and filial disrespect, sexual adventures and circuitous travels are evoked. We note the Irishness of the fallen hero ("O'Cronione"), and the tripleness of his offspring ("sunsunsuns") who, in two contrasting stories that depend on the ambiguity of "tumble," either dance on his grave, or, in their turn, fall as well. Yet in none of these stories do we make any narrative *progress*; we know their beginnings and ends already (and where there is more than one end in the tradition, Joyce usually gives us both, simultaneously and undecidably). What provides the special pleasure of reading *Finnegans Wake* is the way these stories in so many different registers map onto one another, and the way the power and fascination of narrativity is by this means instanced, exploited, and ironized. When we consider sections of the text larger than the short sentence, of course, this complex texturing of narrative, and resultant heightening of narrativity, operates even more intensely and (if you're in the right frame of mind) enjoyably.

One cannot read *for* narrativity, however; it's like that dim star in the corner of the sky that disappears as soon as you look directly at it. *Narrative* is what one reads for: the particular narrative or simultaneously unrolling narratives that are engaging the attention at the moment of textual contact, with the exercise of recognition, memory, and prediction that they entail. Even in the *Wake*, narrativity is never present as such, but its effects are more strongly felt than anywhere else in literature, as the narratives keep short-circuiting, overlapping, exploding into multiple destinies, and blocking any attempt to turn them into transparent accounts of how it is with people and events in the world.

Does this pushing of narrativity as far as it will go make the *Wake* unlike any other fictional text? I don't think so—as I've argued before in relation to other features of the book, the *Wake* represents an extreme of the literary that reveals with particular clarity the characteristic modes of literature's functioning.[4] Foregrounded narrativity is that which marks literary narrative as distinct from other kinds of narrative (though this is not to make any "high art"/"popular art" distinction—foregrounded narrativity can be found in the productions of the mass media as much as in those of the exclusive salon, as Kimberly Devlin has demonstrated—in a response to an earlier version of this argument—in using the concept to discuss the endless and multilayered narratives of television soaps). Thus it is not merely a question of fictional as opposed to nonfictional narrative: we might find no staging of narrativity in a wholly uninventive story or anecdote. At the same time, there are nonfictional narratives of which we might wish to say that in them narrativity is being performed and tested, though only, I would argue, if they had a certain "literary" quality and thereby encouraged a "literary" reading. The accurate recounting of a sequence of real events—even a story-shaped sequence—would not be likely to produce the experience of foregrounded narrativity I have been describing; but Rousseau's *Confessions* or Gibbon's *Rise and Fall* might. We might risk the assertion that a *literary* narrative—fictional or not—is a narrative in which narrativity is played out at some distance from itself, a process which does not in any way inhibit its power to excite, to move, to delight.

Finnegans Wake is thus the limit case of literary narrative—as it is the limit case of literature in so many other ways. We put it down and turn with pleasure to other fictional constructions where narrative is strong and narrativity weak. But our pleasure in these other stories is not entirely that of relief, since reading the *Wake*, learning how to enjoy its excess of narrativity, is also a schooling that can enhance all the other narratives we encounter—not because it gives us lessons on what narrativity *is*, but because it diminishes our dependence upon what Joyce called "goahead plot" and attunes our faculties to the dance of narrativity wherever it is to be found.

NOTES

1. Michael H. Begnal, who has worked assiduously to find within the overdeterminations of the *Wake* a relatively straightforward account of the actions and speeches of a determinate set of characters, offers the following as the "basic plot of *Finnegans Wake*" (after the preliminary material of book 1):

> II.1, the children are outside in the yard, playing a game after school until their parents call them in at dusk for supper; II.2, after dinner, Shem and Shaun do their homework, while Issy sits on a couch, knitting and kibitzing; II.3, Earwicker presides in his pub until closing time, finishes off the drinks left around by the patrons, falls down drunk, and staggers up to bed later; III.4, the Earwickers are awakened by the cries of Shem in the throes of a nightmare, and they soothe him, return to bed, make love, and once again fall asleep as dawn is breaking; IV.1, Anna Livia awakens, and her thoughts form the monologue which concludes the book. (51–52)

Not much narrative drive or proairetic complication there. And some of the connecting links that produce a linear account of domestic life derive more from a tradition of commentary initiated by Edmund Wilson and by Campbell and Robinson than from clearly articulated statements in the text—for example, the "supper" or "dinner" that joins II:1 and II:2, the continuity of the name "Earwicker," and the event of the publican's staggering up to bed (presumably so that he can be found there in III:4).

2. Joyce owned the French original, *Les trente-six situations dramatiques*, published in 1912; see Ellmann 48, 124. (Thanks to Jorn Barger for bringing this book to my attention.)

3. A parallel in another medium might be the heightened apprehension of the possibilities and the limits of the dodecaphonic tonal system in an inventive piece of music (even if the hearer possesses no technical musical knowledge at all), where we might say that we enjoy not only the unfolding of harmonic sequences and melodic patterns but also the staging of harmonicity and melodicity. On the question of inventiveness, see Derrida's "Psyche," an essay to which I am much indebted in my thinking about Joyce.

4. See chaps. 7 and 8 of *Peculiar Language*.

WORKS CITED

Attridge, Derek. *Peculiar Language: Literature as Difference from the Renaissance to James Joyce*. Ithaca: Cornell University Press, 1988.

Barthes, Roland. *The Semiotic Challenge*. Trans. Richard Howard. New York: Hill & Wang, 1988.

Begnal, Michael H. *Dreamscheme: Narrative and Voice in "Finnegans Wake."* Syracuse: Syracuse University Press, 1988.

Campbell, Joseph, and Henry Morton Robinson. *A Skeleton Key to "Finnegans Wake."* New York: Harcourt, Brace, Jovanovich, 1944.

Derrida, Jacques. "Psyche: Invention of the Other." In *Acts of Literature*, ed. Derek Attridge. New York: Routledge, 1992.

Ellmann, Richard. *The Consciousness of Joyce*. New York: Oxford University Press, 1977.

Polti, Georges. *The Thirty-Six Dramatic Situations*. 1912. Trans. Lucille Ray. Ridgewood, N.J.: The Editor Company, 1917.

Prince, Gerald. *A Dictionary of Narratology*. Lincoln: University of Nebraska Press, 1987.

Wilson, Edmund. "The Dream of H. C. Earwicker." In *The Wound and the Bow: Seven Studies in Literature*. Boston: Houghton Mifflin, 1941.

Contributors

Derek Attridge teaches and directs the graduate program in the English Department at Rutgers University, New Brunswick. His books include *Peculiar Language: Literature as Difference from the Renaissance to James Joyce* (1988), *The Cambridge Companion to James Joyce* (editor; 1990), and *Post-Structuralist Joyce: Essays from the French* (coedited with Daniel Ferrer; 1984). A book on English verse rhythm and a collection of essays on recent South African writing are forthcoming.

Ruth Bauerle is the author of *The James Joyce Songbook* and *A Word List to Joyce's "Exiles"* as well as editor of *Picking Up Airs: Hearing the Music in Joyce's Text*. Her essay "Bertha's Role in *Exiles*" appeared in *Women in Joyce;* she has also contributed to several collections of studies of Joyce and various journals. With Matthew J. C. Hodgart she is completing a study of Joyce's use of opera in *Finnegans Wake*. Before retirement, she taught at Ohio Wesleyan University.

Morris Beja is professor of English at the Ohio State University and the Executive Secretary and past President of the International James Joyce Foundation. He is the author of *Epiphany in the Modern Novel* (1971), *Film and Literature* (1979), *James Joyce: A Literary Life* (1992), and many articles on film and on British, Irish, and American fiction. He has edited volumes of essays on Joyce, Virginia Woolf, Samuel Beckett, and Orson Welles. His edition of *Mrs. Dalloway* for the Shakespeare Head Press Edition of Virginia Woolf is forthcoming. He coordinated the academic program for the International James Joyce Symposium from which the present volume derives.

Zack Bowen is professor and chair of the English Department at the University of Miami. His publications include *Padraic Colum: A Critical-Biographical Introduction, Mary Lavin, Musical Allusions in the Works of James Joyce: Early Poetry through Ulysses, A Companion to Joyce Studies, Ulysses as a Comic Novel, A Reader's Guide to John Barth,* and *Bloom's Old Sweet Song,* as well as approximately one hundred essays, more than half on Joyce. He is editor of Critical Essays on British Literature at Twayne, the James Joyce Series at the University Press of Florida, and the *James Joyce Literary Supplement*.

Austin Briggs is Hamilton B. Tompkins Professor of English at Hamilton College, where he teaches courses in composition, the Gothic tradition in British and American literature, modern British literature, and the language of cinema. He is the author of *The Novels of Harold Frederic* (1969) and articles on Joyce and cinema, and his work in progress includes a study of Joyce and Dickens.

Sheldon Brivic of Temple University is the author of *Joyce between Freud and Jung,*

297

Joyce the Creator, The Veil of Signs: Joyce, Lacan, and Perception, and the forthcoming *Joyce's Waking Women: A Feminist Introduction to Finnegans Wake.*

Thomas L. Burkdall is an assistant professor in the English Writing Department at Occidental College. He is currently revising his manuscript, "Joycean Frames: Film and the Fiction of James Joyce," and exploring the relationship of other modernist authors to the cinema.

Vincent J. Cheng is professor of English at the University of Southern California. His most recent book is *Joyce, Race, and Empire* (1995). He is also the author of *Shakespeare and Joyce: A Study of "Finnegans Wake"* (1984), *"Le Cid": A Translation in Rhymed Couplets* (1987), and numerous articles. He coedited *Joyce in Context* (1992).

Robert Adams Day, who died while this volume was in proofs, was professor of English and comparative literature at Queens College and the Graduate Center, City University of New York. He has written numerous articles and reviews on Joyce and other modernist authors, including "Joyce's Waste Land and Eliot's Unknown God"; he also wrote on eighteenth-century literature and at his death was working on an intellectual biography of the English divine and polymath William Wotton (1666–1727).

Paul Delany is professor of English at Simon Fraser University. His books include *The Neo-Pagans: Rupert Brooke and the Ordeal of Youth* and, as editor, *Vancouver: Representing the Postmodern City.* He is completing a book on English literature and the financial culture.

Maud Ellmann is a university lecturer and a fellow in English of King's College Cambridge. She is the author of *The Poetics of Impersonality: T. S. Eliot and Ezra Pound* (1987), *The Hunger Artists: Starving, Writing, and Imprisonment* (1993), and the editor of *Psychoanalytic Literary Criticism* (1994).

Daniel Ferrer is director of the Institut de Textes et Manuscrits Modernes (ITEM-CNRS, Paris) and editor of the journal *Genesis.* He is the author of *Virginia Woolf and the Madness of Language* and has coedited *Post-Structuralist Joyce: Essays from the French* (with Derek Attridge), *L'écriture et ses doubles: Genése et variation textuelle* (with C. Jacquet and A. Topia), and *Genéses du roman contemporain: Incipit et entrée en écriture* (with B. Boie). He is now writing on the theory of genetic criticism and working on the problems of hypertextual representation of Joyce's drafts.

Sebastian D. G. Knowles (associate professor of English, the Ohio State University) is the author of *A Purgatorial Flame,* a study of seven writers in the Second World War, and the coauthor with Scott Leonard of *An Annotated Bibliography of T. S. Eliot Criticism: 1977–1986.* His lecture recital of songs in *Ulysses* has been heard, with and without Zack Bowen, in Vancouver, Dublin, Montreal, and elsewhere. In 1994, with Patrick Woliver, he reconstructed *The Heart of the Matter,* a program of verse and music by Edith Sitwell and Benjamin Britten, which was performed at Carnegie Hall and at the Forty-seventh Aldeburgh Festival. He is currently at work on *The Music of Modernism,* a study of the cross-relations between music and literature in the modern period.

Contributors

James D. LeBlanc is a catalogue librarian at the Cornell University Library. He has published essays on Céline and Moravia, as well as articles on cataloguing. His contribution to this volume is his first published work on Joyce.

Louis Lentin is one of Ireland's foremost theater and television producer-directors. A former head of Television Drama for RTE (the Irish national network), he has also directed in the United States, Israel, Great Britain, and France. Joyce productions include *The Voice of Shem*, adapted by Mary Manning from *Finnegans Wake* and produced for the Dublin Theatre Festival and also in Paris and London; and, for television, his own adaptations from *Ulysses* and the *Wake*. He now manages his own television production company, Crescendo Concepts.

Jennifer Levine teaches at Victoria College in the University of Toronto, where she is co-ordinator of the Literary Studies program. Her articles on Joyce and narrative have appeared in the *James Joyce Quarterly*, *PMLA*, and the *University of Toronto Quarterly*.

Patrick McGee teaches at Louisiana State University. He is the author of *Paperspace: Style as Ideology in Joyce's Ulysses* (1988) and *Telling the Other: The Question of Value in Modern and Postcolonial Writing* (1992). He is currently finishing a book entitled *Negative Autonomy: The Politics of Responsibility in Adorno, Derrida, and "The Crying Game,"* and he is working on another book manuscript, *History's Echo: Joyce and the Postcolonial Situation*.

Laurent Milesi teaches literature and critical theory at Cardiff University of Wales. He has written widely on Joyce, and his forthcoming book deals with Joyce's treatment of language(s) in *Finnegans Wake*. He is also the author of studies of Pound, Olson, Whitman, and postmodern poetry; Heaney, T. S. Eliot, Poe, Sterne, and Diderot; and usury in Dante, Shakespeare, Pound, and Derrida. He is a member of the Paris ITEM-CNRS research group working on Joyce's manuscripts and an editorial adviser for *A Finnegans Wake Circular*. He is currently editing a volume of essays called *Joyce's Language(s) at the Crossroads*.

David Norris, who teaches at Trinity College, the University of Dublin, is also a member of the Upper House of the Irish Parliament and a bureau member of the Committee on Foreign Affairs. He is the author of *James Joyce's Dublin* (1982) and *Beginner's Guide to James Joyce* (1994), and coeditor of *James Joyce: The Centennial Symposium* (1986). He has also published on the Anglo-Irish short story, the novels of E. M. Forster, and a variety of legal, social, and political topics. He is chairman of the James Joyce Cultural Centre in North Great George's Street, Dublin. With Augustine Martin and Sean J. White, he directed the Irish arrangements for the 1992 Symposium.

Mark Osteen is associate professor of English at Loyola College (Baltimore) and the author of the forthcoming *The Economy of Ulysses*. He has published articles on twentieth-century fiction in such journals as *Modern Fiction Studies*, *Twentieth Century Literature*, the *James Joyce Quarterly*, *Joyce Studies*, *Critique*, and *Review of Contemporary Fiction*. He is currently at work on a study of Don DeLillo's fiction.

Richard Pearce, chair of the English Department at Wheaton College, Massachusetts, is the editor of *Molly Blooms: A Polylogue on "Penelope" and Cultural Studies.* His recent publications include *The Politics of Narration: James Joyce, William Faulkner, and Virginia Woolf* and "Simon's Irish Rose: Famine Songs, Blackfaced Minstrels, and Women's Regression in *A Portrait,*" in Susan Stanford Friedman, ed., *Joyce: The Return of the Repressed.*

Ralph W. Rader is currently professor of Graduate Studies and chair of the English Department at the University of California, Berkeley. He is the author of *Tennyson's Maud: The Biographical Genesis* and of various articles on genre and the concept of form in the novel, including a number of essays on the structure of *Portrait* and *Ulysses,* which he plans to bring together as a book.

John S. Rickard is assistant professor of English at Bucknell University. He has published essays on *Ulysses* and has edited a special issue of the *Bucknell Review* on *Irishness and (Post)Modernism.* His book, *Joyce's Book of Memory: The Mnemotechnic of "Ulysses,"* is forthcoming.

Jeffrey Segall teaches at Kent State University. He has been a Mellon Research Fellow at the Harry Ransom Humanities Center, University of Texas at Austin. He is the author of *Joyce in America: Cultural Politics and the Trials of Ulysses* (1993). He is completing research on the impact of the 1933 obscenity trial of *Ulysses* on the early American critical reception of the novel.

Adriaan van der Weel (Leiden University) and **Ruud Hisgen** (Direct Dutch) have published a Dutch translation of Joyce's *Pomes Penyeach and Other Poems* and an anthology of contemporary Anglo-Irish writing, also in Dutch translation. They edit *Conversion,* an international newsletter on translating Samuel Beckett, and are working on critical editions of *Pomes Penyeach* and Beckett's *Worstward Ho.*

Philip Weinstein is Alexander Griswold Cummins Professor of English at Swarthmore College. He is the author of *Henry James and the Requirements of the Imagination* (1971), *The Semantics of Desire: Changing Models of Identity from Dickens to Joyce* (1984), and *Faulkner's Subject: A Cosmos No One Owns* (1992), and editor of the forthcoming *Cambridge Companion to Faulkner.* He is currently working on a book on Faulkner and Toni Morrison that will explore questions of race, gender, and value.

Index

Index

Chandler, Thomas Malone ("Little
  Chandler"), 7, 140, 160, 186–88
Chaplin, Charlie, 264, 269n
Chodorow, Nancy, 131, 134n
Chomsky, Noam, 87
Citizen, the, 37, 40, 124, 126, 128
Citron, 195–96
Cixous, Hélène, 111, 282
Clark, Eleanor, 19
"Clay," 141
Cleopatra, 214, 217
Clery, Emma, 171
Clery, Mary Elizabeth, 276n
Clifford, James, 39
Clifford, Martha, 184, 217, 219–20,
  222–28, 235n
Clongowes Wood College, xii, 5, 9, 10,
  11, 210, 267
Clongownian (school magazine), 72
Cohen, Bella, 245
Cohn, Alan, 289n
Cohn, Dorrit, 113n
Collins, Joseph, 233n
Collins, Wilkie, 233n; *The Moonstone*,
  220
Colum, Mary, 100n
Colum, Padraic, 85, 98n, 99n
Commitments, The (film), 41n
Communist Party (American), 56
Compagnon, Antoine, 280
Conroy, Father Bernard, 116
Conroy, Gabriel, 142, 143, 169, 211,
  250, 261
Conroy, Gretta, 142, 211
Cook, E. T., 249n
Cope, Jackson I., 14
Corcoran, Neil, 254, 257
Corley, John, 140, 248n
Corrington, John Williams, 149n
Cosgrave, Vincent, 173, 271–72, 276n,
  277n, 278n
Costello, Francis, 241
Costello, Peter, 6, 276
Cotter, 138
"Counterparts," 140–41
Cowley, Father, 200, 217–18, 222–28,
  231, 234n

Craig, Richard, 277n
Crane, Hart, 4
Cranly, 272–73, 275, 277n
Crawford, Myles, 182–85, 188, 200
Critical Writings of James Joyce, The, 21,
  22, 27, 31, 32, 35, 37, 40, 174n
Cromwell, Thomas, 255
Cronos, 293
"Croppy Boy, The" (song), 214,
  230–31, 253
Crosby, Harry, 77
Crotthers, J., 244
Crumb, Michael, 232n
Cuchulain, 37
Cuff, Sergeant, 220
Culler, Jonathan, 133
Cummins, Maria, *Lamplighter, The*, 110
Cumpiano, Marion W., 54, 98n
Curran, Constantine, 45
Curtis, L. P., 21, 22, 23, 32, 36, 37–38,
  39, 41n
Cusack, Michael, 37, 38 fig. 10, 41n

Dail Eireann, 62
Dante Alighieri, 77, 102n, 137; *The Divine Comedy*, 22, 81n, 251–58, 258n,
  280, 285, 286n; *De Vulgari Eloquentia*, 286n, 288n
Day, Robert Adams, 13, 150, 165
Davin, 23, 41n
"Dead, The," 8, 88, 138, 142–43, 169,
  211, 250, 261
Deane, Seamus, 41, 287n
Dean of studies, 11, 31
Deasy, Garrett, 63, 193–94
de Certeau, Michel, 286n
Dedalus, Dilly, 14
Dedalus, Mary ("May"), 6, 11, 207, 208,
  211, 231, 232n, 233n, 246, 253, 262,
  271
Dedalus, Maurice, 10
Dedalus, Simon, 10, 208, 213–19,
  222–30, 233n, 234n, 246, 273, 275,
  277n
Dedalus, Stephen, 3, 4, 6, 9–15, 16, 19,
  31, 36, 41n, 44, 45, 79, 80, 81n, 87, 88,
  91, 108–9, 124, 138, 166, 167, 171, 182,

Dedalus, Stephen (*continued*)
    184, 185, 187, 188, 188n, 193–95, 199,
    205–11, 219, 231, 232n, 238, 245–46,
    248n, 251, 253, 261, 262, 264, 265–68,
    270–75, 276, 276n, 277n, 282, 291
Delaney, Frank, 5
de Lauretis, Teresa, 113, 133
Deleuze, Gilles, 133
De Man, Paul, 284, 287n
Deming, Robert, 84, 86, 92, 165
Dent, Edward, 233n
Derrida, Jacques, 22, 133, 194, 238,
    282, 283–84, 286n, 287n, 295n
Devil and the Statue, The (film), 262
Devlin, Kimberly, 117, 123, 294
Dickens, Charles, 87; *David Copper-
    field,* 241; *A Tale of Two Cities,* 132
Dignam, Paddy, 200, 250, 253
Dionysus, 12, 148
Disraeli, Benjamin, 21, 32, 34, 36
Dollard, "Big" Ben, 214, 217, 228
Donoghue, Denis, 53
Doran, Bob, 140
Doran, George, 99n
Dostoyevsky, Fyodor, *Notes from Un-
    derground,* 145
Douce, Lydia, 130, 214, 216–18, 221,
    222–28, 231
Douglas, Posey, 189
Dowden, Edward, 273
Dowson, Ernest Christopher, 274
Doyle, Jimmy, 8, 139
Dragnet (television show), 144
Dreiser, Theodore, 5
Dreyfus, Alfred, 67
Driscoll, Mary, 233n
Dubliners, 7, 8, 9, 76, 137–43, 146, 147,
    148, 165, 166, 182, 185, 250, 252,
    260–61, 291. *See also individual stories*
Duffy, Charles Gavan, 36
Duffy, James, 141, 144–49, 149n
Dujardin, Edouard, 100n
Dunleavy, Janet Egleson, 101
Dürer, Albrecht, 171

E——. C——., 211, 272, 276n
Egan, Kevin, 267

Eliot, George, *Middlemarch,* 291
Eliot, T. S., 4, 57, 92, 254–58,
    258–59n; *Prufrock and Other Obser-
    vations,* 7–8, 10; *The Waste Land,* 8;
    "Little Gidding," 251–52, 255
Ellmann, Maud, 8, 180, 180n
Ellmann, Richard, 31, 32–33, 35, 45,
    47, 52, 81n, 85, 86, 88, 89, 93–94,
    98–99n, 100n, 102n, 166, 168, 169,
    174n, 179, 221, 232n, 237, 251, 276n,
    277n, 295n
Emmet, Robert, 37
"Encounter, An," 8, 139
Enobarbus, 214
Epstein, Edmund, 289n
Ernst, Morris, 56
Euclid, 183
Eugénie, Empress, 96
"Eveline," 8–9, 48, 139
Exiles, 7, 17, 85, 150–62, 152 fig.1, 153
    fig. 2, 162n, 163n, 168, 169, 170,
    171, 172, 174n, 260

Fahy, Catherine, 17, 45
Fanon, Frantz, 39
Fastroeve, Jarmel, 58
Faulkner, William, 71
Ferguson, Sir Samuel, "Mesgedra," 5, 6
Ferrer, Daniel, 180, 180n, 288n
Feshbach, Sidney, 9
Finnegans Wake, xii, xiii, 3, 4, 6, 7, 8, 9,
    12, 15, 17, 18, 19, 25, 34, 40, 47, 59,
    61, 67, 79, 80, 81n, 84, 85, 88, 93,
    94–96, 97, 98n, 100n, 101n, 102n,
    125, 126–27, 127n, 137, 150–51,
    162, 163n, 194, 196n, 234n, 238,
    261, 266, 268, 279–85, 286n, 287n,
    290–95, 295n
Fischinger, Oscar, 264
FitzGerald, Edward, 22
Fitzgerald, F. Scott, 71
Flanders, Michael, 233n
Flaubert, Gustave, 5, 144; *Bouvard and
    Pécuchet,* 78; *Madame Bovary,* 78,
    130, 221; *The Temptation of St. An-
    thony,* 267
Fleischmann, Marthe, 79, 171, 172, 251

Havel, Vaclav, 57–58
Hawthorne, Nathaniel, *The Scarlet Letter*, 130
HCE (Humphrey Chimpden Earwicker), 61, 81n, 125, 268, 280, 295n
Heaney, Seamus, xii, 250–58, 258–59n; *Field Work*, 251, 254; *North*, 254; *Seeing Things*, 253, 256–58; *Station Island*, 251, 253, 254–57, 258n
Heath, Stephen, 106, 113, 119, 286n
Heidegger, Martin, 287n
Heinzelman, Kurt, 247n
Hely, Wisdom, 263
Henke, Suzette A., 85, 95, 115, 163n
Hera, 12
Herring, Phillip F., 15, 16
Higgins, Ellen, 64
Hochman, Stanley, 134n
Hoffmann, E. T. A., "The Sand-Man," 205–6
Hoffmeister, Adolf, 85
Homer, 35, 87, 110, 123, 251; *The Odyssey*, 11–12, 59, 65, 68, 81n, 112, 168, 170, 172, 174, 193, 198, 200, 219, 222, 234, 246, 252, 293
Hooker, Richard, 240
Howard, Richard, 233n, 235n
Hübner, Wilhelm, 220, 233n
Huebsch, B. W., 76
Hunter, Alfred, 274, 277n
Hutchins, Patricia, 94, 95, 99n
Hutchinson, G. Evelyn, 86, 88, 96, 100n
Hutchinson, Margaret, 96, 100n, 102n
Huxley, Aldous, 82n
Hyde, Douglas, 37; *Love Songs of Connacht*, 167
Hynes, Samuel, 89

Ibsen, Henrik, 95; *Rosmersholm*, 98
Icarus, 11, 13
Ino, 12
"Ireland, Island of Saints and Sages," 21, 22, 27
"Ireland at the Bar," 27–31
Irish Book Lover, 72

Irish Civil War, 62
Irish Land League, 24
Irish Literary Revival, 36, 40
Irish Melodies of 1807 (Moore), 17, 220
Irish Statesman, 165
"Ivy Day in the Committee Room," 141–42

Jackson, Selwyn, 164, 174n
Jakobson, Roman, 283
James, Henry, 57, 83, 246
Janusko, Robert, 242
Jardine, Alice, 113
Jauss, Hans Robert, 71
Jeffrys, Charles, 232n
Jindra, Mirek, 53–56, 58–59
Johnson, Georgina, 14
Johnson, Samuel, 19n
Jolas, Maria, 3n
Jonson, Ben, 247n
Joyce, Giorgio (son), 47, 164, 170, 275
Joyce, Helen (daughter-in-law), 47
Joyce, John Stanislaus (brother), 9, 164, 165, 166, 247n, 271–72, 275, 276n, 278n
Joyce, John Stanislaus (father), 245, 275
Joyce, Lucia Anna (daughter), 18, 45, 47, 48, 51, 164, 168, 170
Joyce, Mary Jane ("May") Murray (mother), 48, 244, 271, 275
Joyce, Myles, 28, 31
Joyce, Nora Barnacle, xviii, 5, 8, 16, 17, 46, 47, 48, 79, 80, 137, 164, 165, 166, 169, 173–74, 246, 270–72, 276n, 277n
Joyce, Stephen James (grandson), 44
Jung, Carl, 92, 95, 100n, 252
Justice, Beatrice, 151–62, 152 fig. 1, 153 fig. 2, 156 table 1, 163n

Kaempffer, Gertrude, 81n
Kafka, Franz, 179; *The Penal Colony*, 201
Kain, Richard M., 10
Kavanagh, Patrick, 255, 258
Keats, John, 4

O'Faoláin, Sean, 88
Ofri, Dorith, 67
O'Hehir, Brendan, 17
Old Father Ocean, 13, 16
Old Gummy Granny, 253
O'Molloy, J. J., 63
O'Neill, Shane, 37
"On the Beach at Fontana," 164, 170
Opper, Frederick B., 30 fig. 7
Orage, A. R., 93
Orel, Harold, 98
Oriana, Alfredo, 170
Ozymandias, 293

"Painful Case, A," 88, 144–49
Palmer, Molyneux, 165
Pannwitz, Rudolf, 287n
Parker, Alan, *The Commitments,* 41n
Parnell, Charles Stewart, 11, 15, 35, 40, 141–42, 261
Parr, Mary, 269n
Parrinder, Patrick, 88, 99n
Pascal, Blaise, 145
Pater, Walter, 97
Paul, Saint, 279, 280, 286n
Pavlov, Ivan Petrovich, 84, 86, 89, 90, 91, 99n
Pearce, Richard, 121n, 130, 131
Penelope, 123, 173, 246
Penrose, 200
Peterson, Robert F., 289n
Petrocchi, Giorgio, 288n
Picasso, Pablo, 59
Piccolo della Sera, Il, 27
Pindar, 4
Pinker, James B. "Ralph," 46, 76
Pipe Dream, A (film), 262
Plato, 145
Plutarch, 179
Poe, Edgar Allen, 266
Pollock, Henry J., 289n
Polti, Georges, 292, 295n
Polyphemus, 12
Pomes Penyeach, 86, 87, 88, 90, 91, 94, 97, 164–74
Popper, Amalia, 164, 168, 171, 172, 174n

Portrait of the Artist as a Young Man, A, 3, 6, 9, 10, 11, 12, 13, 23, 31, 41n, 71–72, 76, 79, 85, 98–99n , 165, 166, 167, 170, 171, 173, 187, 190, 205, 206–11, 261, 264, 272, 276n, 277n, 282, 291
Poseidon, 12
Potts, Willard, 4, 18, 101n
Pound, Ezra, 4, 84, 167
Pratt, Mary Louise, 39, 42n
"Prayer, A," 172–73, 174
Prescott, Joseph, 219, 232n
Prince, Gerald, 290–91
Proteus, 12, 13, 14
Proust, Marcel, 77, 90, 95, 115
Puck, 29 fig. 6, 30 fig. 7
Punch, 23, 24, 24 fig 1, 25 fig. 2, 26 fig. 3, 32, 34 fig. 9
Purefoy, Mina, 237, 241–44, 245–46
Purefoy, Mortimer, 246
Purefoy, Theodore, 237, 241–46

Rabaté, Jean-Michel, 180n, 189n, 289n
Rabelais, François, 16
Radway, Janice, 131, 134n
Rahv, Philip, 56
Ransom, John Crowe, 258
Raphael, 8
Ray, Gordon, 85, 90
Rea, Joanne, 277n
Reagan, Ronald, 137
Reid, Stephen, 149n
Renan, Ernest, 36–37
Revue des Deux Mondes, 74
Reynolds, Mary T., 85, 252–53
Richardson, Dorothy, 77
Riffaterre, Michael, 238–39
Rimbaud, Arthur, 252
Riquelme, John Paul, 289n
Risset, Jacqueline, 286n
Robinson, Henry Morton, 295n
Roe, Sue, 102n
Rogers, Margaret, 213
Rose, Danis, 17
Rose, Jacqueline, 212n
Rossi-Landi, Ferruccio, 247n